Gardens AND *Neighbors*

LAW AND SOCIETY IN THE ANCIENT WORLD

The study of law in ancient societies has a distinguished tradition in both Anglo-American and continental scholarship. Many of our fundamental ideas about ancient society were built on research into legal sources. These traditions continue to provide a foundation for newer approaches to law and society. More recent scholarship draws on a range of methodologies to analyze legal practices, including critical legal studies, sociology of law, economics, and literary criticism.

This series, distinguished by its emphasis on interdisciplinary approaches to law and society, seeks out innovative approaches to ancient legal studies that bring new perspectives to legal topics as well as to broader questions concerning the impact of law on commercial, political, and cultural practices in the ancient world.

Gardens AND *Neighbors*

PRIVATE WATER RIGHTS

IN ROMAN ITALY

Cynthia Jordan Bannon

The University of Michigan Press / Ann Arbor

Published in the United States of America by
The University of Michigan Press
Manufactured in the United States of America
♾ Printed on acid-free paper

2012 2011 2010 2009 4 3 2 1

A CIP catalog record for this book is available from the British Library.

Library of Congress Cataloging-in-Publication Data

Bannon, Cynthia Jordan.
Gardens and neighbors : private water rights in Roman Italy / Cynthia Jordan Bannon.
p. cm. — (Law and society in the ancient world)
Includes bibliographical references and index.
ISBN-13: 978-0-472-03353-9 (cloth : alk. paper)
ISBN-10: 0-472-03353-0 (cloth : alk. paper)
1. Water (Roman law) 2. Riparian rights (Roman law) 3. Water rights—Italy—History. I. Title.
KJA2489.R57B36 2009
346.45'6320432—dc22 2009004566

For Michael

ACKNOWLEDGMENTS

I owe many thanks for the generous help that friends and colleagues have given me as I wrote this book. I have learned much from Dennis Kehoe's publications on Roman law and the economy, and I am grateful to him for reading my manuscript and giving me invaluable criticism and encouragement. I began work on this project while teaching at the Intercollegiate Center for Classical Studies in Rome and I am grateful to Tom McGinn for the opportunity to work in Rome and visit many of the rural areas that this book discusses. My thanks also go to Laura Plummer, who read an earlier version of this book, and to Sander Goldberg and Susan Martin, who each read drafts of chapters. I also appreciate the careful work of Chris Hebert, the editor at the University of Michigan Press who acquired my project and found a pair of very helpful anonymous readers, whose comments and questions helped me to make my argument stronger and clearer. Warm thanks, too, to Ellen Bauerle for adopting my book and seeing it through to publication. Brian Smith at Indiana University's Instructional Support Services made the attractive map of the places that I refer to in my discussion of local water systems; the Department of Classical Studies at Indiana University provided funding for the map. In 2003, this project was supported by a Summer Faculty Fellowship from Indiana University. Throughout the project, I have been fortunate to have supportive colleagues, especially Matthew Christ and William Hansen. Finally, I give my best thanks to Michael Lundell for the usual husbandly things and also for his fine work as my one-man editorial and technical support team.

CONTENTS

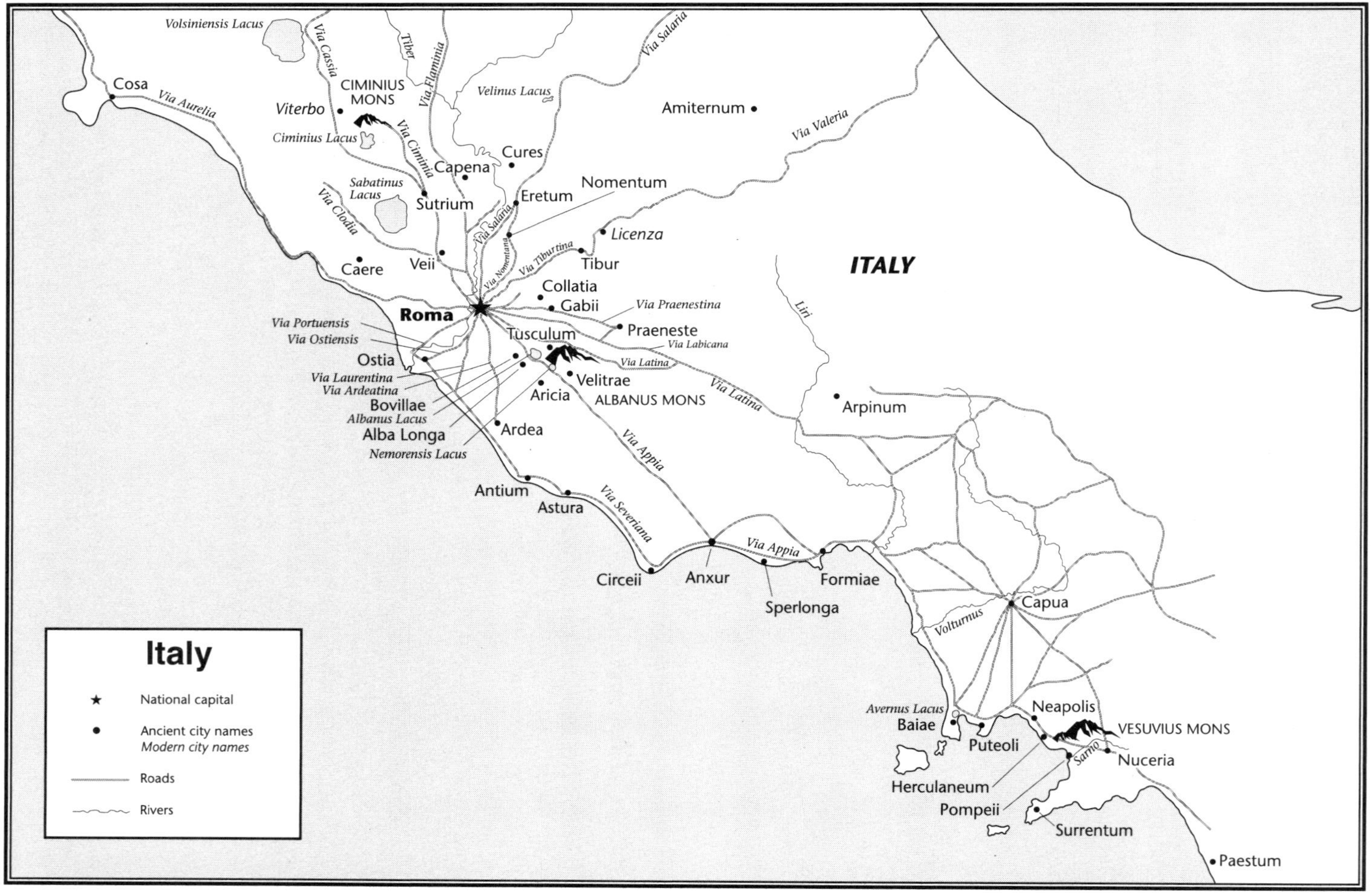
Italy
National capital
Ancient city names
Modern city names
Roads
Rivers
ITALY
Roma
Cosa
Via Aurelia
Volsiniensis Lacus
Via Cassia
Viterbo
CIMINIUS MONS
Ciminius Lacus
Via Ciminia
Tiber
Via Flaminia
Velinus Lacus
Via Salaria
Amiternum
Via Valeria
Sabatinus Lacus
Via Clodia
Capena
Cures
Sutrium
Eretum
Nomentum
Via Salaria
Via Nomentana
Licenza
Via Tiburtina
Tibur
Caere
Veii
Collatia
Gabii
Via Praenestina
Praeneste
Tusculum
Via Labicana
Via Latina
Via Portuensis
Via Ostiensis
Ostia
Via Laurentina
Via Ardeatina
Bovillae
Albanus Lacus
Alba Longa
Nemorensis Lacus
Velitrae
Aricia
ALBANUS MONS
Ardea
Via Latina
Liri
Arpinum
Via Appia
Antium
Astura
Via Severiana
Circeii
Anxur
Via Appia
Sperlonga
Formiae
Capua
Volturnus
Avernus Lacus
Baiae
Puteoli
Neapolis
VESUVIUS MONS
Sarno
Nuceria
Herculaneum
Pompeii
Surrentum
Paestum

INTRODUCTION

Private water rights were a valuable asset on Roman farms and villas. This study investigates the development and operation of private water rights during the late republican and early imperial eras. This is a book about law and how it worked for the Romans—in particular, how the law accommodated social, economic, and environmental constraints. Two questions drive the inquiry: how did rural landowners use legal institutions to secure an adequate supply of water, and how did economic, social, and environmental interests shape the development of water rights? Answers to these questions begin with the analysis of legal cases concerning water rights and then go beyond the courtroom, out into the countryside, where landowners negotiated and used their water rights.

Streams, springs, and wells located on privately owned land were treated as property in Roman law and belonged to the landowner. Other landowners who wanted to share their neighbor's water supply might do so informally or could make a legal arrangement granting access to the water. In Roman law, such private water rights were established through servitudes. A servitude was a kind of property right that gave a landowner the right to use some of his neighbor's property as his own. Roman servitudes were similar to easements in modern law. When power lines run across private property, for example, the power company has an easement that grants it a right of access to the lines. In Roman law, servitudes governed different kinds of property (e.g., land and water), and there were two servitudes that created rights to water, either to draw or to channel it from or across a neighbor's property.

This study explains both the legal development of servitudes for water use and how these servitudes worked in practice.

Servitudes were created to provide the resources necessary for cultivation and raising livestock, that is, to achieve self-sufficiency. Since water resources—springs, streams, and lakes—were unevenly distributed across the landscape, neighbors had to share and even compete for water. Servitudes thus articulated these informal patterns of water sharing, providing a legal mechanism to protect access to water and to resolve dispute. As the market for agricultural produce grew, water came to have an economic value of its own, and legal protection became more important. Roman landowners adapted servitudes to support their commercial interests when they relied on water rights to raise a surplus crop that could be sold for a profit on the market. There was competition for water, then, because access to natural resources was uneven and because landowners needed water to make their land productive, both to support the household and to participate in local markets for produce. Some landowners probably also wanted water for lavish display (splashy fountains, ornamental gardens), but these pursuits were, for the most part, beyond the scope of private water rights, because a servitude could exist only where it was connected with productivity and cultivation of the land.[1]

Because servitudes engaged with social and economic practices, this study of private water rights yields broader perspectives on Roman culture and society. First, servitudes address the relationship between farmers and the land—what we think of, in modern terms, as environmental issues, the allocation and conservation of natural resources. Second, understanding servitudes offers insight into rural communities, revealed in the ways neighbors shared water and how status and social morality shaped these arrange-

1. Two legal cases, both concerning the interdict for daily and summer water, seem to connect to servitudes with uses other than agricultural. In *D.* 43.20.1.11 Ulp. 70 *ad Ed.*, the interdict may be used to protect water both inside and outside the city for its different use in each place, irrigation and other uses and convenience (*usum quoque et commodum nostrum*). Similarly, in *D.* 43.20.3 pr. Pompon. 34 *ad Sab.*, the right to channel water may be used for irrigation, for herds, or for *amoenitas*, which could include almost anything. Servitudes were defined by their connection with cultivation of the land, and the legal cases focus on monetary compensation for damage caused by loss of water; that is, legal practice was oriented around agricultural and commercial uses of water, rather than display. Capogrossi Colognesi (*Servitù d'acqua*, 141–44) notes the connection between servitudes and irrigation in the development of the praetor's protection of servitudes for channeling water only in summer months, the so-called interdict for summer water, on which see chapter 1 in the present study. On *utilitas* generally, see chapter 3.

ments. Third, since water rights were treated as an economic commodity, the legal approaches shed light on Roman economic behavior, specifically the ability of Roman landowners to calculate and plan the use of water in farming. These issues are interrelated; often one legal case involves all three, though the emphasis varies in the chapters that follow.

WHY DID PRIVATE WATER RIGHTS MATTER?

The Romans knew that the best way to secure access to water was to have a source on the land that they owned. All the writers of agricultural treatises recommended a property with a water supply. For Cato, the site should be good land and well watered, *bonumque aquarium* (*Agr.* 1.3). Running water was especially desirable, and Varro described the options.

> The villa should be built if possible so that it has water inside the villa's walls, or if not, as close as possible. First choice is water that rises there; second best is water that flows in [i.e., onto the land] all year round. If there is no running water at all, cisterns should be constructed under the roofs and a reservoir open to the sky, so that people can use [water] from one place, and animals from the other.
>
> [*Villa aedificanda potissimum ut intra saepta villae habeat aquam, si non, quam proxime; primum quae ibi sit nata, secundum quae influat perennis. Si omnino aqua non est viva, cisternae faciendae sub tectis et lacus sub dio, ex altero loco ut homines, ex altero ut pecus uti possit.*] (*RR* 1.11.2)

The advice of the agronomists matched the priorities of Roman landowners. For example, Pliny wrote rapturously about the pure well water on his property at Laurentum and the delightful fountains at Tifernum, and when he was considering buying the adjacent estate at Tifernum, water was a key factor: "now, for the main point of my consideration, the fields are fertile, rich and watered" [*iam, quod deliberationis nostrae caput est, agri sunt fertilies pingues aquosi*] (*Ep.* 3.19.5; cf. *Ep.* 2.17.25 and 5.6.36–40 on Laurentum and Tifernum). Likewise, Cicero was enthusiastic about an estate near Arpinum, which his brother planned to purchase, because its water supply was rich enough for both charm and irrigation (*Q.Fr.* 3.1.3).[2]

Water may have seemed abundant to the Romans. Pliny the Elder re-

---

2. For a discussion of Cic. *Q.Fr.* 3.1.3, see chapter 3 in the present study.

marks on the number of lakes, streams, and springs in his praise of Italy's fertility: "so many lakes, so great an abundance of streams and springs flowing through all of it [sc., Italy]" *[tot lacus, tot amnium fontiumque ubertas totam eam perfundens]* (*NH* 3.41). But climate, topography, and farming practices made water a scarce resource that required careful management if Roman landowners were to cultivate their land successfully. Columella described the ideal farm site as being near a river; on a hillside, with terracing for grain; with streams flowing down to the meadows, fields, willow groves, and reed beds (1.2.4). But Columella also acknowledged that not every property had these resources. Smaller farms especially could lack a spring or stream, and even larger estates might not be able to meet their needs with the resources on site.[3] The distribution of water sources in relation to settlement (topography) was the first factor that limited access to water on rural land.

Some owners of rural property supplemented their supply with water from one of the city aqueducts, legally or otherwise.[4] Already in 184 BC, Cato, as censor, cut off all public water flow to private houses or fields, in an effort to stop the illegal appropriation of public land and water (Livy 39.44.4). Again in 144 BC, the urban praetor was charged with curbing abuse (Front. *Aq.* 7.1). The problem did not go away. By the first century AD, rural taps were depriving the city of its water. According to Pliny, the owners of villas and suburban estates were motivated to take water from the city aqueducts by competition and greed (*ambitione avaritiaque, NH* 31.42). These motives point both to cultivation and the profits it could earn (greed, *avaritia*) and to the use of water for luxurious display in fountains and baths (competition, *ambitio*). Frontinus, curator of the imperial aqueducts in AD 97, took pride in cracking down on such illegal taps and the dishonest officials of the imperial water service, *aquarii,* who facilitated these abuses (*Aq.* 74.4, 87.2, 114).[5] Some water from the urban aqueducts

3. The location of water sources in relation to farmsteads has been charted by survey archaeology for some areas of central Italy, the region that is the focus of this study, and this evidence is presented in chapter 1.

4. Some villas (e.g., those near Tivoli) received supplementary water from the city aqueducts by imperial authorization. See Evans, "In Tiburtium Usum"; in general, Wilson, "Deliveries *extra Urbem.*"

5. Property irrigated illegally from the public aqueducts was to be confiscated, though there is no direct evidence that this rule was ever enforced: see Front. *Aq.* 97.3, with Rodgers, *Frontinus,* 262, 173–77. See also Taylor, "Torrent or Trickle?" 471; Evans, *Water Distribution,* 57–58. There is possible additional evidence in an inscription from the second century BC (*CIL* 10.8236 = *ILS* 5742) that Mommsen thought concerned a dispute about a tap on an urban aqueduct; see aus Caiatia "Inschrift." See also Robinson, "Water Supply of Rome," 53.

was allocated by imperial grant to properties outside but near the city (in Rome's *suburbium*). While this water could be used for fountains and baths, it was also used for irrigation, as has been argued on the basis of an inscription about a grant of water from the Aqua Alsietina (*CIL* 6.31566).[6] When Martial wrote his poetic petition to Domitian for a private tap on the Aqua Marcia, he made his case with an image of his thirsty garden and the swing-bucket that drew water from a stream for it (9.18). But not many of these private grants served properties outside the city where the land was likely to be cultivated, and the number of these grants did not increase much until the second century AD.[7] The limited number of imperial grants and the persistent problem of illegal taps on the city aqueducts are both signs that the demand for water in the areas near the city exceeded supply. For this reason, the control of water sources on private land was critical to owners of rural land in the late republican and early imperial eras. The lack of an adequate public water supply intensified competition for water in areas outside the city.

Climate also made water a scarce resource in Roman Italy. Many streams were (and are) rain-fed, and rainfall varies by season, so during the dry summer, water was in limited supply.[8] To compensate, summer crops required irrigation and frequent manuring.[9] Water was also needed year-round by the livestock that generated manure.[10] Even though the Romans used farming methods that made the most of a limited water supply (e.g., dry farming and selecting crops to suit the land), they cultivated many crops and raised animals that needed water.[11] According to Trevor Hodge, the combined effect

---

6. For a discussion of *CIL* 6.31566, see chapter 1 in the present study.

7. De Kleijn, "Fundorte der Fistulae," 156.

8. Leveau, "Dal paesaggio naturale al paesaggio coltivato," 73; Semple, *Geography*, 85–93, 438–41.

9. For ancient Italy, see Semple, *Geography*, 93, 377; for medieval Italy, Squatriti, *Water and Society*, 79–96; for a dramatic account of the effects of drought on a local irrigation system in medieval Spain, Glick, *Irrigation and Society*, 132–45.

10. The agricultural writers give instructions about the water requirements of various plants and animals, and these sources are collected by topic in appendix A. On drainage and irrigation, see White, *Roman Farming*, 146–72.

11. For references to the agricultural writers' advice about selecting crops and manuring, see appendix A. Some grain crops could be and were grown with only rainwater: Pliny says only millet and panic could be grown with minimal water (*aquis minime*): see *NH* 18.101, with White, *Roman Farming*, 155. For dry farming, see White, *Roman Farming*, 157, 173; Horden and Purcell, *Corrupting Sea*, 201–2. In general on Roman practices to manage soil fertility, see Kron, "Roman Ley-Farming."

of climate and irrigation had a greater impact on local water supplies than has usually been recognized.

> Irrigation must have consumed vast amounts of water, and had an importance out of all proportion to what we actually know about it. . . . [T]wo factors argue persuasively for our consideration of agricultural irrigation as a major factor in water supply. One is that very dryness of the climate. . . . The second factor is that irrigation, in comparison with other forms of water use, requires water in quite enormous quantities, so that quite a modest local scheme would yet use as much as the whole city of Rome.[12]

Similarly, Horden and Purcell write, "Water has some claim to be the most important variable in Mediterranean food production."[13] Vergil's image of the farmer opening the sluices to an irrigation ditch dramatizes what must have been a regular chore: "why should I tell . . . when the field is parched and ablaze with dying crops—/ look! the farmer coaxes a stream from the top of the sloping channel?" [*quid dicam . . . et, cum exustus ager morientibus aestuat herbis, / ecce supercilio clivosi tramitis undam / elicit?*] (*G.* 1.104, 107–9). Though it can be hard to even find the physical remains of dirt channels like the one Vergil describes, the importance of irrigation can be assessed indirectly on the basis of the cultivation that it supported.[14]

Farming produced food, of course, but more than that, agriculture was the mainstay of the Roman economy. Cultivating the land was the primary source of income not only for elites who owned villas but also for landowners of more moderate means.[15] Grain, olives, and vines were the basic crops, and irrigation was an important strategy for reducing risk in the production

12. Hodge, *Roman Aqueducts,* 246–47; Capogrossi Colognesi, *Servitù d'acqua,* 141–49; White, *Roman Farming,* 146–47. Aristotle's comparison of irrigation ditches to veins in the body may not exaggerate their importance: see *Part. An.* 668a14–15, with Hanson, *Other Greeks,* 63 (cf. 60 for watering trees and vines). Plato (*Laws* 6.8, 761a–b) instructs the country wardens to contain runoff in a system of streams and channels for irrigating agricultural land. See appendix A in the present study for a collection of Roman sources on use of water for crops and livestock.

13. Horden and Purcell, *Corrupting Sea,* 237; cf. 237–57 on irrigation.

14. For the difficulty in documenting dirt channels, see Hodge, *Roman Aqueducts,* 249. The archaeological evidence for small local water systems in Rome's *suburbium* and Campania is discussed in chapter 1.

15. Agriculture dominated the Roman economy. Jongman (*Pompeii,* 65) explains that "food represented by far the largest proportion of production and consumption" and that "between 65 and 90% of the population was actively engaged in agriculture" (see also, in general on specialized farming, *Pompeii,* 57–62). See also Duncan-Jones, *Economy of the Roman Empire,* 33; Erdkamp, *Grain Market,* 12.

of these staple crops. A garden or even a few fruit trees in the farmyard required irrigation.[16] But a dependable water supply could also encourage specialization—for example, growing garden crops or raising pigs for local markets.[17] Starting in the early second century BC, the Roman agricultural economy diversified in just this way in response to a growing population and an influx of wealth from foreign conquest.[18] Roman landowners took a more commercial approach to farming, producing not only goods to support the household but also a surplus to be sold in local markets. Both large and small farms raised a variety of produce and livestock and participated in some market-oriented farming.[19] On large estates, this intensive farming often involved what we might consider luxury crops, such as the produce of the infamous fishponds, or turtle doves and thrushes, or the flowers raised by the Bay of Naples for garlands and perfume. Less exotic items, like vegetables and fruits and chickens, were also raised as cash crops on modest farms. All these crops required a steady water supply: for example, sheep and chickens needed water to drink year-round, vegetables and flowers needed water during the dry summer months, and all cultivated trees and vines needed watering when they were planted and for the next two years. Thus,

---

16. Irrigated gardens figure in literature (e.g., Ovid, *Fasti* 2.703–4; Mart. 9.18, discussed previously). For the importance of irrigation to gardens, see Farrar, *Gardens of Italy,* 20–27. Though Farrar focuses on pleasure gardens, water was at least as important for food crops and livestock, and many gardens will have had a dual purpose of pleasure and productivity, on which see n. 23 in the present introduction. More generally, see Jashemski, *Gardens of Pompeii,* 32–48 (ornamental gardens), 188–94, 238, 247–50, 253, 278–88, 289–335 passim (irrigation in gardens with mixed use, i.e., both pleasure and production); Broise and Jolivet, "Il giardino e l'acqua"; White, *Roman Farming,* 153–57.

17. On irrigation to reduce risk and encourage specialization, see Horden and Purcell, *Corrupting Sea,* 241–42.

18. On change in the Roman economy spurred by political conquest, see Weber, *Agrarian Sociology,* 317–18. More recently, see Frederiksen, "Strutture agrarie"; Gabba and Pasquinucci, *Strutture agrarie,* 29–38 (self-sufficiency and markets in Cato's *de Agricultura*), 38–46 (Hannibalic War as turning point); Lo Cascio, "Forme dell'economia," 327–34 (growth of a commercial sector in the Roman economy during the first and second centuries AD), 347–51 (role of urban markets in this development). The change probably began earlier in the fourth century BC, reaching a critical point only after the Second Punic War: see Cornell, *Beginnings of Rome,* 385; Frayn, *Subsistence Farming,* 73–87. For further references, see n. 82 in the present introduction.

19. Erdkamp, *Grain Market,* 46–54, 95–105; see, generally, the second chapter, "The World of the Smallholder," 55–105. For a poetic vignette of a small-scale farmer who sold his produce at Rome, see Tib. 1.7.61–62: in Tibullus's birthday poem to Messala, the travelers heading to the party at Messala's Tusculan villa see a farmer on his way home from the city along the Via Latina (Putnam, *Tibullus: A Commentary,* 125). For a collection of epigraphic evidence for gardeners and other laborers in the *suburbium,* see Friggeri, "Epigrafi sull'agricoltura."

the diversification in Roman farming put additional strains on local water supplies because landowners were raising more crops and animals that required a steady water supply. The opportunity to make a profit from selling this produce no doubt intensified the competition for water in some areas, especially near Rome and other towns with markets.

Rural properties located near Rome and other market towns were well positioned to participate in commercial agriculture. Truck gardens or livestock were especially profitable when the farm was close to a city: transportation was costly, and perishables do not ship well without refrigeration.[20] Already in Cato, we find recognition of the importance of an urban market for fruit, vegetables, and flowers. He ranks an irrigated garden as the second-best type of cultivation (after a vineyard) and recommends growing fruit trees and a garden of vegetables and fruits on a suburban farm.

> Near the city there is every kind of [vegetable] garden, every kind of [flower for] garlands—grape hyacinths; myrtles, variegated, white, and black; Delphic, Cypriot, and forest bay; walnuts, filberts, hazelnuts, almonds. Make sure that these are grown. A farm near the city, especially if someone has only this farm, should be prepared and sown in this way so as to keep it as productive as possible.
>
> *[Sub urbe hortum omne genus, coronamenta omne genus belbos magaricos, murtum coniugulum et album et nigrum, loream, Delphicam et Cypream, et silvaticam, nuces calvas, Abellanas, Praenestinas, Graecas: haec facito uti serantur. Fundum suburbanum, et qui eum fundum solum habebit, ita paret itaque conserat, uti quam solertissimum habeat]* (*Agr.* 8.2)[21]

The variety of produce that Cato expects—"every kind of vegetable garden, every kind of [flower] for garlands"—hints at the specialized produce that was grown on suburban properties. The specification of a suburban property (*suburbanum fundum*) points to the city market as the source of profit.[22]

20. See Col. 7.2.22 on the high price of land transport. In general on land transportation, see Martin, "Roman Law and the Study of Land Transportation."

21. Cf. Cato, *Agr.* 7–8; Varro, *RR* 1.16.3, with Kolendo, "Praedia suburbana." For profitability of various crops, see Duncan-Jones, *Economy of the Roman Empire,* 34–38; on the development of gardens around Rome, Carandini, "Orti e frutteti."

22. Cato's interest in profitable farming was familiar to Romans of Cicero's era. In *de Senectute,* Cato reports an old adage in which a salted ham symbolizes the produce and profit of the *hortus:* "now farmers themselves call the garden [*hortum*] a second joint of salt pork" *[iam hortum ipsi agricolae succidiam alteram appellant]* (Cic. *Sen.* 56). Gourmet hams, known already in the time of Cato the Elder, were imported to Rome from as far away as Gaul (Varro, *RR* 2.4.10–11; cf. Cato, *Agr.* 162 [Cato's recipe for salting ham]).

Cato's interest in profit may seem incompatible with the luxurious villa gardens familiar from literature, but suburban villas were usually also productive farms, where pleasure was combined with productivity, as Varro knew when he recommended both orchards and flower gardens (*RR* 1.23.4; cf. *RR* 3.2.7–18).[23] The Roman word for garden, *hortus,* and its etymology illustrate the ambiguity. As the Romans explain it, *hortus* was derived from *heredium,* the word for the inherited plot of land that supported the family and therefore had a clear economic importance (Pliny, *NH* 19.49, citing the *Twelve Tables*). The word *horti* (plural), when used to mean "villas," was also connected with productive farming, even after the rise of showplace estates. The dual nature of suburban *horti* is also reflected in the legal sources—for example, when the second-century AD jurist Ulpian defined "city properties" (*urbana praedia*) and gardens by both location (in or near town) and function (pleasure).

> In the same way gardens should be said to be included in the category of urban properties, if they are located within buildings. Clearly if a garden is mostly productive, vineyards perhaps or even vegetable gardens, these are not really "urban."
>
> [*Proinde hortos quoque, si qui sunt in aedificiis constituti, dicendum est urbanorum appellatione contineri. Plane si plurimum horti in reditu sunt, vinearii forte vel etiam holitorii, magis haec non sunt urbana.*] (*D.* 50.16.198 Ulp. 2 *Om. Trib.*)

Neither location nor function was an exclusive category for defining rural or urban properties. *Horti* could be *urbani,* "in the city," but not if they were primarily for profit. That some *horti* were designed solely for pleasure did not mean that "rustic" and "urban" were exclusive categories. In fact, many rural villas combined luxurious vacation accommodations with profitable cultivation, and the garden was often at the center of that productivity, as Columella recognized.[24] Similarly, Pliny connected the villa's irrigated garden

23. Noteworthy for its pleasing appearance and contribution to productivity was the planting of trees and vines in geometrical array (see Varro, *RR* 1.4.2 [cf. 1.7.2]; Cic. *Sen.* 59; Vergil, *G.* 2.277–78; more fancifully, the old man of Tarentum's garden in Vergil, *G.* 4.125–46). On the combination of pleasure and productivity on Roman estates, see especially Purcell, "Roman Villa," revising earlier views that downplayed production on villas, such as that of D'Arms (*Bay of Naples,* 11–13), whose innovation was in recognizing that some villas were not working farms.

24. For the central place of the garden in Columella, see Henderson, "Columella's Living Hedge," 113; more generally, Horden and Purcell, *Corrupting Sea,* 221. For continuity of the pattern in medieval Italy, see Squatriti, *Water and Society,* 80–89.

with commercial agriculture in the introduction to his catalogue of plants (*NH* 19.49–60). For Pliny, the garden was an opportunity to moralize, and he contrasts contemporary cultivation with old-fashioned garden plots: wild asparagus has been replaced by monstrous, cultivated varieties; salads are now rejected in favor of vegetables cooked with imported spices and expensive oil; gourmet groceries divide rich and poor, threatening another secession of the plebs.[25] The rhetoric and moralizing draws on economic realities: garden produce, plain and fancy, was an important part of Rome's economy.

Rome's hinterland, or *suburbium,* and the rich farmland near the towns of Campania were prime locations for villa gardens and farms that participated in local produce markets. Columella marked out a garden belt from northern Campania to the *suburbium* in his catalogue of places where cabbage thrives (10.127–35; cf. Mart. 7.30).[26] Indeed, this region of central Italy—Campania and the area around Rome, sometimes referred to as "Tyrrhenian Italy"—is associated with a specific type of rural estate whose cultivation was oriented toward the market (Carandini's "central" type of villa).[27] As the city grew during the late republic, there developed "a large and wealthy market for all kinds of commodities, especially foodstuffs, fuel and building materials," as Morley describes it. This market in turn shaped agricultural practices in rural areas that supplied this market. Morley explains, "It is within the immediate hinterland of the city, the region with the best access to the urban market, that we can expect to find the most significant and visible changes in agricultural practice; a greater degree of orientation towards the market, with specialization in a particular set of crops and more intensive cultivation."[28] This commercially oriented agriculture increased the de-

25. For other cultural interpretations of the garden, see Pagán, *Rome and the Literature of Gardens.*

26. For Rome's garden belt, see Horden and Purcell, *Corrupting Sea,* 223.

27. Carandini, "Columella's Vineyard," 195; Carandini, "Paesaggi agrari," especially 168; Vallat, "Structures agraires," 182–205. For the early history of the area, see Cifani, "Notes on the Rural Landscape." In general on the relationship between location and participation in the monetary economy, see De Neeve, "Price of Agricultural Land," 84–96.

28. Morley, *Metropolis and Hinterland,* 52 (urban market), 83 (impact on hinterland); "Transformation of Italy," 57. Horden and Purcell (*Corrupting Sea,* 238 and see 238–55) give a similar assessment of the relationship between local markets and specialization, recognizing the role of irrigation: "Spring-fed summer production is inevitably local, though it may, of course, make a disproportionate contribution to a microregional economy." The pattern was noted already by Rawson ("Ciceronian Aristocracy," 94–95). See also Kolendo, "Praedia suburbana," 59–61; De Neeve, *Peasants in Peril,* 16–22; Marzano, *Villas in Central Italy,* 108–10

mand for water from local streams and springs in central Italy, which led neighboring landowners to compete for an adequate supply. The competition for water is nicely described by Morley in his discussion of agriculture in the areas closest to Rome, the *suburbium.*

> A few privileged residents of the *suburbium* also benefited from the [urban aqueduct] system; the remainder were left to assert their objections through water-stealing or vandalism, and to compete amongst themselves for the water that remained after the city had drunk its fill. This competition, for both productive and leisure uses of water, must have been fierce, especially in a dry year. The Roman jurists produced a detailed set of rulings on the administration of water rights, which must reflect the likelihood of litigation in this area; the word "rivals" derives from *"rivales,"* those who drew water through the same channel and who were thereby liable to come to blows.[29]

Morley's "detailed set of rulings on the administration of water rights" refers to servitudes and the legal cases about them that are preserved in the *Digest of Justinian.* Many of these cases involved competition for access to water, as the word *rivales* suggests. Originally, a person who shared a water channel, *rivus,* was known as a *rivalis,* a rare technical term that occurs only four times in this sense—twice in the *Digest of Justinian,* once in Aulus Gellius's *Noctes Atticae,* and also in the inscription recording Augustus's grant of water from the Aqua Alsietina (mentioned earlier).[30] *Rivalis* is more often used metaphorically of rivals in love, emphasizing the competitive sense of the

(more generally, 102–28). For similar patterns in southeastern Italy, see Yntema, "Greeks, Natives, and Farmsteads," 88. For a longer perspective on this phenomenon, we might also compare the analysis of Laertes' garden in *Odyssey* 24.226–47 as a prototype of intensive agriculture, as discussed in Hanson, *Other Greeks,* 48–50.

29. Morley, *Metropolis and Hinterland,* 106. See also Bruun, "Water Shortage."

30. In the introduction to his discussion of the Chaldean astrologers, Gellius (14.1.4) introduces legal business involving servitudes (*aquae ductus* and a shared wall) as an example of the kind of thing that is not controlled by the stars. *Rivalis* occurs in *CIL* 6.31566, on which see chapter 1 in the present study. The term does not otherwise seem to be common in inscriptions; this is the only example that I have found searching *CIL,* the indexes of *ILS,* the Epigraphische Datenbank Heidelberg (http://www.uni-heidelberg.de/institute/sonst/adw/edh/indexe.html), and the secondary literature. In the *Digest, rivalis* occurs in *D.* 43.20.1.26 Ulp. 70 *ad Ed.* and *D.* 43.20.3.5 Pompon. 32 *ad Sab.* (see chapters 1 and 2, respectively, in the present study).

word.[31] In one of the passages from the *Digest,* the competition is explicit, as two landowners challenge each other for the use of a watercourse (*D.* 43.20.1.26 Ulp. 70 *ad Ed.*). In all the passages where *rivalis* is used in the technical sense, a dispute or potential dispute about private water rights is involved, clear evidence not only of competition for water but of the role of law in mediating this competition.

This study investigates the institution of Roman law, servitudes, that regulated the privately owned sources of water for which landowners competed. Romans adapted servitudes to define private water rights in ways that served their economic interest in the water supply. Servitudes, or private water rights, developed at a time when Roman ideas about farming and markets were evolving. By the second century BC, landowners had access to the Roman legal system to create and enforce their rights and were interested in using the law to articulate and defend their access to local water sources.[32] Many of the key legal cases are ascribed to republican jurists whose views are important points of reference for the later classical jurists. Investigating the legal problems surrounding water rights opens approaches to social and economic issues surrounding servitudes for water. Roman law is at the heart of this exploration of water use in agriculture, but the new perspectives on rural life, the Roman economy, and the law itself emerge only through the analysis of literary and archaeological sources for the culture and society that informed legal practice.

SERVITUDES AND PRIVATE WATER RIGHTS

Servitudes were the main legal mechanism for articulating and protecting private water rights in ancient Rome.[33] They belonged to the *ius civile,* the law based on the *Twelve Tables,* which applied to Roman citizens. A servitude was

31. See *OLD,* s.v. *rivalis* 2. The metaphorical sense (first in Plautus, *Bac.* 1210) is attested nearly two centuries earlier than the technical usage. For the technical sense, see *OLD,* s.v. *rivalis* 1, which cites only Gellius 14.1.4 and *D.* 43.20.1.26.

32. Brunt, *Italian Manpower,* 531–33 and, in general, appendix 3, "Italian Municipal Autonomy before 90 BC."

33. For a quick overview of servitudes, see Buck, *Agriculture and Agricultural Practice,* 36–38. See, more authoritatively, Kaser, *RP* 1:143–44, 440–47; Franciosi, *Servitù prediali,* 4–17. Specialized literature on legal topics relating to servitudes is extensive, and references are available in Kaser, *RP,* as well as in the following major studies: Biondi, *Categoria;* Franciosi, *Servitù prediali;* Grosso, *Servitù prediali;* Solazzi, *Tutela e il possesso;* Solazzi, *Specie ed estinzione;* Saliou, *Les lois des bâtiments;* Rainer, *Bau- und Nachbarrechtliche Bestimmungen;* Palma, *Iura vicinitas.*

a kind of property right, specifically a right to use someone else's property. For example, a right-of-way was a servitude in Roman law that allowed one person to walk across his neighbor's property. There were two types of servitude governing water: the right to channel water, *aquae ductus,* and the right to draw water, *haustus.* Water that arose on a property—springs, streams, wells—was treated as private property in Roman law and belonged to the person who owned the property. By contrast, the ocean, rivers, and the city aqueducts were treated as public.[34] The public water supply was governed by imperial laws and decrees, whereas water on private property was regulated by Roman private law generally and by servitudes in particular. Servitudes were an old and, in some ways, odd institution that was connected with traditional ways of life—farming, neighborly cooperation, and an organic concept of the land and its resources.

Servitudes were known as *iura praediorum,* or predial servitudes, because they were attached to a property, *praedium.* They were also classified as rustic or urban. "Urban" was the exclusive category limited to city landscapes (e.g., the right to insert a beam into someone else's wall). Rustic servitudes were connected with the cultivation of the land, though some rustic servitudes, such as right-of-way, could also be established in the city (e.g., a path across someone's backyard).[35] The rustic servitudes developed before the urban, and in early Roman law, there were just four rustic servitudes—two rights-of-way (*via* and *iter*), the right to drive animals (*actus*), and the right to channel water (*aquae ductus*).[36] It is possible and not unlikely that all four "origi-

34. No servitude was needed to draw water from a public river, though a right-of-way to the river could be needed if the river was bordered by private land (*D.* 8.3.3.3 Ulp. 17 *ad Ed.*). On legal categories for the ownership of water (public vs. private), see Costa, *Le acque,* 1–12; Capogrossi Colognesi, *Servitù d'acqua,* 52–70. Cf. Shaw, "Lamasba," 92–93, citing Mommsen's early work on the Augustan inscription from Venafro ("Romische Urkunden," 309–12 = *Gesammelte Schriften,* 3:88–90). Hinker ("Grundzüge des öffentlichen Römischen Wasserrechts," 179) cites *D.* 43.12.1.2 Ulp. 68 *ad Ed.* to support a strict classification of waters—perennial = public, torrent = private—without reference to legal discussions of this classification.

35. On the distinction between rustic and urban servitudes, see *D.* 8.4.1 Ulp. 2 *Inst.,* with Kaser, *RP* 1:441–42, 444 n. 54; Grosso, *Servitù prediali,* 167–75; Capogrossi Colognesi, *Servitù d'acqua,* 101–6. On the essential connection between a servitude and the property it serves, whether a building (*superficies*) or land (*praedia*), see Biondi, *Categoria,* 355–57 (in general, 350–65).

36. *D.* 8.3.1 pr.-1 Ulp. 2 *Inst.,* with Kaser, *RP* 1:440–41; Biondi, *Categoria,* 653–59; Franciosi, *Servitù prediali,* 26–28, 38–42. These four servitudes were included in the praetor's edict. Servitudes were classified as rustic and urban in classical and postclassical legal sources.

nal" rustic servitudes were already in existence in the fifth century BC, at the time of the *Twelve Tables* (ca. 450 BC). The fragmentary state of the *Twelve Tables* makes it impossible to know for certain, but one of the servitudes for right-of-way (*via*) is mentioned by name, and the *Twelve Tables* contains many provisions to protect farming and rural land—for example, penalties for casting a spell on crops (*XII Tab.* 8.8).[37] Already in this era, landowners were using law to resolve disputes about water, at least when the problem was too much water: the *Twelve Tables* includes the *actio aquae pluviae arcendae,* which provided compensation when runoff caused damage.[38]

In the early law, servitudes were treated as a kind of ownership rather than as a property right as in classical law. For this reason, they were included in the category of *res mancipi,* an important kind of property.[39] The category of *res mancipi* was defined in two ways, procedurally and by example. Procedurally, *res mancipi* were things whose title could be transferred only by *mancipatio,* an early form of conveyance or formal legal transfer of title. The types of property transferred by *mancipatio* were defined by example. In addition to servitudes, *res mancipi* included real estate in Italy and corporeal objects important for the cultivation of the land, such as slaves, cattle, horses, donkeys, and mules.[40] Classifying servitudes as *res mancipi* recognized their key role in making the land productive. Rights-of-way provided necessary access to fields for work and transport, while water channels brought water for irrigation, livestock, and human consumption. The connection between productivity and natural resources is expressed in discussions of servitudes through the legal concept of *utilitas:* a servitude could be set up only for activities that were useful to the estate and tightly connected with the cultivation of the land.[41]

---

37. The rule for the width of *via* is mentioned in *XII Tab.* 7.6, reconstructed on the basis of Varro, *LL* 7.15; Festus 371L (which concerns repairs to *via* and is also cited as *XII Tab.* 7.7); and *D.* 8.3.8 Gaius 7 *ad Prov. Ed.* Cf. also *D.* 8.6.6.1d Cels. 5 *Dig.* For provisions related to farming, see *XII Tab.* 6.8 (vineyard), 6.9 (vines), 7.9 (trees), 7.10 and 8.7 (acorns), 8.8 (penalties for casting a spell on crops), and 8.9 (grain crops).

38. *XII Tab.* 7.8, based on *D.* 43.8.5 Paul. 16 *ad Sab.;* see Crawford, *Roman Statutes,* 2:673–74. See also Kaser, *RP* 1:441; Biondi, *Categoria,* 653–59; Franciosi, *Servitù prediali,* 38 (generally, 25–53).

39. Grosso, *Servitù prediali,* 14–19.

40. Gaius, *Inst.* 2.14a, 17, with Kaser, *RP* 1:123–24, 381–82, 441.

41. For a good general introduction, see Grosso, *Servitù prediali,* 97–108; cf. 42–45. On servitudes and utility to the estate, see *D.* 8.1.8 pr. Paul. 15 *ad Plaut.* See, in general, chapter 3 in the present study.

As property rights, servitudes were conceptualized in physical terms and in relation to the land. Only a landowner could hold a servitude, and it was attached to his property (*D.* 8.4.1 Ulp. 2 *Inst.*). A servitude was conceived as unified; that is, it could not be divided or owned in shares. Nor could water governed by a servitude be shared with a third party. Servitudes for channeling or drawing water could be established only on a perennial or permanent source; the key element here seems to have been a natural source, as opposed to a man-made cistern or aqueduct, because an exception was made to allow a servitude on a seasonal torrent.[42] The apparent permanence of a servitude—it was attached to a property permanently or at least until its owner decided to modify or remove it—was useful because it made the water supply reliable and predictable.[43]

The mechanisms for transfer of ownership, *mancipatio* and *in iure cessio*, were used to establish servitudes and to transfer ownership of them.[44] In addition, ownership of a servitude could be defended in *vindicatio*, the standard legal procedure for deciding questions of ownership (*D.* 8.3.5 pr. Ulp. 17 *ad Ed.*).[45] In fact, in early law, the water servitudes seem to have involved a combination of a right-of-way and actual ownership of the spring from which the water flowed. This development may explain why servitudes were treated as a kind of property right.[46] In postclassical Roman law, the term *servitude* was also used of personal rights, but these later servitudes were different from the water rights studied here.[47] In classical law, the servitude to channel or draw water was a property right, different from an imperial grant to tap the city aqueduct, which was personal, belonging to the person (not

---

42. For the types of sources that could be governed by a servitude, see *D.* 8.3.9 Paul. 1 *Sent.* and *D.* 43.20.1.5–8 Ulp. 70 *ad Ed.*, with Capogrossi Colognesi, *Servitù d'acqua*, 52–70; Palma, "Derivazioni di acqua." On an apparent exception, *D.* 8.4.2 Ulp. 7 *ad Ed.* (which seems to allow a servitude on a waterwheel or cistern), see Grosso, *Servitù prediali*, 181; Biondi, *Categoria*, 615.

43. Horden and Purcell (*Corrupting Sea*, 239) note that perennial rivers are "the most promising providers of abundant water."

44. Gaius, *Inst.* 2.17, 29; Paul. *Vat.* 45, with Kaser, *RP* 1:443–44; Franciosi, *Servitù prediali*, 5–7.

45. On the development of *vindicatio* for servitudes, see Franciosi, *Servitù prediali*, 8–17; Solazzi, *Tutela e il possesso*, 1–50.

46. Franciosi, *Servitù prediali*, 4–5, 18–21; Capogrossi Colognesi, *Servitù d'acqua*, 52–53.

47. *D.* 8.1.1 Marc. 3 *Reg.* distinguishes personal and predial servitudes. For a quick overview of this distinction, see Nicholas, *Introduction to Roman Law*, 140–48; see also chapter 3 in the present study.

his land) and lasting only as long as he lived (though it was usual for the grant to be transferred; in late law, it was often treated the same way).[48] By contrast, servitudes remained attached to the property and were transferred to the new owner when land was sold.[49] The status of servitudes as property rather than personal rights afforded some advantage when they were contested in court. In a lawsuit based on a personal right, *in personam,* the plaintiff could claim only a debt; even if he won his suit, he joined a group of unsecured creditors waiting for the defendant to pay. But when a servitude was at issue in an action for property, *in rem,* the plaintiff claimed ownership of the property; if he won, his claim came ahead of the unsecured creditors, so he was more likely to get satisfaction.

A servitude created a relationship between two properties: the servient estate provided a resource to the dominant estate. In a servitude for channeling water, *aquae ductus,* for example, the owner of the dominant estate had a legal right to use the water from the servient estate and, in this sense, owned the water. This arrangement was asymmetrical: the holder of the servitude exercised his right at the expense of his neighbor and gave nothing in return; at least, nothing was legally required. The owner of the dominant estate had a broad right to use his neighbor's property, including repairs and maintenance, while the owner of the servient estate had a negative duty not to interfere with the use of the servitude. Both parties were expected to respect each other's property. Local custom influenced the rules governing servitudes as well as the establishment of these rights. A servitude could be created when long-standing practice was recognized as a legal right. In addi-

48. In general, on private grants to use the public aqueducts, see Bruun, *Water Supply,* 64–96; Evans, *Water Distribution,* 8–10; Peachin, *Frontinus,* 118–34; Taylor, *Public Needs and Private Pleasures,* 67–76. On the assimilation of public grants to private servitudes, see Palma, "Derivazioni di acqua," 448–52.

49. A few legal cases refer to what appears to be sale of a servitude separate from land: see *D.* 8.3.14 Pompon. 32 *ad Q. Muc.* (see Capogrossi Colognesi, *Servitù d'acqua,* 80–81 n. 149 on emending the text to remove the reference to sale); *D.* 8.4.6.3a Ulp. 28 *ad Sab.; D.* 8.5.16 Iul. 7 *Dig.; D.* 19.1.3.2 Pompon. 9 *ad Sab.; D.* 19.1.6.5–6 Pompon. 9 *ad Sab.; D.* 21.2.10 Cels. 27 *Dig.* These cases are probably postclassical (i.e., later than the period under examination here) and probably deal with personal servitudes: see Capogrossi Colognesi, *Servitù d'acqua,* 77, 80–81 n. 149. In addition, a few inscriptions refer to the sale of water, but these concern assessing fees for use of water in municipal systems (see Eck, "Wasserversorgung," 79–81). The legal cases of apparent sale may in fact concern such fees for use, since there are three cases on this topic as well: see *D.* 7.1.27.3 Ulp. 18 *ad Sab.; D.* 19.1.4.1 Papin. 3 *Resp.; D.* 30.39.5 Ulp. 21 *ad Sab.* On fees for use, see also chapter 1 in the present study. It also appears to have been possible to purchase freedom from a servitude, as indicated in an inscription from Pompeii, *CIL* 10.787 (see Biondi, *Categoria,* 104–5; Solazzi, *Specie ed estinzione,* 144–45).

tion, it was usual for the parties to a servitude, the owners of the dominant and servient estates, to agree to a *modus* or terms limiting the exercise of a servitude.[50] In the case of water servitudes, the parties might specify the materials that could be used to repair a water channel or set up a schedule for channeling water.

Water was not, however, the only resource that might be in scarce supply, and over time, servitudes were developed to regulate other activities and resources. By the early first century BC, there were servitudes for, among other things, pasturing and watering herds, storing crops, gathering stakes for a vineyard, and piling up debris for later removal.[51] Like the original four, the new rustic servitudes were conceived as property rights attached to the land itself and considered predial servitudes. This rule was articulated for the right of drawing water, *ius hauriendi,* one of these new servitudes: "the right of drawing water belongs not to a person but to a property" [*hauriendi ius non hominis, sed praedii est*] (*D.* 8.3.20.3 Pompon. 33 *ad Sab.*). The new servitudes seem to have quickly come into common use, as *haustus* is mentioned in paragraph 79 of the *lex Coloniae Iuliae Genetivae,* the constitution of a triumviral colony in Spain created by Octavian and Antony (*CIL* 2.5439 = *ILS* 6087). Though the inscription recording this constitution is Flavian, the rules regarding

50. The *modus* did not affect the basic conception of the right as unified (see Biondi, *Categoria,* 638–44; Grosso, *Servitù prediali,* 159–63, with references). Furthermore, the *modus* or terms governing the exercise of a servitude are to be distinguished from conditions because a servitude could not be created on a contingency of any kind, temporal or otherwise (*D.* 8.1.4 pr.-2 Papin. 7 *Quaest*). There is some variation in the form of these agreements (see, e.g., *D.* 8.5.9.1 Paul. 21 *ad Ed.; D.* 8.6.11 pr. Marcel. 4 *Dig.*), which Franciosi (*Servitù prediali,* 109–18) explains historically: in their early forms, the three rights-of-way (*via, iter, actus*) were not defined as strictly as in classical and postclassical law. For an exceptional type of temporary servitude, see E. Caiazzo, "In tema di servitù *ad tempus.*" See also chapters 1 and 2 in the present study.

51. There were new rustic servitudes for raising the height of a building/obstructing light (*D.* 8.3.2 pr. Nerat. 4 *Reg.*); pasturing oxen, collecting and storing farm produce, collecting stakes for a vineyard, making a pile of debris from quarrying (*D.* 8.3.3 pr.-2 Ulp. 17 *ad Ed.*); pasturing and watering oxen (*D.* 8.3.4 Papin. 2 *Resp.*); drawing water, watering oxen, digging clay, burning lime (*D.* 8.3.5.1 Ulp. 17 *ad Ed.*); quarrying stone, digging sand, taking timber to support vines, having a shepherd's hut as part of servitude for pasturing or watering cattle (*D.* 8.3.6.1 Paul. 15 *ad Plaut.*); and making a dung heap, though the case does not specify whether this should be treated as rural or urban (*D.* 8.5.17.2 Alf. 2 *Dig.*). On the date of the newer servitudes, particularly *haustus,* or the right to draw water, see Capogrossi Colognesi, *Servitù d'acqua,* 108; cf. 70–78. The earliest sources for these new servitudes are late republican (Varro, *LL* 5.27; Cic. *Leg.* 114; Cic. *de Orat.* 179; cf. Cic. *Caec.* 74), yet the dramatic date of Cicero's *de Oratore* suggests that they were already in use toward the end of the second century BC.

servitudes, along with most of its other provisions, are thought to belong to the period of the colony's foundation. Even if, as Capogrossi Colognesi has argued, the provision refers to local custom rather than to the actual Roman legal concept, the simple use of the legal term attests to wide familiarity with the new, praetorian servitudes.[52] It is probably also at this time that rustic servitudes came to be treated as incorporeal rights rather than as corporeal assets of an estate (all the other *res mancipi* were corporeal); urban servitudes, created in this later era, were probably not ever treated as *res mancipi*.[53] The change affected practice more than classification: the rustic servitudes were still classified as *res mancipi* and property, but their intangible nature was recognized in legal rules. For example, a *lex Scribonia,* dated usually to the late republic, created a ban on acquiring servitudes and other intangible rights by *usucapio*—that is, by long possession, usually two years for real property and one year for other kinds of things.[54]

The coexistence of the older concept of a servitude as physical property alongside the new abstract right created some apparent contradictions in the rules for servitudes. For example, though a servitude was conceived as a unified whole, it could be governed by terms or a *modus* that effectively divided it, as when water was channeled on a daily or hourly schedule (e.g., *D.* 43.20.4 Iulian. 41 *Dig.; D.* 8.6.16 Procul. 1 *Epist.*). More dramatically, when a dominant estate was divided into parcels that were sold separately, the whole servitude went with each parcel, although clearly, unless the water supply was augmented, the water had to be divided between the two properties (*D.* 8.3.25 Pompon. 34 *ad Sab.*). The water could be divided, but the right remained whole. The apparent inconsistency between a property right and an abstract right of use emerges most clearly in what I call the "use-it-or-lose-it" rule. According to this rule, a servitude was lost if the right was not ex-

52. Capogrossi Colognesi, *Servitù d'acqua,* 118–19, with note 215.

53. On the classification of urban servitudes, see Kaser, *RP* 1:441. Capogrossi Colognesi (*Servitù d'acqua,* 149–57) argues that the concept of incorporeal rights arose in the early first century BC. Our sources are not definitive, but other legal developments of this period involve the same kind of thinking, such as the creation of urban servitudes, which were never considered as corporeal, and of usufruct, another kind of right in someone else's property (discussed in chapter 3 in the present study). See also Biondi, *Categoria,* 662, 665–70. In general on these types of right in another person's property (i.e., servitudes and usufruct), see Kaser, *RP* 1:440, 449–50.

54. For the *Lex Scribonia* as it applied to servitudes, see *D.* 41.3.4.28 Paul. 54 *ad Ed.,* with Grosso, *Servitù prediali,* 18–19. Kaser (*RP* 1:444–45) dates the *Lex Scribonia* to the late republic.

ercised for two years or for the period of time agreed on by the parties to the servitude.[55] Applying this rule to a servitude for channeling water seems straightforward: if a person did not channel water for two years, he lost his right. But what if the servitude was regulated by a seasonal, daily, or hourly schedule? The exercise of the right no longer conforms to a clear, unified concept of property; rather, it relies solely on the abstract notion of a right to use, which exists all the time, even though it is used only intermittently.[56]

Because these contradictions were accepted by the Roman legal system and the landowners who relied on it, servitudes became a flexible tool for managing access to scarce resources—a more flexible system than is typical of irrigation schemes. In anthropological studies of irrigation communities, two basic patterns have been observed. In one type of system, associated with large rivers, water rights are inseparable from land rights, and water is allocated in proportion to land. In the second type, water rights are separable from land rights and are allocated in fixed units of time.[57] Both patterns were known in the ancient Roman world, but they were not implemented in the same ways. The public water supply was allocated in proportion to land allotments, though, as noted earlier, these imperial grants were personal and could be separated from the property. An example of proportional distribution of a municipal water supply in the Roman era can be found in an inscription from Roman Spain, the *lex rivi Hiberiensis*.[58] This decree from the time of Hadrian records the resolution of a dispute within a local irrigation community located on the right bank of the middle branch of the river Ebro. In the decree, water is allocated in proportion to the amount of property, as are responsibilities for maintenance and the right to police the system. A local system in Roman Africa known from an inscription also allotted water in proportion to landholdings.[59] A proportional distribution could be used when servitudes were involved, but it was a default allocation

55. *FIRA* 2.333 = Paul. *Sent.* 1.17.1–2, with Kaser, *RP* 1:446 at n. 68; Solazzi, *Specie ed estinzione*, 159–63 (see, in general, chapter 4, "L'estinzione," 157–82); Grosso, *Servitù prediali*, 249–50. See also chapter 1 in the present study for the rule applied to a servitude exercised on a seasonal or daily or hourly schedule (*D.* 8.6.7 Paul. 13 *ad Plaut.*).

56. On the development of this concept of use in relation to the praetorian interdicts, see Capogrossi Colognesi, *Struttura della proprietà*, 391–435.

57. Hunt and Hunt, "Canal Irrigation," 391. Throughout their article, Hunt and Hunt work with concepts developed in Glick, *Irrigation and Society*.

58. *Lex Riv. Hib.* 1.24–26, 1.60, with Beltrán Lloris, "Irrigation Decree," 170–71. For the discovery of the inscription, see *AE* (1993): 295–96 (no. 1043).

59. *CIL* 8.18587 = *CIL* 8.4440 = *ILS* 5793, with Shaw, "Lamasba," 82–84. For more discussion of proportional allotments, see chapter 4 in the present study.

that took effect only if the parties did not negotiate distribution of the water. As noted earlier, servitudes could be regulated by schedules based on volume or fixed units of time, on a seasonal, daily, or even hourly schedule, yet they were attached to the land. Thus the law of servitudes offered flexible configurations of water use, adapting the legal rules to the needs of landowners and the constraints of the local water supply.

In the late republic, economic and cultural factors also spurred the development of new legal mechanisms related to servitudes, most notably interdicts created by the urban praetor and included in his annual edict (i.e., list of all the causes of legal action under the *ius civile*). During the second century BC, the praetor's edict came to include several interdicts aimed specifically at protecting servitudes for water use. These interdicts are covered by several chapters of book 43 of the *Digest* (daily and summer water, *D.* 43.20; water channels, *D.* 43.21; springs, *D.* 43.22; drains, *D.* 43.23; cf., on rivers, *D.* 43.12–15). The role of the praetor in protecting servitudes and in transferring them from one owner to another is part of a larger pattern of the urban praetor using his edict to respond to economic needs and interests.[60] In the same era, the urban praetor was also concerned with the public water supply: Q. Marcius Rex, urban praetor in 144 BC, repaired aqueducts and built the Aqua Marcia (Front. *Aq.* 7.1–4; Pliny, *NH* 31.41; cf. Livy, *Epit.* 188–90).[61]

An interdict served as a preliminary phase, a legal mechanism that could be used before a full lawsuit about ownership of a servitude (*vindicatio*). The interdict provided immediate relief (like a restraining order) and could prevent loss due to interruption in the water supply.[62] For example, if a neighbor cut off a water channel, the owner could ask the praetor for an interdict to restore the flow pending the outcome of the suit over ownership. This im-

60. For the praetor's interest in water rights, see *D.* 8.3.1.2 Ulp. 2 *Inst.;* Cato, *ORF* 42–43. More generally, on the praetor's response to social and economic issues, see Frier, "Urban Praetors"; Watson, *Law Making,* 31–62; Brennan, *Praetorship,* 1:130–33, 442–53.

61. For the date of interdicts *de rivis* and for daily and summer water, see Capogrossi Colognesi, *Servitù d'acqua,* 137, and more generally Watson, *Law Making,* 41 (based on Ter. *Eun.* 319), contra Robinson, "The Water Supply." Most praetorian reforms, including the interdicts, belong to the period of greatest economic change in Rome, c. 200–50 BC, see Kaser, *RP* 1.141, 206–7. See also Gaius, *Inst.* 4.138–60 with de Zulueta II.289–93; on Q. Marcius Rex (*pr.* 144 BC) and his work on the water supply, Brennan, *Praetorship,* 1.218–19.

62. Kaser, *RP* 1:447; on *vindicatio,* see 1:128–29, 49, 446. The aim seems to have been to preserve the *status quo ante* while the matter was pending; see *D.* 43.20.7 Paul. 5 *Sent.* and chapter 3 in the present study.

mediate relief served the needs of landowners whose crops needed water to thrive: for example, if the water were restored only after the violets had wilted, the loss would be greater and more difficult to recoup.

Other than servitudes, there is little Roman law about private water rights, though some late imperial statutes do deal with them.[63] The public water supply was regulated by numerous public laws, some of which are collected by Frontinus (*Aq.* 94–115).[64] Among these statutes and decrees, only two touch on the private water supply. Frontinus begins his catalogue with an old law that offers indirect evidence for private water use.

> Among our ancestors all water was designated for public uses and it was specified thus: "no private citizen should conduct any water other than what falls on the ground from a basin." (For these are the words of the law), that is, the water that overflows from the basin: this water we call windfall.
>
> [*Apud antiquos omnis a qua in usus publicos eroga<ba>tur et cautum ita fuit: 'ne quis privatus aliam ducit<o> quam quae ex lacu humum accidit' (haec enim sunt verba eius legis), id est quae ex lacu abundavit; eam nos caducam vocamus.*] (*Aq.* 94.3)

This rule clearly applied to the public water supply, reinforcing the idea that in the good old days, all the water from the city aqueducts was reserved for the public good. But the very existence of the law suggests that the reality was less than ideal. This rule may be connected with the action of the censors in 184 BC when, as part of a general assault on luxury and extravagant behavior, they attempted to stop Romans from using public land and water (Livy 39.44.4). There may also already have been private channels involved in this illegal use of city water, as Bruun suggests.[65]

The second law that seems to concern private water use is the so-called *lex Rivalicia,* mentioned by Festus in his definition of the Greek term *sifus* (σίφων, "siphon").

> A siphon works through the pipes themselves. This is what is called σίφων in Greek, and in the same way in the *lex Rivalicia,* which was en-

63. For late imperial statutes about servitudes, see Biondi, *Categoria,* 656.

64. On Frontinus's selective collection, see Peachin, *Frontinus,* 77, 146–50. See also Crawford, *Roman Statutes,* nos. 42–43. See, in general, Bruun, *Water Supply;* Evans, *Water Distribution.*

65. On Livy 39.44.4 and Front. *Aq.* 94.3 as evidence for early private water channels, see Bruun, "Roman World," 586.

acted when Servius Sulpicius brought the bill to the people. . . . Let the *montani* or *pagani* divide the water by siphons, and so long as they divide the water among themselves, let this be the judgment.

[Sifus [usurpatum est pro tu]bis ipsis, id quod Graece [dicitur σίφων, *in le]ge rivalicia sic est, [quae lata est rogant]e populum Ser. Sulpi[cio]. . . . [mon]tani paganive si[fis aquam dividunto], donec eam inter se [diviserint, ... s] iudicatio esto.]* (*FIRA* 1.81 = Festus p. 458L)

The fragmentary state of Festus's citation makes secure interpretation and dating impossible,[66] but it does give some clues to the law's historical context. We can determine that the law was probably from the republican era, on the basis of the partially preserved name *Ser. Sulpi*———, possibly the name of the sponsor of the law, who can be identified either with Servius Sulpicius Galba (cos. 144 BC) or with the jurist Servius Sulpicius Rufus (cos. 50 BC). The law may be even older, and if it is, it could have applied to the entirely private system of water distribution that existed before the construction of the Aqua Appia in 312 BC. The aim of the law is a little easier to reconstruct. Its title, *lex Rivalicia,* suggests that it regulated private water distribution: *rivalicia* is probably to be connected with the nouns *rivus,* "channel," and *rivales,* designating neighbors who shared a channel. Ulpian's etymology of *rivus* is suggestive: "a 'rivus' is an area depressed lengthwise where water flows down and whose name comes from 'flowing'" *[rivus est locus per longitudinem depressus, quo aqua decurrat, cui nomen est* ἀπὸ τοῦ ῥεῖν] (*D.* 43.21.1.2 Ulp. 70 *ad Ed.*).[67] In addition, the involvement of *pagani* and *montani* points to some kind of public management of the water supply shared by the *rivales.* Comparative evidence from the *lex rivi Hiberiensis,* a later inscription from Roman Spain, supports these interpretations, where *pagani* were responsible for ensuring that participants in the irrigation community complied with rules for water use and provided the necessary materials and funds for upkeep of the channels (*lex rivi Hib.* 4.2.b). Though this Spanish decree is later

66. For a discussion of the text and its chronology, see Crook, "*Lex 'Rivalicia.'*" More recently, Crawford (*Roman Statutes,* 2:727–28), agrees with an earlier date, on the basis of the language of the law, which he finds similar to that of the *lex Plaetoria* from before 241 BC. If the fine was recorded in *sesterces,* however, the law would have to be later than ca. 141 BC, though it is likely that Frontinus or his source modernized the denomination, according to Crawford.

67. As discussed in the preceding section of this introduction, *rivalis* occurs only four times in this technical sense.

and clearly concerns a public water supply, it suggests that the *lex Rivalicia* mentioned by Festus was not unparalleled and that these kinds of arrangements may have been common not only in Italy but around the Mediterranean. Some of these irrigation communities were administered through the local government, as in the Spanish decree, but others may have involved privately owned water systems. In any case, these public decrees do fit a larger pattern of using law to regulate water-sharing arrangements, and this pattern can be traced back at least to the early second century BC, when servitudes began to take shape.

THEORETICAL APPROACHES

Climate and landscape made water a limited resource on Roman farms, and the economic activities of Roman landowners increased competition for water. Servitudes are not an obvious response to these social, economic, and environmental challenges. In fact, the asymmetrical nature of the institution begs for explanation. A servitude gave its holder the right to use his neighbor's property in exchange for nothing.[68] On the face of it, this legal relationship seems to require a idealistic altruism that is hard to reconcile with modern notions of economic rationality, much less with the competitive nature of Roman society.

The allocation of resources is typically an economic or environmental problem, and in the case of servitudes, managing the local water supply also involved social and cultural norms. Because water was unevenly distributed across the landscapes of central Italy, access to water depended on social relationships, on neighbors sharing a stream or spring and channeling water from one property to the next. These unequal exchanges were embedded in the social networks of rural communities and sustained by social morality and by the shared aim of agricultural productivity. Agricultural lease law developed in a similar way. Frier explains, "Early classical lease law was solidly founded in prevailing agricultural practice. . . . The jurists raised commercial practice into law and protected it as law. They were strongly sympathetic to traditional patterns of production, and to the social establishment which these patterns served to support."[69] Like lease law, servitudes institutional-

68. On the asymmetrical allocation of rights in servitudes, see the discussion earlier in this introduction and, in general, chapter 2.

69. Frier, "Law, Technology, and Social Change," 226; cf. *Landlords and Tenants*, 198. For a more in-depth appraisal of imperial policy and its accommodation of local practices, see Kehoe, *Law and the Rural Economy*, 93–129.

ized the social patterns that promoted agricultural productivity as they formalized relations among people in rural communities. In this way, servitudes can be considered an institution of "customary law." Parisi defines the phenomenon this way: "Custom thus amounts to a spontaneous norm which is recognized by the legal system and granted enforcement as a proper legal rule . . . customary rules derive their force from the concurrence of a uniform practice and a subjective belief that adherence to them is obligatory."[70] Though, in the sources, the origins of servitudes cannot be traced back to ancient customs, the relationship between law and society in servitudes follows the patterns of customary law in important respects.

When neighbors shared a local water supply, their ongoing relationships provided a moral framework to support informal equity and an efficient allocation of water. The community might come together to build or repair a local aqueduct system on occasion.[71] But servitudes involved more intensive interaction, even day-to-day contact, at least to the extent of entering a neighbor's property to draw water from a spring. These interactions fostered cooperation between neighbors, generating a network of one-on-one relationships that could involve nearly everyone in the community. In close-knit communities, shared values and ongoing relationships provided the means of balancing the asymmetry and generating an equilibrium of costs and benefits. These social and economic relationships have been modeled in sociological studies that offer key parallels for servitudes. For example, Gallant has used a similar approach to investigate the strategies used by ancient Greek households to manage scarce resources.[72] In the modern world, Ellickson's study of relations between ranchers and "yuppies" in northern California shows how neighbors used a variety of methods—gossip, self-help violence, and legal action—to sustain their traditional grazing practices.[73] The same pattern has been observed specifically in irrigation systems, as described, for example, in Fernea's comparative analysis: "the point is that the social and cultural attributes of which I speak—shared norms and values,

70. Parisi, "Spontaneous Emergence of Law," 603.

71. Thomas and Wilson, "Water Supply for Roman Farms," 190–91. See also chapter 3 in the present study.

72. Gallant, *Risk and Survival*, 143–69. Erdkamp (*Grain Market*, 55–71, especially 63–64) accepts Gallant's approach as valid for the Roman Empire, despite some problems with his method. For a more pessimistic view of the role of elites and the law in negotiating water sharing in local communities in the ancient world, see Horden and Purcell, *Corrupting Sea*, 255; for medieval Italy, Squatriti, *Water and Society*, 89–96.

73. Ellickson, *Order without Law*.

mutual social relations and institutions, however few or many, simple or complex—precede active participation in the development and maintenance of the technical social controls which together constitute systematic use of natural resources."[74] These sociological approaches complement more traditional models of Roman society; in fact, Palma's study of urban servitudes in Rome considers social contexts without the sociological models and comes to similar conclusions. According to Palma, the oldest legal institutions (including servitudes) are characterized by group solidarity, which functions in a normative way to resolve conflict and to preserve the community and its shared values.[75]

Servitudes were an old institution, but they persisted in part because law is inherently conservative and in part because Roman society itself was conservative. Their persistence also indicates that the social practices and shared values surrounding servitudes remained productive for Roman landowners, even as their aims and methods of farming changed. Rather than a straightforward evolution from social control to legal rights, servitudes represent an ongoing dialogue among competing interests and values in allocating the rural water supply. My investigation reconstructs and analyzes this dialogue, in much the way McGinn assesses the "social adequacy" of law in his study of prostitution in ancient Rome. His approach to legal questions proceeds along three trajectories, as he explains, "first, the social and legal forces that contribute to law-finding; second, the structures and rules that make up the 'law'; and, third, the impact the law has on behavior in society."[76] These three interrelated aspects of legal analysis also guide my study of servitudes.

As part of my investigation into the social adequacy of servitudes, I include economic attitudes and behaviors, because the Romans recognized that access to water was critical to agriculture, the largest sector of their economy. In the chapters that follow, I examine how Roman landowners adapted the legal institution of servitudes to make the most of available resources while maintaining good relations with their neighbors and making their land productive, even profitable. Commons theory provides a helpful model for understanding these dynamics. A "commons" is a communally owned resource

74. Fernea, "Conflict in Irrigation," 77.

75. Palma, *Iura vicinitatis,* 109; cf. 30–42 (an ideal of neighborliness could mediate tensions between rural neighbors), 46–54 (the role of the good neighbor in sustaining servitudes for right-of-way and other questions of property rights), 55–109 (archaic legal institutions other than servitudes and how they were embedded in close-knit communities).

76. McGinn, *Prostitution, Sexuality, and Law,* 5–6 (insufficiency of evolutionary theories to explain the role of law in society).

that is likely to be destroyed when everyone exploits it in pursuit of individual gain. The problem of the commons was first discussed in connection with shared grazing land: everyone who grazes animals has an incentive to add one more animal to his herd, then another and another, because each additional animal brings him more profit. This pursuit of individual profit harms the other people who share the pasture, since it takes away from what their animals can eat, limits the number of animals they can graze, cuts into their profits, and, finally, if carried to its logical extreme, destroys the pasture and everyone's livelihood. Managing a common resource depends on the effective application of two principles: *subtractability* (each use subtracts from the common supply) and *excludability* (to insure supply to some people, others need to be excluded, even when controlling access is difficult).[77] When the community manages its common resources effectively, it conserves the resource by limiting access to sustainable levels. The Romans used servitudes in just this way to structure water-sharing arrangements.

Commons theory was developed around communally owned resources; that is, the people who shared the pasture in the herdsman's dilemma also owned the land jointly. In such a community, the limits are enforced through shared social norms, and community norms played an important role in defining and enforcing local water-sharing systems in the Roman world, as reflected especially in inscriptions that describe these systems. But in a community with a legal system, law is often used to support the social morality that underlies a commons.[78] The regime of private water rights in Roman law functions in this way. Recall that a servitude was a kind of property right in which the landowner owned the water governed by the servitude. Even though the Romans treated water as private property, they continued to rely on social constraints to enforce the water-sharing arrangements that were articulated in servitudes. This aspect of commons theory fits with the concept of customary law, where the force of legal rules derives from social norms.[79] A similar combination of legal and social sanctions was deployed

---

77. On subtractability and excludability, see Feeny et al., "Tragedy of the Commons," 76–80, especially 78. For a summary of the herdsman's dilemma, see Hardin, "Tragedy of the Commons," 6–8.

78. On the use of law to buttress a commons system, see Ostrom, "Reflections on the Commons," 100, 104–8; Feeny et al., "Tragedy of the Commons," 84–87. See also Ostrom, "Private and Common Property Rights."

79. Parisi ("Spontaneous Emergence of Law," 610–11) discusses the balance between common good and self-interest in customary law, using the prisoner's dilemma, which explores reciprocity in much the same way as the dilemma of the commons.

to manage local irrigation systems in the region of Valencia in medieval Spain. Though there were municipal regulations governing the water supply and though the system was administered by town officials, much of the real control was vested in the people who actually used the water. Glick's study of this medieval irrigation community is a seminal work for anthropological approaches to the water supply and in some ways prefigures the concepts more recently articulated in commons theory.[80] Because commons theory embraces social, economic, and legal perspectives on the allocation of water resources, it helps to answer Traina's call for a wholistic understanding of approaches to the environment in the ancient world.[81]

Commons theory directly addresses social and environmental aspects of the water supply, and it also offers a starting point for exploring the economic contexts of servitudes. Managing a commons involves allocating a scarce resource, a function that markets can also accomplish. The concepts of excludability and subtractability assume some kind of calculations about the need for water and its value to those who share the local supply. In fact, economic issues had a direct bearing on the water supply and the legal institutions that Romans developed to manage it. After the war with Hannibal (218–201 BC), Roman agriculture became more oriented toward the market rather than aiming at only subsistence, though self-sufficiency continued to be a goal, alongside commercial agriculture.[82] The crops most likely to earn a profit required irrigation or a steady supply of water. In these new economic circumstances, landowners reevaluated their interest in water, treating it as an economic commodity and not simply as a resource to be shared among neighbors. At the same time, the fashion for luxury villas put strains on the rural water supply and changed social conditions in rural areas. The real estate market for rural land also tended to disrupt traditional practices, those long-standing, close relationships that supported servitudes and other water-sharing arrangements.[83] As landowners competed with new neighbors

---

80. Glick, *Irrigation and Society,* ix, 31 (description of the irrigation community), 187–97 (see particularly 192–97 on the parallels between irrigation practices in medieval Valencia and ancient Rome). For a similar application of Glick to Roman conditions, see Horden and Purcell, *Corrupting Sea,* 250–52.

81. Traina, *Paludi e bonifiche,* 18, 21.

82. On the mix of crops for market and self-sufficiency, see Erdkamp, *Grain Market,* 46–54, 95–105; De Neeve, "Price of Agricultural Land," 84–97; Duncan-Jones, *Economy of the Roman Empire,* 34–36; Love, *Antiquity and Capitalism,* 59–109. For the change in Roman economic horizons after the Hannibalic War, see n. 18 in the present introduction.

83. On the demand for estates near Rome and in Campania, see Rawson, "Ciceronean Aristocracy," 95–96.

for water for their market crops, they adapted servitudes to advance not only their social interests but also their economic ones.

An investigation of the economic interests surrounding servitudes raises methodological questions about the nature of economic activity and attitudes in ancient Rome. Our own assumptions about economic behavior, ancient and modern, shape our explanations of why the Romans spent money as they did and how they understood their decisions about property and trade. Scholarly discussions of the Roman economy have at times become polarized around two positions that are often referred to as "modernist" or "primitivist." For the modernists, there are few, if any, significant differences between ancient and modern economic activity and attitudes. The primitivist view assumes that the ancients made decisions about money, trade, and agriculture not on the basis of what we would recognize as economic interests but for other reasons. For example, the decision to purchase a rural estate would be understood as a capital investment by the modernists, whereas a primitivist would see the acquisition as an expression of social status. Two scholars whose early work on the ancient economy is still influential are often presented as standard-bearers of these two views: Moses Finley (primitivist) and Michael Rostovtzeff (modernist). But as Saller has recently argued, polarizing discussions of their work has misrepresented both their views.

> The contrast between Finley and Rostovtzeff is commonly summed up in the following polarities: primitivist versus modernist, no-trade versus long-distance trade, autarky versus integrated markets, technological stagnation versus technological progress; no-economic-growth versus growth, non-rational traditionalist versus rational individualists. These polarities are grossly misleading for two related reasons: 1) they seriously misrepresent the views of both Rostovtzeff and Finley, and 2) the polarities are very far from representing the full spectrum of possibilities, as both Rostovtzeff and Finley knew.[84]

In fact, Rostovtzeff and Finley agreed on the basic contours of the ancient economy, according to Saller, and both emphasized the limits on economic activity. Agriculture was the mainstay of the economy and was market-oriented to some degree, but markets were not integrated by long-distance trade, as they are in the modern world. Limited trade was stimulated in part by taxation that requisitioned grain for Rome and supplies

84. Saller, "Framing the Debate," 252; see 252–61 for analysis of Finley's and Rostovtzeff's positions and the points of agreement about the ancient economy. See also, more recently, the nuanced picture of Rome's market economy in Temin, "Market Economy."

for the army.[85] Local markets provided an outlet for specialized produce that could earn a cash profit.[86] Landowners, large and small, shared a common goal—steady productivity—that included both supplying the household (self-sufficiency, or autarky) and producing a surplus to sell on the market (commercial agriculture), though the scale of this commercial activity varied.[87] These shared assumptions are important because they provide the foundation for most scholarship on the Roman economy, whether it tends toward the modernist or primitivist view.

My approach to the economic issues relating to servitudes starts from this common ground. Private water rights helped to secure the resources a landowner needed to make his land productive, that is, to provide the steady income to support his household, large or small. But a servitude could also allow a landowner to participate in local markets or to increase his participation in these markets by cultivating specialized produce for sale. In studying the impact of local markets on water rights, I adopt the modified "consumer city" model developed in Morley's study of Rome's markets and hinterland. Rather than a simple country/city dualism, Morley assumes a more complicated exchange between Rome and the *suburbium*, one that encouraged specialized farming in the areas with access to urban markets: "The demands of Rome for perishable goods like fruit and vegetables and for luxury foodstuffs supported the development of particular forms of production in the *suburbium*."[88] Growing produce for the market and for the household involved satisfying basic material needs, an important factor recognized already by Finley and emphasized recently by Tchernia in his analysis of responses to Finley's model.[89] In this way, my study contributes to the developing picture of Roman economic practices, with their aim of "satisficing," as Kehoe has described it, and limited participation in markets.[90]

---

85. Hopkins, "Rome, Taxes, Rents and Trade"; Erdkamp, *Grain Market*, 206–57.

86. For Rome's produce markets, see Morley, *Metropolis and Hinterland*, 83–107.

87. For the assumption that steady productivity was a shared goal, see Kehoe's "Approaches to Profit and Management" (46–47) and, more generally, his *Investment, Profit, and Tenancy*. For the participation of small-scale landholders in local markets, see Morley, *Metropolis and Hinterland*, 166–74; Erdkamp, *Grain Market*, 95–105.

88. Morley, *Metropolis and Hinterland*, 107; see also 13–32 for a nice review of the "consumer city" model and its applicability (or not) to Rome.

89. Tchernia, "Quelle rationalité?" 290.

90. See Kehoe, *Law and the Rural Economy*, 29–52 (economic models for the Roman economy), especially 37–38 (satisficing), 39–43 (rationality in the Roman economy). Erdkamp (*Grain Market*, 101–5) argues that selling and buying on the market might be a rational approach to achieving long-term security but does not necessarily reflect a fully capitalistic approach to farming.

My analysis of private water rights also moves beyond this consensus view of the Roman economy to address two of the central issues in economic discussions: growth and rationality. The legal evidence allows us to generate a more nuanced understanding of these issues, as encouraged by Saller in his analysis of approaches to the ancient economy (cited earlier). Though I do not argue for dramatic growth in the Roman economy and cannot calculate the amount of growth on the basis of legal cases, my work contributes to a growing body of scholarship that examines the ways that Romans participated in markets and how they approached productivity. My study provides the possibility of limited growth supported by the use of law to develop the natural resources that could increase productivity. In modern legal studies, it is generally recognized that treating a natural resource, such as water or land, as private property can facilitate economic development. Getzler notes in his recent history of water rights in common law, "In today's world private property in goods such as land and water is commonly justified by the theory that clearly defined, assignable, and enforceable legal titles to appropriable goods are a critical feature of productive market economies."[91] In relation to Roman society, Kehoe has demonstrated that law was effective in protecting property rights and encouraging economic activity, and his conclusions are apposite to my argument about servitudes.[92] In a servitude, water was treated as private property and as an economic commodity. Unlike the law of sale, where the structure of the legal institution limited commerce (e.g., long-distance sale was impossible), private property law was a flexible tool for economic development.[93] Servitudes in particular accommodated Roman landowners' ideas about natural resources and their role in making the land productive.

By introducing a modern concept like the commons, I do not mean to signal that I take a purely "modernist" approach to the Roman economy. In fact, my interest in commons theory stems from a belief that Roman law responded to social as well as economic factors. As noted earlier, according to commons theory, in a society with a developed legal system, private property rights can be used to support the social systems that regulate common resources. By combining the insights of commons theory with legal theory that recognizes the economic impact of water rights, I include in my discus-

91. Getzler, *History of Water Rights*, 1.

92. Kehoe, *Law and the Rural Economy*, 18, 53–91, 93–129.

93. On the law of sale and its limiting effect on economic activity, see Tchernia, "Quelle rationalité?" 289.

sion both economic and noneconomic issues that affected the development of servitudes. Indeed, my approach echoes the recommendations of a recent analysis of the economics of water published by the International Irrigation Management Institute.[94] According to this analysis, water is treated as both a public good and an economic commodity in most modern societies, and each system brings its own set of benefits and costs. Though water for basic needs can best be delivered by a public system, the allocation of water beyond basic needs (e.g., for irrigation) involves complicated questions about economic factors, practical matters of infrastructure, and moral issues. Thus, modern, sociological approaches to the water supply include issues that have been classified as both modernist and primitivist in the scholarship on the Roman economy. For this reason, I am able to chart a middle ground—between primitivist and modernist approaches to the Roman economy—where, I argue, we can find a fuller understanding of how Roman law responded to the desires of landowners to improve the productivity of their land through investment and careful management.

Roman attitudes toward farming, investment, and economic activity in general involve a consideration of rationality in the technical sense associated with economic behavior. In modern economic theory, rationality is defined in terms of maximizing profit and pareto efficiency (or the zero-sum game). It is assumed that economic agents make rational choices, weighing costs and benefits in terms of their final, financial outcome, with clear and complete information about the issues. This kind of rationality aims at utility defined by pareto efficiency, that is, an efficient allocation of resources in which one person's utility cannot be increased without decreasing someone else's utility, the zero-sum game. Using this theoretical concept of rationality to understand the ancient economy has been problematic and has contributed to the primitivist-versus-modernist divide. This concept of rationality, however, is best understood as an ideal type against which to measure economic behavior and attitudes, a principle articulated by De Neeve and more recently by Tchernia in his analysis of the various approaches to rationality in studies of the Roman economy.[95] For Tchernia,

94. Perry, Rock, and Seckler, *Water as an Economic Good.*

95. See Tchernia, "Quelle rationalité?" 286–91 (idea of a continuum), 283 (questions about calculation). Cf. De Neeve, "Price of Agricultural Land," 97–98: "modern 'economic man' aiming at maximizing income and to this end acting fully rationally is an ideal type, i.e. a conception drawn from reality for analytical purposes, with an overemphasis on certain characteristics and neglect of others." Though more pessimistic, Lo Cascio allows that some sectors of Rome's economy were more rationalized than others ("Forme dell'economia," 315,

the opposition between primitivist and modernist approaches can be understood as part of a continuum of economic and social attitudes toward property and commerce. While the views of primitivists (no rational calculation) and modernists (idealized rationality) stand at the extremes of this continuum, there is room in between for the more complex and comprehensive approaches to the ancient economy that both Saller and Tchernia advocate. The key question is, what do we mean when we say that the Romans made or did not make decisions based on calculated policy? Or what sort of rational calculations did the Romans make, and how did they evaluate the outcome of their decisions?

In assessing the nature of rationality in private water rights, I draw from scholarship on both the ancient and modern economy that offers alternatives to the purely idealizing concept of rationality. My approach has been influenced in important ways by Dennis Kehoe's work on Roman law and economics. In his book *Law and the Rural Economy,* Kehoe uses new institutional economics to develop a beautifully theorized model for investigating the nature of rationality in the Roman economy and how Roman law encoded and promoted economically efficient practices.[96] Though the scope of Kehoe's study is somewhat broader than mine, I adopt and build on several parts of his model. As already outlined in relation to commons theory, the interplay of formal (i.e., legal) and informal institutions is key to understanding private water rights. Moreover, the law in general and private property rights in particular promote bargaining that leads to economically efficient decisions by individuals and to a legal institution (i.e., servitudes) with an economically effective design. Like Kehoe, I work from the premise that the Roman legal system played a real role in social and economic life, despite limitations generated by the ad hoc nature of lawsuits and the uneven quality of judges and judgments. Finally, I argue that Romans engaged in rational economic behavior; that is, they made systematic efforts to make calculated economic decisions despite asymmetrical and imperfect information about costs and benefits. Describing the nature of this rationality—where it falls on Tchernia's continuum and what features characterize it—is part of my project. The rules and legal cases about servitudes can inform us

---

323–27; cf. Jongman, *Pompeii,* 43). Cf. also Carandini, "Columella's Vineyard," 182 (presenting Kula's conclusions): "*Any economic activity is in fact to a certain extent both traditional and rational. . . .* Economic analysis could thus measure the degree and type of rationality present in a given historical reality and identify the conditions which discouraged or favoured its growth."

96. Kehoe, *Law and the Rural Economy,* 29–52.

about economic rationality both because water was understood by the Romans as a component in economic activity and because the law responded to these economic interests.

To explore the economic interests that shaped servitudes, I rely on the concepts of bounded and procedural rationality, developed by Herbert Simon. Bounded rationality, in contrast to a rationality defined in terms of an abstract utility, takes into account empirical evidence to understand the constraints and limitations on human goals and the means of achieving them. Simon explains the differences.

> Global Rationality, the rationality of neoclassical theory, assumes that the decision maker has a comprehensive, consistent utility function, knows all the alternatives that are available for choice, can compute the expected value of utility associated with each alternative, and chooses the alternative that maximizes expected utility. Bounded rationality, a rationality that is consistent with our knowledge of actual human choice behavior, assumes that the decision maker must search for alternatives, has egregiously incomplete and inaccurate knowledge about the consequences of actions, and chooses actions that are expected to be satisfactory (attain targets while satisfying constraints).[97]

Bounded rationality thus provides a framework for a systematic examination of economic decisions—the reasons behind the rationality. The related concept of procedural rationality focuses on the decision-making process—how people generate options and choose among them. The field of behavioral economics offers complementary approaches, with a focus on factors that complicate such concepts as rationality and maximizing; for example, in *Quasi Rational Economics,* Richard Thaler suggests categories for sorting out motives, distinguishing final outcomes from the more limited aims that more typically motivate decisions.[98]

Simon's concepts help to shift the discussion of rationality away from an all-or-nothing approach by providing a framework for characterizing rationality and exploring the middle ground on the continuum. This less idealizing approach to rationality is well suited to studying the Roman economy, where it is generally agreed that access to markets and information was far from perfect and that economic behavior was influenced by goals other than

97. Simon, *Empirically Based Microeconomics,* 17; see, in general, 3–31.
98. Thaler, *Quasi Rational Economics,* 43–50.

strict financial maximization, as formulated in Kehoe's *Law and the Rural Economy*.

> Given the lack of information surrounding any economic decision, and the impossibility for any economic actor to know fully the consequences of any particular action, we cannot analyze economic decisions in terms of wealth or utility maximization. Instead, we need to recognize that people or institutions will find various strategies to pursue what they perceive to be their utility in a changing world that they understand imperfectly.[99]

Applying this approach to servitudes, my study explores the strategies that Romans used to manage local water supplies. Some of these strategies are recognizably economic—for example, schedules that allot water by time or volume. In this way, privately owned water was treated like other resources on agricultural land, to judge by Rathbone's analysis of the management of the properties owned by Appianus in Roman Egypt. A large archive of records documenting the management of these properties provides evidence of rational calculation: for Rathbone, record keeping is itself a kind of rational activity, the careful accounting of costs that is also recommended in all the ancient agricultural handbooks.[100] Managing a local water supply also involved other kinds of strategies, such as cooperating with neighbors and bargaining with potential purchasers of land. Roman landowners had a range of priorities that led them to adopt various strategies that express a kind of rationality based on limited knowledge (would the spring dry up?) and using the available technology (e.g., dirt channels and, sometimes, the natural alternation of day and night). Overall, decisions about the water supply involved landowners in calculations that can be characterized as bounded rationality, and the contours of this economic behavior are reflected in the legal cases concerning water rights. My study of servitudes, then, advances our understanding of rationality in ancient economic activity by presenting new evidence for rational decisions about raising crops to earn a profit and investing in infrastructure to secure the water supply. Though

99. Kehoe, *Law and the Rural Economy,* 38; cf. *Investment, Profit, and Tenancy,* 17. For a qualified endorsement of Simon's ideas for the study of the ancient economy, see Tchernia, "Quelle rationalité?" 286.

100. Rathbone, *Economic Rationalism,* 400. Tchernia ("Quelle rationalité?" 288–89) qualifies Rathbone's conclusions.

literary anecdotes about individual landowners and their choices do not necessarily add up to a coherent system of rational economic planning, the legal cases institutionalized practice and thus represent a broader pattern of economic decisions that depend on rational expectations and calculations.[101]

To understand the rationality of private water rights, I have turned to commons theory because it accommodates both economic and social factors that affected the allocation of scarce resources. Commons theory bridges the divide between "primitivist" and "modernist" approaches to the ancient economy, by insisting on the role of community in managing resources. In addition, commons theory relies on an alternate rationality of not maximizing to both conserve water and secure access to it, allowing individuals to pursue their own economic aims in a limited way—a strategy that responds to social competition and environmental constraints. Most important for my investigation of servitudes, there is a place in commons theory for legal institutions to complement and extend the social systems that operate in a true commons. In the cases about servitudes, legal practices illustrate the balancing act between self-sufficiency and profit seeking, self-interest and neighborly duties—the same ambivalence about change that characterizes the rhetorical moralizing common in Roman literature, even the agricultural treatises. These competing aims are sometimes resolved when, for example, getting along with one's neighbor turns out to yield long-term profit despite a short-term cost.

Voluntary cooperative efforts may be virtuous, but they can also be economically efficient, however that efficiency is defined in a given social and cultural setting. In a seminal study, Kenneth Arrow analyzed altruism, self-interest, and social cohesion as rationales for exchange both in and outside the market, in response to R. Titmuss's *The Gift Relationship: From Human Blood to Social Policy* (1971). Arrow examined transactions surrounding the supply of blood available for transfusions in the United States and the United Kingdom and found that the commercialization of the blood supply discourages

101. On using legal sources to investigate the ancient economy, see Kehoe, *Investment, Profit, and Tenancy*, 9–15. He explains (13–14), "Thus the economic assumptions made by the jurists are not just to be considered within the framework of developing rules within a legal system subject to its own logic and hence divorced from the real world. Rather, these assumptions present us with an idealized view of the overall conditions to which all economic activities on the part of upper-class Romans were subject. . . . An analysis of the economic assumptions in the juristic sources, then, should allow us to construct a model describing the general principles that guided upper-class Romans in managing their wealth."

altruism and has a negative impact on medical care as well as social ethics. Arrow revises Titmuss's more radical position that gifts work better than economic exchange in allocating scarce resources. For Arrow, the two systems are compatible in the management of resources, a "class of unilateral transactions in which there is no element of payment in any direct or ordinary sense of the term." We expect intangibles, such as love and respect, to be outside the monetary economy, but as Arrow explains, tangible resources and services are also given away when "there is uncertainty about the quality of services and a difference between the degrees of knowledge possessed by buyer and seller."[102] It is interesting to note that Arrow's work, redefining rationality, appeared one year before the first edition of Finley's *Ancient Economy,* which has, in the end, led classicists to develop more sophisticated approaches to economic behavior and rationality in the ancient economy. For my study of water rights, Arrow's ideas are important because they provide a basis for the nonmaximizing rationality that commons theory endorses and that also characterizes the Roman law of servitudes.

Among Roman landowners, the local water supply was treated as a common, a scarce resource, but also as a commodity that had economic value and could best be managed through enlightened self-interest. Lest we idealize the relationships between rural neighbors, it should be acknowledged that the practices of these landowners, documented in legal cases about water rights, show a variety of choices and behaviors—greed, restraint, imagination, and plodding literalism—all of which contribute to a complex picture of farming and rural life. For this reason, this study of Roman law paints on a large canvas: close analysis of legal issues opens new perspectives on social relations, economic behavior, and the landscapes of ancient Italy.

A NOTE ON SOURCES

This study relies on an interdisciplinary mix of sources to investigate private water rights in relation to rural water use and agricultural markets. Law, literature, and archaeology, including inscriptions, all contribute valuable information about the ways that rural landowners used water. Combining these diverse sources yields robust arguments (if, in some places, circumstantial) about the practices of rural landowners as well as the development of legal ideas about water rights.

The main legal source for water rights is the *Digest of Justinian,* a sixth-cen-

102. Arrow, "Gifts and Exchange," 345.

tury AD compilation of writings by legal experts known as jurists, reporting and commenting on legal cases. The *Digest* presents a wide spectrum of approaches to servitudes, because it collects the opinions of many different jurists from a period of nearly five hundred years (from the second century BC to the third century AD) and because these opinions are excerpted from several different kinds of legal books and are connected with different kinds of legal cases. For example, a legal textbook might give a simplified definition of servitudes, whereas a commentary written for other jurists would lay out the points of disagreement on vexing legal questions. Some of the cases are hypotheticals devised to explore problematic situations, while others contain quotations from statutes and the praetor's edict, actual law that was used in Rome. A third type of case reports real legal disputes, and these sometimes include imperial rescripts, the responses from the emperor's legal office to queries from Roman citizens across the empire. Though these lawsuits can rarely be connected with specific people or places, one case about water rights does provide remarkable details about a lawsuit between Statilius Taurus and his neighbors at Sutrium. Where the jurists comment on law or cases, their opinions may be only that—opinions rather than law that was actually enforced. They nevertheless offer valuable insight into legal approaches and concepts as well as the social and economic interests that shaped the law.[103] Taking these different kinds of juristic writings together, we can gain insight into the system of rules that governed private water rights as well as the larger issues that influenced the law. To apply Kehoe's approach to water rights, an analysis of the economic assumptions in the jurists' writings should allow us to construct a model to describe the general principles that guided Romans in managing local water resources.[104] Since this model represents an idealized view, I test it against other kinds of evidence—literary, epigraphical, archaeological—to gain a clearer picture of how private water rights worked in practice.

Literary sources of all kinds contribute to our understanding of law in Roman society. Even though legal topics are seldom the focus of poems or even Cicero's speeches, there is enough mention to show that Romans who enjoyed literature also knew and used legal institutions in managing their

103. Changes in the exact form of the legal rules were more likely to be influenced by patterns of legal thinking, even when these changes responded to social and economic concerns. On the relationship between social factors and jurisprudence in the process of legal change, see Frier, "Why Law Changes," 888.

104. See n. 101 in the present introduction.

rural properties. An anecdote dating to the Second Punic War suggests an early integration of law and farming. When Regulus requested to be relieved of command so that he could return to his farm, the Senate refused but contracted the cultivation of his farm.[105] Legal parodies abound in Roman comedy.[106] Cicero's letters discuss the management of his estates and related legal issues. In their agricultural treatises, both Cato and Varro provide model contracts for lease and sale relating to agricultural work.[107] In addition, Varro cites Manilius's compilation of legal formulas, an apparently well-known handbook whose existence argues for common knowledge of at least some aspects of the law.[108] Moreover, Varro's advice to avoid boundary lawsuits by planting trees along the land line shows that law was perhaps too commonly used by Roman landowners (*RR* 1.15). The variety of sources—publicly performed comedy, technical writing, and literary letters—attests to the widespread familiarity with law among Romans in the late republican and early imperial eras.

Servitudes, in particular, seem to have been commonly known, even though, like many other areas of Roman private law, water rights are not much discussed in traditional literary sources.[109] A few passages from Cicero's writing (discussed in the chapters that follow) are of special impor-

105. On the contract to cultivate Regulus's farm, see Pliny, *NH* 18.27–28, 39; Col. 1.4.2; Val. Max. 4.4.4.; Livy, *Epit.* 18; Sen. *ad Helv.* 12.5; Heitland, *Agricola,* 139–40.

106. For a collection of literary parodies of legal language, see Meyer, *Legitimacy and Law,* 66–74.

107. Cato, *Agr.* 14.1–2 (in construction contracts, what the contractor supplies), 14.3 (what the owner supplies, including water), 16 (contract for burning lime on shares), 136 (lease of land), 137 (lease of vineyard), 144 (contract for gathering olives), 145 (contract for milling olives), 146 (contract for sale of olives on the tree), 147 (contract for sale of grapes on the vine), 148 (contract for sale of wine in jars), 149 (lease of winter pasture), 150 (sale of increase of the flock). See Brehaut, *Cato the Censor on Farming,* 123 n. 1. For *formulae* for the sale of livestock, see Varro, *RR* 2.1.15 (cattle), 2.2.5–6 (sheep), 2.3.5 (goats), 2.4.5 (pigs), 2.5.10–11 (cows), 2.7.6 (horses), 2.8.3 (mules), 2.10.4 (slaves); cf. *RR* 2.9.7 (when dogs were purchased, title was transferred on delivery), 2.10.4–5 (six ways to acquire title in the purchase of slaves; guarantees). At *RR* 2.3.7, Varro refers to leasing a farm: often such a lease prohibits keeping goats because of the damage done by their indiscriminate grazing.

108. Varro refers to Manilius' *actiones* in *RR* 2.3.5, 2.5.11, and 2.7.6. Cf. Cic. *de Orat.* 1.246, 212, for the identification of Manilius (cos. 149 BC) as a legal expert; see also Schulz, *Roman Legal Science,* 90.

109. There are possibly two literary puns involving servitudes in Stat. *Silv.* 2.2.73–74 and Pliny, *Ep.* 1.3.1 (see Sherwin-White, *Letters of Pliny,* 92). Cicero mentions them in passing in the *pro Caecina* and refers to a jurist as an expert in servitudes in the *pro Balbo* (*Caec.* 74; *Balb.* 45). On literary passages that do not refer to servitudes (including Front. *Aq.* 18; Pliny, *NH* 26.64, 70; and the *agrimensores* in general), see Biondi, *Categoria,* 584–87.

tance for this study, as they deal with servitudes and water use on rural land.[110] Servitudes are also mentioned in *de Legibus,* where Cicero cites them as an example of technical legal knowledge different from the profound problems of government, though useful in their own way (*Leg.* 1.14, 2.47). But when he considered servitudes in relation to property rights (his own and others'), it is clear that this practical legal institution was familiar to Cicero and other Roman landowners. One passage from Cicero's third speech in *de Lege Agraria* shows what a typical audience might have been expected to know about law in general and servitudes in particular. Cicero takes issue with chapter 40 of Rullus's land bill, which directs a redistribution of land confiscated under the dictator Sulla. He criticizes Rullus's ability to draft effective legislation and impugns his motives at the same time. Quoting the bill phrase by phrase, Cicero "explains" its technical terms—what they really mean, rather than what Rullus would have the Romans believe. For example, Rullus's bill described the land to be allotted as *optimo iure,* a legal phrase reminiscent of the terms of a sale contract—in particular, the clause guaranteeing that property is not burdened with a servitude (*Agr.* 3.7–8).[111] Cicero's audience is meant to appreciate sarcasm based on an understanding of servitudes and how they are handled when land is sold. Not only is Rullus a fool, argues Cicero, but his ignorance of the law is destructive: if the land were to be handed over *optimo iure,* all preexisting arrangements, including servitudes, would be erased, much to the disadvantage of new and old residents alike. The sarcasm deflates Rullus as it pumps up Cicero's audience, drawing them into his mastery of the law: Cicero presumes that they surely know how to use the law to their own advantage better than Rullus does. Even if some of the audience missed the finer points of the legal reference, the rhetorical strategy assumes familiarity with the law and a positive view of that familiarity.

Agricultural practices, including the use of water on villas, are treated in literary sources, especially the technical works by Pliny the Elder and the agricultural writers Cato, Varro, and Columella. These sources help to contextualize legal approaches to water rights, and there is much common

110. See his discussion of servitudes on his own and his brother's land (Cic. *Att.* 15.26.4; *Q.Fr.* 3.1.3) and his account of Gratidianus's suit over a servitude against Sergius Orata, famous for oyster ponds (Cic. *de Orat.* 1.178; *Off.* 3.66–67). Cicero's treatment of servitudes does not deal with legal technicalities: see Grosso, *Servitù prediali,* 57–60.

111. For the interpretation of *optimo iure* as referring to servitudes, see Jonkers, *Social and Economic Commentary,* 143. On the *uti optimus maximusque* clause, see chapter 4 in the present study.

ground between literary and legal sources. In both, there is a balancing between traditional approaches to farming and awareness of market concerns. The successful farmer is open to new ideas, whether learning from his neighbors, as Cato advises; making a study of "scientific" methods of farming, as Columella advocates; or paying attention to the new market opportunities for selling the goods of the farm, as Varro's approach assumes.[112] Where such writers as Varro tend to respond to the new economic situation with moralizing that emphasizes traditional ideals, the jurists also often take a conservative approach, preserving older concepts while responding to new ideas about rational planning and market orientation. The jurists, like other Romans, incorporated social values into their economic thinking and legal remedies, so that many of the working assumptions behind servitudes correspond to the advice about neighbors offered by Cato and Columella.[113] Legal solutions to problems of water sharing take into account both self-sufficiency and market orientation, and these sometimes contradictory aims motivate much of the instruction in the agricultural treatises. Because the legal sources tend to be problem-oriented—a landowner brings suit to challenge his neighbor's use of water—they reveal the dynamics of the economic and social interests of rural landowners as they used Roman law to make their land productive and to negotiate the exploitation of common resources. The interplay of tradition and innovation in law and agriculture may have continued into later eras, but it was first articulated when the rules for servitudes were being adapted to serve the market, in the same era to which much of the literary evidence belongs.

While literary sources offer valuable perspectives on the culture and society that shaped servitudes, the physical environment was also a factor in managing the water supply. The best material evidence for local water supplies comes from inscriptions that provide valuable comparisons for the legal cases discussed in the chapters that follow. In his study of servitudes for water use, Capogrossi Colognesi has used inscriptions to explain the development of the servitude to channel water (*aquae ductus*) and of the praetorian servitudes to draw from a spring and to water animals (*haustus* and *adpulsus*). The fully developed servitudes were unified rights that combined a right to

112. Cato, *Agr.* 1.4: *caveto alienam disciplinam temere contemnas;* Col. 1.praef. passim (the importance of knowing what you're doing), 1.1.4–6 (how to select from both new and traditional methods), 1.2. (the necessity of *scientia*).

113. For a similar approach to the relationship between law and the agricultural treatises, see Steinwenter, *Fundus cum instrumento,* 72–73.

use water from a source with a right-of-way across the property to reach the source (either to channel the water or to walk or drive animals).[114] In all three cases, the unified right to draw water and channel it arose from two separate rights: ownership of the spring and a right to channel. The language of the inscriptions indicates the original separation of these two rights and also shows the diversity of legal practices, even after the concept of a servitude had been unified. The legal situations in these inscriptions vary: some involve public water, others private; the water may be a gift (e.g., from an individual to his town), purchased, or organized in a servitude. There are also several inscriptions (some about municipal water) that describe a shared channel and a schedule for water use. These complement the legal cases about servitudes with schedules for privately owned water. Finally, there are three long inscriptions about public irrigation schemes: one from Lamasba in Roman North Africa and two from Roman Spain, the *lex rivi Hiberiensis* and the *Tabula Contrebiensis.*[115] The *Tabula Contrebiensis* records the legal proceedings that arose from a dispute about building an aqueduct for a local irrigation system and thus provides new evidence for the operation of civil law, while also confirming widespread competition for water. The other two long irrigation decrees, the Lamasba inscription and the *lex rivi Hiberiensis,* each describe in detail a system for distributing and regulating a local water supply. These irrigation decrees offer unparalleled information about the social contexts and the technical details of rural water use, which are directly relevant to servitudes, even though the decrees concern public, not privately owned, water. In both public and private systems, many of the same strategies are used to balance the interests of individuals and the community in a valuable local resource. Though the inscriptions represent a variety of situations, they are part of larger social and legal dialogues about rural water use. In fact, the variety itself is instructive, a good reminder that practice could be diverse and that a legal case might represent just one possible solution.

In addition to inscriptions, other kinds of archaeological evidence enhance our understanding of the use of water in rural areas and the role of law in exploiting this valuable resource. Many villas and farms have been excavated and studied in the regions of central Italy where agricultural markets affected the system of water rights. Archaeology allows us to reconstruct the

114. Capogrossi Colognesi, *Servitù d'acqua,* 88–121.

115. For the irrigation decree from Lamasba in North Africa, see n. 59 in this introduction. For the *Lex Rivi Hiberiensis,* see n. 58 in this introduction. For the *Tabula Contrebiensis,* see Richardson, "Roman Law in Spain."

landscapes—social and physical—onto which water rights were mapped. Like legal sources, archaeological evidence is largely anonymous: it cannot tell us which site near Sutrium was owned by Statilius Taurus, for example. But, the remains of hydraulic installations at individual sites show how landowners invested in infrastructure to exploit the water supply. These efforts to improve resources can then be evaluated in relation to the legal measures that landowners took to secure a water supply. Also, archaeology can indicate which crops or animals were raised on villas and rural sites. This information allows us to assess the demand for water and to draw some inferences about competition for the local water supply. Finally, the maps of rural settlements generated by survey record the physical environment in which servitudes operated and, when combined with the literary evidence, allow us to reconstruct the social relationships that made servitudes work. Although the evidence presents something of a patchwork, it does allow us to observe congruities between legal solutions and the situation on the ground. Legal analysis offers a valuable method of interpreting material evidence, bringing to life the practices that shaped the physical and social environments for rural water use and commercial agriculture.

Private water rights were most valuable when they served farms located near urban produce markets, especially in the areas near Rome and in Campania, in western Italy from southern Etruria to Campania, along the coast, and inland to the *suburbium* of Rome—a region that is sometimes referred to as "Tyrrhenian Italy." As noted earlier, this region of Italy is associated with a specific type of rural estate whose cultivation was oriented toward the market.[116] Private water rights can be studied in relation to the archaeological evidence from this region, because much is known about villas and land use (even about smaller farms) on the basis of archaeological excavation and survey. This archaeological research tends to corroborate the literary descriptions of villa agriculture and livestock raising on suburban villas, allowing us to bring back an "otherwise invisible memory" of local water-sharing arrangements and to probe the complexities of the legal approaches to this problem.[117] The combination of these various types of evidence provides a firm basis for investigating the social, economic, and physical envi-

116. See nn. 23 and 27.

117. On this use of archaeology, Alcock (*Archaeologies of the Greek Past,* 35) writes, "Material evidence can help us watch for phantoms of otherwise invisible memory, and can thus prevent over-easy acceptance of overly tidy versions of the past." Though Alcock's project aims to restore memories effaced by overtly political influences on society, the method can be applied more broadly.

ronments that influenced the development of water rights in Roman law. Thus this project leads to a more realistic view of the Roman countryside, countering the simplified pictures familiar from literary polemics—an idyllic and idealizing retreat from the evils of the city or an unsophisticated (not to say primitive) and undeveloped wilderness. Considered together, the legal, literary, and archaeological evidence show that rural land was cultivated by Romans who knew the law and had a vested interest in sustaining traditional ways of life as they exploited natural resources in the pursuit of their economic and social aims.

CHAPTER TOPICS

My investigation of private water rights begins from the allocation of natural resources and the limits imposed by the physical environment. In chapter 1, "Rationality and Rationing a Common Resource," I consider the strategies that Romans adopted to manage privately owned water supplies, a scarce resource in the countryside around Rome. In examining the regulatory aspects of private water rights, I use commons theory to better understand how Roman landowners used legal rules to limit water use, so as to both conserve the resource and secure a reliable supply for themselves. Some of the legal rules were general and applied to all servitudes; others were crafted for individual situations. Among the specific rules for water use, schedules (seasonal, daily, and hourly) are an important tool. These schedules assume the principle of subtractability and provide a mechanism for excludability, in accord with commons theory. Schedules are also preserved in inscriptions and in Frontinus's description of Tusculum's water supply, and these other sources fill out the picture suggested by the legal evidence. Through an analysis of these schedules—their terms and physical contexts—we can observe the Romans attempting to rationalize the use of a natural resource while at the same time preserving the traditional social structures that made servitudes work. Schedules and other mechanisms for regulating water use are rational because they efficiently allocate a scarce resource, limiting waste as they insure fairness. Moreover, they provide a framework in which landowners can calculate their needs for water and negotiate to acquire the necessary supply.

Chapter 2, "Law and Neighborly Practice," examines the social contexts that shaped and supported servitudes. Local water systems drew neighbors into cooperative and competitive relationships. As servitudes developed, traditional ideas of neighborliness were integrated into the legal rules, creating a sort of etiquette for sharing natural resources and a kind of equity in their allocation. The "etiquette" of servitudes incorporates excludability and subtractability, the organizing principles of commons theory. Commons theory also provides an approach to understanding the social relationships and norms that communities rely on to manage natural resources. The lawsuit between Statilius Taurus and his neighbors illustrates these dynamics, and it is particularly interesting because it shows that the legal system could empower a small holder by guaranteeing his access to water. Cicero's letter about a servitude on his land at Tusculum (*Att.* 15.26.4) also lends insight into the ways that landowners balanced proximity and distance as they shared a local water supply.

In chapter 3, "Utility, Productivity, and Planning," I investigate a central concept in servitudes: *utilitas*, or "utility"—namely, the principle that a servitude must serve some need related to cultivation of the land. The concept of utility embodies Roman assumptions about the environment and natural resources and also about the relationship between landowners and these resources. Here again, commons theory advances the discussion, but the focus shifts more toward economic issues relating to the market for agricultural produce. A comparison between servitudes and another similar legal institution, usufruct, helps to broaden our view of Roman economic practices, showing that traditional ideas about self-sufficiency coexist with market-driven behavior and a growing emphasis on monetary exchange. The legal cases offer a glimpse of the economic decisions made by Roman landowners. In this way, they illustrate systematic approaches to farming within the constraints of natural resources and limited participation in the market. Examples of this systematic commercial activity include setting up a servitude to support specialized farming or to secure a water supply that would make it worthwhile to invest in hydraulic infrastructure. Cicero's improvements to the water supply of his garden at Tusculum are a case in point. Here, as elsewhere, the legal evidence is used to contextualize such anecdotes and to show that they are part of a broader pattern of economic behavior.

Economic interests are also at play in the legal cases that are the focus of chapter 4, "Servitudes and the Sale of Land." Water supply was a key factor in the sale of rural land, and a servitude for water use could make a property more desirable or not, depending on whether it was dominant or servient. But how did landowners know what resources were available when they considered buying a property? What happened to traditional neighborly water-sharing arrangements when land changed hands? How was a landowner's investment in the resources on a new property protected? In the first part of this chapter, I present the rules that governed the transfer of servitudes when land was sold. In the second and third sections, I analyze how the law of sale was adapted to take account of private water rights when land was sold. The law of sale provided a mechanism through which landowners could address these questions—namely, clauses or guarantees added to the sale contract and describing any servitudes connected with the land. For this reason, the sale of rural land was an occasion for landowners to articulate their needs for water and to craft legal protections for that supply. After the sale, the guarantees in a sale contract could be the basis for litigation if the water resources were different than the parties had claimed. In the last section of chapter 4, I consider a famous lawsuit brought by G. Sergius Orata about a servitude on the property at Baiae that he purchased from M. Marius Gratidianus. Orata is perhaps best known for his invention of artificial oyster ponds, built to raise shellfish for the gourmet grocery market, and these commercial interests may have motivated his claim against Gratidianus. This lawsuit and the legal cases about servitudes in the sale of land show how Romans adapted the law of sale to protect their economic interest in the water supply on their rural land. My analysis of these legal cases suggests that at least some landowners took a systematic approach to farming, calculating their need for water and using the law to secure access to this valuable resource.

In these four chapters, the argument proceeds in a roughly chronological way, from the possible origins of servitudes in informal social practice sometime in the midrepublican period to the well-documented late republican and early imperial period, when the law was also shaped by the economic interests of Roman landowners. Throughout the chapters, I integrate literary, epigraphical, and archaeological sources into my discussion of legal cases. The discussion of fish farming in chapter 4, for example, depends on an analysis of the archaeological remains of fishponds and the channels that supplied them with freshwater. Both archaeological and literary evidence helps us to know what crops were grown where, and these sources are introduced, where I analyze the ways that law responded to landowners' interest in the market for specialized produce. More generally, my argument about competition for local water supplies draws on archaeological survey results that allow us to reconstruct the physical landscape in which servitudes operated—that is, the distribution of springs and streams across the land and the location of farms and villas in relation to these natural resources. In chapter 2, this reconstructed landscape helps to explain the legal rules for servitudes and the related social networks. In chapter 1, the importance of competition for local water supplies is likewise motivated by an analysis of the relationship between settlement patterns and water resources. Key evidence also comes from inscriptions; those recording schedules for water use are directly relevant to servitudes, while the inscriptions describing public water-sharing systems contextualize the private legal arrangements. In all the chapters, I draw on literary sources to gain insight into the cultural and social ideas that influenced the development of legal institutions. Though some of this evidence is anecdotal, the legal cases allow me to reconstruct a system of logic and expectations, broader patterns that provide a framework for interpreting the episodes reported in letters and literature. Throughout, the focus is on the law and how Roman landowners developed flexible legal institutions that served their interest in maintaining local, privately owned water supplies on their rural land.

ONE

RATIONALITY AND RATIONING A COMMON RESOURCE

What happens when one of the people using a scarce resource takes more than his share? This issue was controversial for jurists and landowners alike. A case preserved in the *Digest of Justinian* reflects the competition for water on rural property and is a signal for my approach to this competition, because it recalls the classic formulation of the tragedy of the commons, the herdsmen's dilemma.

> Trebatius [writes] that the whole herd may rightly be denied [access to water] when a larger number of animals is driven to water than should be, because adding one animal to the herd invalidates the right to water for the whole herd to which it is owed. Marcellus says, however, if the holder of a servitude for watering the herd drives more animals [to water], he should not be prevented from watering in the case of individual animals; and this is correct, because herd animals can be separated.
>
> [*Trebatius, cum amplior numerus pecoris ad aquam appelletur, quam debet appelli, posse universum pecus impune prohiberi, quia iunctum pecus ei pecori, cui adpulsus debeatur, totum corrumpat pecoris adpulsum. Marcellus autem ait, si quis ius habens pecoris ad aquam appellendi plura pecora adpulserit, non in omnibus pecoribus eum prohibendum: quod est verum, quia pecora separari possunt.*] (*D.* 43.20.1.18 Ulp. 70 *ad Ed.*)

In the Roman countryside, water was a scarce resource and in high demand for agriculture and livestock. Bruun has noted, "The relative scarcity of water for irrigation purposes sometimes led to sophisticated schemes of resource-sharing."[1] The legal case effects the competition and report the flexible strategies that allowed landowners to satisfy their need for water while at the same time conserving it, achieving the goals of commons theory through legal mechanisms.

This chapter presents an analysis of the rules for servitudes that mediated competition for water. It explains how these rules were applied and reconstructs their underlying rationales. Three types of rules led to efficient allocation and conservation of water: rules that restricted servitudes to adjacent property, those that enforced schedules for use, and those that prohibited informal sharing of water. A related legal mechanism, the praetorian interdict for summer and daily water, also served this function when disputes about schedules arose. An inscription recording a schedule could function in a similar way to enforce a rationing scheme and, indirectly, to reflect the social constraints on the use of resources. Several inscriptions of this sort have been found in the areas near Rome, and they are examined in the second part of this chapter, along with a well-known inscription from Roman North Africa that records a local irrigation scheme and the two inscriptions from Roman Spain that involve disputes over the water supply. The inscriptions also describe the distribution of water resources in relation to settlement and, for this reason, are discussed in relation to archaeological evidence for local aqueducts in central Italy. Together, archaeological and epigraphical evidence allows us to reconstruct the landscape of resources that servitudes regulated and to show how the physical environment motivated competition. The material evidence—physical remains of local aqueducts and inscriptions—serves as a bridge between the first and last parts of this chapter, both of which focus on legal cases. In the first section, the three key types of rules are analyzed, to develop the notion of rationality that underlies servitudes. The last section considers legal cases about schedules, drawing on the preceding discussion of inscriptions and local aqueduct systems.

LIMITS IN THE STRUCTURE OF SERVITUDES

The legal structure of servitudes itself provided a basis for mediating com-

1. Bruun, "Roman World," 580–81, with references to the four inscriptions with schedules that are discussed later in the present chapter.

petition for water, specifically in three rules that limited access to the resources governed by servitudes. First, a servitude was conceived as an indivisible right that was permanently attached to a property. Second, a rustic servitude could be established only on adjacent property. Third, informal sharing of servitudes was prohibited. Thus, while the legal right was indivisible, the resource itself might be divided so that more than one landowner held a servitude to the same resource. In this way, the rules allowed the possibility of shared channels, and this circumstance provided a setting for competition as well as a framework for resolving it. With this practical (if apparently paradoxical) approach, the jurists adapted the legal concept to the constraints of both the physical and social environments, where water sources were scarce and landowners needed to share them. As these rules restricted the scope of servitudes, they also helped to curtail greedy landowners who sought to control all resources in a region. The ban on informal sharing had a similar effect: the holder of a servitude to channel water could not share the water with his neighbor unless the neighbor had a servitude of his own. While the owner of a servitude held an exclusive right to the resource, he might be required to share the resource with others who had servitudes to use it. Although these rules may have developed as the jurists attempted to systematize the concept of servitudes, they nevertheless point beyond the legal scholarship to real issues that confronted the owners of rural property who had to share a water supply. In turn, the legal approaches reflect the strategies of landowners, thus revealing the kinds of rational or social motivations that shaped their solutions to water sharing.

A servitude was conceived as indivisible, even if the resource could be divided or shared among several people. There seems to have been no direct limit on the number of people who could hold a servitude to use the same channel. The Hadrianic jurist Julian argued that it was possible to have more than one servitude on the same channel, just as more than one person can have a right-of-way over the same ground.

> I have granted to Lucius Titius [a servitude] to channel water from my spring. It is asked whether I may also grant [a servitude] to Maevius to channel water through the same [aqueduct]; and if you think that [a servitude] to conduct water through the same aqueduct can be granted to two people, how should they exercise [their rights]? He replied: just as a right of *iter, actus,* [or] *via* can be granted either simultaneously or in turn to many people, so the right of channeling water may be rightly granted. But if there is no agreement among the people to whom the

[right to] water is granted, about how they should exercise [their rights], it will not be unfair to allow an analogous action, just as is used for those to whom a usufruct applies; and many [jurists] agreed that an analogous action for dividing common property should be granted.

[Lucio Titio ex fonte meo ut aquam duceret, cessi: quaesitum est, an et Maevio cedere possim, ut per eundem aquae ductum aquam ducat: et si putaveris posse cedi per eundem aquae ductum duobus, quemadmodum uti debeant. respondit: sicut iter actus via pluribus cedi vel simul vel separatim potest, ita aquae ducendae ius recte cedetur. sed si inter eos, quibus aqua cessa est, non convenit, quemadmodum utantur, non erit iniquum utile iudicium reddi, sicut inter eos, ad quos usus fructus pertinet, utile communi dividundo iudicium reddi plerisque placuit.] (*D.* 43.20.4 Iulian. 41 *Dig.*)

Those who shared a right-of-way or a servitude to channel water could use it at the same time or in turn (*vel simul vel separatim*). If the parties could not agree on how to exercise their rights, Julian prescribes a legal remedy: they should file a lawsuit similar to the one used for dividing common property. This remedy reflects the definition of a servitude as a kind of property right. The very mention of a remedy presupposes the potential for dispute or competition over a shared water supply. But the legal remedy also seems to be an alternative to social negotiation, something to try when other approaches to dispute resolution fails. Julian, at least, anticipated that some disputes could be resolved informally, relying on social relationships to facilitate water sharing. When this informal cooperation was defined in a legal standard, the rule seems to have been "Do no harm." This rule appears in another case ascribed to Julian, in which several people all drew water from a river (a public water supply rather than a private servitude): "several people can channel water from a river, so long as they do not harm the neighbors or, if the channel is narrow, even someone [i.e., a neighbor] who is on the opposite bank" *[ex flumine aquam ducere plures possunt, ita tamen, ut vicinis non noceant, vel, si angustus amnis sit, etiam ei, qui in alia ripa sit]* (*D.* 43.20.3.1 Pompon. 34 *ad Sab.*). Those who shared a channel were expected to cooperate in much the same way as the parties to a servitude: the person who holds the servitude should exercise his right without damaging the servient estate, and the owner of the servient estate should allow peaceable exercise of the servitude; these issues are explored in more detail in chapter 2.

Social norms might inform some of the guidelines for sharing a channel, but the physical environment was also a factor in the rules that limited competition for water. While more than one person could use the same channel, granting a right-of-way and a waterway in the same place was prohibited, and this legal restriction seems to arise from logistics: how could one walk or drive animals through a waterway (*D.* 8.3.14 Pompon. 32 *ad Q. Muc.; D.* 8.4.25 Paul. 1 *Epit. Alf.*)? In another case, the water supply itself was seen as self-limiting: additional servitudes could be established as long as there was enough water (*si aquae ductus vel haustus aquae sufficiens est, D.* 8.3.2.2 Nerat. 4 *Reg.*; see, similarly, the interdicts for summer and daily water: *D.* 43.20.1.3–4, 30–31, 35 Ulp. 70 *ad Ed.*). In these rules, the law raises the natural situation to a legal standard, but it does not provide much protection for the water supply.

The restriction to adjacent property, which was also based in the physical landscape, could help to conserve the water supply. Rustic servitudes, unlike urban servitudes, could be imposed only on adjacent property (*in rusticis autem praediis impedit servitutem medium praedium, quod non servit, D.* 8.3.7.1 Paul. 15 *ad Plaut.*).[2] By limiting the potential number of users, this rule addressed subtractability and rationed water among local users, strategies compatible with commons theory. In addition, the restriction to adjacent property coheres with traditional Roman ideas about neighborly interactions. For example, Cato sets strict limits on exchange with neighbors: borrow only with two or three neighbors and nothing critical, for example, no money and no seed (*Agr.* 5.3). Similarly, Columella advises against too much borrowing (Col. 1.8.8; cf. 11.1.20). All three agricultural writers (Cato, Varro, and Columella) recommend that interactions with neighbors should be limited and aimed at assuring self-sufficiency, the farmer's traditional goal. This conservative attitude, when applied to a valuable resource like water, could also support commercial agriculture, providing secure access to the water a landowner needed to raise a surplus to sell on the market. Columella recognized the economic value of water even as he privileged a free supply: well-watered land brings a profit without investment "because it is possible to return a profit without expense" [*quia sine impensa fructum reddere potest*] (Col. 2.2.6). Whether landowners aimed at self-sufficiency or profit, the restriction to adjacent property protected access to local water supplies for the benefit of neighboring landowners. Environmental concerns dovetail with

2. Other cases about the restriction to adjacent property include *D.* 8.4.7.1 Paul. 5 *ad Sab.* and *D.* 8.3.5.1 Ulp. 17 *ad Ed.* For two cases that assume a neighboring farm, cf. *D.* 8.3.3.1–2 Ulp. 17 *ad Ed.* (*in vicini villa*) and *D.* 8.3.23.1 Paul. 15 *ad Sab.* (*ad fundum vicinum*); see also *D.* 39.3.17.4 Paul. 15 *ad Plaut.* (*tuus proximus*). For urban servitudes with an intervening property, see *D.* 8.5.4.8 Ulp. 17 *ad Ed.* (right to obstruct a view may be held by someone whose house is at a distance) and *D.* 8.5.5 Paul. 21 *ad Ed.* (the right to have an unobstructed view).

economic aims in the restriction to adjacent property, just as they do in the second limit, the ban on informal sharing.

If a landowner held a servitude, he was generally prohibited from sharing his right with anyone else. This ban on informal sharing reflects efforts to manage competition for scarce resources while balancing landowners sometimes conflicting interests: self-sufficiency and market-oriented farming, neighborly cooperation and individualistic economic success. The interplay of social and economic motives can be glimpsed in a legal case that reports a difference of opinion about informal sharing. The legal case asks whether a landowner with a channel can give his water to a neighbor? Two jurists give two different answers. Labeo says yes, but Proculus says no.

> Labeo writes that I can (provide [water] to) any neighbor from my waterway; alternatively, Proculus [writes] that it is not possible to use this water in another part of my land than the one for which the servitude was acquired. Proculus's opinion is more correct.
>
> [*Ex meo aquae ductu Labeo scribit cuilibet posse me vicino commodare: Proculus contra, ut ne in meam partem fundi aliam, quam ad quam servitus adquisita sit, uti ea possit. Proculi sententia verior est.*] (*D.* 8.3.24 Pompon. 33 *ad Sab.*)

These two opinions demonstrate the flexibility in legal approaches to informal sharing and to private water rights in general.[3] The law could work with social norms or could respond to the economic priorities of Roman landowners. Though the case does not preserve arguments for either position, we can offer a plausible reconstruction that sheds light on both social and economic issues. Labeo allows sharing, which would promote neighborly reciprocity but could also threaten the self-sufficiency of the servient estate. His opinion seems to assume that social norms can effectively regulate the water-sharing system. The limits worked because neighbors lived close enough to form a close-knit community that could sustain social norms of sharing. Proculus adopts a more formalistic approach, following the letter of the law to restrict informal sharing among neighbors. His ban on informal sharing supported the goal of self-sufficiency by limiting the landowners' discretion in using the water that he gets from a servitude.[4] This

3. For a similar rule in the sale of land with servitudes attached, see *D.* 8.4.5 Iavol. 2 *Epist.*

4. In *D.* 8.3.24 Pompon. 33 *ad Sab.*, Proculus's opinion has also been interpreted in connection with the concept of *utilitas*, the idea that a servitude must provide something useful for and permanently connected to the dominant estate (Grosso, *Servitù prediali*, 98–99, 104–8; Capogrossi Colognesi, *Servitù d'acqua*, 158–72). For more on *utilitas*, see chapter 3.

limit protected the water supply for both the dominant and the servient estate, as commons theory prescribes, and is also consistent with the practice in larger local systems: if there was more than one servitude on the same source, these additional landowners were protected. The comparative evidence from medieval Valencia shows the power of this rule, since it was enforced in the Spanish irrigation community, even in times of drought, when compassion might otherwise motivate neighbors to share their allotment of water.[5] In the law of servitudes, both rules conserve the water supply by limiting access. In some cases, sharing might not affect the overall supply; for example, where water use was measured by time or volume, a landowner could share his allotment without affecting the others who shared the supply. But in a less formal arrangement, sharing with a friend could lead to an abuse of the system that would decrease the water supply.

The ban on informal sharing created an all-or-nothing situation where a landowner had to choose between the freedom to dispose of his property in informal sharing and legal protection for the water supply. This rule might be attractive to a landowner with commercial interests, for a couple of reasons. First, since informal sharing could make the water supply less predictable, it could also interfere with a landowner's calculations about his needs for water and could affect productivity and profit from his crops. Second, the ban on informal sharing provided a mechanism for obtaining compensation for damage caused by loss of water, monetary compensation that could take the place of the profit he expected to earn from his water-dependent crops. Proculus's strict interpretation of the law thus turns out to be economically efficient as well as environmentally conservative.

Both the restriction to adjacent property and the ban on informal sharing limit competition for water and preserve this scarce resource in ways that are consistent with commons theory. Both rules assume the principle of subtractability, because they control the water supply by limiting the number of users to a known group. The rules also provide a mechanism for excludability that could be verified easily in the face-to-face relationships between neighbors. Moreover, the typical size and distribution of farms—close enough to be neighbors and with uneven access to streams and springs—created physical and social contexts that both supported cooperation and led to competition for water.[6] Commons theory offers insight into

---

5. On Valencia, see Glick, *Irrigation and Society,* 81; for the whole saga of conflict between those upstream and those downstream along an irrigation canal, see 74–85.

6. For landholding patterns near Rome in the late republic and early empire (i.e., a patchwork of small plots rather than large, contiguous holding), there is evidence in survey

the logic underlying these rules. More generally, it suggests the kind of rationality that guided Roman landowners' approach to the water supply. Rather than aiming to maximize access to water, these legal rules construct a rationality that takes into account social values, which may include getting along with your neighbor and conserving the water supply. Both these goals also support the economic well-being of Roman landowners, whether or not they engaged in commercial farming.

This kind of rational approach also characterizes a rather long case about a shared channel and what happens when one person drops out of the system.

> Several people were accustomed to channel water, which had its source on a neighbor's farm, through the same channel by right, in such a way that each conducted [water] on his own day from the source, first through the same, common channel, and then as each was further along [the channel], in his own waterway. One [of them] did not conduct [water] for the prescribed period of time in which the servitude was lost. I think that he lost his right of channeling water and that his right was not acquired by the others who conducted [water in the same channel], for the right belonged individually to each of them and could not be acquired for another person. But if a right-of-way for [drawing] water was owed to a farm owned by several people, [the right] could be acquired by one of them for all those whose common property the farm was. And so if one of them, to whom the servitude for channeling water was owed and who channeled water through the same water-

archaeology: see Duncan, "Sutri," 96–98; Carandini, "Orti e frutteti," 67–69; Castagnoli, "Resti di divisioni agrarie . . . Lazio," 51–52 (Cures Sabini), 61–62 (Sabine region); Dyson, "Settlement Patterns in the *Ager Cosanus*," 272–83; Gilkes, Martin, and Matheus, "Prati San Martino, Sutri"; Jones, "Capena, Part II," 147; Kahane, Threipland, and Ward-Perkins, "Ager Veientanus," 145–58; Manacorda, "Produzione agricola . . . nel'*ager Cosanus*," 85–90; Mills, "Luni," 266; Quilici, "Campagna romana," 429–32; Rathbone, "Agriculture in the 'Ager Cosanus,'" 10–23; Tomei, "Il suburbio di Roma," 107–9; Ward-Perkins, "Luni," 184. For related studies, see Buonocore, "Insediamenti e forme economiche"; Camilli and Vitali Rosati, "Nuove ricerche nell'Agro Capenate," 406–8; Carandini, *Romanizzazione dell'Etruria*, 49 (Vulci), 60, 78–79 (Valle del Fiora), 81 (Statonia); Vallat, "Structures agraires," 182–204; Vera, "Dalla 'villa perfecta'"; Champlin, "Owners and Neighbors." Coastal Lazio offers some variation, with fewer small sites, perhaps because there were more towns where citizens of modest means could dwell: see Arthur, *Romans in Northern Campania*, 64–65. The evidence from Tusculum, the Ager Romanus, and the coast of Lazio is discussed later in this chapter; for Sutrium and southern Etruria, see chapter 2.

way, lost the right of channeling water by not conducting it, no right accrued from his account to the others who used the waterway; but the benefit, which was lost on the part of one of them by nonuse, belonged to the man through whose farm the route for water [went], for he enjoyed freedom from this part of the servitude.

> *[Aquam, quae oriebatur in fundo vicini, plures per eundem rivum iure ducere soliti sunt, ita ut suo quisque die a capite duceret, primo per eundem rivum eumque communem, deinde ut quisque inferior erat, suo quisque proprio rivo, et unus statuto tempore, quo servitus amittitur, non duxit. existimo eum ius ducendae aquae amisisse nec per ceteros qui duxerunt eius ius usurpatum esse: proprium enim cuiusque eorum ius fuit neque per alium usurpari potuit. Quod si plurium fundo iter aquae debitum esset, per unum eorum omnibus his, inter quos is fundus communis fuisset, usurpari potuisset, Item si quis eorum, quibus aquae ductus servitus debebatur et per eundem rivum aquam ducebant, ius aquae ducendae non ducendo eam amisit, nihil iuris eo nomine ceteris, qui rivo utebantur, adcrevit idque commodum eius est, per cuius fundum id iter aquae, quod non utendo pro parte unius amissum est: libertate enim huius partis servitutis fruitur.]* (*D.* 8.6.16 Procul. 1 *Epist.*)

In this legal case, the jurist Proculus deals with what was probably a typical situation. Several landowners each hold a servitude to conduct water from the same spring and along a channel shared at least part of the way to their respective properties. One of the landowners did not exercise his right and so lost it on the basis of the use-it-or-lose-it rule.[7] Once one landowner is removed from the arrangement, what happens to the water that he is no longer consuming? When one of the landowners loses his right, none of the others can take it. Instead, the water reverts to its source, and any benefit accrues to the owner of the servient estate: he gets the extra water that is left behind when one fewer person is drawing on his spring.[8] The rule is modified to cover the case of a jointly owned property, where any of the co-owners can exercise the right and thus preserve it. The decision in the case conforms to a spirit of equity; that is, all the holders of servitudes are treated equally. Arguably, the same result could be achieved by dividing the

7. For the use-it-or-lose-it rule, see the introduction in the present study. See also the discussion later in this chapter on *D.* 8.6.7 Paul. 13 *ad Plaut.*, for the rule applied to a servitude exercised on a seasonal or daily or hourly schedule.

8. For the interest of the owner of the servient estate, Proculus uses the same language (*commodum*) that Ulpian uses in his discussion of the utility, or usefulness, of the water. See chapter 3 in the present study.

extra water among the other holders of servitudes, but the logistical difficulties of this solution probably made it unattractive; rotating among the users would work, but there is no evidence for this kind of schedule. While equity often characterizes legal solutions that balance the interests of the parties to a servitude, other issues seem to motivate Proculus's decision in this case.

Managing competition for water emerges as the main benefit of Proculus's approach. Each servitude is conceived as independent of the others, so that the sharing arrangement is not conceived as a zero-sum game. In the zero-sum situation of pareto efficiency, what one landowner lost would be appropriated (*usurpari*) by the others, and the total supply of water would be constant. Instead, the volume of water supplying the servitudes is decreased by the amount of water granted in the lost servitude. This extra water reverts to its source, possibly to be used by the owner of the servient estate. Proculus, anyway, assumes that the extra water is an advantage for the owner of the servient estate. Though he recognizes the benefit of having this extra water (or perhaps because he recognizes this), his decision addresses the potential for conflict over allocating the additional water. In effect, Proculus creates an opportunity for the other users of the water to negotiate with the owner of the servient estate for this boon. Rather than a zero-sum formulation that could lead to wasteful competition for water, this kind of rationality conserves water and promotes efficient use of the resource.[9] Compare Columella's advice about dealing with tenants: it is more profitable, he says, to emphasize good cultivation than to claim all that he legally can [i.e., in payment of rents] (Col. 1.7.1–2). More explicit concern with the environment was expressed about erosion (see, e.g., Varro, *RR* 1.16.3; Col. 2.17.5; and, somewhat less seriously, Hor., *Serm.* 2.4.15–16). In the legal case, rationality was bounded by a concern for the water supply, as it puts some of the water in reserve, available to the owner of the servient estate but not dedicated to a specific use. Conservation is not explicitly invoked in this or the other legal cases about servitudes for water use. Nevertheless, the jurists did recognize the natural constraints on the water supply, and these environmental factors shaped their approaches to servitudes. In particular, in the development of the praetorian interdicts to protect water servitudes, the jurists took environmental conditions into account as they defined servitudes involving schedules for water use. These interdicts are examined in the last section of

9. A similar approach characterized the irrigation systems of medieval Valencia. See Glick, *Irrigation and Society*, 13.

this chapter. The next section presents archaeological evidence of competition for water and the "natural" constraints on the development of servitudes. The law did not exist in isolation: the physical environment set the parameters for the legal rules governing servitudes. The archaeological evidence for this environment—settlement patterns, land use, and the distribution of water resources—corroborates the interpretation of servitudes as a mechanism for conservation and for negotiating competition over a limited resource.

RECONSTRUCTING THE LANDSCAPE: ARCHAEOLOGY AND LITERATURE

Material evidence from the Roman countryside makes it possible to reconstruct a picture of the landscapes where landowners shared and sometimes competed for the water from nearby streams and springs. Archaeological surveys allow us to map farms and villas onto the physical landscape to show the relationship between settlement and the natural sources of water, namely, springs and streams. This pattern was recognized already by the Roman land surveyors (*agrimensores*), who noted that streams could flow across a property or serve as its boundary, and boundary stones were marked to indicate that the boundary lay at a stream or spring.[10] Further information about local water sharing comes from the physical remains of local aqueducts, arches, and underground channels (or *cuniculi*). Both archaeological and literary sources provide information about land use, suggesting what kinds of crops and/or animals were raised on the property. In the areas near Rome, intensive cultivation of garden crops created a steady demand for water. Though there are gaps in the evidence, it is consistent enough to reconstruct the landscape of the *suburbium*, where many landowners competed for water as they worked to make their land productive.

A typical pattern of suburban settlement is found in the Tor Sapienza

---

10. For the various relationships between streams and property holdings, see Campbell, *Roman Land Surveyors*, 116.11–22 (Siculus Flaccus, *de Condicionibus Agrorum*) = *grom.* 114.7–24. For examples of a stream (*rivus*) serving as boundary, see Campbell, *Roman Land Surveyors*, 60.17 and 68.13–16 (Agennius Urbicus, *de Controversiis*) = *grom.* 61.7–12 and 66.13–17, 94.8 (Hyginus (1), *de Generibus Controversiarum* = *grom.* 91.9–11). For boundary stones marked to indicate a stream or spring, see, e.g., Campbell, *Roman Land Surveyors*, 226.4–5, 9–18 (*ex Libris Latinis de Terminibus*). For a similar appraisal of the topography and the potential for irrigation or water sharing, see White, *Roman Farming*, 151; Semple, *Geography*, 438.

area, near ancient Collatia, on the northwest side of the Alban volcano, where most sites are located near the tops of long gentle ridges, not directly adjoining streams. Streams were probably diverted for irrigation in the wider valley to the north. The high density of sites suggests little grazing. The landscape of the hills, as described by Thomas and Wilson, shows that neighbors would be engaged in sharing the water supply.

> The small size of the farms, taken in conjunction with the agronomists' emphasis on vegetable growing as yielding a high return, suggests that most farms and farm-villas had vegetable gardens which would have required water from time to time during the year.
>
> It is unlikely that many of the houses or settlements were able to use water from the aqueducts which cross the area on their way to Rome because the aqueducts were mostly below ground at this point, except at deeper stream crossings. . . . A number of conduits—whether for drainage or supply is uncertain—have been discovered at a rural settlement agglomeration just to the north of the Alexandrina, but in this case, the conduits may have been part of an independent network, as the settlement is at a higher level than the Alexandrina. . . .
>
> The abundance of water sources, coupled with the numerous ridge-top villas and cisterns, raises the possibility that small springs may have been developed along these stream valleys to capture the water rising into them and taken by conduit downstream to farms or villas along the ridge tops. Conduits seem frequently to have been laid along the lines of roads where conveniently located, and the coincidence of Roman roads and ridge tops suggests that many conduit systems also followed the general line of the ridge tops to supply a line of properties on the ridge. . . .
>
> In summary, the farms and farm-villas in this area probably all had underground cisterns for roof-runoff, many certainly had wells or wells with adits where ground water conditions were favourable, and others used locally developed springs or adits. The above ground cisterns in the cases of some of the villas situated at the highest levels, and the very large underground cisterns at sites on the flatter lower slopes, could in some cases have been supplied from roof-runoff, but along many ridge tops they were probably parts of water supply networks for groups of houses and farms. These small aqueduct systems (tunnels and conduits) were supplied from developed springs and lakes upstream, and perhaps soil water runoff. A few villas obtained water

from the Rome city aqueducts where a gravity supply was possible, and if the owners could afford it.[11]

This pattern of settlement in relation to water resources is typical of the *suburbium* and demonstrates the natural constraints on the local water supply.

The water supply was critical because much of the land in the *suburbium* was cultivated. The region was home to prized villas because they were so close to Rome—weary senators could retreat there after a long day at the forum. In the area along the Tiber, for example, just outside the city, in the traditionally Sabine district, villas generated produce for the urban markets, transported readily down the river to Rome and described by Pliny (*NH* 3.54).[12] In this region, there are two familiar examples from literary sources as well: Cato the Elder's family property (Cic. *RP* 3.40; Nep. *Cato* 1.1) and a villa belonging to Varro's aunt, where thrushes were raised for the gourmet market (Varro, *RR* 3.2.14–15). The *suburbium* was also ideal for transporting fragile produce to market, as Carandini notes. Indeed, he describes the *suburbium* as perfect for gardens and orchards.[13] Quilici's earlier interpretation that the density of sites precluded agriculture does not take into account the possibility of gardens and aviaries integrated into the villa, as described in the Roman literary sources.[14] For example, Varro indicates that doves could be raised even inside the city itself (*RR* 3.7.7). We need not assume that villa cultivation required large acreage, but some properties near the city must have been large: Varro reports the frustrated ambitions of one equestrian,

11. Thomas and Wilson, "Water Supply for Roman Farms," 183–86. For other interpretations of the settlement pattern that take into account both natural features and types of cultivation, see Castagnoli et al., "Resti di divisioni agrarie"; Zaccagni, "Lo sfruttamento agricolo del suburbio"; Musco and Zaccagni, "Carrateri e forme di insediamenti rustici."

12. For discussion of this literary example, see Reggiani, "La villa rustica nell'agro Sabino."

13. Carandini, "Orti e frutteti." On the archaeological evidence for agricultural production, see Corrente, "Alcuni esempi di forme economiche"; Vallat, "Structures agraires," 199–200; Thomas and Wilson, "Water Supply for Roman Farms, 184." For similar evidence from two other sectors, see Tomei, "Il suburbio di Roma"; di Mazano, Messineo, and Staffa, "Le ville nel settore Nord-est del suburbio." For a survey of sites between the Via Latina and the Via Ardeatina that illustrates mixed use (i.e., cultivation combined with residential villas) from the late republic through the second century AD, see Spera, *Il paesaggio suburbano di Roma,* 341–64; Spera's conclusions (459–62) build on Carandini's argument in "Orti e frutteti."

14. Quilici, "Campagna romana," 431. Even earlier, Ashby (*Roman Campagna,* 20) expressed surprise that vegetables and garden produce for the city were not grown on suburban properties.

Gaberius, who attempted to raise a large herd of goats (one thousand in all) on one thousand *iugera* near the city and lost most of them to disease (*RR* 2.3.10). Modern studies of the archaeological remains tend to confirm the Roman sources, as they show that the region between the Alban Hills and Rome was dotted with villas and cultivation of various sorts: gardens and vineyards, fishponds and dovecotes.[15]

Literary sources, mostly Pliny's *Natural History* and the agricultural treatises, report that water-dependent garden crops were grown in areas near Rome. According to Pliny, the mulberries of Ostia and Tusculum were not much different in size from those grown in Rome, and Tusculum was the only place near Rome where peach and almond trees could be grown. Tusculum, with its reliable water supply and proximity to the city, would also have been a good place to grow cherry trees, because fruit trees required intensive watering when young and during dry spells. Lucullus may have grown them at Tusculum, as he imported the cherry tree from Pontus after his military victory there, according to Pliny (though Pliny does not indicate where he planted them). Flowers were also grown in Tusculum. A type of violet, with broad petals but faint perfume, was named for Tusculum. The area was also connected with a variety of onion, and nearby Aricia was known for leeks, which required moist soil.[16] All these garden crops depended on a good water supply, as Columella recognized: "a site should be chosen [for the garden], if the lay of the land allows, near the villa, especially rich [soil] and one which can be watered with a stream flowing in, or if not running water, from a well" [*locum autem eligi conveniet, si permittit agri situs, iuxta villam, praecipue pinguem, quique adveniente rivo, vel si non sit fluens aqua, fonte puteali possit rigari*] (11.3.8). Columella also recommends planting the orchard and garden where it will catch runoff from the barnyard and baths (1.6.24; cf. 2.17.7).

---

15. Tortorici, in his introduction to the *Forma Italia* Regio I, vol. 11 *Castra Albana* (17–18), argues that the archaeological remains corroborate descriptions in literary sources of villas with farms in the Alban Hills. See also the studies cited in nn. 11 and 13 in the present chapter.

16. On the produce at Tusculum, see Pliny, *NH* 15.97 (mulberries), 16.138 (peaches and almonds), 15.10 (Lucullus's cherry trees), 21.27 (violets), 19.110 (leeks); Col.10.139 (*mater Aricia porri*), 3.2.14, 3.8.5 (vines). Columella (3.3.2) boasts of fruitful Aminean vines grown on his properties at Alba, Ardea, and Carseoli; cf. Varro, *RR* 1.2.7, citing Cato, *Origines.* See also Carandini, "Orti, e frutteti." Almond trees could have been grown on terraced slopes in the Alban Hills, with vines in between, even if no evidence of their processing remains (cf. Shaw, "Water and Society," 149). For the specific water requirements of different crops, see appendix A in the present study.

Mixed cultivation—garden crops sown among fruit trees and vines—was probably common in the areas near Rome, as it was in the gardens at Pompeii, some large enough to be commercial enterprises, others growing food for the household. The Pompeian gardens were irrigated, either by cistern or by municipal aqueduct. In fact, for Jashemski, archaeological evidence of irrigation is a sure sign that fruit, vegetables, and/or flowers were cultivated: "These provisions for irrigation make it appear almost certain that vegetables were raised in this garden [a shophouse garden near Porta di Nocera]."[17] Many of the gardens investigated by Jashemski have a cistern that was used for watering plants. Such a private supply could be critical to a garden because water from the imperial aqueduct was distributed unevenly across the city. Gardens on suburban villas will have been equally dependent on a steady supply of water, since many areas were inaccessible to the city aqueducts, as Thomas and Wilson point out in the passage previously quoted. Additional archaeological evidence from the areas near Rome attests to this pattern of cultivation and local water systems. I discuss some of the more important sites here, in more or less detail, depending on the available sources.

At Monte Savello in the Alban Hills, the connection between local water supplies and cultivation for the urban market can be traced in the archaeological remains of the villa and its surroundings. The site of Monte Savello has been variously connected with Bovillae and Apiola, and the nearby spring is probably to be identified with the Aqua Ferentina and the Lucus Ferentinae.[18] This spring was channeled into a *cuniculus* (underground channel) with several branches leading toward the villa site, which also includes a cistern. Cisterns could be used to store rainwater and/or water collected from springs as insurance against the dry summer months, as is assumed in Varro's recommendation to build reservoirs and to find a property

17. Jashemski, *Gardens of Pompeii,* 192; for examples, see 32 (gardens with a cistern), 53 and 45–48 (house of Loreius Tiburtinus), 190–91 (shophouse garden near Porta di Nocera), 253 (large orchard west of garden of fugitives); see also 238 and 278–88, with similar conclusions about the larger (probably commercial) gardens at the house of the ship Europa and the Garden of Hercules and for the impact and uneven distribution of water from the Augustan aqueduct (i.e., pools and fountains became the focal point in ornamental gardens).

18. The site was continuously occupied until the middle of the eighteenth century, when the water supply failed. For the description in general and the identifications with Bovilla and Apiola, see De Francesco, "Monte Savello," 219, with sources cited there. For the cistern, see Valenti, "I *loca Albana,*" 82. Other examples appear in Carandini, "Orti e frutteti."

with running water (*RR* 1.11.2).[19] The site was occupied at least from the midrepublic through the Augustan era and also probably through late antiquity, when it was given to the basilica at Alba by Constantine. The villa may have had olive trees and a vineyard—growing the grapes for which the region was famous—if the land was cultivated in the same way through the medieval period, when the records describe a *fondo oliari* (or *olivella*) and a *fundus Sabellus* that included a *vinea dissertina* with access to a public road. Access to water and transportation made the villa well suited to serve the urban market, as well as its own needs and perhaps those of its neighbors. At many of the villas scattered over the Alban Hills there are remains of hydraulic installations: pipes, fragments of fountains, a small aqueduct crossing the town of Alba.[20] The imperial villas in Alba also relied on local supply.[21] Collatia, like Gabii further east on the Via Praenestina, may also have had its own municipal aqueduct. An epitaph found near the town describes a burial in relation to a water supply (*proxime . . . aquae est*), but the text is too fragmentary to reveal more.[22] Small local distribution systems seem to have been common in the Alban Hills.

In southern Etruria, the patterns of settlement and water use are similar to those in the Alban Hills. Before the Roman conquest, the Etruscans managed streams and developed springs with *cuniculi* or rock-hewn channels

19. Tilly, *Varro the Farmer*, 163.

20. For example, Lanciani (*Le acque e gli acquedotti*) describes an epitaph found in the Vigna Bevilacqua that refers to an Aqua Albana (332), the Villa dei Quintilii, which drew on a source in the Alban Hills (393–96), and a private aqueduct found at castel San Gregorio on monte di S. Silvia (591). Other sites have been identified through the study of Lanciani's unpublished notebooks (Codd. Vat. Lat. 12045 and 113046), as reported by Valenti ("I *loca Albana*"): notable are, near the Villa Doria, structures that include pipes and fittings, a terrace, and a cryptoporticus (75); near Ariccia, peperino foundations and traces of a fountain (81); on a side road from the Via Appia past the outflow of the Lago di Albano, an Augustan villa (84); near Rocca di Papa, an aqueduct in the valley of the Arcioni stream (86–87); and pipes near remains of the aqueduct that crossed the ancient city (89). See also, in general, Del Nero, *Tusculum and Algidus Areas;* Borda, *Tuscolo.*

21. Bruun (*Water Supply*, 281–82) concludes from an examination of pipe inscriptions that the imperial villas (or villas of imperial date?) were supplied not by a city aqueduct but from a local reservoir and that there was still a local system in the first century AD.

22. For the epitaph at Collatia/Tor Sapienza, see *AE* (1974): 38 (no. 166), lines 7–8; for Hadrian's restoration of the aqueduct at Gabii, *AE* (1982): 40 (no. 142). On the remains of a small aqueduct on the Via Tuscolana and of a fountain near the Via Labicana (with an inscription naming M. Decumianus and Celius Latiniensis as its builders and dating probably to the late first century BC), see Del Nero, *Tusculum and Algidus Areas*, 54–55, 57.

through the tufa, which could be used equally for drainage or water supply as the need arose, sometimes serving both functions at once.[23] Much of the Etruscan infrastructure continued in use through the Roman period, and there was strong continuity of settlement into the Roman period. The pattern is clear in the territories of Veii and Capena, where good information is available from surveys done by the British School at Rome.

Near Capena, there were a few large villas, but the majority of sites were small holdings, close to neighbors; typical is one of these sites, which is fairly well known because it has been more fully excavated than others.[24] This residence appears to have been built around the time of the resettlement by Caesar's veterans in 46 BC and to have continued in use through the Hadrianic period. There are Etruscan *cuniculi* that were inherited and used by the Romans along with barrel-vaulted cisterns.[25] All of these *cuniculi* systems except one belong to the republican period, before the development of large-scale aqueducts and the mastery of barrel vaulting for conventional cisterns. The use of *cuniculi* to tap springs and groundwater indicates an early exploitation of water resources, in the same period when servitudes were taking shape. In addition to *cuniculi*, other types of infrastructure suggest fishponds or irrigation: solid concrete building platforms on ridges and outbuildings, which could have included cisterns and farmyard pools, were ideally located to distribute water to the lower parts of the property, as the agricultural writers recommend. Southern Etruria may have supplied fish to Roman tables; three of the four lakes that Columella lists in his discussion

---

23. See Bizzarri, "Bonifica idraulica," classifying two types of *cuniculi* for supply and for drainage; these *cuniculi* were built by the Etruscans and seem to have continued in use during the Roman period. Drainage and supply channels have been found at several Etruscan sites dating from the sixth and fifth century BC; see Wikander, "Iron Age," 629–30, with references. Wikander sees the Roman project to drain the Alban lake in 397 BC as evidence of their adoption of the Etruscan hydraulic facilities. In coastal Etruria, where excess water was more of a problem, *cuniculi* (from the fourth through third century BC) were used primarily for drainage (Rendeli, *Città aperte*, 124). For a system of *cuniculi* draining the hills and serving a fountain at Portonaccio, see Stefani, "Veio," 87–92.

24. On site 154, a small, well-excavated farm site in the territory of Capena, see Jones, "Capena, Part II," 147–58 (in general, 127–58). On the status of Capena and its citizens' rights in Roman law (*civitas sine suffragio* before the Social War, rights by treaty perhaps as early as 395 BC [Livy 5.24.3]), see Baronowski, "Roman Treaties," 174–75.

25. The hydraulic infrastructure is less developed in the Ager Capenas than in the territory of Veii, because it lacked a centralized political power in the Etruscan period: see Jones, "Capena, Part II," 141.

of raising fish are found here.[26] Also in Capena's territory, another villa, near the modern farm *I Cassini,* has elaborate hydraulics, including a small aqueduct that Jones describes as "a rare instance of what must have been a regular feature of many of the larger sites."[27] These installations are consistent with the practice of mixed and intensive farming of the sort that Varro describes on his aunt's property at Cures in Sabinum, across the Tiber from the Ager Capenas (*RR* 3.2.14–16).

Similar patterns of settlement and distribution of water resources are found in the territory of Veii. Despite literary sources depicting Veii as empty forgotten ruins, archaeological survey has restored a picture of a populous countryside.[28] Farmsteads located along the roads tend to be larger sites whose accessible location made them both profitable for cultivation and attractive retreats for pleasure. These sites usually have a cistern, probably rain-fed, for domestic use; and many have grain mills or kilns, which indicate a water supply for agricultural production as well.[29] A typical site is the villa on the cliffs over Fosso della Vacchereccia, along the Via Veientana, where there are several structures on a rise, including terracing, a cistern, and probably related buildings, which are dated not later than the end of the first century AD.[30] The cistern was likely fed by a well twenty meters away, and since the cistern was located on high ground, it could serve not only the villa but also several smaller sites nearby along the Via Veientana, which provided a transport route to the markets in Rome.

To the south of Rome, local water resources were developed as early as the second century BC. Some of these projects involved the public water supply, while others were clearly private installations. There could also be confusion, intentional or otherwise, about the intention of such a project, as happened in an early case from the area near Anxur/Tarracina. In 179 BC, M. Aemilius Lepidus (cos. 187) built a breakwater on his property, which in-

---

26. Columella (8.16.2) lists the Velinus (Piedi di Luco in Umbria), the Sabatinus (Lago di Bracciano), the Volsiniensis (Lago di Bolseno), and the Ciminius (Lago di Vico). Higginbotham (*Piscinae,* 72–112) includes fishponds on only coastal sites in Etruria. For more on fishponds, see chapter 4 and appendix B in the present study.

27. Jones, "Capena, Part II," 145.

28. For poetic descriptions of Veii's territory as a wasteland, see Prop. 4.10.27–30; Lucan, *BC* 7.391–93. For the correction based on archaeological evidence, see Liverani, *Municipium Augustum Veiens,* 157–59.

29. Kahane, Threipland, and Ward-Perkins, "Ager Veientanus," 154 (location of roads), 158–59 (cisterns, mills, kilns); De Neeve, *Peasants in Peril,* 22–29 (Veii's location and the agricultural market).

30. Ward-Perkins, "Notes on Southern Etruria," 50–52.

cluded both a residential villa and land under cultivation, according to D'Arms's analysis.[31] Since the property was on the coast, "cultivation" could mean raising fish, and the breakwater could have been part of a fishpond complex, as suggested by the modern description assigned to the remains of one such site near Circeii, *piscina detta di Lucullo,* but this may be influenced by the reputation of the famous fishponds built by Lucullus in the next century.[32] In Livy (40.51.2), Lepidus is criticized for using public funds to pay for construction on his own property; he may have claimed that the project benefited other landowners in the region, though Livy does not report the debate. In any case, the misappropriation of funds shows that Lepidus was eager to limit his own expenses, like any good landowner. More important, it suggests that building hydraulic infrastructure was an expensive investment.

Lepidus's breakwater is not the only evidence of local water management near Anxur. In the late republic and Augustan era, two ancient aqueducts served the villas inland and along the coast near Anxur. The older aqueduct was part of a municipal system that extended from the hilltop spring of S. Stefano down to the coast.[33] Along the route of the aqueduct, on hillsides and in the valley, are the scattered remains of villas, many of which have hydraulic installations. There was also a small aqueduct on a terraced site that was probably a private installation of the republican era.[34] Anxur's territory was also traversed by a canal that provided irrigation; at least one republican villa with a reservoir abuts the canal (site 78). Another republican villa, this

31. D'Arms, *Bay of Naples,* 5; D'Arms argues that in later eras the land was not cultivated.

32. Lugli, *Circeii,* site 9.

33. Lugli, *Anxur-Tarracina,* map 2. The republican aqueduct from the Fonte di San Stefano ran along the Via Appia on the coast past villas at sites 24, 25, 28, 50 (with reservoir 51), 38 (with reservoir 39), 43 (with reservoir 42), 45, and 55. A second aqueduct (Trajanic), from the northwest, ran past villas at sites 4, 8, 11, 13, 16, 18, 20, 24, 25, 26, 27, 28 (with a reservoir), 31, 32, and 45; and reservoirs at sites 2, 5, 9, 21, and 33. For discussion, see also Lugli, *Anxur-Tarracina,* cols. 45–46. Two later aqueducts also cross the territory, one built by Pio VI following the route of the republican aqueduct (and still used for watering horses) and the other built in the late nineteenth century. The earliest aqueduct probably served a municipal system, based on three inscriptions (Borsari, "Terracina," 234; Vaglieri, "Terracina," 145; *CIL* 10.6335).

34. Lugli, *Anxur-Tarracina,* site 12. The site has polygonal masonry that is likely to be republican and could predate the Roman presence. Tarracina was first captured by the Romans in 406 BC (Livy 4.59.4–11; Diod. 14.16.5) and was brought into the Roman orbit with a colony in 329 BC (Livy 8.21.11; Vell. 1.14.4; see Oakley, *Commentary on Livy,* ad loc.). See also Lugli, *Anxur-Tarracina,* cols. 13–14; Salmon, *Roman Colonization,* 58, 175 n. 70, 170 n. 11, with plate 3 for centuriation.

one on the Via Appia, filled its cistern from a hillside spring improved with *cuniculi* (site 93). The pattern is similar near Circeii (just to the northwest along the coast from Anxur/Tarracina), where villas are located on both sides of the Sisto River, many with reservoirs and channels (both *cuniculi* and open streams)—some for drainage, others for water supply.[35]

Along the coast to the north, closer to Rome, the area between Circeii and Antium was also equipped with hydraulic infrastructure that both drained marshy areas and provided water for irrigation. Trenching and terracing were commonly used to control the flow of water, preventing damage from drainage and, at the same time, collecting water for irrigation, as the agricultural writers all recommend.[36] In the region from Velletri (in the hills to the southeast of the Alban volcano) to the coastal swamps, there are pre-Roman *cuniculi* along the slopes of valleys, connected with both drainage and irrigation, like similar systems in Etruria.[37] Similarly, on the marshy coast in the Ager Pomptinus, survey archaeology has identified drainage works to improve the land for cultivation, some of which may be connected with the building project of M. Cornelius Cethegus (cos. 160) in 160 BC.[38] Around the same time, G. Lucretius Gallus (pr. 171) built a channel from the Loracinto to his lands near Antium. Like Lepidus's breakwater, Gallus's channel was connected with his service in public office in Livy's account, because Gallus was praetor at the time. After he failed to supervise elections, he claimed to have been out of town on public business, but he was in fact supervising the construction of his channel.

---

35. Lugli, *Circeii*, sites 1 (*fossa Augusta*), 9 (*piscina detta di Lucullo*), 12 (cistern near a lake, possibly connected also with the villa at site 11), 21 (developed spring with *cuniculus*), 30 (*cuniculus*, probably part of a drainage system), 39 (Lucus Feroniae, shrine to the goddess Feronia with a developed spring), 41 (portion of an aqueduct running from the Amaseno Valley to Tarracina/Astura, built by Trajan and the Antonines), 44 (large villa with cisterns and *cuniculus* for drainage), and finally a large site that has been identified as Domitian's estate at Circeii.

36. For the recommendations about drainage and using the lay of the land in the agricultural writers, see appendix A. See also Treacy and Denevan, "Creation of Cultivable Land," 95; Oleson, "Irrigation," 211; Horden and Purcell, *Corrupting Sea*, 234–37.

37. For the pre-Roman *cuniculi* at Velletri, see Ashby, *Roman Campagna*, 24. For their continuous use into the republican period, see Quilici Gigli, "Sistemi di cunicoli." For the study of one villa that has its own hydraulic installations and also illustrates this continuity, see Lilli, "La villa alla Civiatana."

38. On Cornelius Cethegus's drainage system in the Ager Pomptinus, see Livy, *Epit.* 46; Frederiksen, *Campania*, 165; Koot, "Marching through Marshes," 13. For local rivers in coastal Latium, see Pliny, *NH* 3.57, 59, with Frederiksen, *Campania*, 17–23. Compare the drainage and irrigation works in inland Campania, classified as private endeavors by Arthur (*Romans in Northern Campania*, 69–71).

The tribunes of the plebs attacked Lucretius because he was absent during busy elections, although he made the defense that he was away on state business; but then, even the nearby regions were so unfamiliar that he was on his land at Antium at that time and was building a water channel to Antium from the river Loracinto with the spoils [of his victory in Greece; cf. 43.4.5]. (7) The work is said to have been contracted at a cost of three hundred thousand bronze coins; he also adorned the doors to the temple of Asclepius with painted tables from the spoils.

> *[Lucretium tribuni plebis absentem contionibus adsiduis lacerabant, cum rei publicae causa abesse excusaretur; sed tum adeo vicina etiam inexplorata erant ut is eo tempore in agro suo Antiati esset, aquamque ex manubiis Antium ex flumine Loracinae duceret. (7) id opus centum triginta milibus aeris locasse dicitur; tabulis quoque pictis ex praeda fanum Aesculapi exornavit.]* (Livy 43.4.6–7)

For Livy, the channel episode illustrates Gallus's failure to fulfill his duties as praetor, but it is possible to see Gallus's attention to his water channel in a more positive light, as an indication of its importance for the cultivation on his coastal property. Livy also reports the cost of the project, perhaps because the funds came from Gallus's campaign in Greece and also to suggest extravagance. In the juxtaposition of the water channel with his gift to the temple of Asclepius, there may be an insinuation that Gallus was irresponsible not just in missing the elections but also in spending more of his spoils on a private project than on his gift to the god. The cost of Gallus's channel is given as HS 30,000, which seems small by comparison with the few figures we have for larger, public aqueduct projects. In 144 BC, the first Roman aqueduct, the Aqua Marcia, cost HS 180,000,000 (Front. *Aq.* 7.4), or about HS 600 per foot.[39] Both of these figures may be conventionally stylized rather than accurately reported, but even with room for exaggeration and inaccuracy, they give some idea of scale.[40] By comparison, Quintus Cicero had a bid to build a water channel at three *denarii* (or HS 48) per foot (*Q.Fr.* 3.1.3). The difference between the two prices can probably be explained by the size and scope of the project: the Aqua Marcia

---

39. The price per foot of the Aqua Marcia is based on the calculation of price per kilometer in Leveau, "Research on Roman Aqueducts," 153–54. On the cost of building aqueducts in general, see Hodge, *Roman Aqueducts,* 6; Eck, "Wasserversorgung," 71–79. For more on Quintus Cicero's water channel, see chapters 3 and 4 in the present study.

40. The cost of Gallus's channel (HS 30,000) and of the Aqua Marcia are both multiples of thirty; on conventional figures, see Scheidel, "Finances, Figures, and Fiction," 244, 226, and table 2.

crossed varied terrain over almost 62,000 paces, 54,247 1/2 paces underground and 7,463 on structures aboveground (Front. *Aq.* 6.8). Presumably, the two private projects were smaller and may not have involved either tunnels or arches. Gallus's channel may have been to connect his property with a larger regional system that supplied the area around Antium. Water was brought from the Alban Hills through a system of channels, *cuniculi,* and collection reservoirs that may once have been private, though it appears to have been publicly administered by the Flavian era.[41] Some of this water was doubtless spent on luxury distribution, like the fountains celebrated by Martial on Domitian's estate at Astura (between Antium and Circeii), but not all of it went for display: in another poem, Martial describes a retreat at Formiae where fish were raised.[42] On the coast, as in the suburban areas near Rome, luxury villas were also working farms that made demands on the water supply.[43]

The reconstructed landscape of the *suburbium,* as described here, can be at best a patchwork, because of the nature of the sources—a short stretch of arches belonging to a local aqueduct, Pliny's sampling of local varieties. Yet even this impressionistic view helps us to understand the constraints on local water supplies. First, the distribution of springs and streams relative to farms and villas constituted a real physical limitation on access to water. Second, most of the land near the city was used for gardens and other types of cultivation that relied on a steady water supply, including fish farming along the coast. The need for water for farming was critical because landowners needed to make their land productive, even when it was part of a luxurious estate. Thus, the reconstructed landscape also helps to explain the economic interests that contributed to competition over a local water supply. Both physical and economic factors affected the strategies that landowners adopted to manage competition for water, both informally and through servitudes. The inscriptions presented in the next section also con-

41. Portions of these channels and reservoirs as well as arcades from the raised channel have been identified. Also, inscribed water pipes (*fistulae*) show that there was a public distribution system in the Flavian era. For details, see Brandizzi Vitucci, *Antium,* 77–79 ("Acquedotti").

42. For the retreat with a fish farm at Formiae, see Mart. 10.30; for Domitian's villa at Axur, Mart. 10.51.7–10, 10.58.1, 5.5.1 (possibly with sulfur spring). Lugli, *Circeii,* cols. 12 and 71–76 identifies a number of hydraulic installations with Domitian's villa. For villas at Astura, see Cic. *Att.* 15.10; Suet. *Aug.* 16; Suet. *Tib.* 72; Lugli, *Circeii,* cols. 8–10. See also Andreussi, "Stanziamenti agricoli," 353–54; Marzano, *Villas in Central Italy.*

43. For sources and details, see appendices A and B.

tribute to our understanding of these strategies as they relate to the physical environment and competition for water among owners of rural properties.

INSCRIPTIONS AND LOCAL WATER DISTRIBUTION

Several inscriptions from Roman Italy and the provinces attest to local water-sharing arrangements like those outlined in the preceding section on the basis of the material remains of hydraulic infrastructure. The circumstances surrounding these inscriptions vary. They are from various places in Italy and the Roman provinces, and they involve both public and private water supplies, as well as different legal situations. Some of these inscriptions have been used by Capogrossi Colognesi in his study of the history of servitudes, to explain the developments in the legal concepts.[44] Similarly, public and private water supplies are compared here—first the private, then the public—because the similarities outweigh the differences. Though there are differences in detail, the overall pattern is consistent in confirming competition for water. Moreover, the inscriptions document practice on the ground, illustrating the strategies for managing competition over water—particularly the use of legal rights and schedules, which are the focus of the legal cases in the last section of this chapter.

In several cases, an inscription regulating water was found with archaeological evidence—for example, near a spring or the remains of an aqueduct. This was the case with one stone from Tor Sapienza, the area near Rome previously described, where hillside farms shared streams and springs. This puzzling and fragmentary text, of republican date, seems to indicate local control over water and some dispute among those sharing the supply. The inscription, in two lines of rough-cut letters around a cylindrical stone, is partially preserved and reads: *rivei a (. ?.) /(. ? .) ere non licet.*[45] It is a prohibition of some sort, related to water from a channel, probably the Aqua Mariana (or Maranna), a perennial stream in the area. The nature of the prohibition depends on how the text is reconstructed. Five reconstructions have been proposed. Two reconstructions protect open access to the stream.

---

44. On epigraphical evidence and the development of the unified concept of the servitude, see Capogrossi Colognesi, *Servitù d'acqua*, 88–96 (*aquae ductus*), 114–21 (*haustus*).

45. See Coste and Schutzmann-Bolzon, "Il cippo arcaico," 370 (reconstructions), 366 (the date, based on the material [tufa], the genitive ending *-ei*, and the letterforms). In discussing the reconstructions, Coste and Schutzmann-Bolzon do not indicate where the line break should be, and as I have not been able to examine the stone, I present the reconstructions without line breaks.

Keeping anyone from water from the stream is not allowed.
[rivei a[qua quemvis prohib]ere non licet.]

Preventing access to the stream is not allowed.
[rivei a[dditum interdic]ere non licet.]

These reconstructions suggest a public waterway and should probably be rejected, because the rural location fits better with a private source. Another reconstruction limits access to the stream.

Drawing or taking water of the stream is not allowed.
[rivei a[quam haurire sum]ere non licet.]

If this reconstruction is accurate, the inscription aims at excludability, keeping those outside the system from using the water. Such a reconstruction would be consistent with a closed private system where only a few people were allowed to use the water, perhaps only the landowner. The last two reconstructions, which address interference in the stream, are consistent with either a private or a public water supply. In any case, these prohibitions suggest that the community was engaged in policing the stream, protecting either the purity of the water or its flow along the channel.

Spoiling the water of the stream is not allowed.
[rivei a[quam corrump]ere non licet.]

Blocking the channel of the stream is not allowed.
[rivei a[lveum obstru]ere non licet.][46]

Although it is not possible to determine, on the basis of these reconstructions, whether or not the water supply was public or private, the rural location suggests a private system. Presumably, the person or persons who set up the inscription used the water in the stream—by custom, if not by right. The presence of the inscription, however it is restored, is a sign that other people were meddling in the stream's use, presumably without right. Even though it is impossible to fully reconstruct either the text or the situation, this inscription shows that a small stream could be the focus of dispute about access to a local water supply.

---

46. Coste and Schutzmann-Bolzon ("Il cippo arcaico") reject this reconstruction on the basis of incompatible letterforms, arguing that the fragmentary letter at the end of the first line cannot be reconstructed as a *v*.

A clearer picture of competition for water can be constructed from another, less fragmentary inscription from the Gracchan era (late second century BC), which documents the use of law to protect access to a spring. This stone was found and is still located near a spring and the remains of the aqueduct that carried its waters, in the province of Caserta, inland from the coast of Campania. This inscription reports a declaration about water, made by one Q. Folvius before the urban praetor.

> Quintus Folvius, son of Quintus, grandson of Marcus, declares this water before Publius Atilius, son of Lucius, the urban praetor.
>
> *[Q(uintus) Folvius Q(uinti) f(ilius) M(arci) [n(epos)*
> *hance aqua[m*
> *indeixit apu[d*
> *P(ublium) Atilium L(ucii) f(ilius)*
> *Pr(aetorem) Urb(anum)]*
> (*CIL* 10.8236)

The expression is a bit compressed, but it probably concerns private, rather than public, water, as will be argued shortly, though this inscription has been interpreted as evidence for a public water supply.[47] The involvement of the urban praetor points to private law, which was his jurisdiction, and to private ownership, rather than to a municipal aqueduct, which the censors would have supervised. By declaring the water before the praetor, Folvius claimed ownership of the spring, and with that claim, he may also have established a servitude to draw water from it (*haustus*), because this right could be expressed as ownership, even after the servitudes were conceptualized as abstract rights. According to Capogrossi Colognesi's interpretation, the servitudes for *aquae ductus* and *haustus* were not always conceived as unified rights that included both a right of access and a right to use water; instead, they developed from a combination of two separate rights: a right-of-way and ownership of the source of water. His argument is based on several inscriptions that refer to a right-of-way along with ownership of a spring (but not this one).[48] For Capogrossi Colognesi, the language of these inscrip-

47. Folvius's spring (*CIL* 10.8236) was interpreted as a public water supply in its first publication, by Mommsen ("Inschrift aus Caiatia," 497), and more recently by Pagano ("Alcuni aquedotti romani," 104–6). The spring is now known as the Fontana di Caiazzo or Fontana "Fistola," and until recently, it was the main source of running water for the residents of the town of Caiazzo.

48. Inscriptions cited by Capogrossi Colognesi (*Servitù d'acqua*, 114–21) for the development of a unified concept of *haustus* include, in addition to *CIL* 9.4791 = *ILS* 6013 (discussed

tions reflects the development of the legal concepts of *aquae ductus* and *haustus*. In some cases, the claim to the water is implicit, as, for example, in the following text from the Sabine region near Rome.

> The road or field below the spring belonging to Quintus Maelius Cerdo, 1,200 feet long and 10 feet wide all the way to the Consuletus stream, is private [property] of Quintus Maelius Cerdonis.
>
> *[via sive ager est*
> *infra fontem*
> *Q. Maeli Cerdonis*
> *longum p(edes) ∞ CC latum*
> *p(edes) X usque ad rivom*
> *Consuletum privata*
> *est Q. Maeli Cerdo / nis.]*
>
> (*CIL* 9.4791 = *ILS* 6013)

Folvius's inscription follows the same pattern, claiming ownership without explicit reference to a servitude, so it is not unlikely that his declaration before the praetor also secured a servitude (i.e., not just ownership of the spring but also access to the water). If a servitude was involved, Folvius's inscription would provide a public record of his right to share the water and, by implication, the exclusion of those without such a right. If Folvius's declaration implies simple ownership and not a servitude, then it established his exclusive access to the spring. In any case, the declaration before the urban praetor implies that there was some dispute about the water and that his inscription was aimed at deterring rival claims to the water. Finally, the public record of Folvius's legal action—in the naming of the urban praetor on the stone—suggests that Folvius and his rivals for the water recognized that private property rights were an effective way to secure access to water. Similar

---

shortly in the present chapter), *CIL* 5.3849 = *ILS* 8356 (Verona, possibly a right-of-way and right to draw water for a tomb) and *CIL* 13.7252 (fragmentary inscription from Germany, right to a spring and right-of-way) and for comparison, two provincial statutes, the lex Coloniae Genetivae *CIL* 2.5439 = *ILS* 6087, line 99 and the Augustan edict de *aquaeductu Venafrano*, *CIL* 10.48.42= *ILS* 5743. In arguing for the same development in *aquae ductus*, Capogrossi Colognesi (*Servitù d'acqua*, 88–96) cites four inscriptions that record the gift of water supply to a town, that is, a public supply: *CIL* 13.966 = *ILS* 5756; *CIL* 11.5942 = *ILS* 5762; *CIL* 12.2493–94 = *ILS* 5768; *CIL* 12.1882–89. He includes one inscription that relates to privately owned water, *CIL* 11.3003 = *ILS* 5771 (quoted and discussed shortly in the present chapter).

expectations motivated a much more elaborate inscription about a private aqueduct built more than two hundred years later.

In the late first century AD, Mummius Niger Valerius Vegetus owned an aqueduct that is described in detail in an inscription from Viterbo, in northern Etruria.[49] The aqueduct began at a source on the Fundus Antoninanus and brought water to Vegetus's villa Calvisiana. In the inscription, the villa is said to be near the Aqua Passeriana, a famous hot spring, mentioned by Martial (6.42.5–6), though its location is not now known. When the inscription was discovered in the seventeenth century, it was built into an aqueduct near the convent of S. Maria in Viterbo, where it entered what was thought to be an ancient *cuniculus.* This structure may have been part of Mummius's water channel, and another part may survive as part of a small aqueduct serving a villa near Viterbo.[50] The inscription, on a peperino slab now in the museum at Viterbo, describes the route of Vegetus's aqueduct, naming the landmarks it crossed (public roads and private estates) and reporting its length and physical features.

> Mummius Niger Valerius Vegetus, a man of consular status, built his own aqueduct (Aqua Vegetiana), [to channel water] that arose on the larger Antonine farm of Publius Tullius Varro, after <the place> in which the spring arose was [purchased and] conveyed, [he built it] across 5.95 miles to his own villa Calvisia, which is near the Aquae Passerianae, after the places [*locis;* sc., land] and rights of access [*itineribus*] were purchased and conveyed to him by the possessors, each of his own farm, across which the aqueduct described above was built, across [a strip of land] ten feet wide for the arches and six feet wide for the pipes. [It was built] across the greater and lesser Antonine farms of Publius Terentius Varro and the Baebian and Philinian farm of Avileus Commodus, the Petronian farm of Publius Terentius Varro, the Volsonian farm of Herennius Polybius, the Fundanian farm of Caetennus

49. For the date of *CIL* 11.3003 = *ILS* 5771 and the identification of Vegetus, see Capogrossi Colognesi, *Servitù d'acqua,* 93 n. 174. On this inscription as evidence for using lead pipes in the last stretch of an aqueduct, see Bruun, *Water Supply,* 126, 133. For another local aqueduct in Etruria, probably serving the town of Ferentium, compare the aqueduct at Aquarossa that ran underground, probably from a source in the Monte Cimini (Östenberg and Pallottino, *Case Etrusche,* 35–36). For more on the Vegetus inscription, see chapter 2 in the present study.

50. On the villa and aqueduct near Viterbo, see Lanciani, *Le acque e gli acquedotti,* 591.

Proculus, the Cuttolonian farm of Cornelius Latinus, the lower Serran farm of Quintinus Verecundus, the Capitonian farm of Pistranus Celsus, the left embankment of the public road, the Via Ferentiensis and the Scirpian farm of Pistrania Lepida and the Via Cassia into his own villa Calvisia, and likewise through roads and public rights-of-ways through the fields by a grant according to a decree of the Senate.

[Mummius Niger Valerius Vegetus consular(is) / aquam suam Vegetianam, quae / nascitur in fundo Antoniano / maiore P(ubli) Tulli Varronis cum † eo loco † / in quo is fons est emancipatus, duxi[t] / per millia passuum VDCCCCL in vil / lam suam Calvisianam, quae est / ad aquas Passerianas suas, compara / tis et emancipatis sibi locis itineri / busque eius aquae a possessoribus / sui cuiusque fundi, per quae aqua / s(upra) s(cripta) ducta est, per latitudinem structu / ris pedes decem, fistulis per latitudi / nem pedes sex, per fundos Antonian(um) / maiorem et Antonianum minor(em) / P(ubli) Tulli Varonis et Baebianum et / Philinianum Avilei Commodi / et Petronianum P(ubli) Tulli Varonis / et Volsonianum Herenni Polybi / et Fundanianum Caetenni Proculi / et Cuttolonianum Corneli Latini / et Serranum inferiorem Quintini / Verecundi et Capitonianum Pistrani / Celsi et per crepidinem sinisterior(em) / viae publicae Ferentienses et Scirpi / anum Pistraniae Lepidae et per viam / Cassiam in villam Calvisianum suam / item per vias limitesque publicos / ex permissu s(enatus) c(onsulto).] (*CIL* 11.3003 = *ILS* 5771)

Vegetus's aqueduct ran for almost six miles through a combination of arches and pipes, built on a strip of land of varying width (ten feet for arches, six feet for pipes). More important, his inscription provides a public record of his ownership of the facility and the water it provided to his estate. Indeed, it specifies that Vegetus purchased the spring where the water arose and the strip of land on which the aqueduct was built as well as rights-of-way: *cum † eo loco † / in quo is fons est emancipatus, . . . compara / tis et emancipatis sibi locis itineri / busque eius aquae a possessoribus / sui cuiusque fundi, per quae aqua / s(upra) s(cripta) ducta est.* Instead of establishing a servitude, Vegetus chose to purchase the spring and the land on which he built his aqueduct. This arrangement corresponds to a form of private water rights that was used for at least two centuries (roughly 100 BC to AD 100), until the servitude for channeling water (*aquae ductus*), which unified control of the channel and the source, became the dominant legal mechanism, according to Capogrossi Colognesi.[51] Pur-

51. For the interpretation of *CIL* 11.3003 = *ILS* 5771 as the purchase of a spring and the land for an aqueduct (not a servitude), see Capogrossi Colognesi, *Servitù d'acqua*, 93–94; cf. 88–96.

chasing land also seems to have been the usual practice for the city aqueducts, as a way of protecting both private and public property rights (*ut in suis finibus priprium ius <tam> res publica quam privati haberent,* Front. *Aq.* 128.1).[52] Vegetus, too, may have chosen to purchase the land and spring, instead of setting up a servitude, because ownership effectively secured a monopoly on this source of water. As in Folvius's case, setting up the inscription helped to enforce his monopoly, as a reminder of his rights as owner and his legal power to enforce those rights.

In each of these four inscriptions, a privately owned source of water is the object of competition. All the inscriptions presuppose that someone other than the person who set up the stone was interested in or was in fact interfering with the water supply, because they aim to restrict access to water—creating a monopoly in Vegetus's case and at least limiting use in the others, where brevity or uncertainty make it impossible to say more. Whether these inscriptions claim ownership or a servitude for water use, they all reflect a fundamental similarity between public and private water systems: the fact of competition over water and systematic efforts to respond to competition. Further insight into the strategies for managing competition can be gained from five inscriptions about the distribution of municipal or publicly owned water among rural properties. One of these inscriptions, like the Vegetus inscription, describes the route of an aqueduct, while the others contain schedules or maps for small distribution systems.

A long inscription from the town of Amiternum in southern Italy describes the route of the town's municipal aqueduct, which was either built or repaired in the first century AD when the stone was erected.[53] The route of the aqueduct is represented as if one were walking along it, with a series of entries reporting the distance from one reservoir to another—for example, "from the *castellum* to the hill near the vineyard of the Ancharii . . . feet from the vineyard of the Ancharii to the reservoir which is opposite the vineyard of the Pacii 320 feet" *[ab castello ad con= / [. . .]lum ad vinias Anchariorum ped(es) / [. . . af vin]ieis Ancharum ad castellum qui / [est contra vin]ias Pacianias p(edes) CCCXX]* (lines 4–8). There seems to be a *castellum,* or reservoir, on each

52. See Rodgers, *Frontinus,* 315, 321–22 (use of private property rights to demarcate public and private water). For the parallel between Vegetus's private arrangements and public practice, see Eck, "Wasserversorgung," 59–60; see 61 for a nice photograph of the Vegetus inscription.

53. *ILS* 5792=Segenni, "Amiternum," 101–3, n. 50. The inscription commemorated a cleaning, according to Buonocore, "Fra topografia ed epigrafia, 187, or recorded a plan for routine cleaning, Wilson, "Extra Urbem," 318.

property, suggesting that water was delivered to each property along the route of the aqueduct, and the presence of a *castellum* probably indicates a legal right to use the water. Although this inscription describes the distribution of a municipal water supply, it nicely illustrates the topography that is assumed in the legal cases where several landowners have the right to use water from a shared channel.

The same pattern appears even more clearly in the four inscriptions that describe shared channels with a map and/or in a schedule allocating water by day and time. Three of these are from areas close to Rome; the fourth is an inscription from Lamasba in Roman North Africa and is discussed in the next chapter as well, in relation to local custom. Although the Lamasba inscription (AD 218–22) is probably about a century later than the Italian ones, it makes a good starting point because it has been carefully studied by Shaw, whose conclusions are apposite to this discussion of servitudes. The Lamasba inscription preserves a schedule for irrigation that used water from a perennial stream.[54] Each entry in the schedule lists the name of the landowner to whom water is allocated, the amount, and the time of day for channeling the water. The entries are probably arranged as the land itself was; that is, the water flowed from the source to the first property in the schedule, then to the next, and so on in order down the line, as in the inscription from Amiternum. Though there is no pictorial map, the text itself reflects the landscape and the landowners' interest in the water. The schedule was inscribed on stone and exists only because there was some dispute about the distribution, as Shaw infers from the preamble to the inscription. In arid North Africa, it is not surprising to find competition for a limited water supply, and Shaw notes that many similar irrigation systems have been identified in the region, though this is the only inscription of its kind from Africa. In Italy, however, three similar inscriptions are also known, and Pliny knew about scheduled water distribution in Africa (*NH* 18.188), so it seems that disputes over water were well known and that the use of inscriptions to record the resolution was not uncommon. In comparing the African and Italian inscriptions, Shaw notes that the allotments are more flexible in Italy, because the channels were different sizes, whereas they are uniform in the Lamasba inscription. Flexibility also characterizes the schedules connected

54. *CIL* 8.18587 = *CIL* 8.4440 = *ILS* 5793; Shaw, "Lamasba," 68–71 (the decree as a local resolution of dispute over allocation); 72–73 (the schedule); 88 (abbreviations and the numbers in the inscription and calculations of the time units); 61–62 and 95–100 (narrative of discovery and reconstruction).

with servitudes, which will be examined in the next section of this chapter. Because the three Italian inscriptions describe conditions near Rome, they can be interpreted in the context of the city aqueducts and the competition for this public supply. In fact, one of these inscriptions concerns the use of water from one of the city aqueducts.

The first Italian inscription gives the most general indications about competition for water. In this early imperial inscription (AD 4–37), Augustus confirmed permission for private individuals to use water from the Aqua Alsietina, an aqueduct built primarily to supply the naumachia.[55] Like the Lamasba inscription, this one was probably in response to a dispute or disagreement about water use, because it confirms a previously existing system. The water came from the Alsietina's supplementary channel, the Forma Mentis, and was delivered to people who shared its channel, the *rivalibus*. This inscription is one of the three texts where the term *rivalis* is used in its technical sense.[56] These *rivales* used water from the Forma Mentis, presumably every day, for a set period of time, until a specified signal.

> The emperor Caesar Augustus, son of a god, Pontifex Maximus, added the channel of Mens (flowing) to the channel of the Aqua Augusta [i.e., the Alsietina], which goes to the grove of the Caesars, so that [it would flow] to the people sharing a channel who were receiving (water) until a specified signal.
>
> *[[Imperator Caesar*
> *divi f.] Augustus*
> *[p]ontif(ex) max(imus)*
> *[for] mam Mentis attrib(uit)*
> *[r]ivo aquae Augustae*
> *[q]uae pervenit in*
> *nemus Caesarum*
> *[ut] ex eo rivalibus qui*
> *[ad b]uccinam accipieb(ant).]*
>
> (*CIL* 6.31566)

The phrase *ad buccinum* probably refers to a fixed schedule of distribution, according to Ashby's interpretation, which makes reference to one of the Ital-

55. *CIL* 6.31566 = *CIL* 11.3722a = *ILS* 5796. My text and translation follow the reconstructions in Ashby, *Aqueducts*, 183.

56. For the usage of *rivalis*, see the introduction in the present study.

ian inscriptions with a schedule for water use (*CIL* 6.1261, discussed shortly).[57] Frontinus describes delivery of water from the Alsietina to properties outside the city: "[Augustus] granted what had begun to be surplus for the naumachia to the properties nearby and to the use of private citizens for irrigating" [*quod naumachiae coeperat superesse hortis adiacentibus et privatorum usibus ad inrigangdum concessit*] (*Aq.* 11.1; see 71.2 and 85 for the volume of water). These private properties probably used the water during the day, when it was in less demand, because the naumachia was refilled at night.[58] A special channel of the Alsietina, the Forma Mentis, seems to have been dedicated to this private distribution of water for irrigation.[59] Private grants to imperial aqueducts, then, serve some of the same needs as local supplies, whether private or municipal; and the situation described in this inscription is consistent with a pattern of competition for shared local water supplies that were used to irrigate private property in the *suburbium.*

The second Italian inscription (*CIL* 14.3676) describes a shared channel related to the municipal water supply at Tibur, and it confirms the demand for water in rural areas near Rome. The stone is built into the church of St. Peter at Tivoli, and it preserves part of the text and part of a map depicting two channels. The text lists people to whom the water goes (in the dative), the volume of water due to each, and the time of day when it may be channeled. This local distribution system was independent of the Roman aqueducts that passed through Tibur's territory, though branch lines from the city aqueducts also supplemented the water supply at Tibur.[60] At least one illustrious landowner, Manilius Vopiscus, had an imperial grant to use water from the Aqua Marcia and piped it to his land across the Anio River (Stat. *Silv.* 1.3.66–69). If the engineering of Vopiscus's pipes was singular, his desire for water was not, and not everyone who used the city water did so legally. Frontinus's attention to illegal taps suggests that some landowners used ag-

57. Ashby (*Aqueducts,* 184 n. 1) explains, "The phrase *ad buccinum* was common as meaning 'at a given signal,' and it is not necessary that it should refer to anything more than the regulated system in use on the Aqua Crabra."

58. For daytime irrigation and refilling the naumachia at night, see Taylor, "Torrent or Trickle?" 473.

59. Rodgers, *Frontinus,* 180. Alternatively, the Channel of Mens may be the conduit bringing water from the Lago di Bracciano to supplement the Alsietina (Front. *Aq.* 11.3–4, with Ashby, *Aqueducts,* 184).

60. Evans, "In Tiburtium Usum," 447–48, 450 (the branch from the Anio Vetus), 452–53 (Manilius Vopiscus's pipes from the Aqua Marcia), 453–54 (the branch from the Anio Novus), 454–55 (demand for water in Tibur in general).

gressive tactics to satisfy their demand for water. Even if, as Frontinus asserts (*Aq.* 87–88), the imperial aqueducts brought an ample supply in his time, the persistent problem of stealing the city's water shows that not everyone who wanted an imperial grant could get one and that, as Peachin writes, "the lion's share . . . rightly belonged to the emperor and the elite."[61] Illegal taps on the city aqueducts were not new in Frontinus's day: he compares his contemporary situation to a speech, *de Aquis,* given by M. Caelius Rufus in his curule aedileship in 50 BC, which apparently accused *aquarii* (officials in the city water administration) of accepting bribes.[62] The *aquarii* were often complicit in the theft of water, but they also facilitated a market for water. Because the right to use water from a city aqueduct was personal (unlike a servitude), it ceased when the person died or sold the property. In these situations, the imperial watermen were able to sell this "extra" water, until it was allocated to someone else (Front. *Aq.* 109.1–2). In at least one instance, the watermen appropriated a local water supply for their off-the-books market, and this episode also concerns the last Italian inscription documenting a shared channel. This shared channel was part of the local water at Tusculum and was based on a stream called the Crabra.

The town of Tusculum was nestled on the slopes of the Alban volcano, land that was fertile and watered by springs and streams. These local sources were important to the people of Tusculum because most of its territory was on too high an elevation to tap the city aqueducts. Pipes associated with many of the villas near Tusculum have inscriptions showing that they were supplied from a local reservoir rather than by one of the urban aqueducts. This local system was in operation through the first century AD and probably longer, based on the evidence from Frontinus, who describes the situation at Tusculum in the context of Agrippa's development of the Aqua Julia to supplement the Aqua Tepula.[63] Agrippa did not tap the Crabra, which

61. Peachin, *Frontinus,* 133–34; see 118–26 on the interpretation of Frontinus.

62. On contemporary illegal water use in comparison to Caelius's speech, see Front. *Aq.* 76, with Rodgers, *Frontinus,* 240–42. Caelius, as curule aedile, was dealing with a scandal in which tavern keepers bribed *aquarii* to secure a water supply, on the basis of Cic. *Fam.* 8.6.4 (written in February of 50 BC): *nisi ego cum tabernariis et aquariis pugnarem, veternus civitatem occupasset.* Alternatively, Caelius may have been faced with two separate scandals, one involving watermen, the other shopkeepers; for this interpretation, see Shackleton Bailey, *Ad Familiares,* 1:416. On illegal tapping, see Bruun, *Water Supply,* 55–58, 106–9; Taylor, "Torrent or Trickle?" 470–71, 490–91.

63. See Bruun, *Water Supply,* 281–82; Thomas and Wilson, "Water Supply for Roman Farms," 184–85.

was used by the people of Tusculum, but subsequently, the dishonest *aquarii* sold the water of the Crabra for their own enrichment. Frontinus imagines the surprise of the people of Tusculum when the emperor ordered the Crabra's water restored to them: "they now perhaps draw it [sc., water] not without marveling, because they are do not know to what cause they owe this unaccustomed abundance" [*qui nunc forsitan non sine admiratione eam sumunt, ignari cui causae insolitam abundantiam debeant*] (*Aq.* 9.7). The unaccustomed abundance of water suggests a situation where demand more usually exceeded supply, as does Frontinus's description of the distribution scheme that operated at Tusculum.

> Beyond the source of the [Aqua] Julia flows a stream that is called the Crabra. . . . This is a stream from which all the villas along its course draw water allotted in turn by day and specified amounts.
>
> [*Praeter caput Iuliae transfluit aqua quae vocatur Crabra. . . . Haec namque est quam omnes villae tractus eius per vicem in dies modulosque certos dispensatam accipiunt.*] (*Aq.* 9.4–5)[64]

Water from the Crabra, a local stream, was distributed to residents according to a daily schedule and specific amounts, just as in the inscription from Tivoli. A similar inscription found in Rome on Monte Maria has been associated with the Crabra system since Mommsen suggested the connection, even though the text does not mention Tusculum or the Crabra (*CIL* 6.1261).[65] This inscription is also fragmentary, but it clearly contained the map of a channel, along with the names of the people who shared the channel, the volume of water, and scheduled times for channeling it. Frontinus

---

64. The full text of Front. *Aq.* 4–7 reads: *Praeter caput Iuliae transfluit aqua quae vocatur Crabra. (5) Hanc Agrippa omisit, seu quia improbaverat sive quia Tusculanis possessoribus relinquendam credebat. Haec namque est quam omnes villae tractus eius per vicem in dies modulosque certos dispensatam accipiunt. (6) Sed non eadem moderatione aquarii nostri par[tem] eius semper in supplementum Iuliae vindicaverunt, nec ut Iuliam augerent, quam hauriebant largiendo compendi sui gratia. (7) Exclusa ergo Crabra et tota iussu imperatoris reddita <est> Tusculanis, qui nunc forsitan non sine admiratione eam sumunt, ignari cui causae insolitam abundantiam debeant.*

65. Mommsen ("Römische Urkunden," 307 = *Gesammelte Schriften* 3:87–88) cites *CIL* 6.1261 to illustrate a typical distribution scheme for local aqueducts. Mommsen dates this inscription to the Augustan era because it names one C. Iulius Hymetus, probably a freedman from the imperial household. He bases the connection with Tusculum on this passage from Frontinus (*Aq.* 9.4–5) but also suggests Tibur as a possibility, with reference to *CIL* 14.3676 (previously discussed in the present chapter).

seems impressed that the system worked: he characterizes the behavior of the people of Tusculum as involving restraint (*moderatio*), which suggests that there was some incentive not to be virtuous; that is, there was competition for water at Tusculum. The behavior of the Tusculans may have been reinforced by financial considerations if they paid a fee for use, as Cicero seems to have done: "I should pay a tax to the people of Tusculum for the aqua Crabra," he writes, "because I acquired the property by sale" [*ego Tusculanis pro aqua Crabra vectigal pendam, quia mancipio fundum accepi*] (*Agr.* 3.9).[66] Based on Cicero's explanation, it appears that the local water supply was attached to the property, like a servitude, though the system was clearly municipal. The practice of transferring private grants to tap the public supply was usual in Rome, at least in Frontinus's day.[67] Whatever the status of the Crabra system (public or private), it was characterized by a dynamic of competition similar to the pattern connected with servitudes.

At Tusculum, competition for water was managed with a daily schedule that conserved a limited resource and enforced a systematic distribution. The schedule involves economic rationality, since it presumes the ability to calculate water use. Indeed, the technology to measure and control the flow of water was known and used by the Romans (see, e.g., the detailed measurements of water allotments in Front. *Aq.* 78–86).[68] In addition, the fee for use, since it was a monetary assessment, shows that these calculations were also financial: the people of Tusculum were able to put a price on water. In terms of mediating competition, a fee for use could serve to ration the water, though in a wealthy community, only a sizable fee could affect consumption, and it seems likely that the fee was related to the use of water for economic purposes.[69] Such fees for use are known from a few other inscriptions from Italy describing municipal aqueducts, but the sources do not

66. Cf. *D.* 19.1.41 Papin. 3 *Resp.*, a case involving an annual fee (*pensistatio*) for use of water in the city and how that fee should be handled when property is sold. Freedom from a servitude could also be purchased, at least on one occasion recorded in an inscription from Pompeii (*CIL* 10.787; see Biondi, *Categoria*, 104–5; Solazzi, *Specie ed estinzione*, 144–45). For more on the water supply to Cicero's Tusculan property, see chapters 2 and 3 in the present study.

67. On the transfer of private grants to use the public aqueducts, see Evans, *Water Distribution*, 8–10; Bruun, *Water Supply*, 64–96; Peachin, *Frontinus*, 124–27.

68. On Frontinus's measurements and the physical device for controlling flow (*calix*), see Bruun, *Water Supply*, 39–58; see also his discussion of methods for saving water in "Water Shortage" (219–21).

69. For a list of the villas and their owners that were likely served by the Crabra, see Lanciani, "Le acque e gli acquedotti," 322–23.

specify the fee or how its proceeds were used.[70] These fees might have helped a community recover the costs of building a local aqueduct, as suggested by Eck.[71] Fees may also have financed maintenance of the system; for example, those who used the water in the Spanish irrigation community described by the *lex Rivi Hiberiensis* did the maintenance work and contributed to the costs.[72] In Rome, private use of surplus water from the city aqueducts was also subject to an annual fee or tax. According to Frontinus, this was an old practice, from a time when there were no private grants and when overflow water was available only for commercial use in baths and laundries (*Aq.* 94.2–4). Presumably, the city expected to earn revenue from the fee, indicating that businesses were willing and able to pay, probably because the cost was offset by profit, the fee was less costly than other alternatives, or there were no good alternatives. At Tusculum, landowners probably also had an economic interest in using water to cultivate crops for the garden markets in Rome, as was typical of suburban villas. The location of Tusculum, ideal for a quick getaway from the city, was also convenient for transporting produce to the urban market.[73] But the rationality of this system was not maximizing; or at least, there is insufficient evidence to prove that it was. A schedule for use could help these landowners to satisfy their need for water by securing access. The organization of a schedule suggests, in turn, that these landowners were able to calculate how best to use the water, including what crops and how many they could raise with their allocation. The schedule is thus a sign of the systematic approach that Roman landowners could take to exploiting the resources they needed to make their land productive.

Frontinus includes the people of Tusculum and the Crabra system to illustrate the integrity of his administration. For this study, he provides a rare literary description of what was a typical phenomenon in rural areas, that is, a stream or spring shared by a local community. This kind of distribution system was common in the *suburbium*, where villas and farmhouses were lo-

---

70. *CIL* 9.5144 (from the ruins of a bath at Castrum Novum in Abruzzo); *CIL* 10.4842, 4875 = *ILS* 5743, lines 37–41 (Venafro); *ILS* 6087 (*lex Urso*, ch. 100). Vitruvius's reference to a tax on private use (8.7.2) probably refers to these municipal systems.

71. Eck, "Wasserversorgung," 79–81. On fees and the apparent sale of water, see the introduction in the present study.

72. *Lex Rivi Hib.* 1.9–15; cf. 2.50–3.2 on fines for noncompliance, with Beltrán Lloris, "Irrigation Decree," 171, 173–74, 179.

73. Silverio ("Iconografia delle acque antiche," 174) argues that the inscriptions with schedules should be connected with irrigation, with reference to *CIL* 6.1261 (Rome) and 7.448 (Tivoli).

cated to take advantage of springs and streams. The situation at Tusculum, as described by Frontinus, corresponds to inscriptions recording shared channels and schedules for distributions. Though most of these inscriptions involve a municipal water supply rather than the private water sources governed by servitudes, both types of system were subject to the same competition for a scarce resource. In fact, boundary disputes were more likely when a stream marked the boundary, as observed in the writings of the Roman land surveyors: "I have marked [a boundary line] . . . along a stream, which rather often tends to come into question," [*dereximus . . . per rivum, quod frequentiore solet in questionem deduci*] (*grom.* 365.12–15).[74] Where inscriptions present a snapshot of a shared channel, the legal sources for servitudes illustrate the ongoing process of negotiation over a local water supply. The legal cases are particularly important for showing how Romans viewed schedules or what goals a schedule could serve.

LEGAL SCHEDULES FOR SERVITUDES

Landowners could manage competition for water by arranging specific terms to regulate servitudes on their land. These specific terms took the form of contracts between the individual landowners and supplemented the built-in restrictions discussed in the first section of this chapter.[75] A schedule for use, based on time or volume, was a common way to regulate water rights when more than one landowner drew on the same water supply or used the same channel, as illustrated by the inscriptions in the third part of this chapter.[76] A schedule was one kind of *modus* that governed the use of a servitude but did not affect its unified nature.[77] When a schedule was formalized in a legal agreement attached to a servitude, it provided a legal mechanism for enforcement and monetary compensation when social coer-

74. See also Campbell, *Roman Land Surveyors*, 268.4–5.

75. On terms generally, see the introduction in the present study; for terms as an expression of neighborly norms, see chapter 2.

76. For legal cases with various schedules, see *D.* 8.1.4.2 Papin. 7 *Quaest.*; *D.* 8.3.2.1–2 Nerat. 4 *Reg.*; *D.* 8.3.15 Pompon. 31 *ad Q. Muc.* (on which see chapter 2 in the present study); *D.* 8.6.7 Paul. 13 *ad Plaut.*; *D.* 8.6.10.1 Paul. 15 *ad Plaut.*; *D.* 43.20.5 pr. Jul. 4 *ex Minucio.* The last three cases are discussed in the present chapter. In the schedules (both legal and epigraphical), water use was allotted by time and/or by amount, measured and controlled by the size of the pipe or fixture (*foramen*): see n. 68 in this chapter.

77. On schedules as a *modus* of servitude for *aquae ductus*, see Capogrossi Colognesi, *Servitù d'acqua*, 152–53, 138 n. 235; Grosso, *Servitù prediali*, 159–66.

cion failed. In this part of the chapter, legal cases involving schedules are analyzed for what they reveal about landowners' strategies to manage competition for water. Their strategies take into account the natural constraints of the landscape, social dynamics, and the landowners' economic interest in a reliable water supply. The emphasis on these factors varies from case to case, as the jurists develop flexible rules to accommodate the changing aims of landowners, whether that means maximizing access to water, conserving the supply, sharing with a neighbor, or carefully calculating the monetary cost of lost water. In their approaches to schedules for water use, the jurists treat water both as an economic commodity and as a shared resource that is defined in natural or environmental terms.

Typical schedules are described in the sections of the *Digest* that deal with the praetorian interdicts. An interdict was an order issued by the praetor in an administrative hearing where questions of fact were considered. It protected possession, rather than ownership, and served as a preliminary to a lawsuit in which ownership was contested (*vindicatio*).[78] For example, if a plaintiff alleged that his neighbor was interfering with his servitude to channel water, the praetor would determine the validity of this claim, usually on the basis of the plaintiff's testimony.[79] If there appeared to be a violation of rights that should be taken up in a trial, he issued an interdict prohibiting the offensive action until the matter could be resolved through further legal procedure, which could take some time. If more than one landowner was claiming a servitude, as must often have been the case where neighbors shared channels, each could be protected from the other's aggression by an interdict. The possibility of such a legal duel is discussed in one of the two legal cases where the technical term *rivalis* occurs, suggesting both the underlying tensions in shared water systems and the importance of equity in the legal approaches to them (*D.* 43.20.1.26 Ulp. 70 *ad Ed.*). The double interdict gave both parties protection and the same opportunity to find a legal solution to their dispute. Because an interdict, like a restraining order, provided immediate relief, the aim seems to have been to preserve the status quo ante while the matter was pending (see, e.g., *D.* 43.20.7 Paul. 5 *Sent.*). When a

---

78. *D.* 8.5.2.3 Ulp. 17 *ad Ed.* For the distinction between *vindicatio* (questions of law) and *interdict* (questions of fact) and in general on interdicts, see Kaser, *RP* 1:408–13. On the interdicts relating to servitudes, see Grosso, *Servitù prediali*, 304–13; Solazzi, *Tutela e il possesso*, 51–92.

79. *D.* 43.20.1.44 Ulp. 70 *ad Ed.*, which seems to say otherwise, in fact belongs to a section on the interdict *de castellis*, that is, private grants to use water from the city aqueducts: see Palma, *Iura vicinitas*, 153–55, with references.

servitude for water use was at stake, an interdict could prevent loss due to interruption in the water supply.

Several different interdicts governed servitudes for water use, and the oldest of these, the interdict *de rivis,* protected the right to channel water from the end of the second century BC.[80] There were two separate interdicts for "daily" and "summer" water.[81] These categories are discussed together by Ulpian, who adopts Neratius's approach to summer water (*D.* 43.20.1.2–3 Ulp. 70 *ad Ed.; D.* 43.20.6 Nerat. 3 *Membr.*). Daily water either is or can be channeled every day, whether it is used continuously or on an intermittent schedule. Similarly, summer water either is or can be channeled during the summer. Though both definitions appear unproblematic at first glance, they raise certain legal problems, especially concerning the use-it-or-lose-it rule and how to apply it to intermittent use. In resolving these questions, the jurists recognize nature as a key factor in competition for water, and they consider nature in relation to human practices and legal concepts.

In legal terms, the discussion of daily and summer water responds to two defining features of servitudes—*perennitas* and *utilitas*—that seem to contradict the categories of daily and summer water. For *perennitas,* summer water is more problematic. According to *perennitas,* a servitude can be established only on a permanent or perennial source, that is, a spring or flowing water.[82] How can water that flows only during the summer be considered perennial, that is, how can it be possible to have a servitude on a seasonal torrent? Neratius shows that the contradictions are only apparent when law accommodates natural circumstances. According to Neratius, there were four criteria that might be invoked to define summer water:

1. A right to channel only in the summer
2. The plans of the landowner
3. The nature of the water (e.g., a torrent that flows only in summer)
4. The usefulness (*utilitas*) to the place into which the water is channeled

In defining summer water, the first two of these criteria (right and plans) are rejected, while the last two (nature and *utilitas*) are selected. Neratius invokes the nature of the water to define its *perennitas* in seasonal terms, though use-

80. See n. 61 in the introduction to the present study.
81. For the wording of the interdict on summer water, see *D.* 43.20.1.31 Ulp. 70 *ad Ed.*
82. *D.* 8.3.9 Paul. 1 *Sent.*, with Capogrossi Colognesi, *Servitù d'acqua,* 2–10.

fulness turns out to be more important. Summer water flows in the summer and thus is available on a constant basis (like any other perennial source) whenever the servitude is used. As Neratius explains.

> When we look into the interdict on summer water, and likewise the interdict on daily water, we think that it must first be established what is the summer water for which there is usually provided a special interdict related to the period of the previous summer. The [question] is whether it should be called "summer water" on the basis of the right of using it only in the summertime; or on the basis of the plan and intention of the person who channels it (the fact that he had a plan to channel it in the summer); or on the basis of the nature of the water itself, because it can be channeled only in the summer; or on the basis of the use of the places to which it is channeled. It seems right, then, that the water is properly called ["summer" water] because of two factors, its own nature and the use of the places to which it is channeled, [and] so in this way it is rightly called "summer" [water] whether its nature will be that it cannot be channeled except in the summer, even if it is needed also in the winter, or whether its own nature allows it to be channeled at any time of year, if the advantage [*utilitas*, or "usefulness"] to the persons onto whose land it is channeled requires its use only in the summer.
>
> [*De interdicto de aqua aestiva, item cottidiana quaerentes primum constituendum existimabamus, quae esset aqua aestiva, de qua proprium interdictum ad prioris aestatis tempus relatum reddi solet, hoc est aestiva aqua utrumne ex iure aestivo dumtaxat tempore utendi diceretur, an ex mente propositoque ducentis, quod aestate eam ducendi consilium haberet, an ex natura ipsuis aquae, quod aestate tantum duci potest, an ex utilitate locorum, in quae duceretur. Placebat igitur aquam ob has duas res, naturam suam utilitatemque locorum in quae deducitur, proprie appellari, ita ut, sive eius natura erit, ut nisi aestate duci non possit, etiamsi hieme quoque desideraretur, sive omni tempore anni duci eam ipsius natura permitteret, si utilitas personis, in quam ducitur, aestate dumtaxat usum eius exigeret, aestiva recte diceretur.*] (*D.* 43.20.6 Nerat. 3 *Membr.*)

While Neratius and other jurists recognize natural constraints, human practices have a greater influence on legal categories of water. Neratius's second criterion, *utilitas*, directly addresses human practices: if the water is useful to the dominant estate only in the summer, it is summer water. In other cases, *utilitas* often encompasses planning, a separate category in Neratius's analysis—and a topic that is explored in chapter 3 of this study. Reading the broader context into this case, human needs dominate the category of summer water. Similarly, Ulpian's definition of daily water gives priority to human practices with analogies to summer clothes and summer pastures (*D.* 43.201.2–3 Ulp. 70 *ad. Ed.*).[83] While a seasonal schedule may depend on natural circumstances (water that can be channeled only in summer), these schedules are designed to serve utility or the landowner's interests; that is, they are established on perennial sources that flow in all seasons. The priority accorded to *utilitas* in definitions of daily and summer water is consistent with the legal concept of servitudes: a servitude could only be established if it served the needs of the landowner. Furthermore, it demonstrates self-conscious attention to the relationship between human and natural factors in managing the water supply.[84]

Natural and human factors may be interrelated in legal definitions of summer water, but they are not interdependent. For both Neratius and Ulpian, the categories of use (*utilitas*) and nature are alternatives. Summer water can be defined by either nature or use: summer water may flow all year round but be useful to the landowner only during the summer months. This dichotomy uncouples natural and human factors, so that they are treated independently in legal decisions. In fact, summer water becomes an abstract category that is defined by human practices. The process of abstraction is taken to an extreme in a rule that allowed a plaintiff to use the interdict for summer water to protect water that he channeled only during the winter (*D.* 43.20.1.35 Ulp. 70 *ad Ed.*). This is not the only redefinition of use that adapts natural categories to human use. As suggested earlier, the concept of *perennitas* was also modified to accommodate agricultural practices. As Palma has argued, a servitude could be established on a *castellum,* because the legal concept of the source, or *caput,* could be separated from a "natural" source.[85]

83. See Capogrossi Colognesi, *Servitù d'acqua,* 138; Palma, "Derivazaioni di acqua," 442–45.

84. Similarly, the legal sources also include a precise description of "summer" itself as the period beginning with the spring equinox and ending with the fall equinox (*D.* 43.20.1.32 Ulp. 70 *ad Ed.*). This description is ascribed to the experts (*sic peritiores tradiderunt*), indicating a degree of self-consciousness in dealing with the environment. Compare handbooks reporting traditional practices that emphasize seasonal schedules; for example, Varro (*RR* 2.2.11) reports that the summer feeding/watering schedule for sheep should be in effect from the rising of the Pleiades to the autumn equinox.

85. Palma, "Derivazioni di acqua."

Similarly flexible was the concept of a servitude as a unified right. When the holder of a servitude used even part of the right-of-way, he kept his right to the entire route. Or in the case of water rights, "if water flows in part of the waterway, even if it does not reach to the final destination, it has made use of all parts all the same" [*aqua si in partem aquagi influxit, etiamsi non ad ultima loca pervenit, omnibus tamen partibus usurpatur*] (*D.* 8.6.9 Iavol. 3 *ex Plaut.*). Partial use is the same as full use, it seems, because the servitude is indivisible. In a case at the limit of the rule, even if the owner did not actually use the water, the servitude was maintained as long as water flowed naturally in the channel (*et si aqua per rivum sua sponte perfluxit, D.* 8.6.12 Cels. 23 *Dig.*). The natural flow of the water takes the place of the owner's exercise of his right: use seems to be defined as "water flowing naturally." This definition strains common usage, as it attempts to reconcile the corporeal with the incorporeal concept of a servitude. The purpose of a servitude was to provide resources needed by the property, and as long as the water was available to be used, it fulfilled its purpose. The owner's actions were secondary: if the water could be used, it was as good as used. The legal reasoning manipulates the relationship between humans and their environment to generate a consistent concept of use for servitudes, even though actual use might vary.[86]

In the legal concepts of summer and daily water, natural categories are defined in terms of human practices. The interdicts for daily and summer water apply to different schedules for intermittent use—daily and seasonal, respectively. While the terms daily and summer water correspond to familiar time units that exist in the natural world, the legal categories are focused on human practices, specifically, the way Romans used objective measures to manage the water supply.

Schedules represent a rationalizing approach to water use that includes landowners' ability to measure water use in a way that served agricultural practice. Though this discussion has so far focused on daily and seasonal schedules, it was also possible to organize a schedule based on the volume of water, "since it is agreed that water can be allotted not only by times but also by measures" [*cum constet non solum temporibus, sed etiam mensuris posse aquam dividi*] (*D.* 43.20.5 pr.-1 Iulian. 4 *ex Minucio,* discussed shortly). In fact, the schedule in the inscription from Tivoli prescribes both time and volume for each person who participated in the system. Similarly, water from the city aqueducts

---

86. Compare Augustus's ruling in the lawsuit against Statilius Taurus (*D.* 8.3.35 Paul. 15 *ad Plaut.,*), where natural factors also shape the definition of use (on which see chapter 2 in the present study).

was measured by volume; Frontinus describes the detailed measurements of pipes and fittings and how they were used to measure and regulate delivery from individual aqueducts (*Aq.* 36–63). Pipes for private deliveries from the city aqueducts were stamped with their measurement, though this system was something less than standardized.[87] The schedules that are discussed in the legal cases are all based on time, daily or seasonal—possibly because measuring volume is more precise and therefore less likely to prompt dispute. It seems more likely, however, that time schedules were more common because they required less technology, relying on easily observed and familiar benchmarks—days and seasons—that were already used to organize the farming work that a water supply served. Seasonal markers were used in a similar way to define the period for lease of rural land: the lease of a meadow was coordinated with time when the pear tree bloomed and the neighbors irrigated their land (see chapter 2). In the irrigation community in Roman Spain, described by the *lex Rivi Hiberiensis,* the schedule for water sharing was organized around annual cleaning and maintenance of the channels (*lex Rivi Hib.* 1.38–46).[88] Both farming practices and natural cycles are deployed to organize the rules of this public irrigation system, much as they are in the definitions of summer and daily water. Although the time schedules for water use are less precise, perhaps, than measures of volume, they were a useful standard that could be easily enforced because they relied on practices and information that landowners could be expected to know.

While schedules cohere with farming practices in a broad sense, they also reflect landowners' ability to calculate their need for water and to negotiate a distribution scheme that protected their access to a scarce resource. The general rule on *perennitas*—that a servitude could be established only on a perennial stream—provided some stability in the water supply by ensuring that the natural supply was constant.[89] In addition, the flexible concept of summer water helped to increase supply, another kind of security, by channeling summer torrents as well as perennial streams. But a schedule specified the needs of individual landowners, protecting their access against others who shared the local supply. A schedule also, like an inscription, by the mere fact of recording allotments of water, provided a guarantee of access. Glick

87. On Frontinus's pride in newer, more careful measurements, see Evans, *Water Distribution,* 62–64; and on measures of water volume, see n. 68 in the present chapter.

88. See Beltrán Lloris, "Irrigation Decree," 176–77. On *D.* 8.6.12 Cels. 23 *Dig.,* see chapter 4 in the present study.

89. Capogrossi Colognesi, *Servitù d'acqua,* 131. See the discussion later in the present section on the servitude for watering animals; see also chapter 3 in the present study.

has described the arrangements in medieval Spain: "Another guarantee of stability was the recording of the measurements of divisors in a legal document."[90] The divisors, physical barriers that diverted the water from the main canal to individual properties, were designed to regulate the flow of water so that each property received its due allotment. The record of allotments had similar import in the Lamasba inscription, where the lists of amounts and daily times for channeling created a kind of virtual ownership of the water, as Shaw argues: "The Africans viewed the water itself as property, divisible into precise time units to be allotted to each proprietor and 'owned' by him"; "The water consciously appropriated by artificial diversion and retention schemes was not an unlimited, commonly available resource, but property of the highest value."[91] While an inscription may have been intended to make the arrangement permanent, a servitude brought actual legal ownership, with its stronger protections. Community enforcement played a role in supporting servitudes (as will be argued in chapter 2), just as it did in informal irrigation systems. But a legal right to water gave the individual landowner a tool for protecting his own economic interests against those of his neighbors. Thus, while a schedule might serve as a rationing mechanism that conserved the water supply, it also expressed the underlying competition for water that could be resolved, at least temporarily, by a legal agreement.

Competition and conservation are also at issue in cases where the use-it-or-lose-it rule is applied to schedules for water use. It is not immediately clear how to apply the use-it-or-lose-it rule to a servitude that is exercised on an intermittent basis in a schedule. For this rule and for servitudes in general, "use" means constant, continuous use, as in water flowing along the channel all day every day. If the right is not "used" for two years, it is lost. How can this rule be applied to a servitude that is exercised for just an hour a day or only in the summer? How can you tell if someone is not exercising his right when he does not use it all the time? The jurists solve the problem by creating a new definition of use that separates the existence of the right from its terms of use. Servius is credited with this approach, in a case that accommodated varying practice and at the same time preserved the legal

90. Glick, *Irrigation and Society*, 88, and see 87–93.

91. Shaw, "Lamasba," 80–81; "Water and Society," 167. Similarly, in the irrigation decree from Roman Spain, representation on the board that administered the canals was in proportion to the size of property (*lex Rivi Hib.* 1.1-18, with Beltrán Lloris, "Irrigation Decree," 170). On the division of water in proportion to property when land was sold in parcels, see chapter 4 in the present study.

concept of a servitude as a unified right, even when the right was exercised over intervals of time.

> If [a servitude for] water is so arranged that it is channeled either only in the summer or in one month, it is asked how [the right] can be lost by not using it, because the time period [for use] is not continuous, in which he does not use it since he is not able to use it. Thus, if someone has [a servitude to channel] water in alternate years or months, it is lost in twice the specified time, and likewise [the right] for passage is protected, if either alternate days or all day or only at night, [but the right] is lost in the period of time established in the agreements, because the servitude is a unified thing. For if he should have a servitude in alternate hours or every day for one hour, Servius writes that he loses the servitude by not using it, because it was a daily right that he had.
>
> [*Si sic constituta sit aqua, ut vel aestate ducatur tantum vel uno mense, quaeritur quemadmodum non utendo amittatur, quia non est continuum tempus, quo cum uti non potest, non sit usus. itaque et si alternis annis vel mensibus quis aquam habeat, duplicato constituto tempore amittitur. idem et de itinere custoditur. si vero alternis diebus aut die toto aut tantum nocte, statuto legibus tempore amittitur, quia una servitus est: nam et si alternis horis vel una hora cottidie servitutem habeat, Servius scribit perdere eum non utendo servitutem, quia id quod habeat cottidianum sit.*] (*D.* 8.6.7 Paul. 13 *ad Plaut.*)

For daily schedules, the standard rule can thus apply directly: if there was a daily schedule for intermittent use (alternate days or at a specific time of day), the period of nonuse was the two years set by statute;[92] if the schedule extended longer than a day (alternate months, summers, or years), the right was lost if it was not used for twice the prescribed period (e.g., for four summers). This flexibility in the law allows quick response to changing needs of landowners. The legal rule reflects rational calculations by landowners about their needs for water and their desire to capitalize on a neighbor's error or change in usage. It also seems to assume active engagement in managing the local water systems—that is, neighbors who would notice if someone was not following the schedule. The rule for longer schedules thus assumes both economic and social rationality in approaches to the water supply.

92. See n. 55 in the introduction to the present study.

Applying these rules to daily and summer water could promote either conservation or competition for the local water supply. A schedule can control access to water both by limiting what each user takes and by excluding those who do not follow the schedule—that is, achieving excludability, a necessary component of managing a common resource. Legal schedules are also consistent with the other principle of the commons, subtractability—the notion that each user takes away from the common supply. The use-it-or-lose-it rule provides some security for that access by preventing surprise claims for servitudes that had not been exercised for a while. As will emerge in the Statilius Taurus lawsuit, discussed in chapter 2, long-standing practice could trump this rule. But the use-it-or-lose-it rule took a carrot-and-stick approach to compliance. If landowners failed to comply, the rule punished them by dropping them from the system, thus denying them access to water and creating an opportunity for someone else to have access to the water. The possibility of additional water could motivate landowners to police the schedule, and this motive could be stronger if there was already competition over the local water supply. The use-it-or-lose-it rule thus reflects not only competition for water but also a zero-sum approach to the water supply, where each participant in a local system sought to maximize his access to this valuable resource.

Though schedules were generally enforced according to these rules, one unusual ruling raises the possibility of other solutions to both economic and environmental concerns. Underlying this case is a discussion and possibly a disagreement about how a schedule should be implemented, how it should affect the right established through a servitude. Two landowners held servitudes to channel water in the same waterway, one every day all year, the other only in the summer. This was a reasonable arrangement that probably served the cultivation of each estate: the one that needed water only in the summer may have grown delicate produce, while the other may have had livestock that needed water all year; or the farm with the summer water may have had an alternate supply that satisfied its needs during the winter. The legal wrinkle arose when the landowners did not stick to the schedule but instead swapped their scheduled times for channeling water. Applying the use-it-or-lose-it rule, we would expect them to lose their rights, as happened in another case where someone with a servitude to channel at night lost his right because he used it during the day instead (*D.* 8.6.10.1 Paul. 15 *ad Plaut.*). But when the landowners swap schedules, they do not lose their rights, according to Julian's report of the case. This opinion is drawn from his commentary on the writings of an earlier jurist, Minucius, that focused on legal problems, and so the nature of the sources may account for the puzzle in this case.[93] The situation probably represents a limiting case for the rule and may well be a hypothetical case rather than an actual lawsuit, but the details seem drawn from the real world of shared channels, and the legal opinion responds to these constraints as well. I quote the case in full because it offers hints about the legal logic and its relationship to social and economic contexts.

> Since it is agreed that water can be shared not only by times but also by measures, one person can channel water at the same time on a daily basis and another only during the summer, so that in the summer the water is divided between them while in the winter only the one who has the right of daily [water] channels. (1) It was agreed between two people, who conducted water in the same channel separately at specific hours, that they would exchange times and continue to use the water. I ask, since they had conducted [water] for a longer period of time than established for the servitude in this way, such that neither one of them used his own time, whether they lost their right of use. He said that they had not lost [the right].
>
> [*Cum constet non solum temporibus, sed etiam mensuris posse aquam dividi, potest eodem tempore alius cottidianam, alius aestivam aquam ducere, ita ut aestate dividatur inter eos aqua, hieme solus ducat is qui cottidianae ius habeat. (1) Inter duos, qui eodem rivo aquam certis horis separatim ducebant, convenit, ut permutatis inter se temporibus aqua uterentur: quaero, cum amplius tempore servitutibus praefinito ita duxissent, ut neuter eorum suo tempore usus esset, num ius utendi amisissent. Negavit amisisse.*] (*D.* 43.20.5 pr.-1 Iulian. 4 *ex Minucio*)

Though both landowners have channeled water at the wrong time for longer than the two years that define nonuse, they keep their right (*cum amplius tempore servitutibus praefinito ita duxissent, ut neuter eorum suo tempore usus esset. . . . Negavit amisisse*). It is not clear whether the decision in this case superseded the usual application of the rule, but the persistence of both rules in the *Digest*

93. On the nature of Julian's commentary on Minucius, see Schulz, *Roman Legal Science,* 228; cf. 223, 216–17 (on Minucius). The arrangement of the list on Schulz's p. 228 suggests a late first-century AD date for Minucius.

suggest that both could be used or that there were at least some cases in which the strict application of the use-it-or-lose-it rule was not the best choice.[94]

The specific circumstance of this case may have made it an exception to the rule. One servitude involved daily water, the other summer water. During the summer, both landowners used the channel, each during scheduled hours. The only change they made was in the hours that each used; they did not change the basic arrangement of summer water for one, daily water (i.e., all year round) for the other. The cooperation between landowners itself may have been a factor in the legal reasoning as well. Their right may have seemed worth protecting in part because they agreed to swap hours (*[i]nter duos . . . convenit, ut permutatis inter se temporibus aqua uterentur*). The terms governing servitudes were simple legal agreements between the two parties, separate from the right itself. The ruling, then, recognizes a new agreement to replace the old. This flexibility in the legal system allowed the neighbors to renegotiate their terms to suit changing needs.

The decision in this case is also consistent with the legal concept of the servitude as a continuous right. What stayed the same, after the exchange of hours, was more important than what changed. The equal exchange of hours did not affect the allocation of water—the same amount of water was used either way—but it was assigned differently to the two landowners: one had daily use, the other only summer. The one who traded summer water for daily water increased his supply, while the other lost water. For the landowner who increased his supply, this reconstruction implies a rationality aimed at maximizing access to a scarce resource, even if he gave some other form of compensation to his neighbor. This logic accords with an economic approach to allocating resources, maximizing access and a zero-sum concept of the water supply. While the landowners may not have used these terms themselves, their choices reflect an understanding of the principles and are, to that extent, rational in the classical economic sense. But their rationality is more complex, because the exchange of hours also achieves subtractability and conserves water, following commons theory. These two approaches—maximizing and conserving—may appear to be contradictory, but they are in fact two aspects of the same, larger calculation: the landowner's need for a secure supply of water. One of the parties in this case was willing to limit his own consumption of water according to

94. For the uncertainty as to whether *D.* 43.20. 5.pr.-1 Jul. 4 *ex Minucio* set out a new rule or applied only to the particular case, see Grosso, *Servitù prediali*, 162.

the schedule because it provided more security for his supply. This dualistic concept of rationality is bounded by the real environmental constraints that landowners faced when they relied on a local water supply. Even if this case derives from legal scholarship rather than actual litigation, it illustrates the constructive role that law could play in allocating a scarce resource. In managing a servitude, maximizing access for individual landowners was a rational strategy for conservation when the parties shared an interest in conserving the supply. Not all conflicts over access to water were, however, resolved so easily.

In a case about the servitude for watering a herd, the need to conserve water also comes into conflict with individual interests in the water supply. The situation in this case recalls the "herdsman's dilemma," the classic formulation of the problem of a commons,[95] though water, rather than pasture, is at stake. Several landowners watered their herds at the same stream; each held a servitude for *adpulsus* (the right to drive animals to water) and had agreed to terms that specified how many animals he could water at the stream. What should happen when one of the parties tried to water more animals than the terms allowed?

> Trebatius [writes] that, when a greater number of herd animals is driven to water than should be, the whole herd may be rightly prevented, because an animal added to the herd, to which the right of watering is owed, invalidates the whole right of watering the herd. Marcellus says, however, if the holder of a servitude for watering the herd drives more animals [to water], he should not be prevented from watering individual animals; and this is right, because herd animals can be separated.
>
> *[Trebatius, cum amplior numerus pecoris ad aquam appelletur, quam debet appelli, posse universum pecus impune prohiberi, quia iunctum pecus ei pecori, cui adpulsus debeatur, totum corrumpat pecoris adpulsum. Marcellus autem ait, si quis ius habens pecoris ad aquam appellendi plura pecora adpulserit, non in omnibus pecoribus eum prohibendum: quod est verum, quia pecora separari possunt.]* (*D.* 43.20.1.18 Ulp. 70 *ad Ed.*)

The case reports the opinions of three different jurists: Trebatius, Marcellus, and Ulpian. The earliest jurist, Trebatius, ruled that the party who did

95. On the herdsman's dilemma and commons theory, see the introduction in the present study.

not follow the terms lost his right—in fact, invalidated it—and should not be allowed to water any of his animals (*posse universum pecus impune prohiberi . . . totum corrumpat pecoris adpulsum*). Trebatius's opinion is in line with the rule about schedules attributed to the jurist Servius, who is roughly contemporary with Trebatius: when one party disregards the schedule, he loses his right altogether.[96] In the view of these jurists, the servitude seems to apply to the herd as a whole, and the herd has the same number of animals as specified in the terms. When one animal is added, the herd now exceeds the limit, and so the right is lost. In contrast, the later jurists, Marcellus and Ulpian, have a more flexible conception of the herd and how the limit should be applied to it. Paradoxically, their flexibility depends on a strict interpretation of the terms. It does not matter, in this later view, how large the herd is. What counts is the number of animals that are watered at one time: as long as this number complies with terms of the agreement, the right remains. As Ulpian points out, the animals can be separated (*quod est verum, quia pecora separari possunt*).[97] In effect, the landowner could have a larger herd and still observe the terms of the agreement by watering only part of the herd at any given time. The difference between the earlier and later jurists could be explained in terms of legal development. The terms specifying the number of animals were part of the *modus*, or method of exercising the right, and the application of *modus* evolved over time.[98] But since Trebatius's view is preserved in the *Digest*, it seems more likely that the two opinions represented issues that continued to be debated in cases involving servitudes, namely, how best to reconcile environmental constraints with landowners' needs.

Both interpretations respond to competition over a local water supply and the need to conserve it. If the servitude holder in this case watered too

96. Both jurists were active in the first century BC. Trebatius was Augustus's advisor, C. Trebatius Testa. Servius is the consul of 51 BC, Servius Sulpicius Rufus. For biographical details, see Schulz, *Roman Legal Science*, 42–43; see also the helpful chart of republican jurists in Frier, *Rise of the Roman Jurists*, 146.

97. Solazzi (*Tutela e il possesso*, 77–78) argues that *D.* 43.20.1.18 Ulp. 70 *ad Ed.* should be interpreted along with the preceding extract, *D.* 43.20.1.17 Ulp. 70 *ad Ed*, which addresses the question of divisibility: if the holder of a servitude mixes different water into the channel's regular water, he loses his right to use the regular water in the channel. In *D.* 43.20.1.18, Ulpian provides a contrasting example of divisibility: where the new water cannot be separated from the regular channel supply, the herd of animals can be divided into individual animals. This interpretation does not, however, adequately account for the division of water by time or volume that was allowed in terms, or *modus*, of a servitude. Both kinds of terms, both methods, involve a deal dividing water and provide a coherent system for allocating a scarce resource.

98. For the development of the legal concept of *modus*, see Grosso, *Servitù prediali*, 159–63.

many animals and lost his right, the extra water remained unallocated until someone else arranged a new servitude. The legal agreement thus served as a gatekeeper, regulating access to the scarce resource and excluding those who do not abide by the rules, just like a schedule. Strict enforcement of the limit on the number of animals was a mechanism for excludability and thus conservation. While the outcome encourages conservation, the circumstances of the case reveal the underlying competition for water. The person who waters too many animals is aggressively pursuing his own interests at the expense of others who share the stream. Even if the actual supply was sufficient, there was a perceived threat to the local supply, which suggests that the parties in this case saw the water supply as a zero-sum situation. Their agreed-on limits are a mechanism to ensure a consistent allotment of the water and to control aggressive self-interest; the lawsuit provided enforcement. The law provided a flexible response that both protected the water supply and allowed the landowner to pursue his interest in having a larger herd. Raising livestock was particularly profitable for the Romans, and they took a systematic approach to this profitable activity. This broader context also contributes to our understanding of the landowners' interests that were at stake in this legal case.

In the raising of livestock, there were economic incentives to aggressive exploitation of the water supply. Livestock could bring a good profit, in addition to providing manure that improved agricultural production. Herd animals were traditionally associated with wealth,[99] but more immediate and realistic opportunities existed. Throughout his treatment of livestock, Varro is conscious of prices and profit; his recommendations about what kinds of and how many animals to purchase are based on their potential to produce revenue: their offspring could be sold, as well as such products as meat, milk or cheese, and wool.[100] He also reports the ambitions of one Roman knight, a Gaberius, who hoped to earn one thousand *denarii* a day in profit from his herd of goats, until it was lost to disease (*RR* 2.3.10). All these animals needed regular watering, and for the most part, the agricultural writers assume a natural source, a stream or spring;[101] the animals' food could also be soaked in water. In addition, adequate, clean water was essential for prevent-

99. Consider, for example, the familiar etymology of *pecunia* from *pecus* (Varro, *RR* 2.praef.6–12).

100. Columella has a similar perspective. For references to both Columella and Varro, see appendix A.

101. An exception is Columella's recommendation (6.22) that man-made pools filled by rainwater are better for watering cattle than rivers and streams, because cold water from natural streams can cause miscarriages.

ing the diseases that could ruin a landowner's investment in livestock, especially sheep and pigs.

Both the agreement limiting the number of animals that could be watered and its strict enforcement fit into a larger pattern of systematic practices for raising livestock. It is clear from Varro that at least some landowners took this kind of calculating approach. To manage the size of a herd of cattle, he advises the landowner to cull his herd every year, removing sick animals that take the place of others that could bring a profit (*RR* 2.5.17).[102] When purchasing cattle for a new herd, the landowner should calculate the size of the herd based on access to pasture. The number of animals should be maximized, but not so as to exhaust the available pasture: "for the man who cares for the herd should also determine the count, how many herd animals and how many he should graze, lest the pasture fail or be excessive and for the same reason its produce go to waste" [*nam et qui parat pecus necesse est constituat numerum, quot greges et quantos sit pasturus, ne aut saltus desint aut supersint et ideo fructus dispereant*] (Varro, *RR* 2.1.24; cf. Pliny, *NH* 18.39–40). Varro's recommendation echoes the herdsman's dilemma, and it is not unlikely that Varro's readers would have taken a similar approach to the limited supply of local water. Like Cato and Columella, Varro emphasizes cost control as a way to maximize profit, but he also offers specific examples of how a landowner should calculate the cost of resources and their effect on profits. As noted earlier, other water-sharing systems adopted a similar approach; for example, in Roman North Africa, water was allocated in proportion to the number of trees on the property or to the size of the property. Likewise, landowners who held servitudes for *adpulsus* could arrange terms for a specific number of animals, planning ahead in a systematic way. This approach coheres with the bounded rationality that shaped the legal case about exchanging hours. Though the landowners may not have had complete information about the

102. Similarly, in the case of pigs (Varro, *RR* 2.4.22), the farmer should calculate the number based on profit (*ab sua utilitate*) and on the nature of the animal; on wild boar for game parks, see, in general, Pliny, *NH* 8.210–12. Varro seems to see such calculation as an important human intervention that manages nature, because he recognizes "natural" factors in considering the number of sheep: he says there is no natural limit on the size of a flock (*RR* 2.2.20), though the ratio of sheep to shepherd could affect cost (cf. *RR* 2.10.11; for a similar calculation for the number of birds in a flock, see Col. 8.2.7). For the advantages of a small flock of goats (limiting loss in case of disease), see Varro, *RR* 2.3.9–10. Compare also the approach to equipment and staff for the farm at *RR* 1.18.1–8 (the number of slaves should be in proportion to the size of the farm, citing Cato at 1.18.3) and 1.19.1–3 (how many yoke of oxen for farms of different acreage, citing Cato).

markets for their livestock, they understood the need for water to raise animals and the effects of competition over a limited supply of water. For these landowners, servitudes and the additional agreements about terms were a flexible tool that expressed their strategies for conserving water, thereby securing access to this resource for the farms.

CONCLUSION

The archaeological evidence for settlement in the rural areas near Rome indicates that Roman landowners frequently shared a local water supply. This natural constraint led to competition for water. Servitudes provided mechanisms for mediating this competition. The basic structure of the institution—the restriction to adjacent property and the ban on informal sharing—responded to the need to manage competition. When a servitude was established, the parties could agree on additional terms regulating the right. Schedules were a common mechanism for rationing the local water supplies, and they are known from both inscriptions and legal cases. Schedules, set out in terms attached to the servitude, helped to manage competition but did not end it completely. The interdicts reflect the ongoing process of negotiation over the water supply, providing protection for as many parties as shared a water supply: "if a dispute about the use of water should arise between those who share a canal, that is, those who channel water in the same canal, a double interdict is appropriate for each of them when they both claim that the use [of the canal and water] is his" [*si inter rivales, id est qui per eundum rivum aquam ducunt, sit contentio de aquae usu, utroque suum usum esse contendente, duplex interdictum utrique competit*] (*D.* 43.20.1.26 Ulp. 70 *ad Ed.*).

A local water supply could draw landowners into a zero-sum game as they competed for a limited amount of water: what one landowner channeled away was no longer available to his neighbors. As we saw in Proculus's decision in the case concerning a shared channel, the law of servitudes could provide an alternative paradigm that helped to conserve the limited supply of water. The rules of servitudes both conserved the water supply and protected individual access to it, achieving the two aims of resource management described in commons theory. This approach also served the economic interests of landowners. A schedule organizing water use by the day, hour, or season could make the water supply more predictable, so that landowners could plan ahead, calculating how best to use the available water. While an informal water-sharing arrangement, supported only by social networks, could achieve the same ends, servitudes provided real property rights that reflected the economic value of water. Legal remedies became more attractive to Roman landowners as their interests became more oriented toward the market. In the cases about schedules and terms for use, the jurists responded to landowners' interests in market-oriented activities, such as raising livestock. The legal solutions reflect the systematic approaches that landowners adopted as they engaged in commercial farming.

This analysis of legal limits on servitudes contributes to an understanding of the nature of property rights and their role in Roman agriculture. The legal cases illustrate various strategies adopted by landowners and jurists in managing a scarce resource. Some of these strategies respond to environmental constraints; others respond to the market for agricultural goods that was expanding during the period when the interdicts took shape; many balance conflicts between limited resources, social relations, and economic interests. Schedules, for example, can represent neighbors' cooperation in managing a common resource with an alternate rationality that is not strictly zero-sum, while at the same time providing a mechanism that recognized the economic value of water. The rules governing servitudes are thus characterized by a rationality that treats water as an economic commodity and, at the same time, recognizes the environmental limits on local water supplies.

TWO

LAW AND NEIGHBORLY PRACTICE

A servitude depended on a fine balance in relations between neighbors. In a case preserved in the *Digest of Justinian,* the owner of a servient estate shared water from an open channel with the holder of a servitude on the same channel, and the owner of the servitude wanted to convert it to an underground passage. The case reports the opinions of two jurists who disagree about whether the holder of the servitude should be allowed to bury the channel.

> Labeo says that an underground channel cannot be made out of an open channel because the landowner loses the convenience of watering his herd or drawing water. Pomponius says that this does not seem right to him because the landowner has it [i.e., the use of the channel] more by circumstance than by right, unless it was specified from the start when the servitude was imposed.
>
> [*Labeo non posse ait ex aperto rivo terrenum fieri, quia commodum domino soli auferetur appellendi pecus vel hauriendi aquam: quod sibi non placere Pomponius ait, quia id domino magis ex occasione quam ex iure contingeret, nisi si ab initio in imponenda servitute id actum esset.*] (*D.* 43.21.2 Paul. 66 *ad Ed.*)

Labeo and Pomponius offer different solutions to this legal problem and their views reflect two important factors in managing a local water supply: social negotiation and legal rights. Labeo gives priority to social negotiation.

In his opinion, the holder of the servitude could exercise his right, but he had to consider the convenience of his neighbor and should not make changes that put his neighbor at a disadvantage. Pomponius disagrees, writing that a legal right requires more respect than mere circumstances. Although a servitude granted its holder broad rights to use his neighbor's property, there were limits, and these were defined by both legal rules and social morality.

This chapter investigates how the law developed and operated within the social relationships that surrounded a local water supply. Because sources of water were unevenly distributed in Roman Italy, neighbors often needed to share the water supply and probably just as often competed for it, as indicated by the inscriptions discussed in chapter 1. These disputes could be resolved through social exchange either with or without a legal agreement—that is, a servitude that recorded their arrangements. The law institutionalized an advantage for the holder of the servitude (i.e., his legal right), as Pomponius's opinion indicates, yet the legal cases show that practice was more nuanced and involved both tacit and explicit rules, an etiquette of sharing resources that was codified and adapted in the rules of servitudes. The etiquette of water sharing depended on stable and reliable cooperation between neighbors, a pattern that conforms to traditional ideas about neighborliness reflected in the agricultural treatises and, more generally, in the literary sources for Roman society. It may be that these social patterns preceded their expression in the legal institution of servitudes and that local water sharing took the form of a true commons before the development of servitudes. Alternatively, the jurists may have constructed a teleological perspective as they systemized the legal rules. While the archaeological evidence for settlement patterns is suggestive of this pattern of legal development, the sources for the early period are not full enough to corroborate it. The ideal of stability may be connected more closely with discussions in legal textbooks than with actual litigation, though Palma argues, in his study of servitudes, that an ideal of neighborliness could mediate tensions between rural neighbors.[1] In any case, social relations are a consistent theme in legal cases about servitudes, showing that even in a society where natural resources were treated as private property, the law could accommodate social priorities, as commons theory predicts.

In most of the legal cases about servitudes, the jurists assume a dynamic relationship between neighbors. The legal cases show how these landowners

1. Palma, *Iura vicinitatis,* 30–42.

used servitudes to spell out the terms of their cooperation, first generally and then in response to specific needs—for example, new neighbors and repairs and improvements to hydraulic installations. The second part of this chapter considers how the jurists balanced the rights of neighbors—the owners of both servient and dominant estates—who pursued varied and sometimes incompatible interests in the local water supply. These variable interests may be related to changes in farming practices, specifically, commercial farming of specialized crops. Of course, traditional social morality itself had an economic aspect, the traditional ideal of self-sufficient farming. This ideal was one of the shared social values that supported the social negotiation over local water supplies, and it continues to influence legal approaches even as they take into account commercial activity. In general, the law attempted to balance landowners' economic interests with the social relationships that were critical to the operation of servitudes. This balancing act is also illustrated by three situations involving water rights and identifiable historical persons. First, the *Digest* reports a legal case about access to a spring on Statilius Taurus's property near Sutrium. Second, Cicero's property at Tusculum had a servitude attached, and one of his letters reports his efforts to smooth out relations with the neighbor who owned the servient estate. Third, Vegetus's private aqueduct near Viterbo, discussed in the previous chapter, illustrates an alternative to servitudes that created a different social dynamic around a local water supply. Because these three landowners can be situated historically and topographically, their stories allow us to more precisely describe the relationship between landscape, law, and social relations.

BROAD RIGHTS AND GOOD NEIGHBORS

A servitude created an asymmetrical relationship between two estates and their owners. It gave its holder a broad, indivisible, and asymmetrical right to use his neighbor's resources—land, water, lime, brush—and he might give nothing in return. The owner of the servient estate had a negative duty: he could not be compelled to do anything except let the servitude be exercised.[2] This meant

---

2. *D.* 8.1.15.1 Pompon. 33 *ad Sab.* See *D.* 8.5.6.2 Ulp. 17 *ad Ed.* for a similar case about the urban servitude for a support wall (*oneris ferendi*), though there was some disagreement about this particular servitude. In some cases, the owner of the servient building could be compelled to repair the wall (*D.* 8.5.8 pr. Ulp. 17 *ad Ed.*) The owner of the servient estate should not let conditions deteriorate to the point that exercising the right was impossible (*D.* 8.5.6.7 Ulp. 17 *ad Ed.*). More generally on repairs and rustic servitudes, see the next section of the present chapter.

doing nothing that interfered with the water supply—no digging, sowing, cutting down, or pruning (*D.* 43.20.1.27 Ulp. 70 *ad Ed.*). Passive tolerance could be a substantial responsibility when it meant allowing extensive repairs to a waterway or road on one's property.[3] At the same time, the broad rights created by the servitude were limited to protect the owner of the servient estate, based not on the servitude but on his rights as a property owner. Ideally, balancing these rights would result in a stable equilibrium that allowed both parties to make their land productive.

The broad right of the servitude was also limited by the social expectations of neighborly respect and cooperation. The parties could agree on terms to restrict the exercise of the right, but even without specific terms, the holder of the servitude was expected to observe some limits in the exercise of this right.[4] The most basic limit applied to the route of the servitude: the holder of the right should pick a route for his water channel and stick to it.[5] This limit is first defined for a water channel, probably because a channel was harder to relocate than a path. These expectations are set out in a long legal case that is worth quoting and discussing in detail because it explicitly defines legal duty in terms of social values.

> If a right-of-way through another person's estate is granted or bequeathed to someone without qualification, he may go or drive over really any part he likes without limit, but in a civil manner, for these [terms] are understood tacitly in the expression. For he is not allowed to go or drive through the villa itself or through the middle of a vineyard, when he could just as conveniently do this across another part [of the property] with less harm to the servient estate. But it is agreed that he should go or drive where he first made a route and he does not have the authority to make it wider: so it seemed right also to Sabinus, who

3. When a servitude was left as a legacy, the legatee (i.e., the holder of the servitude) was allowed to excavate and build foundations on the servient estate if the servitude could not be exercised without this work (*D.* 8.1.10 Cels. 18 *Dig.*).

4. On the *modus,* or terms, generally, see the introduction in the present study; for examples relating to schedules, see chapter 1.

5. Grosso (*Servitù prediali,* 165–66) sees this case as expressing the origin of the legal concept of a *modus* for exercising a servitude. See also Franciosi, *Servitù prediali,* 34 n. 108. For the same rule, cf. *D.* 43.20.8 Scaev. 1 *Def.; D.* 43.21.1.11 Ulp. 70 *ad Ed.* The same logic seems to underlie the rule that co-owners of a servitude should agree on its route (*D.* 8.3.28 Iul. 7 *Dig.*). If there was disagreement at the start about the route, an arbiter could be brought in to resolve the difference; see *D.* 8.3.13.1–3 Iavol. 10 *ex Cassio,* calling in an arbiter to settle disputes about the width and location of *iter* and *actus.*

used the case of a channel, which [was allowed] wherever it first had been allowed to be routed, after the water had been channeled, and it was not allowed to shift it [to another place]. It is right that this rule should also be observed for a right-of-way.

> *[Si cui simplicius via per fundum cuiuspiam cedatur vel relinquatur, in infinito, videlicet per quamlibet eius partem, ire agere licebit, civiliter modo: nam quaedam in sermone tacite excipiuntur. Non enim per villam ipsam nec per medias vineas ire agere sinendus est, cum id aeque commode per alteram partem facere possit minore servientis fundi detrimento. Verum constitit, ut, qua primum viam direxisset, ea demum ire agere deberet nec amplius mutandae eius potestatem haberet: sicuti Sabino quoque videbatur, qui argumento rivi utebatur, quem primo qualibet ducere licuisset, posteaquam ductus esset, transferre non liceret: quod et in via servandum esse verum est.]* (*D.* 8.1.9 Cels. 5 *Dig.*, citing Sabinus)

Legally, a servitude could be exercised on any part of the servient estate when it was established without additional agreements specifying terms (*simpliciter* or, in this passage, *simplicius*). But this right is not as broad as it might seem, since it is restricted by everyday practice: the phrase *in sermone,* "in the expression," represents the shared understanding of social morality and neighborly expectations, akin to our tag "as everyone knows." Exactly what social morality prescribed is developed through a series of definitions. At first, *simplicius,* "without qualification," seems to mean "without limit" (*in infinito*) and "anywhere he likes" (cf. *per quamlibet eius partem*). It turns out that these phrases are not to be construed in their strongest or even most usual sense. In fact, they mean something quite different: the right should be exercised "in a civil manner" (*civiliter modo*). This abstract formula is defined by example: the servitude should stay away from buildings and crops (*Non enim per villam ipsam nec per medias vineas ire agere sinendus est*).[6] The rule is not, however,

---

6. For the general rule concerning a water channel when no route is specified (*non destinata parte*), see *D.* 8.3.21 Paul. 15 *ad Sab.*; *D.* 8.3.22 Pompon. 33 *ad Sab.* The latter reads, *Si mihi concesseris iter aquae per fundum tuum non destinata parte, per quam ducerem, totus fundus tuus servit: (22) sed quae loca eius fundi tunc, cum ea fieret cessio, aedificiis arboribus vineis vacua fuerint, ea sola eo nomine servient.* More generally, exercising a servitude must not harm crops: *si modo fructus non laedat* (*D.* 8.3.7 pr. Paul. 21 *ad Ed.*). Palma (*Iura vicinitatis,* 53, on *D.* 8.6.6 pr. Cels. 5 *Dig.*) observes a similar principle in urban servitudes, that the jurists aim to provide maximum use of the servitude with minimum inconvenience to the landowners. Even a right-of-way could interfere with cultivation, for example, of a meadow where the grass should grow long, and changing the route would cause even more damage; as Varro recognized, all traffic should be kept out of a meadow: *solum enim hominis exitium herbae et semitae fundamentum* (*RR* 1.47).

absolute. Instead, it depends on the servitude holder's judgment and sense of responsibility. He should avoid these places if he can exercise his right just as well in some other place, so as to minimize harm to the servient estate (*cum id aeque commode per alteram partem facere possit minore servientis fundi detrimento*). In a related case, the holder of the servitude was liable for any damage to the servient estate, except what arose from natural causes—for example, when rainfall floods a water channel.

> A servitude may, through natural circumstances, harm the servient estate but not through human intervention: for example, if the water in a channel rises because of rain or flows from the fields into the channel or a spring of water is later discovered alongside the channel or in it.
>
> [*servitus naturaliter, non manu facto laedere potest fundum servientem: quemadmodum si imbri crescat aqua in rivo aut ex agris in eum confluat aut aquae fons secundum rivum vel in eo ipso inventus postea fuerit.*] (*D.* 8.3.20.1 Pompon. 33 *ad Sab.*)

These rules may seem like nothing more than common sense, and that is what they represent: the shared assumptions about how neighbors should respect each other's property.[7] The law here reflects both practice and norms: neighbors should not destroy each other's crops when they cross each other's land or channel water over it, and they probably could not get away with doing so very often.

The holder of the servitude was expected to behave in certain socially prescribed ways when he exercised his legal right on his neighbor's property. Stability (the channel should not be moved) and mutual respect are key elements in the legal rule. This rule provided an easy-to-apply, legal standard, and it was also economically efficient: building a new channel was costly. These expectations also accord well with Roman cultural ideals of neighborly practices and good farming as expressed, for example, by the elder Cato in his advice to the prospective buyer of rural land.

> Pay attention to how prosperous the neighbors are; in a good area they should be very successful. You should also enter the property and look

7. Similarly, Zuccotti ("*Locus Servitutis*") sees these legal rules emerging from actual cases that reflect agricultural practice. Much as property rights supported social negotiation around servitudes, administrative institutions and tribunals supported this kind of consensus in medieval Spain (see Glick, *Irrigation and Society*, 64–68).

around, make sure you can get out. The land should have a good climate and not be liable to storms; it should thrive in its good soil and quality. (3) If possible, the land should be at the foot of a hill, with a southern exposure in a healthy place. There should be plenty of labor and a good water supply. There should be a thriving town nearby, or the sea or rivers where boats travel, or good, well-traveled roads. (4) It should be among those rural areas that do not change owners often, and where those who do sell property in these areas regret having sold.

[*Vicini quo pacto niteant id animum advertito: in bona regione bene nitere oportebit. Et uti eo introeas et circumspicias uti inde exire possis. Uti bonum caelum habeat; ne calamitosum siet; solo bono, sua virtute valeat. (3) Si poteris, sub radice montis siet, in meridiem spectet, loco salubri. Operariorum copia siet bonumque aquarium; oppidum validum prope siet, aut mare, aut amnis qua naves ambulant, aut via bona celebrisque. (4) Siet in his agris qui non saepe dominos mutant: qui in his agris praedia vendiderint, quos pigeat vendidisse.*] (*Agr.* 1.2–4)

Checking out the neighbors should be the first priority for prospective buyers: the most desirable properties are located where the neighborhood is stable. Even if the neighbors' appearance should be interpreted as a reflection of the quality of the land, as Pliny the Elder assumes, their prosperity involves more than fertile soil, as he also acknowledges: Cato's most useful advice is to cultivate one's neighbors (Pliny, *NH* 18.44; cf. 18.26–27). A landowner's reaction to his neighbor might be sheer delight (Cic. *Verr.* 2.2.7)[8] or something quite different, as suggested by a legal case that allowed a buyer to call off the sale of land if the seller had concealed a neighbor's name when that identity would deter the buyer: "If in selling property a seller concealed [the name of] a neighbor, he will be held liable if the seller, had he heard the name, would not have purchased the property" [*si quis in vendendo praedio confinem celaverit, quem emptor si audisset, empturus non esset, teneri venditorem*] (*D.* 18.1.35.8 Gaius 10 *ad Prov. Ed.*).

Cato further encouraged the farmer, after he moved in, to be a good neighbor. If he was, he would have an easier time selling his surplus to his neighbors and contracting with them for jobs and labor.[9] They would be more likely to help him with workmen, draft animals, and materials in

8. In the *Verrines* passage, Cicero evokes a landowner's delight in his neighbor's fruitful estate to illustrate the Romans' view of the province of Sicily in general.

9. Peasants and small-scale landholders might regularly work as craftsmen in addition to farming their own land; see Erdkamp, *Grain Market*, 79–95.

building projects; and they would stand by him in times of trouble (*Agr.* 4). Cato connects this idealized, unchanging neighborhood with successful farming and a community of landowners united in their shared pursuit of productivity.[10] In fact, these community values seem to underwrite agricultural productivity.

Similar assumptions underlie Columella's advice about neighbors, though he recognizes Cato's unchanging neighbor as an ideal. The neighborhood may change through death and other causes, and the connections with the community could be sustained by a local tenant (Col. 1.3.5, 1.7.3), but some values remain constant. For Columella, a neighbor's greatest virtue is passive tolerance. He should let trees grow on the land line, leave unmolested seedbeds and stakes for the vineyard, and allow cattle to graze undisturbed (Col. 1.3.7). A landowner might cut brush on his neighbor's land for the compost heap, as long as he did so with care and without harm (*sine iniuria, etiam cum officio*, Col. 2.14.6). Stable and limited interactions are recommended; for example, the *vilicus* should allow no new paths across the property (Col. 1.8.7).[11] This last recommendation implies its converse: existing paths and other types of sharing, such as servitudes, should presumably be tolerated but not expanded—the same rule that is formalized in the law of servitudes. The evidence from Columella applies not only to the owner of the dominant estate but also to that of the servient estate. Like the holder of the servitude, the owner of the servient estate had a culturally defined role to play in regard to servitudes on his property.

While the holder of the servitude enjoyed a broad right to use his neighbor's property, the owner of the servient estate had limited protection, and his actions were restricted: he was prohibited from doing anything that interfered with the exercise of the servitude. The asymmetrical roles of the parties to a servitude are discussed in an interesting case that also illustrates the degree of interconnectedness between rural neighbors. The case is a bit confusing because it involves two kinds of property rights, servitude and usufruct, both of which granted the holder a right in someone else's property. A servitude involved a property right that was permanently attached to the property, whereas usufruct, which created a personal right to use and en-

10. Though Love (*Antiquity and Capitalism*, 77) writes that Cato's notion of profitability in this passage may not be modern, he concedes that Cato aims at reducing costs and increasing revenue.

11. For the duty of the *vilicus* to preserve stable and limited interactions with neighbors, see also Col. 11.1.23, 11.3.62, with Palma, *Iura vicinitatis*, 31–34 (on occasional loans of tools).

joy property, was attached to the person and could not be transferred. In this long legal case, the owners of two properties exchange rights of use. One landowner grants the other both a servitude and usufruct on his land, making his estate servient. Then the other landowner (who owns the dominant estate) transfers back the usufruct. As a result, both owners have rights to use the servient estate, but different kinds of rights. How should this arrangement work? Which right—usufruct or servitude—should take precedence if there is a conflict? What happens, as in this case, if the holder of the usufruct (i.e., the owner of the servient estate) wants to build something that would interfere with the servitude? The description of the situation is a bit confusing, in part because it is framed in negative comparisons and probably also because of changes made in compilation. But Pomponius's ruling is clear enough.

> If you granted to me a right to go and drive across your land [i.e., servitude] and at the same time also a right to its produce [i.e., usufruct], and then I granted to you that the usufruct was not mine, you would have a right to use and benefit from this no differently. Likewise, if I have a right-of-way across your land. The situation is the same, if I have a right to channel water across your farm and you have no legal right to build there without my permission, or if I grant you the right to build, you should make this servitude available to me and build only in such a way that my water channel remains [as it is]. The situation of the whole property should remain such as it was, provided that the grant [of the servitude] was made at the start together [with the grant of the usufruct].
>
> *[Si mihi eodem tempore concesseris et ire agere per tuum locum et uti frui eo ius esse, deinde ego tibi concessero ius mihi uti frui non esse: non aliter eo loco uteris frueris, quam ut ire agere mihi recte liceat. Item si et ducere per tuum fundum aquam iure potuero et in eo tibi aedificare invito me ius non fuerit: si tibi concessero ius esse aedificare, nihilo minus hanc servitutem mihi praestare debebis, ne aliter aedifices, quam ut ductus aquae meus maneat, totiusque eius rei condicio talis esse debet, qualis esset, si una dumtaxat initio concessio facta esset.]* (*D.* 8.3.20 pr. Pompon. 33 *ad Sab.*)

The servitude takes precedence over the usufruct, and the holder of the usufruct might exercise his rights so long as he did not interfere with the servitude. Any construction had to leave the property as it was when the servitude was established. Similarly, if the holder of the servitude allowed the owner of the servient estate to build something that interfered with the servitude, he lost his right: his agreement to the construction was interpreted as release of the servient estate.[12] The rule in this case assumed the basic roles of the parties. The holder of the servitude had broad rights but had to respect the servient estate. In turn, the owner of the servient estate must allow the exercise of the servitude, though he should be allowed the use of his land. Moreover, the circumstances of the case show how closely neighbors were engaged and how much the success of their farms depended on their cooperation and mutual respect. That cooperation should depend on such unequal relationships might at first seem surprising and even unsustainable. But it can be explained as part of a broader pattern of the social norms and relationships characteristic of small, rural communities organized around agricultural production. The asymmetry of servitudes also fits with the stable patterns of exchange in Roman society in general between patrons and clients, the elites and the lower classes.[13]

The productivity of rural land depended on both natural and social resources, as Cato's advice confirms, and securing access to valuable resources, such as water, required neighborly cooperation. Rural neighbors have various strategies for sharing resources, and a helpful model can be found in Gallant's study of the Greek world of the fifth and fourth centuries BC, the era when servitudes were first developed. Gallant describes the period's social relationships: "The strength of the obligation between individuals is directly related to the way they conceive of the social bond between them. If there are multiple ties between them, then the degree of moral obligation to provide assistance increases: the so-called multiplex relationship."[14] Like the Greek households that Gallant studies, Roman landowners of the early and middle periods of the republic practiced primarily subsistence farming, a

12. For the impact of construction, see also *D.* 8.5.9 pr. Paul. 21 *ad Ed.*, citing Julian (the same rule regarding rights-of-way and the servitude for accepting runoff, *stillicidium*); in this case, the legal argument more clearly reflects the rights of the owner of the servient estate to control his property, on which see previously in this chapter. In a case about the urban servitude for a supporting wall, the servient owner may build as long as he improved the condition of the wall and did not make it worse (*D.* 8.5.6.7 Ulp. 17 *ad Ed.*). In fact, if the holder of the servitude granted his neighbor the right to build on the route of the servitude, he lost his right (*D.* 8.6.8 pr. Paul. 15 *ad Plaut.*).

13. On the economic importance of such social exchange, see Verboven, *Economy of Friends*, especially 103–14.

14. Gallant, *Risk and Survival*, 151–52; cf. 143–69.

shared aim among rural neighbors.[15] Because the parties to a servitude were neighbors, the asymmetry or apparent unfairness of their exchange was offset by other kinds of compensation that created a kind of equity, if not equality, between them. Similar observations have been made about rural communities that shared a water supply drawn from the Euphrates in the early twentieth century: "shared norms and values, mutual social relations and institutions, however few or many, simple or complex—precede active participation in the development and maintenance of the technical social controls which together constitute systematic use of natural resources."[16] Neighbors shared many interests and risks, and these multiple ties could motivate them to help each other. Those also connected in other ways (kinship, status) even more easily sustain unequal exchanges, because they had additional avenues of exchange. Roman landowners of the early and middle periods of the republic probably formed such a homogenous group, the *assidui,* united in their status and, in some cases, also by kinship.[17] Sometime during this early era, servitudes institutionalized the social patterns that promoted agricultural productivity as they formalized relations among people in rural communities. These patterns persisted even after water was treated as private property rather than a communal resource, part of a broader social phenomenon where Roman aristocrats defined themselves at least in part by their ability to bestow benefits on the less powerful. As Verboven describes it, "the social nature of the obligation to give was deeply rooted in the social identity of the Roman aristocrat."[18] These patterns of cooperation are specifically associated with servitudes, as Palma has argued in his study of urban servitudes.[19] In the Roman era, there is evidence beyond servitudes for a water-sharing system that depended on social networks.

Community irrigation systems are known from Roman Spain and North Africa, where social relationships played an important role in the management of a local water supply. In Roman Spain, the social networks also sup-

15. White (*Roman Farming,* 51) observes, "Mixed intensive farming of this type is ultimately based on the need for self-sufficiency, which goes back to the earliest days of Roman husbandry." Cf. Astin, *Cato,* 261.

16. Fernea, "Conflict in Irrigation," 77; cf. 82–83.

17. Cornell, *Beginnings of Rome,* 288. The patterns continue into later eras; see, e.g., Champlin, "Owners and Neighbors."

18. Verboven, *Economy of Friends,* 100.

19. Palma, *Iura vicinitatis,* 42–109.

ported the irrigation system, described in the *lex Rivi Hiberiensis.*[20] In this municipal system, the community's role was formalized as a council of the landowners who shared the water, called *pagani.* This council was responsible for maintenance of the canals and for enforcement of the rules governing water use. There was a complex system of rules and fines, as well as procedures for adjudicating disputes (*lex Rivi Hib.* 1.1–34, 3.18–22). As Beltrán Lloris argues, one of the main aims of this decree was to systematize the regulations for irrigation and to create a community that could enforce the rules.[21] At Lamasba in Africa, there was a large irrigation community, known from a long inscription discussed in chapter 1 (*CIL* 8.18587 = 4440 = *ILS* 5793), which reports the resolution of a dispute about the allocation of water from a local stream to a number of landowners who used the water to irrigate their farmland. The bulk of the inscription records the distribution scheme—a schedule with the names, amounts, and times when water could be used. According to the preamble of the inscription, this schedule restored, revised, and confirmed a distribution system that had existed previously: "of the water that used to be allocated, it is so decreed that the water ought to flow down [the irrigation channels] whenever the spring flows, as the schedule written below indicates" *[[aquarum quae da] / ri solitae sunt, constitit ita debere aquam decurrere si quando fo [ns decurrit, ut monstrat forma infra scripta]* (*CIL* 8.18587, lines 2–3).[22] The local community had appointed one of their own to supervise a commission that would negotiate a settlement. This process did not involve Roman officials or Roman law, but that Roman habit of epigraphy was used to record and reaffirm the new community consensus about water sharing. Shaw explains,

> Conflict is often endemic in irrigation systems, but ordinarily disputes are settled by mechanisms provided by the local society itself and not by external "official" action. Consensus can be broken, but as long as the proprietors are part of a tightly knit and isolated community, and have their own perceived instruments of justice, the basis for effective social control is considerable.

---

20. Beltrán Lloris, "Irrigation Decree," 173–75. For more discussion of the *lex Rivi Hiberiensis,* see chapter 1 in the present study.

21. Beltrán Lloris, "Irrigation Decree," 187–91.

22. For the decree as a local resolution of dispute over allocation, see Shaw, "Lamasba," 68–71. For a discussion of the schedules in this inscription, see chapter 1 in the present study.

Shaw concludes that "in either type of distribution [i.e., by time or volume], the process is controlled by social restraints and supervised by the local *jama'a* or council of elders."[23] At Lamasba, the community was strengthened by various ties—families tended to own contiguous plots of land and consolidated their interests by intermarriage—and the pattern of land tenure and family ties facilitated the exchange and sharing of water. Glick has observed similar social cooperation in the irrigation community of medieval Valencia, where most of the landowners followed the rules of the system; only about one-third of them were involved in disputes (on average about one per year), and they constituted a group of chronic offenders who were repeatedly involved in disputes with their neighbors and with the local water authorities.[24] The social practices connected with the public irrigation systems in the Roman decrees help to reconstruct the role of the community in sustaining servitudes. Although the decrees involve larger communities, similar dynamics are at play among landowners who managed a local water supply with servitudes. As in the public irrigation systems, the parties to a servitude were expected to be vigilant in enforcing their agreements.

In the legal cases about servitudes, there are several features that reflect the broad community involvement characteristic of the commons model. To protect a servitude, its holder could bring suit against anyone who interfered, not just the owner of the servient estate (*D.* 8.5.10 pr.-1 Ulp. 53 *ad Ed.*).[25] When repairs were needed, he could approach his channel by the shortest route, across any neighboring property, not just the servient estate (*D.* 8.4.11.1 Pompon. 33 *ad Sab.*; cf. *D.* 43.21.3.10 Ulp. 70 *ad Ed.*).[26] Perhaps most indicative of the influence of social practice is the legal recognition of longstanding use: if someone had channeled water for longer than anyone could remember, the law would recognize his practice as a legal right.[27] Finally, application of the use-it-or-lose-it rule depended on neighborly cooperation.

---

23. Shaw, "Lamasba," 69, 169; cf. 88–93.

24. Glick, *Irrigation and Society*, 52–64.

25. The interdict for daily water could also be used against anyone who interfered (*D.* 43.20.1.25 Ulp. 70 *ad Ed.*).

26. The owner of the servient estate was in a stronger position than these other neighbors, since he could refuse access by so specifying when the servitude was created (*D.* 8.4.11 pr. Pompon. 33 *ad Sab.*). Later in the present chapter, there is further discussion of this extract.

27. *D.* 43.20.3.4 Pompon. 34 *ad Sab.*; *D.* 39.3.26 Scaev. 4 *Resp.*; *D.* 39.3.1.23 Ulp. 53 *ad Ed. D.* 39.3.2.1, 5, 7, Paul. 49 *ad Ed.*, with Kaser, *RP* 1:445.

According to this rule, a servitude was lost if the right was not exercised for two years or for the prescribed period.[28] An owner could sustain use by having someone else exercise the right, so the neighbors needed to know not just the landowner himself but also his slaves and tenants.[29] In addition, those who used the servitude had to be aware of the legal status of their activity: to avoid the use-it-or-lose-it rule, they had to believe that they were exercising a right.[30] The law assumed informed and self-conscious social practices, where neighbors have specific information about each other and the natural resources that they use and share. Comparative evidence from the irrigation community in medieval Valencia is apposite: the system depended on intensive interaction and local experience, and according to Glick, the local officials responsible for policing the system had to be participants as well, "who knew the topography, regulations, and local traditions intimately."[31] More generally, in a survey of irrigation communities, Hunt and Hunt observed the central role of local social organizations in managing the water supply.[32]

Precisely this type of coordination and shared knowledge is expected by Cato, as evidenced in the terms he gives for the lease of winter pasture, probably as part of seasonal transhumance.

> [The term of lease] for a dry meadow should end when the pear tree begins to bloom; [the term of lease] for an irrigated meadow should end when the neighbors above and below let flow [the water], or set a day agreeable to both sides.
>
> *[prato sicco decedat ubi pirus florere coeperit; prato inriguo, ubi super inferque vicinus promittet, tum decedito, vel diem certam utrique facito; cetero pabulo Kal. Martiis cedito.]* (*Agr.* 149.1)

---

28. See n. 55 in the introduction to the present study.

29. *D.* 8.6.5 Paul. 6 *ad Ed.* (co-owner, usufructuary, possessor in good faith); *D.* 8.6.20 Scaev. 1 *Reg.* (someone in possession—a hired servant, guest, doctor, tenant, usufructuary); *D.* 8.6.24 Scaev. 1 *Reg.* (even use by a possessor in bad faith sustains a servitude). Cf. Solazzi, *Specie ed estinzione*, 165–66. Similarly, Roman law recognized a marriage, without other formalities, if the neighbors knew that a man and woman were living together and trying to have children or that the man had acknowledged the woman's child as his own (*Cod. Just.* 5.4.9). For more on the use-it-or-lose-it rule, see chapter 1 in the present study.

30. *D.* 8.6.22 Scaev. 1 *Reg.*; *D.* 8.6.25 Paul. 5 *Sent.* The jurists do not directly raise the possibility of deceit, though the standard terms of the interdict (*nec vi nec precario nec clam*) could keep a dishonest claimant from winning his suit. See Solazzi, *Tutela*, 73.

31. Glick, *Irrigation and Society*, 37.

32. Hunt and Hunt, "Canal Irrigation," 395.

Dry and irrigated meadows were leased on different terms. Lease of a dry meadow ends when the pear tree blossoms. Lease of an irrigated meadow was coordinated with the neighbors' water use; specifically, the lease should begin (and end) when the neighbors irrigate their meadows. Though both leases are coordinated with seasonal work, the lease of the irrigated meadow emphasizes human factors in cultivation. Meadows were typically watered on an annual schedule (usually in the spring), so Cato's rule aimed to coordinate possession of the leased meadow with the calendar of agricultural work.[33] He assumed that everyone irrigated his meadow at about the same time, and this suggests that neighboring landowners also shared a water supply: they coordinated not only the schedule for irrigation but also the use of the resource itself. This type of neighborly interaction provided a basis for both legal and social practices in Cato and in legal treatments of servitudes. The law of water rights recognized the importance of social practices not only by protecting them but even more by depending on them for its enforcement.

Servitudes could draw an entire community—not just the owners of the dominant and servient estates—into a network of ongoing one-on-one relationships. In such communities, neighbors tend to have a shared interest in making everyone's farm productive. Lirb has discussed cooperation around lease, usufruct, and partnerships in rural communities, and he mentions servitudes in particular as a way of sharing inherited property.[34] Similar, too, are the cooperative regional markets that arose in the "close-knit pattern of distribution of the Campanian agro-towns," discussed in Arthur's study of northern Campania.[35] In sociological studies of modern communities, Ellickson has describe the same phenomenon: "Members of a close-knit group develop and maintain norms whose content serves to maximize the aggregate welfare that members obtain in their workaday affairs with one another."[36] Commons theory also addresses the effectiveness of small groups in enforcing a system of shared resources, as formulated by Olson: "in general, social pressure and social incentives operate only in groups of smaller size, in the groups so small that the members can have face-to-face contact with one another."[37]

---

33. For details and sources on meadows, irrigated and otherwise, see appendix A. It may be that leases were coordinated with irrigation so that those downhill could benefit from runoff water, though limiting the amount of runoff may have been more of a concern (see Shaw, "Water and Society," 137–38).

34. Lirb, "Partners in Agriculture," 278–79, 286–87.

35. Arthur, *Romans in Northern Campania,* 45.

36. Ellickson, *Order without Law,* 167.

37. Olson, "Group Size," 45.

In the Roman world, this kind of rural community could be centered on a small cult site where an ideal of neighborliness could mediate tensions between neighbors.[38] Cato's preference for a stable neighborhood recognizes the value of these social networks (*Agr.* 1.4, quoted earlier in this chapter). Where litigation was an option, Columella acknowledged that long-term residents were less likely to use it. He quoted Saserna's opinion that absentee landlords most often produced lawsuits instead of profit: "Saserna used to say that a lawsuit was earned instead of pay from a man of this sort" [*Saserna dicebat ab eius modi homine fere pro mercede litem reddi*] (Col. 1.7.4). Stable, neighborly communities tend to resolve conflicts through negotiation and cooperative interaction rather than by law, but they may also use legal institutions to reinforce their values and practices. The importance of these social factors is not incompatible with the treatment of water as property, as is illustrated in the Lamasba inscription previously discussed, where a schedule that depended on social cooperation was also predicated on private ownership of the allotments of water. Roman landowners seem to have used the law of servitudes in just this way to craft an equitable balance between the rights of servitude holders and the owners of the servient estates.

REPAIRS AND IMPROVEMENTS

While the community had an interest in supporting local water-sharing arrangements, individual landowners could disrupt the comfortable stability of the neighborhood by pursuing their own needs and interests. Even the idealizing advice of the agricultural writers recognizes the potential for change in traditional patterns, due not just to neighbors moving in and out but also to the recurring need to repair or replace the farm's equipment. When it came to the water supply, a channel might start leaking, or a landowner might want to improve the channel (e.g., by lining it with waterproof cement so that it conserved water better). Because the holder of the servitude had property rights, he was legally allowed to repair and improve his water channel, but these projects could also affect the owner of the servient estate, especially if he shared the channel. In the legal cases about repairs and improvements, the jurists consider both social and practical issues, asking whether there should be any limit on the right to repair and improve a channel, as well as how the interests of the owner of the servient estate should be taken into account.

---

38. Frayn, *Subsistence Farming*, 17–33.

The balancing of social cooperation and individual rights can be traced in legal opinions about repairs, starting with Quintus Mucius in the late second century BC and continuing in the writings of the classical jurists Pomponius and Ulpian. Earlier jurists, such as Mucius and Labeo, put more emphasis on social cooperation than on individual rights, encouraging the holder of the servitude to accommodate his neighbor's needs. Over time, a more individualistic, rights-based approach emerged, which cast the question in more abstract terms. Pomponius emphasized the rights of the servitude holder, while Ulpian used the concept of utility (*utilitas*), a defining feature of servitudes, to articulate a new balance between the interests of the servient and dominant estates. This focus on rights could lead to a more objective legal standard, but it could also obscure the sometimes messy social negotiation that might be necessary when a landowner wanted to change his channel over a neighbor's land. For both earlier and later jurists, practical concerns, such as conserving water, were very important.

Repairs and cleaning were no trivial matter for the holder of a servitude to channel water. If a servitude could not be used because the channel was filled with debris or in poor repair, the right was lost.[39] Carrying out repairs was the right and the responsibility of the holder of the servitude.[40] This right was created tacitly when the servitude was established, and the two parties could also agree to terms governing repairs (*D.* 8.4.11 pr. Pompon. 33 *ad Sab.*; cf. *D.* 8.5.6.2, 5 Ulp. 17 *ad Ed.*). Special interdicts protected the right to repair channels and the infrastructure surrounding a spring.[41] The creation of these interdicts suggests that there was often dispute about repairs, disputes that were not resolved by neighborly negotiation.

Though the holder of the servitude had a right to make repairs, his access to the channel to carry in supplies and do the work depended on the cooperation of his neighbor. When the neighbor shared the channel, he might have an interest in repairs and improvements, and if it seemed likely that the repairs would harm his interests, he might not be so cooperative. What the holder of the servitude saw as an "improvement" might appear very different to the owner of the servient estate—for example, if it meant burying a channel underground so that he could no longer draw water from it, as in

39. *D.* 43.21.1 pr.-1 Ulp. 70 *ad Ed.*; cf. *D.* 43.21.4 Venul. 1 *Interdicts.* In general on the use-it-or-lose-it rule, see the introduction and chapter 1 in the present study.

40. The practice was similar in medieval Valencia; see Glick, *Irrigation and Society,* 48–51.

41. On the interdict protecting the right to maintain and repair a water channel, see Grosso, *Servitù prediali,* 311–12; on its wording, Solazzi, *Tutela e il possessio,* 73–79. See also chapter 1 in the present study.

the case cited at the beginning of this chapter. For this reason, disputes arose about the distinction between "repairs" and "improvements." What sort of covering or substructures could be built around the channel? What did building and mending entail? Or—to rephrase the questions in a way that reveals the underlying issues for social cooperation—would this work improve the water supply for the holder of the servitude while also reducing access to water for the owner of the servient estate? Not all the legal cases address the social issues explicitly, yet these issues underlie the discussion of the practical need for repair.

Despite attempts at definition in the interdict itself and in the legal commentaries, there was some overlap between repairs and improvements, even in Ulpian's explanation of what these terms were to mean in the praetor's interdicts.

> Next the praetor says "repairing and cleaning." Repairing means to restore what is broken to its former condition. Covering, building substructures, mending, [and] building are included in the word repairing, and also carrying and bringing in those things that are necessary for this work.
>
> [*Deinde ait praetor 'reficere purgare.' Reficere est quod corruptum est in pristinum statum restaurare. Verbo reficiendi tegere substruere sarcire aedificare, item advehere adportareque ea, quae ad eandem rem opus essent, continentur.*] (*D.* 43.21.1.6 Ulp. 70 *ad Ed.*)

> Most people consider that the word *cleaning* refers to a channel itself that is in good condition; it clearly pertains also to a channel that needs repair: for most of the time when it needs repair, it also needs cleaning.
>
> [*Purgandi verbum plerique quidem putant ad eum rivum pertinere, qui integer est: et palam est et ad eum pertinere, qui refectione indiget: plerumque enim ut refectione, et purgatione indiget.*] (*D.* 43.21.1.7 Ulp. 70 *ad Ed.*)

That "cleaning" could be included in "repairing" and "building" seems to open a range of possibilities, which could be the source of disagreement or misunderstanding. There is some effort to limit repairs, and the most interesting cases concern activities that were permitted under the rubric of repairs only under certain circumstances—namely, (1) lining an earthen channel with waterproof cement (*opus signinum*), (2) laying pipe in an existing channel, and (3) converting an open channel to a closed one or vice versa. There is no overall solution to these cases; different jurists draw the line around repairs in different places. These different legal approaches might be explained in part as a lack of systematization in Roman private law. Or they might reflect the nature of the sources, that is, the scholarly discussion among jurists of limiting cases as they sought to establish consistent rules. In any case, the variety of approaches seems to reflect actual circumstances and legal disputes where the outcome gave more weight to neighbor's interests than to the rights of the servitude holder.

Early jurists focus on balancing the landowners' interest in the water supply, as illustrated in two cases, one of which is reported twice in the *Digest*. The first case reports an opinion of Q. Mucius (cos. 95 BC) that the holder of a servitude could lay pipe in his channel.

> Quintus Mucius writes, when someone has [the right to a channel water] across someone else's property, by the day or summer or a longer interval, he may lay his own pipe, either ceramic or of whatever sort, in the channel in order to spread the water more widely, and he may do what he likes in the channel, so long as he does not make the water channel worse for the owner of the [servient] estate.
>
> [*Quintus Mucius scribit, cum iter aquae vel cottidianae vel aestivae vel quae intervalla longiora habeat per alienum fundum erit, licere fistulam suam vel fictilem vel cuiuslibet generis in rivo ponere, quae aquam latius exprimeret, et quod vellet in rivo facere, licere, dum ne domino praedii aquagium deterius faceret.*] (D. 8.3.15 Pompon. 31 *ad Q. Muc.*)

The same rule is reported in an abbreviated form in another case that can be traced back to an early imperial jurist, Sabinus. Continuity with Mucius's opinion, if not direct reference to it, is suggested by the repetition of the unusual term *aquagium*.

> A person, who has a right of [channeling] water on a daily basis, can lay pipe in the channel or do anything that he likes, so long as he does not interfere with the owner's use of the [servient] property or with the use of the waterway on the part of those who share the channel.

> [*Is, qui aquae cottidianae ius habet, vel fistulam in rivo ponere vel aliud quodlibet facere potest, dummodo ne fundum domino aut aquagium rivalibus deterius faciat.*] (*D.* 43.20.3.5 Pompon. 34 *ad Sab.*)

This later version of the case hints at difficulties of coordinating land and water use—disputes or potential for dispute—with the term *rivalis.* The term is rare in this technical sense of people who share a channel; in other contexts, *rivalis* expresses competition, and that sense is implicit here.[42] In both versions of the case, the jurists counsel cooperation, even as they acknowledge the potential for dispute.[43]

In the second case showing such balancing efforts, cited at the beginning of this chapter, Labeo determines that an open channel could not be converted to a closed channel if the change adversely affected the owner of the servient estate. Instead of seeking a static ideal of "no change," both Mucius and Labeo base their decisions on the competing needs of the dominant and servient estates. Mucius's language recalls the broad freedom to exercise the rights in a servitude: the holder can lay any kind of pipe he wants and do whatever he wants in the channel, so long as his work does not adversely affect the water supply for the servient estate. Similarly, Labeo takes into account the needs of the servient owner, specifically for agricultural tasks, such as watering animals, and also more generally, since drawing water from the channel could serve a variety of purposes (*appellendi pecus vel hauriendi aquam*). He is willing to curtail the rights of the servitude holder in order to sustain neighborly cooperation. Both opinions presume that the neighbors are sharing the water supply and that the law aims to sustain that cooperation. In these cases from the late republic, the legal rules seem to be emerging from social practice as the jurists recognize informal exchanges of resources as the basis of legal rights. Palma has observed the same emphasis on finding an equilibrium in the interests of neighbors in the writings of the late republican jurists.[44] If this analysis is accurate, servitudes developed as a kind of customary law, where the legal system recognized social practices and accorded them legal protection. Indeed, Capogrossi Colognesi has suggested that Labeo's approach in this case may reflect an older legal approach to the

42. On usage of *rivalis,* see the introduction in the present study.

43. According to *D.* 43.20.3.6 Pompon. 34 *ad Sab.,* similar consideration must be given when raising one's channel on a bridge, so as not to interfere with the channel running under it.

44. Palma, *Iura vicinitas,* 158.

servitude to channel water, namely, that the two neighbors shared ownership of the channel and that both had to agree to any changes. Even after the servient owner lost this legal right, his agreement continued to be important in practical terms, and for this reason, it remained a topic in the legal discussions of these issues.[45]

The second case, however, also includes the comments of the classical jurist Pomponius (late second century AD), who takes a more systematic approach to the balance of interests. Pomponius rejects Labeo's opinion as too circumstantial, though he agrees with Mucius on the question of pipes. Pomponius's and Mucius's decision about pipes may reflect the conventional view of technology: according to Pliny, the best way to develop a spring was to conduct water from it in pipes (*NH* 31.57). Pipes may have been preferred because they could carry the water by means of a siphon, which could cross a valley, going down one side and up the other.[46] In legal texts, *rivus* could be used for a water channel that had pipes, without the pipe necessarily being specified.[47] Whether or not technology was an issue, Pomponius emphasized the issue of rights in a way that Mucius did not. According to Pomponius, the holder of the servitude had a legal right to make repairs, whereas the owner of the servient estate had no rights at all, at least none that should be considered where improving the channel was at stake. Pomponius's argument might be interpreted as evidence of a change in the law, if cases by other classical jurists supported his view. Instead, Pomponius's strict rights-based analysis was rejected by Ulpian in favor of an analysis that considered rights, practicality, and neighborly cooperation.

Ulpian's approach to repairs draws from both strands in the earlier juristic discussion. Like the earlier jurists (Mucius and Labeo), Ulpian balances the interests of the parties to the servitude, recognizing implicitly the role of neighborly cooperation in sustaining servitudes. Like Pomponius, Ulpian attempts to systematize the rule about allowable repairs by using abstract categories. Ulpian develops the legal concept of utility to articulate a kind of equity between the servient and dominant estates. His approach both preserves the asymmetrical nature of the institution and, paradoxically, re-

---

45. On the origins of servitudes in a kind of joint ownership and on the continuing recognition of the interests of the owner of the servient estate, see Capogrossi Colognesi, *Servitù d'acqua,* 53–54 n. 94.

46. On the use of pipes and siphons for crossing valleys, see Trevor Hodge, *Roman Aqueducts,* 33; see, generally, 147–60.

47. Franciosi, *Servitù prediali,* 91 n. 6. For an example in an inscription, see *CIL* 11.3003 = *ILS* 5771, with Bruun, *Water Supply,* 126, 133.

quires equity that gives a legal foundation to social norms. The recognition of social cooperation as a legal right is again suggestive of customary law.

Ulpian's approach to repairs can be analyzed in a case where he responds to the work of two republican jurists (Labeo and Servius). The case is rather long but worth quoting in full to observe the development of ideas. It presents three examples, each about a different type of repair or improvement: opening an underground channel, lining an earthen channel with cement, and laying pipes in a channel. Ulpian cites earlier jurists' opinions on each type of repair and then offers his own comment.

> Servius, however, writes that water may be channeled in a different way—[for example,] if water that was previously conducted through an underground channel is now conducted through an open channel—for if someone does some work in order to retain/contain the water better, he is not prevented with impunity. I would [say the same] also in [the case of] an underground channel, unless a greater usefulness [*utilitas*] for his opponent is involved. (1) Servius and Labeo write, if he wants to make a channel, which from the beginning was earthen, into a cement [channel] because it did not hold water, his case should be heard; but if he afterwards makes this channel, which is raised on structures [arches], or part of it into an earthen channel, likewise he should not be prevented. It seems right to me that urgent and necessary repairs ought to be allowed. (2) If someone wants to place a new tube or pipe in a channel, though it never had one, Labeo says that this interdict will be applicable to him. We also think on this point that the needs [*utilitas*] of the one who channels [water] should be considered [so long as it is done] without inconvenience to him whose field [is crossed by the channel].
>
> *[Servius autem scribit aliter duci aquam, quae ante per specus ducta est, si nunc per apertum ducatur: nam si operis aliquid faciat quis, quo magis aquam conservet vel contineat, non impune prohiberi. Ego et in specu contra, si non maior utilitas versetur adversarii. (1) Servius et Labeo scribunt, si rivum, qui ab initio terrenus fuit, quia aquam non continebat, cementicium velit facere, audiendum esse: sed et si eum rivum, qui structilis fuit, postea terrenum faciat aut partem rivi, aeque non esse prohibendum. Mihi videtur urgens et necessaria refectio esse admittenda. (2) Si quis novum canalem vel fistulas in rivo velit collocare, cum id numquam habuerit, utile ei hoc interdictum futurum Labeo ait. Nos et hic opinamur utilitatem eius qui ducit sine incommoditate eius cuius ager est spectandam.]* (*D.* 43.21.3 pr.-2 Ulp. 70 *ad Ed.*)

Concerning all three examples of repairs, Ulpian works with the concept of *utilitas* to evaluate changes to the channel, but he does so in different ways.[48] The second example, lining an earthen channel with cement, is the most straightforward because it focuses on the practical question of the purpose of the work. The landowner wants to line the channel with cement because it is leaking. Ulpian approves the opinions of both Labeo and Servius, agreeing that this should be allowed. Stopping leaks does seem to fit the category of repair, because the work restores the channel to its former (i.e., leak-free) state, though using different materials. This work could be considered an improvement—in that it changes the channel, lining it with cement and making it more permanent—but in defining the category of repairs, the purpose of the work is more important than its effect on the channel. This makes sense in terms of the broader treatment of repairs. They are intended to facilitate exercise of the right: if the channel leaks too much, it is impossible to conduct water through it. Lining a channel with waterproof cement seems analogous to paving a right-of-way, which was allowed (*D.* 8.5.4.5 Ulp. 17 *ad Ed.*), though the jurists do not draw this analogy. Moreover, this work is not likely to harm the owner of the servient estate. If he shares the channel, it is in his interest that the channel not leak. Because the neighbors share an interest, the efficiency of the channel is the relevant legal issue (this idea is asserted in the first example). Whereas Servius and Labeo base their opinion on practical details (the channel will not hold water), Ulpian creates an abstract category, "necessary and urgent repairs," which could be transferred to another situation where there was a question about repairs.

For the first and third examples of repairs, *utilitas* is less an abstract category than a dynamic function. Ulpian is here concerned equally with the efficient use of water and with balancing the landowners' interests. His opinion broadens the standard of utility in a way that redefines the relationship between servient and dominant estates, taking into account the interests of both landowners. In the first example, where Servius allowed

48. The use of *utilitas* in this case may account for its repetition in *D.* 43.21.1.11 Ulp. 70 *ad Ed.*, which has been rejected as an interpolation (Levy and Rabel, *Index Interpolationum*, 3:303). Compare Ulpian's approach to cutting stone from a neighbor's quarry, which also balances the interests of both landowners as it takes into account local practice: without a servitude, it is possible to use a neighbor's quarry only if this is customary (*consuetudo*) and if a legal guarantee (*cautio*) is provided that the quarry owner's use of stone is protected (*D.* 8.4.13.1 Ulp. 6 *Opin.*).

opening a closed channel, Ulpian also approves closing an open channel if the change allows more efficient use of the water (*quo magis aquam conservet vel contineat*). But efficiency is not the only criterion; the interests of the servient estate must be considered (*si non maior utilitas versetur adversarii*). The *adversarius* is the owner of the servient estate, and his *utilitas* should be taken into account. The argument is compressed, possibly abbreviated in compilation, but the sense is clear. An open channel may be buried only if the change does not put the servient estate at a disadvantage. Ulpian thus undermines the characteristic asymmetry of servitudes because his opinion equates the interests of the servient and the dominant estates. The legal right to water is not given more importance than customary water-sharing arrangements, such as the servient owner's use of the open channel. Instead, Ulpian puts the neighbors on equal footing, redefining in legal terms (*utilitas*) the informal cooperation that earlier jurists recognized as the basis for making servitudes work. Here he disagrees with Pomponius's opinion in the case previously discussed. The record of disagreement suggests an ongoing debate about these priorities, which probably reflects actual instances of neighbors who were negotiating their access to water through the legal institution of servitudes.

For the third example, laying pipe, Ulpian retreats from this wider application of *utilitas* and asserts a rights-based rule more like that of Pomponius. Pipes may be laid in the channel so long as the work meets the needs of the holder of the servitude and does not cause inconvenience to the owner of the servient estate (*Nos et hic opinamur utilitatem eius qui ducit sine incommoditate eius cuius ager est spectandam*). Convenience harkens back to the neighborly cooperation presumed in Labeo's opinion.[49] In Ulpian's treatment, convenience seems less formal, possibly easier to ignore, as the litotes *sine incommoditate* might suggest. The change in language from *utilitas* to *commoditas* marks a revision of Ulpian's opinion in the first example, where he equated the interests of the servient estate with the legal right of the dominant estate. By focusing on the needs of the dominant estate, Ulpian redeploys a traditional feature of servitudes. Usefulness, or *utilitas,* was an old principle, central to the very existence of a servitude: a servitude could exist only if it provided

---

49. Ulpian's rule in this case seems to correct another republican jurist, Ofilius, a student of Servius, whom he cites in *D.* 43.21.1.10 Ulp. 70 *ad Ed.* as the authority for the rule that lining a channel with cement was not permitted as repairs. Ulpian may be restating an earlier rule, since it is found also in the writings of Paul (*D.* 39.3.17.1 Paul. 15 *ad Plaut.*).

something useful to the dominant estate.[50] Ulpian applies this standard to evaluate the competing interests of the landowners, affirming the traditional concept of a servitude and using it to systematize the distinction between repairs and improvements.

While a servitude created asymmetrical legal rights, the legal system recognized competing interests and supported informal equity between dominant and servient properties. In deciding what repairs could be allowed, the earlier jurists focus on balancing the needs of the servient and dominant estates. Labeo comes closest to recognizing a right of access to the channel for the owner of the servient estate. Later jurists, Pomponius and Ulpian, advance a rights-based approach that gives priority to the rights of the holder of the servitude. But even in these later discussions, the jurists consider the impact of repairs on the servient estate, recognizing the real importance of neighborly cooperation. Ulpian's attempt to create an abstract rule based on *utilitas* appears to be part of a jurist's effort to systematize the rules on servitudes—that is, it may be the product of the jurists' debates about hypothetical legal problems—yet it also reflects the ongoing negotiation between neighbors about how best to use the water available to them.

STATILIUS TAURUS AND CICERO: CLASS-CONSCIOUS NEIGHBORS

As the preceding discussion has shown, legal rules for servitudes drew on the traditional ideas about neighborliness and farming that held rural communities together. Social networks were an important mechanism for regulating a local water supply. The law provided an alternate remedy when neighboring landowners were unable to reach a satisfactory agreement through social negotiation. In most of the extant reports of such legal disputes, the parties are anonymous, and the location of the property is unspecified. But there is one lawsuit about a servitude that preserves this information. It involved T. Statilius Taurus and his neighbors and the water they channeled from a spring on his property at Sutrium in southern Etruria (*D.* 8.3.35 Paul. 15 *ad Plaut.*). The case is reported in the *Digest of Justinian* as an imperial rescript, that is, the emperor's decision or opinion about

50. On the development of *utilitas,* see chapter 3. Lining a channel with waterproof cement seems analogous to paving a right-of-way, which was allowed (*D.* 8.5.4.5 Ulp. 17 *ad Ed.*), though the jurists do not draw this analogy.

how a case should be decided. The Statilius Taurus in this case is usually identified as Augustus's "marshal" (as Syme calls him) or one of his sons, and the identification provides a basis for ascribing the response in the case to Augustus or perhaps Tiberius.[51] Because this case can be tied to specific historical circumstances, it can be contextualized both socially and geographically. The social dynamics in the Taurus lawsuit can be illuminated by comparison with two similar situations where an elite landowner is negotiating with less powerful neighbors over a water supply: one discussed in one of Cicero's letters (*Att.* 15.26.4) and the other described in the long inscription from Viterbo about Vegetus's private aqueduct (*CIL* 11.3003, discussed in chapter 1). In addition, the historical landscape of Sutrium, reconstructed on the basis of the British School surveys, tends to confirm the relationship between law and social exchange that is documented in the legal, literary, and inscriptional evidence.

Sutrium, now perhaps most famous for its amphitheater cut into the stone rather than erected on arches, is located in southern Etruria, north of Veii on the Via Cassia. The town is built on the spur of a hill. Around the time of our lawsuit, Strabo describes Sutrium as one of the larger towns of southern Etruria (5.2.9), and dedications to Antoninus Pius and to Caracalla show that it continued to thrive in the second century AD (*CIL* 11.3249, 3250). Its territory extended north to the hills around Lake Ciminius and Lake Sabatinus, over hillsides and gorges that were infamous in the Roman period for impenetrable forests, *invia atque horrenda,* as Livy describes them (9.36.1). Yet settlements grew up along the roads connecting Sutrium with neighboring towns and with Rome, and the region was known for its fine farmland. Livy's account of the Etruscan wars of the late fourth century gives us a charming picture of the consul Q. Fabius Rullianus standing on a ridge of the Monte Cimini just before battle, gazing out over rich Etruscan fields (*opulenta Etruriae arva,* 9.36.11); and after the battle, plunder did not disappoint.

Sutrium first became a colony either when it was captured from the Etruscans by Camillus in 390 BC (Livy 6.3.1–10; Diod. 14.117) or at the same

---

51. On the identification of Taurus, see Nagl, "Statilius Taurus," 2195–97. The family was from Lucania according to Syme (*Roman Revolution,* 237). He was suffect consul in 37 BC and consul in 26 BC; see Syme, *Augustan Aristocracy,* 32, 35, 202, 212, 274 (career), 240, 376–77 (revising the stemma in Nagl: his three sons were all consuls in the first century AD). For the identification of the emperor, see Solazzi, *Specie ed estinzione,* 184; Biondi, *Categoria,* 282 n. 1. Augustus's interest in Taurus's suit may also be related to his systematization of surveying, on which see Gvozdeva, "Land Cadastre of Augustus."

time as Nepi was colonized in 383 BC (Vell. 1.4; cf. Livy 6.21.4). After its recapture by Rullianus in 310, the area was securely in Roman control (Livy 9.32–36). Like other Latin colonies, Sutrium suffered economically during the Second Punic War, was unable to make its annual contributions of troops and grain, and was subsequently punished (Livy 27.9.7, 29.15). There was, however, room to relocate Campanians in 210 BC (Livy 26.34.10). Sutrium became a *municipium* shortly after the Social War, and a new colony was founded there in the triumviral period, after it was occupied by Agrippa in the civil war between Antony and Octavian.[52] By the late first century BC, at the time of the second colony, settlement had spread west and south of town and immediately to the north of town and was also spreading northward toward the Ciminius Lacus (Lago di Vico).[53] In the aftermath of Augustus's defeat of Antony, Caesarians had the opportunity to acquire land in southern Etruria, and it is probably at this time that Statilius Taurus came to own an estate near Sutrium, which subsequently was the focus of a lawsuit about the right to use water from a spring.

The problem in the Taurus case centers on the rule for loss of servitude by nonuse (the "use-it-or-lose-it" rule) and how to apply this rule when the source of water disappears and then reappears due to natural causes. Taurus's neighbors used to channel water from a spring on his property, but then the spring dried up. After the water began to flow again, they resumed channeling it. Presumably, Taurus objected, and when they were unable to settle the dispute amicably, his neighbors took the case to the emperor, who decided in their favor.

> Atilicinus says that the emperor replied to Statilius Taurus with these words: "Those men, who customarily channeled water from the farm at Sutrium, approached me and explained that they were not able to use

---

52. On the triumviral colony, see App. *B.C.* 5.31; cf. Pliny's list of colonies at *NH* 3.51 and *CIL* 11.3254 (*Colonia Coniunc(ta) Iulia Sutrina*). The exact date of this second colony is uncertain: see Keppie, *Colonisation,* 170; Harris, *Rome in Etruria and Umbria,* 310. The only source, Appian, says that Agrippa occupied Sutrium because it was or could be useful to Lucius Antonius. Keppie and Harris agree that the passage from Appian is not decisive proof that Antony founded a colony there for his soldiers.

53. For details about Sutrium, see Duncan, "Sutri," 66–69 (history), 92–95 (growth of settlement in the countryside). See also Potter, *Changing Landscape,* 93–96, 89–91; Salmon, *Roman Colonization,* 172 n. 53; Harris, *Rome in Etruria and Umbria,* 43–44; Brunt, *Italian Manpower,* 352–53; Carandini, *Romanizzazione dell'Etruria,* 38; Torelli, *Etruria,* 47; Keppie, *Colonisation,* 169–70. On continuity in land use before and after late republican colonization, see Campbell, "Shaping the Rural Environment," 94.

the water which they had used for a number of years from a spring on the farm at Sutrium because the spring had dried up, and that afterward, the water began to flow from this spring. They petitioned me to restore the right to them because they had not lost their right out of disuse or their own fault, but because they could not channel the water. Since their petition did not seem unfair to me, I thought that they should be helped. And so I decided that the right that they used to have at that time when the water first was not able to flow to them should be restored to them."

[*et Atilicinus ait Caesarem Statilio Tauro rescripsisse in haec verba: "Hi, qui ex fundo Sutrino aquam ducere soliti sunt, adierunt me proposueruntque aquam, qua per aliquot annos usi sunt ex fonte, qui est in fundo Sutrino, ducere non potuisse, quod fons exaruisset, et postea ex eo fonte aquam fluere coepisse: petieruntque a me, ut quod ius non neglegentia aut culpa sua amiserant, sed quia ducere non poterant, his restitueretur. Quorum mihi postulatio cum non iniqua visa sit, succurrendum his putavi. Itaque quod ius habuerunt tunc, cum primum ea aqua pervenire ad eos non potuit, id eis restitui placet."*] (*D.* 8.3.35 Paul. 15 *ad Plaut.*)

The legal issues can be reconstructed from the emperor's response. Taurus seems to have claimed that his neighbors did not have a servitude and therefore that they had no right to channel water. In response, the neighbors tried to establish that they had a right based on long-standing practice. To gain protection for long-standing use, they had to show either that they had a legal right to the water or that they had used it for a long time in good faith—that is, not by force or fraud or in secret—and had believed that they had a right to do so.[54] The neighbors seem to have covered these points in their presentation, based on the report in the case. The emperor wrote that Taurus's neighbors were accustomed to channel water (*aquam ducere soliti sunt*), that they had used the spring on his land for a number of years (*per aliquot annos usi sunt ex fonte*), and finally that they had asked the emperor to restore their rights (*ut . . . ius . . . his restitueretur*). This was a good strategy, because servitudes could be created on the basis of long-standing practice, in the manner of customary law as previously discussed. The emperor ap-

54. On standards of proof for long-standing practice, see *D.* 8.5.10 pr. Ulp. 53 *ad Ed.* On the requirement that the plaintiff believe that he had a right to channel, see *D.* 8.6.22 Scaev. 1 *Reg.*; *D.* 8.6.25 Paul. 5 *Sent.* On these cases, see nn. 28, 29, 30, 31 in the present chapter.

proved of this logic and gave legal recognition to informal practice. He ruled that the right should be restored to Taurus' neighbors, even though they had lost it by non-use. As Biondi explains, the decision creates a new right in the guise of restoring the old one, which was based in customary practice. The decision fits with Augustus's public image of beneficence, fairness, and reverence for tradition. But it also may have led to a new legal principle that was adopted into subsequent rulings: a servitude lost by non-use should be restored if it was impossible to exercise the right during the prescribed period.[55]

In restoring the neighbors' right, the emperor rejected a strict application of the use-it-or-lose-it rule and introduced a slight modification. Since the neighbors failed to use their right, they should have lost it. The emperor redefines "use" to take into account both ethical and natural circumstances. The neighbors lost their right not "out of disuse or fault, but because they could not channel the water" (*ut quod ius non neglegentia aut culpa sua amiserant, sed quia ducere non poterant*). Augustus's rule may reflect contemporary notions about the natural world.

According to Pliny, springs and streams could be variable, stopping and starting again because of earthquakes (*NH* 31.53–54) or changes in farming; for example, tilling land could free up the water. A few famous springs were reputed to flow and cease on a regular schedule, daily or hourly (*NH* 2.228–29, 232). The same view of use is at play in the views of later jurists, where changes in the natural environment make it impossible to exercise a servitude. In a case about a flood that blocks a right-of-way, the issue is under what circumstance the holder loses the servitude through nonuse (*D.* 8.6.14 Iavol. 10 *ex Cassio*). The answer is not set out in the case, but it seems to be that if the flood washes away the land where the servitude passed, the

55. Biondi, *Categoria;* on Augustus's opinion in this case as the basis for a new rule, see 283–87. The new standard may be reflected in *D.* 39.3.26 Scaev. 4 *Resp.* Judging by later practice, Augustus's ruling influenced later law. Glick (*Irrigation and Society,* 13) observes, "According to a dictate of Roman law universally observed in eastern Spain, non-use did not void a right. (The principle of *rega o pert*—irrigate or lose—applied only to the irrigation turn, not to the underlying right.)" Though Glick does not refer to Roman law on this point. In contrast, Solazzi (*Specie ed estinzione,* 183–89) argues that the case did not set precedent and, moreover, that it did not concern a servitude or a lawsuit about private property but, rather, a grant of imperial water. For Solazzi, the case shows the emperor granting a favor to the petitioners from Sutrium, based on Solazzi's interpretation of *petierentque . . . his restitueretur* as language that does not describe legal proceedings, though he cites no parallels for the usage.

right is lost. Instead of setting out this answer, the case explains when the right is sustained, focusing on situations where there might be doubt. Two situations are considered. First, if the water recedes before the prescribed period of nonuse expires, the right is sustained. Second, if the water recedes after the period expires, the right is lost, but it must be reinstated if the owner desires. This second situation is analogous to the Taurus lawsuit—as the case says, *quod ius habuerunt tunc . . . id eis restitui placet.*[56] Human practices and natural circumstances are interrelated in these rulings as they are in other cases concerning the use-it-or-lose-it rule. As discussed in chapter 2, for example, the use of daily or summer water was defined in terms of human practices with reference to the natural phenomena but not limited by them. In all these cases, the legal right seems to be more constant than the natural environment that it delimits.

Taurus and his neighbors were working within real constraints imposed by the physical landscape: the relative location of their properties and the spring. A general picture of this landscape can be assembled on the basis of archaeological surveys done by the British School. In addition, the surveys also provide information about how landowners used technology to exploit the local water supply. Sutrium's territory is typical of southern Etruria, where hills create valley catchment basins around numerous streams, which could provide water to farmsteads on the hillsides and in the valleys. Settlement patterns were shaped by this topography in the archaic period and, to a large extent, in the Roman period.[57] Both villas and farmsteads are located not just along roads but also near streams. The Etruscans managed these streams with *cuniculi,* or rock-hewn channels through the tufa. *Cuniculi* could be used equally for drainage or water supply as the need arose, and they

56. Cf. *D.* 43.20.3.2 Pompon. 34 *ad Sab.* (*haustus* from public river that changes its banks) and *D.* 8.3.20.1 Pompon. 33 *ad Sab.* (quoted earlier in the present chapter), the rule on damage to the servient estate, which also recognizes natural causes as a kind of *vis maior:* the holder of the servitude is liable for all damage except what is caused naturally, for example, flooding. For more examples and discussion of the development of the legal approaches to loss by nonuse, see Solazzi, *Specie ed estinzione,* 170–79.

57. For the topography and settlement of the countryside, see Duncan, "Sutri," 77, 92–94. On continuity between archaic and Roman periods, see Rendeli, *Città aperte,* 122–25; see also maps on pp. 96, 123, 178, 206, 254, 352. For northern Etruria, there is no overall analysis like Rendeli's, but similar patterns of continuity between pre-Roman and Roman settlement sites are noted by, for example, Fentriss ("Saturnia," 79) and Dyson ("*Ager Cosanus* and the Albegna Valley," 269–71).

sometimes served both functions at once.[58] Throughout Sutrium's territory, large and small sites cluster in the valleys and on the lower slopes along streams, where water was readily accessible. Several farms were located along each stream, positioned to share its water. The settlement pattern is comparable at Narce, just to the north of Sutrium. Despite the steep hillsides, settlers were drawn to the area by abundant natural resources, including a perennial water supply: all valleys carry substantial streams that flow strongly throughout the year; thus even during the hot, dry summer, there was a constant supply of water, as T. W. Potter describes it.[59] Although water was plentiful, the density of settlement in most parts of southern Etruria probably led some residents to share a water supply, as did Taurus and his neighbors.

Most of Sutrium's territory was occupied by small to moderate-sized farmhouses, though there are three larger villas in the region. Duncan's survey reports, "The majority of buildings seem to have been farmhouses of varying sizes, but most of them not very large. Judging from the density of sites, each farm would have been a comparatively small unit and the countryside would have been divided up among a series of such individual holdings. There are only two of the larger sites that could have been centers of estates of any size, namely the villas at 'San Giovanni a pollo' and at Casale Castellaccio."[60] To the larger sites, the villa at Prati San Martino should now also be added.[61] The smaller farms could have been operated by owners, tenants, or slaves of the landowner. In Roman Italy, elite property holdings were often fragmented, that is, a collection of smaller parcels in various locations, a good strategy for reducing risk. But wherever adjacent farms were owned by different people, there is a good chance that they had to negotiate the water supply.[62] In Sutrium's territory, there is archaeological evidence

---

58. Bizzarri ("Bonifica idraulica") classifies two types of *cuniculi,* for supply and for drainage, with examples from near Orvieto. For a system of *cuniculi* draining the hills and serving a fountain at Portonaccio, see Stefani, "Veio," 88–92. See also n. 23 in chapter 1 in the present study.

59. Potter, *Falsican Town,* 3–5.

60. Duncan, "Sutri," 96–97.

61. On the villa at Prati San Martino, see Gilkes, Martin, and Matheus, "Prati San Martino, Sutri," 371–80.

62. On landholding patterns, see Erdkamp, *Grain Market,* 18–22; Kehoe, *Investment, Profit, and Tenancy,* 3–4, with literature cited there. The younger Pliny is a good example of elite landholding patterns; see De Neeve, "Roman Landowner."

that residents built hydraulic facilities that would improve the water supply and could also facilitate sharing. Duncan's survey reports hydraulic technology at about thirty-five residential (or possibly residential) sites: cisterns, *cuniculi* and channels, a fountain or two, or some patches of *opus signinum* (waterproof paving suggestive of a cistern or channel but also used in pressrooms).[63] Wells were either not found or not recorded, perhaps because the groundwater was too deep on the hills where most of the sites are located. Though hydraulic facilities appear at only 18 percent of these residential sites, the evidence may underreport actual practices, especially for the smaller sites where the most likely "facility" was a dirt channel that could disappear without a trace.

Two sets of sites with hydraulic installations illustrate technological solutions to the uneven access to water. First, a pair of farmhouses on a spur north of Sutrium on the Via Ciminia may have shared the aqueduct that was built on the hillside and fed a fountain or trough for watering animals.[64] There are also a couple of smaller sites nearby that may have relied on this aqueduct, if not to channel water, then to draw water from its fountain. A second pair of sites, smaller farmhouses, are also located to share a local water system. There is a cistern on each site, and the cisterns seem to be connected by a *cuniculus;* another *cuniculus* leads from one of these cisterns into a cave, where it may have tapped a spring. Most, though not all, of the evidence for hydraulic installations was found on sites described as "large" or "villa." It is tempting to identify the disputed channel in Taurus's lawsuit with a private aqueduct running to the villa at Prati San Martino or to imagine his villa as one of the large farmhouses on a high spur above a smaller site with a *cuniculus* tapping a spring.[65] Although it is impossible to identify any archaeological site as the properties of Taurus or his neighbors, the uneven distribution of water resources and hydraulic technology allow us to understand what was at stake in their lawsuit. While the larger farms were well equipped to secure their own water supply, many of the smaller sites did not even have a cistern to hold rain water and would have had to rely on

63. My count of hydraulic facilities is based on descriptions in the list of sites in Duncan, "Sutri."

64. See Duncan, "Sutri," 97–98, for the pair of villas (689871, 692872), the aqueduct on the hillside (694873), and the smaller sites with cistern and *cuniculus* (728861, 729860).

65. See Duncan, "Sutri," 99, for the villa on a spur (site 674796) and the smaller site with *cuniculus* (site 673796). For the aqueduct running to the villa at Prati San Martino, see Gilkes, Martin, and Matheus, "Prati San Martino, Sutri," 372.

springs, streams, and small rivers and on cooperation with their neighbors. Such was the situation for Taurus's neighbors. The spring was located on Taurus's property, and this physical reality led to the dispute, though other factors might also have been at play.

Legal and social circumstances contributed to the disagreement between Taurus and his neighbors. Because of his rights as owner, Taurus had the advantage of controlling the spring. He had also some social advantage based on his prominent political position and connections with the emperor, who addressed the rescript to Taurus, even though his neighbors brought the petition (*Caesarem Statilio Tauro rescripsisse . . . Hi . . . adierunt me proposueruntque aquam*). But the neighbors may have had a different kind of social advantage, based on their claim of long-standing use. Taurus was probably a newcomer: his family was from Lucania, as Syme argued, and it seems probable that he acquired the property in the aftermath of the occupation of Sutrium during the Perusine War.[66] When Taurus took possession of the property, his neighbors were not using the spring, because it was dry. New to the neighborhood, Taurus may have been unfamiliar with local practice, including his neighbors' long-standing use of the spring. As Shaw notes in his discussion of the irrigation community in Roman North Africa, the arrival of outsiders could easily contribute to disputes about water.[67] Similarly, a servitude could create resentment because it remained in force even after a property was sold.[68] This seems to be exactly what happened when the water bubbled up in the spring again and Taurus's neighbors began to use it. The neighbors sought legal protection for their access to the spring when neighborly cooperation failed. The case and the emperor's decision both show how deeply embedded in local practice the law was, recognizing informal cooperation, shoring up traditional practices in the face of changes in the neighborhood; new residents, who were not originally involved, are compelled to respect and participate in long-standing relationships. The outcome of the case may be surprising, though, given the relative social clout of the two parties.

Assessing the power dynamics of the case involves the characteristic

66. On the origins of the Statilii Tauri in Lucania, see Syme, *Roman Revolution*, 237; cf. *Augustan Aristocracy*, 44. For Taurus's social and political clout, see Syme, *Augustan Aristocracy*, 211, 387, 393.

67. Shaw, "Lamasba," 69.

68. For this observation, without discussion of sources, see Ellis, "Pooling Resources," 149. For the treatment of servitudes when land was sold, see chapter 4 in the present study.

asymmetry of servitudes. The emperor ruled in favor of Statilius Taurus's neighbors and against a prominent and well-connected defendant. The Statilius Taurus in this case is usually identified as the prominent general of the Augustan era.[69] We know that his neighbors were Roman citizens, simply because they had access to Roman law.[70] They may have been local elites or Roman settlers of an earlier generation, as rich as Taurus, or small-scale landholders. What might seem remarkable here is that these nameless citizens both brought a legal suit to the emperor and won. They may have approached the emperor because of Taurus's prominence, expecting that only a high authority would be reliable when the difference in status between parties was great. A prominent man like Taurus might be expected to use the law to negotiate favorable terms for himself or, more likely, to take advantage of his neighbors. By comparison with the inscriptions discussed in the previous chapter, Taurus does not seem to have chosen the most effective legal strategy. In most of the inscriptions relating to private water supplies, the landowner asserted ownership of the source of water. In Taurus's case, ownership of the spring was to no avail against his neighbor's claim of a servitude. Instead, it appears that the law offered real empowerment, even to anonymous citizens, and the terms of a servitude make this legal equity even more surprising.[71]

Servitudes construct asymmetrical rights, apparently empowering one party at the other's expense. A servitude granted a right to one party in exchange for nothing; that is, the holder of the servitude had a right to channel water and had no obligation to do or give anything to his neighbor in return. Usually, however, other considerations—social or economic exchange, for example (something outside the legal system)—compensated for the one-way advantage of a servitude. Unequal allocations of resources and social power are described by Varro, when he writes about the villa owner and his neighbors. The owner of a villa might find seasonal or occasional workers among his neighbors.

---

69. For the identification, see above p. 126 at n. 51.

70. Most landowners in southern Etruria probably had citizenship by the late republic: citizenship was granted to the entire population of Veii in 384 and at the nearby towns of Capena and Faliscii one year earlier (Livy 6.4.4, with *CAH* 7.7.312–13).

71. For a similar conclusion about the advantages of the legal system for smaller farmers, see Kehoe, *Law and the Rural Economy,* 45. Compare the expectation that "hydraulic technology served the interests of a recognizably powerful section of society, concerned with lucrative redistribution rather than prudence" (Horden and Purcell, *Corrupting Sea,* 242).

> Therefore farmers in this situation have neighbors on yearly contracts—doctors, fullers, craftsmen—rather than having their own in the villa; [for] sometimes the death of one artisan takes away the revenue of the farm.
>
> [*itaque in hoc genus coloni potius anniversarios habent vicinos, quibus imperent—medicos, fullones, fabros—quam in villa suos habeant, quorum non numquam unius artificis mors tollit fundi fructum.*] (Varro, *RR* 1.16.4)

Some of these may have been free persons and landowners themselves, while others could have been slaves on large estates. In any case, the relationship was expected to be regular (*anniversarios*) and unequal (*imperent*), the same terms on which servitudes were exercised. Villa owners were accustomed to exploiting local labor, and they may have expected to monopolize natural resources as well. The broad rights associated with servitudes seem to reflect this sense of entitlement. Similarly, their normative stability, typical in a conservative society, may yet reflect the outlook of elite landowners, who probably had the most to lose when customary practices were abandoned. Varro clearly indicates the importance of these relationships to the economic well-being of the farm.[72] In the Taurus lawsuit, however, law reinforced local custom, and the less powerful neighbor secured access to the water supply. Even assuming that he extorted something from his neighbors in exchange for recognizing their legal right to the water, the case shows the power of the legal arrangement.[73] These unpretentious residents of Sutrium used the law to protect their right to water. The emperor's decision thus enforced the asymmetry of the servitude to improve the resources available to even a weaker neighbor by imposing on Taurus a duty to share water.

The legal success of Taurus's neighbors can be put in perspective by comparison with the situation described in the long inscription from

72. On this passage as evidence of the connection between informal neighborliness and economic relationships, see Palma, *Iura vicinitatis*, 34–35.

73. Similarly, the local administration of irrigation canals in medieval Spain provided protection for the less powerful landowners. Glick (*Irrigation and Society*, 44) explains, "Decentralization of authority among the autonomous communities virtually prevented any meddling by town officials whether they were water users or not. Indeed, there is no evidence that any such meddling took place during the medieval centuries. Within the communities a powerful individual might seek to thwart the will of the commons or cequier [official in charge of a canal], but the success of such a maneuver depended purely on the resources of the individual and could have no institutional support."

Viterbo, in northern Etruria, describing the private aqueduct owned by Mummius Niger Valerius Vegetus in the late first century AD.[74] Vegetus purchased the spring as well as the land on which his channel was constructed. This arrangement represents an alternative to servitudes: a servitude granted the right to use the water, whereas Vegetus acquired legal title to the spring and the land under his aqueduct and the paths giving access to it, presumably for repairs.[75] Vegetus effectively secured a monopoly on the water by buying the land on which the spring rose. Setting up the inscription no doubt helped to enforce his monopoly, a reminder of his rights as owner and his legal power to enforce those rights. Some holders of servitudes used inscriptions in a similar way, to make a public record of their rights, though their position, like that of Taurus, involved more negotiation.[76] Taurus had to share water with his neighbors—they had a servitude to draw water from a spring on his land and to channel it over his property to theirs. Moreover, he was in the less powerful position in legal terms; because Taurus owned the servient estate, he had to allow his neighbors to exercise their right to water unmolested, and the emperor backed up his neighbors. It is fanciful to imagine that Vegetus knew Roman law well enough to know of Taurus's lawsuit and chose to buy the land rather than risk litigation over a servitude, even though he would have been in the more powerful legal position if he had held the servitude. It may be less fanciful to imagine that Vegetus's neighbors knew Roman law well enough to understand that selling the spring would cut off their access to a local water supply. But they may not have needed it, or they may have negotiated a servitude or made some "off the books" deal with Vegetus to use the water. It does not seem likely that Vegetus would agree to a servitude, but an "off the books" deal would serve his interests by increasing his social clout: his neighbors would depend on his goodwill for use of the water, but they, unlike Taurus's neighbors, would have no legal recourse if he reneged.

As in the Taurus lawsuit, there is some uncertainty about the social status of Vegetus's neighbors (even though they are named in the inscription), because there is a mix of Roman and Etruscan names. Like Taurus, Vegetus

74. For the full text of the Vegetus inscription and for further discussion, see chapter 1.

75. The same alternatives were available to individuals who provided a water supply to a municipality, as recorded in inscriptions discussed in chapter 1. See also Capogrossi Colognesi, *Servitù d'acqua*, 88–96.

76. On these inscriptions, see chapter 1.

probably had political connections; he was suffect consul in AD 92. Nothing in the inscription reveals his neighbors' attitude: were they compliant or compelled? Vegetus may have had to contend with the kind of violent opposition suggested in a legal case about wrongful loss, where neighbors demolish an aqueduct (*D.* 9.2.27.31–32 Ulp. 18 *ad Ed.*). Local opposition may have motivated his decision to purchase the land and to memorialize his ownership. In any case, the inscription does describe the legal arrangements that Vegetus made to secure his water supply, and these legal issues lead to a more subtle appreciation of the social context surrounding rural water use.

In the Vegetus inscription and the Taurus lawsuit, the legal analysis allows us to view the social dynamics from the outside looking in, to draw inferences based on the legal powers associated with servitudes and the relative social status of the parties. An inside view is presented in one of Cicero's letters, where he writes about a neighbor and a servitude on his property at Tusculum, revealing the expectations that Taurus and other elite landowners might have brought to managing a shared water supply. Like many properties at Tusculum, Cicero's villa combined luxurious living quarters with for-profit farming—albeit on a small scale, in a garden. Cicero bought his villa at Tusculum from one Vettius, probably shortly before 68 BC.[77] References to the water supply at Tusculum occur throughout his writings from 63 to 44 BC, suggesting that the issue was an ongoing concern.[78] With the exception of a letter to his brother that concerns Quintus's property, it is likely, but not certain, that all his references to water channels involve his property at Tusculum. Two passages in his speeches also refer to the water supply on his Tusculan property. Cicero mentions paying for water from the Crabra, a local stream known from other sources to have supplied the residents of Tusculum (*Agr.* 3.9; cf. Front. *Aq.* 9.4–5: both sources are discussed in chapter 1). He also refers to his own water channel at Tusculum, *de aqua nostra Tusculana,*

77. Cicero's letters from 68 BC show him furnishing the villa at Tusculum (*Att.* 1.4.3, 1.5.7, 1.6.2). Though Cicero put the property on the market in 57, after his return from exile (*Att.* 4.2.7), he did not find a buyer (*Q.Fr.* 2.2.1). He seems to have kept the same property, even though rebuilding was more expensive than buying a new place (see Shackleton Bailey, *Letters to Atticus,* 2:137). He tried to buy a villa at Lanuvium from Phamea, who refused his offer (*Att.* 9.9.4–5, with Shackleton Bailey, *Letters to Atticus,* 4:376–77).

78. Six of Cicero's letters discuss the water supply on his and his brother's properties. On the water supply of Quintus's property, see Cic. *Q.Fr.* 3.1.3. On the water supply of Cicero's own properties, see Cic. *Att.* 5.12.3, 5.13.3, 13.6.1, 15.26.4; *Fam.* 16.18.2–3. For the list of these citations, see Shackleton Bailey, *Letters to Atticus,* 6:274 (on Cic. *Att.* 15.26.4).

where it is a potential topic of inquiry for legal experts in water law, suggesting a servitude or perhaps the Crabra distribution system (*Balb.* 45). Only one letter explicitly locates the water channel on his property at Tusculum (*Fam.* 16.18.2–3).[79] Another letter, which discusses a water servitude, implies that the water supply was located at Tusculum, because the letter was sent to Atticus while he was there, asking him to discuss it with a neighbor (*Att.* 15.26).[80] Because Cicero never connects "his water channel" with any other location, it is likely that his letters about the water supply all concern the Tusculan estate. The fact that he had a profitable irrigated garden there supports this interpretation.[81] In any case, his letters show how a landowner managed social relations around a local water supply.

In several letters, Cicero asked Atticus to help with the water supply, a topic in which the latter took some interest.[82] While Cicero was serving as proconsul in the east in 51 BC, he wrote twice to ask Atticus to keep an eye on a certain Philippus who was involved in the water supply.

> If anything can be done about the water channel, keep the spirit that you usually have about water, which I consider most important naturally myself and because of your discussions [about water]. So, please take care of it. And, in addition, if Philippus should ask for anything, please take care of it as you would for your own property.
>
> [*de aqua si quid poterit fieri, eo sis animo quo soles esse de aqua; quam ego cum mea sponte tum tuis sermonibus aestimo plurimi. ergo tu id conficies. praeterea si quid Philippus rogav<er>it, quod in tua re faceres, id velim facias.*] (*Att.* 5.12.3)

> Please take care of the water, and, if Philippus does anything, keep an eye on him.
>
> [*de aqua sit curae; et si quid Philippus aget animadvertes.*] (*Att.* 5.13.3)

79. Shackleton Bailey (*Letters to Atticus*, 5:358, on Cic. *Att.* 13.6.1) offers a more agnostic view: "Cf. 105 (v.12).3. Perhaps this is the same water, and perhaps it is the Aqua Crabra, which supplied the *Tusculanum* (*Leg. Agr.* 3.9; *Balb.* 45); or perhaps not."

80. Cf. Cic. *Att.* 15.14.1, with Shackleton Bailey, *Letters to Atticus*, 6:272. Letters 402 (15.14), 403 (15.25), and 404 (15.26) were written between 28 June and 2 July 44 BC, while Atticus was at Tusculum and Cicero at Arpinum, according to Shackleton Bailey's dating.

81. On the irrigated garden on Cicero's property at Tusculum, see Cic. *Fam.* 16.18.2–3, discussed in chapter 3 in the present study.

82. Shackleton Bailey observes, "Atticus may have been fond of holding forth about the importance of a good water supply (n.b. *tuis sermonibus*)" (*Letters to Atticus*, 3:121, on Cic. *Att.* 5.12.3, with reference to *Att.* 5.13.3 [from Ephesus, July 51 BC] and 13.6.1 [from Tusculum, June 45]).

In these letters, Cicero may have been concerned with construction or repair to the channel, if Philippus was his contractor or the slave who managed his garden.[83] Alternatively, Philippus could be a neighbor who shared the water supply, and Cicero could be asking Atticus to supervise the servitude, making sure that Philippus did not use more than his share of the water. A later letter indicates that Cicero did have some trouble because of this servitude. In the later letter (quoted shortly), the neighbor who shared the water supply at Tusculum was identified as Aelius, not Philippus. Since the property could have changed hands in the intervening years, it is possible that both letters concern a servitude owed to his Tusculan estate. This later letter also offers insight into the social tensions that shaped the asymmetrical relationship of a servitude.

In 44 BC, Cicero's neighbor Aelius had raised concerns about the water supply, working through Atticus as a mediator. The property in question is probably at Tusculum, because Atticus was in Rome and Cicero had just left Tusculum for Arpinum. Apparently, there were pipes or an underground channel along the land line that were connected with a servitude to channel water.[84] Based on the letter, Cicero owned the dominant estate, Aelius the servient; in other words, Aelius's property could provide water to Cicero's. In his letter to Atticus, Cicero asked him to reassure Aelius that he had no interest in exercising the servitude.

> Please release Marcus Aelius from worry. [Say that] I had thought that there were a few channels on the edge of the property, underground ones at that, which could have some kind of servitude; and that now I do not want [the servitude] and that it is of no great importance to me. But when you speak for me, do so as gently as possible, more so that he will be freed from care than that he will suspect that I am angry about something.
>
> [*M. Aelium cura liberabis; me paucos specus in extremo fundo et eos quidem subterraneos servitutis putasse aliquid habituros; id me iam[iam] nolle neque mihi <quic>quam esse tanti. sed ut mihi dicebas, quam lenissime, potius ut cura liberetur quam ut me suscensere aliquid suspicetur.*] (*Att.* 15.26.4)

---

83. Shackleton Bailey (*Letters to Atticus,* 3:212) suggests that Philippus was a slave manager (*vilicus*) and reports Watts's opinion that Philippus was a contractor.

84. Or there may have been a less formal, nonlegal type of arrangement: see Biondi, *Categoria,* 670; Capogrossi Colognesi, *Struttura della proprietà,* 482–83.

The question about the servitude was focused on a few underground channels that apparently brought or could bring water to Cicero's land. Perhaps Aelius wanted to open them up to gain access to the water for his own property, as some of the parties to the disputes about repairs may have done. There does not seem to have been any dispute in this case. Yet, as Cicero relinquished the servitude, he sent a complicated and somewhat contradictory message about his relationship with Aelius. On the one hand, he seemed to want to keep his distance, both by removing himself from a water-sharing arrangement and by sending Atticus as intermediary. Atticus's involvement may have arisen purely from circumstance—the letter was written from Arpinum—or may have been a typical favor. In addition, his concern for Aelius's feelings—that he be freed from care, with no suspicion of anger—seems paternalistic, as if Cicero felt somehow responsible for his neighbor's well-being. On the other hand, Cicero struck an apologetic tone. Though he was doing Aelius a favor by declining the servitude—leaving him a monopoly on the water—Cicero seems to be on the defensive: "I had thought that there were a few channels on the edge of the property, underground ones at that, which could have some kind of servitude" [*me paucos specus in extremo fundo et eos quidem subterraneos servitutis putasse aliquid habituros*]. The past unreal condition (represented by the perfect infinitive in indirect statement) is almost an apology for presuming that there were channels and that they implied a right to water. But even this apology presents a mixed message. Cicero's description of the channels emphasizes his familiarity with the property and its improvements as well as the legal rights attaching to it. At least ten years earlier, Cicero had consulted legal experts about his water supply at Tusculum. In the *pro Balbo,* from 56 BC, he names the jurists he consulted about his aqueduct: "if we consulted Marcus Tugio and Gaius Aquilius about our aqueduct at Tusculum" [*si nos de aqua nostra Tusculana M. Tugionem potius quam C. Aquilium consulebamus*] (*Balb.* 45). Because Cicero mentions Aquilius, a well-known expert in private law, the water in question is more likely to be the servitude than Cicero's allocation from the Crabra system.[85] Even before the episode with Aelius in 44, Cicero made sure of the legal situation surrounding this water supply. Then, when it came to dealing with Aelius, Cicero could gracefully demur, as he expressed his mastery over

85. See Reid, *M. T. Ciceronis L. Cornelio Balbo Oratio,* 85; Reid assumes that Tugio was an expert in servitudes for channeling water, though he is otherwise unknown.

property and law. He may have also had sufficient control over the water supply through the local distribution system of the Crabra.[86]

Cicero's apologetic tone and sensitivity could be explained in personal terms. Aelius may have been irascible or simply the kind of neighbor who was not good at sharing resources—reason enough not to depend on a servitude. More generally, careful negotiation of his relationship with Aelius reflects the tensions that could arise around a water supply shared by neighbors of different social status, uneasily exchanging resources for other benefits. Cicero's neighbor Aelius is not known to have been a senator, so there was some social distance between them. The situation was typical of Tusculum, where the senatorial elite owned villas side by side with equestrians and even freedmen who could afford the price.[87] These neighbors likely shared a water supply, based on both the archaeological evidence for the region and the inscription recording a water-sharing arrangement (*CIL* 6.1261). The names of participants in the water sharing would corroborate a pattern of neighbors of mixed status, if the inscription is rightly ascribed to Tusculum.[88] The sequence of owners of Cicero's property is itself indicative of the mixed society of Tusculum, as Cicero notes in reference to Balbus's villa there (*Balb.* 56).[89] The Alban Hills were desirable real estate, so expensive that only the wealthy could have bought estates there. Nevertheless, the community was not entirely homogenous—all were well-to-do, but not all were from the senatorial class. Some senators, at least, cared about these distinctions, and Cicero seems to be one of them, judging by his dealings with Aelius. Similar tensions between neighbors of different social classes are involved in an anecdote about the old days (*exemplum antiquitatis*) reported by Pliny (*NH* 18.41–43). The freedman Gaius Furius Chresimus was accused of bewitching his neighbor's crops—his neighbors could not explain the success of his farm in any other way. Chresimus defended himself by explain-

86. Cic. *Agr.* 3.9; cf. *Fam.* 16.18.2–3. Distribution of the Crabra is described by Frontinus (*Aq.* 9.4–7); see also chapter 1 in the present study.

87. Compare Cicero's account (*Leg.* 3.30–31) of Lucullus's competition with his neighbors, a freedman and a knight.

88. Different statuses are represented by the landowners named in *CIL* 6.1261: C. Julius Caesar; Caius Bicoleius Rufus; Thrysus, freedman of Augustus; and Gaius Julius Hymetus Aufidanus. On *CIL* 6.1261 and Tusculum (Mommsen, "Romische Urkunden," 307).

89. Before Cicero bought it, the property had been owned by Q. Lutatius Catulus (cos. 102) (and perhaps also his son [cos. 78]), by Sulla, by one Vettius, and then by Cicero (Pliny, *NH* 22.12; Cic. *Att.* 4.5.2, with Shackleton Bailey, *Letters to Atticus,* 2:185–86).

ing that his tools and hard work were his charms, and this appeal to the values of the idealized citizen-farmer won his acquittal. The hostility toward Chresimus reflects a typical elite view of the small-scale landholder, according to Gabba's reading, and it accords well with Cicero's awkwardness about dealing with Aelius.[90] His approach recalls the careful balancing between interests of the servient and dominant estates in the legal cases.[91] Cicero wants to preserve between himself and Aelius a certain distance that would have to be bridged on a regular basis if they were involved in a servitude. Cicero would cede something by way of social privilege through this contact, in exchange for exercising his right to channel water from Aelius's property. His letters suggest that he is uncomfortable with his relationship with Aelius, yet his behavior is proof that neighborly cooperation was key to making a servitude work.

CONCLUSION

The lawsuit involving Statilius Taurus and his neighbors is a test case for the interaction between local practice and legal norms. The emperor's decision in favor of Taurus's neighbors gave legal status to long-standing use of the spring and probably set a new legal standard for servitudes arising from long use. Servitudes provided Taurus's neighbors with a powerful tool that enabled them to maintain control of their water supply and possibly to resist the influence of their well-connected neighbor. Cicero's letter about Aelius offers an inside view of the social awkwardness that might interfere with the management of a local water supply. But these social relationships were critical to the success of servitudes. Indeed, many legal cases show how servitudes were embedded in social networks, both the one-on-one relationship

90. On Chresimus, see Gabba, *Strutture agrarie,* 119. The Chresimus story dates to the second century BC, see Forsythe, *Calpurnius Piso,* 376–79. Compare the jealousy of Sthenelus's success in renovating Remmius Palaemon's vineyard, discussed in chapter 3 in the present study.

91. In his letter to Atticus about Aelius (*Att.* 15.26), Cicero seems to be living up to the ideals that he advances in his theoretical discussion of generosity in *de Officiis,* where, he argues, taking less than you are entitled to is not just generous but often profitable (*Off.* 2.64). This maxim holds good in all types of legal dealings and with neighbors, and it is consistent with the fiscal responsibilities of the paterfamilias. Though this advice has precedents in Greek philosophy, Cicero sets it in the context of Roman social and legal relationships, generating a context that fits the patterns associated with neighbors and rural servitudes. On Cic. *Off.* 2.64, see Dyck, *Commentary on Cicero, "De Officiis,"* 452–53; Palma, *Iura vicinitatis,* 42–43.

between the owners of the servient and dominant estates and also the larger community.

The community's role in supporting local water systems derives from traditional Roman ideas about the relationship between neighbors and agricultural productivity. This emphasis on social negotiation also coheres with modern approaches to managing resources, as notably argued by Feeny in his review of the development of commons theory.

> Societies have the capacity to construct and enforce rules and norms that constrain the behavior of individuals. In many societies and in many situations, the capacity for concerted social action overcomes the divergence between individual and collective rationality. . . . A diversity of societies in the past and present have independently devised, maintained, or adapted communal arrangements to manage common-property resources. Their persistence is not historical accident; these arrangements build on knowledge of the resource and cultural norms that have evolved and been tested over time.[92]

Small groups have the knowledge and shared values to enforce water-sharing systems, in contrast to government regulation, which often fails because it does not account for local practices and traditions. Private law, however, and legal solutions crafted by the community can bolster normative behavior, as the rules on servitudes did for Romans who shared a local water supply.

In late republican Italy, neighbors observed traditional expectations about sharing resources, even as they used Roman law to articulate these values. It may be that servitudes institutionalized informal practices, as is commonly argued in studies of irrigation. Glick, for example, explains that the water supply uses "institutional patterns of a local nature which exist wherever irrigation agriculture is practiced and which are ecologically, more than culturally, derived."[93] The use of the same technology also tends to create continuity over time. With regard to the social contexts of this chapter, it is not possible to draw any firm conclusions about continuity or the evolution of servitudes from informal practices, because there is not enough evidence

92. Feeny et al., "Tragedy of the Commons," 87.

93. Glick, *Irrigation and Society*, 187; cf. 2–3, 149–74, for continuity in Spain from the Islamic to the medieval period and up to nineteenth-century Spain. For a more theoretical and cross-cultural view of the relationship between social practice and formalized institutions for water sharing, see Hunt and Hunt, "Canal Irrigation," 392–96.

for the early Roman period. Nevertheless, in the historical period, the legal sources assume patterns of social cooperation that are consistent with traditional Roman ideas about neighborliness. These practices continue to operate and are reflected when the legal cases report the "etiquette" of servitudes, that is, how to manage a local water supply with minimal dispute. In these legal cases, social factors are balanced against the legal rights of property ownership. The law accommodated and relied on social norms for enforcement, even as it protected the rights of individual landowners to use water and their own land as they saw fit. Neighbors shared many interests and risks, and these multiple ties motivated them to share water, even if it meant sustaining a sometimes unequal relationship of the sort represented by a servitude. At times, as in the Taurus lawsuit, even a less powerful neighbor might effectively work through the legal system to secure his water rights. In the remaining chapters, the focus shifts to these more individual interests and their relationship to the environmental and economic factors that shaped private water rights.

THREE

UTILITY, PRODUCTIVITY, AND PLANNING

A servitude could be established only if it was useful to the dominant estate but there were questions about what was "useful." The jurists developed the concept of *utilitas* or utility to define what useful meant in cases involving servitudes. In a short legal case reported in the *Digest of Justinian,* Paul lists negative examples that limit the scope of the so-called rustic servitudes, that is, servitudes attached to rural rather than urban property.

> A servitude cannot be imposed for us to pick an apple or go for a stroll or dine on someone else's [property].
>
> *[Ut pomum decerpere liceat et ut spatiari et ut cenare in alieno possimus, servitus imponi non potest.]* (*D.* 8.1.8 pr. Paul. 15 *ad Plaut.*)

Picking apples might be farmwork, but picking just one is clearly not—this is the force of the specific, singular fruit, *pomum.* Similarly, dining and strolling do not directly contribute to working the land. These somewhat fanciful examples highlight, by contrast, the essential connection between rustic servitudes and agricultural productivity: what can be referred to as utility, or *utilitas.* The Latin noun *utilitas* is not used consistently when the jurists write about servitudes; instead they use a variety of expressions, including the adjectives *utilis* (useful) and *commodum* (advantage) and the phrases *opus est* (there is need of) and *interest* (it is useful/advantageous). The term *utilitas* efficiently sums up these ideas and is regularly used in modern legal scholarship on servitudes.

A servitude could exist if it provided something useful to the dominant estate, that is, if it offered *utilitas.* In legal discussions, *utilitas* functioned as an objective standard that limited the scope of servitudes, but the standard was open to interpretation.[1] What was "utility" for the farm? Was it strictly self-sufficiency? Or could it include crops grown for the market? The first section of this chapter addresses the relationship between servitudes and these two goals, as expressed in the concept of *utilitas.* Central to the investigation is the analysis of a long legal case that contrasts servitudes with usufruct (another legal mechanism for having a right in someone else's property). The jurists attempt to distinguish these institutions on the basis of their connection with self-sufficiency and market aims, respectively, but a broader examination of cases involving utility and the purpose of rustic servitudes yields a more nuanced picture of the institution and of the ways that Romans actually used servitudes on their land. As the analysis proceeds, it becomes apparent that these two goals—self-sufficiency and market participation—continue to be entwined in legal approaches to servitudes and private water rights, which is not surprising, since literary sources reveal the same ambiguities.

In the second part of this chapter, the discussion of utility is oriented toward commercial farming, as we consider how landowners adapted servitudes to support specific kinds of cultivation on their property; a case in point is the servitude for collecting vine props. A servitude could make it possible for a landowner to specialize in crops that could be sold on the market. It could provide not only needed resources but also a guarantee for the landowner's investment, because he could claim monetary damages if the servitude was interrupted. In the third section of this chapter, the focus shifts from the landowner's current needs to his future plans. When the jurists considered servitudes for the future, utility came to be broadly defined, open-ended, in a way that allowed landowners to plan ahead for capital investment and to calculate the best use of resources on their property. The jurists' approach is consonant with such modern approaches to utility as that adopted by Jongman in his study of the economy at Pompeii: "Economic behaviour is an aspect of all behavior (as long as there is scarcity), rather than a peculiar sphere of behavior (to the exclusion of other spheres of be-

1. On the case cited here, *D.* 8.1.8 pr. Paul. 15 *ad Plaut.*, see Biondi, *Categoria,* 379–82; Solazzi, *Specie ed estinzione,* 48. See also, in general, Grosso, *Servitù prediali,* 97–108; cf. 42–45.

haviour). We may distinguish economic behavior, but we cannot separate it. In modern theory, utility is a subjective concept. Profit or money are not valuable in themselves."[2]

This chapter takes a broader view of servitudes, examining cases about not only water rights but also several of the other rustic servitudes, where the jurists develop ideas about *utilitas* that are key to all the rustic servitudes. While servitudes for water use depend on the same central concept of *utilitas* as the other rustic servitudes, it is in the area of water rights that there was innovation—notably by the jurist Labeo—that allowed landowners to control resources not just in the present but in the future. These legal approaches are set against anecdotal evidence from the literary sources, documenting the economic concerns of Roman landowners. Cicero's letters in particular provide insight into the motives behind the investment in hydraulic infrastructure (e.g., a local aqueduct). Taken together, the literary and legal sources allow us to characterize the economic behavior of Roman landowners as rational, but not in the strict classical sense of maximizing access to resources. Instead, there is a range of approaches, compatible with commons principles (as we saw in chapter 2), from aggressive attempts to control the water supply to innovative legal opinions that allowed landowners to make calculated choices about the resources they needed for farming.

SELF-SUFFICIENCY AND MARKET INTERESTS

The legal concept of *utilitas,* or usefulness, refers to the purpose for which a servitude was created, and it was defined in terms of the needs of the estate: a servitude could exist only if it served the needs of the estate, which were generally understood to involve agricultural production. But as the number and types of servitudes increased, their connection to the land was sometimes attenuated, especially in the case of urban servitudes, most of which were not connected with farming. With regard to rustic servitudes, including the right to channel water, the cultivation of the land remained central to the concept of *utilitas.* What changed was the context of that cultivation, as landowners' practices evolved from self-sufficiency to a mix of market-oriented interests and traditional aims. This development is clearly etched in the legal cases that address a variety of issues including the comparison of usufruct and servitude, monetary compensation, and the purpose or use of a servitude.

2. Jongman, *Pompeii,* 43.

The lasting importance of farming in legal ideas about water servitudes emerges in the jurists' discussion of the interdict on daily and summer water.[3] The question arose, could someone use the interdict if he channeled water for any purpose other than agricultural? The answer was yes, which seems to separate *utilitas* from cultivation of the land and to define the needs of the estate more broadly. An analysis of the underlying rationale, however, affirms the traditional connection between farming and water channels. Two cases, one ascribed to the Augustan jurist Labeo and another to Pomponius from the late first century AD, demonstrate the lasting importance of this principle. In both cases, the jurists assume that irrigating farmland is the original purpose or use of a servitude for channeling water: they begin with irrigation and compare other possible uses. But both jurists also extend the interdict to cover all water channels serving various aims.

> It is asked whether only water used for irrigating fields is included in these interdicts or any water that serves our use and convenience. I apply the law in such a way that this [sc., convenience], too, is included, because this interdict has a place even if someone wants to channel water onto an urban property. (12) Moreover, Labeo writes, even if the channel does not belong to a farm, because they [*sic*] can be run anywhere, the interdict still applies to it.
>
> [*Illud quaeritur, utrum ea tantum aqua his interdictis contineatur, quae ad agrum irrigandum pertinet, an vero omnis, etiam ea, quae ad usum quoque et commodum nostrum. Et hoc iure utimur, ut haec quoque contineatur. propter quod etiam si in urbana praedia quis aquam ducere velit, hoc interdictum locum habere potest. (12) Praeterea Labeo scribit, etsi quidam ductus aquarum non sit fundi, quia quocumque duci possint, tamen ad hoc interdictum pertinere.*] (*D.* 43.20.1.11–12 Ulp. 70 *ad Ed.*, citing Labeo)

> We use this right so that water may be channeled not only for irrigation but also for the care of the herd or for amenity.
>
> [*Hoc iure utimur, ut etiam non ad irrigandum, sed pecoris causa vel amoenitatis aqua duci possit.*] (*D.* 43.20.3 pr. Pompon. 34 *ad Sab.*)

---

3. For more about the praetorian interdicts relating to servitudes, see the introduction and chapter 1 in the present study.

Though neither case uses the technical term *utilitas,* the jurists in both cases address the topic by example.[4] In the earlier case, Labeo considers irrigation against all other uses. Pomponius limits his argument to three allowable examples: irrigation, watering livestock, and charm or amenity (*amoenitas*). Pomponius's *amoenitas* seems removed from cultivation, evoking ornamental fountains, perhaps, in opposition to the livestock in his second example, *pecoris causa.* Indeed, Pomponius's collection of examples seems to recognize the fact that a channel could bring water both for ornamental fountains and for irrigation or livestock. His opinion is consonant with ideas familiar from literary sources. For example, Cicero praises hydraulic technology for its contribution to the productivity of the land: "why should I bring up irrigation, trenching, or plowing by which the land is made much more productive?" [*quid ego irrigationes, quid fossiones agri repastinationesque proferam, quibus fit multo terra fecundior?*] (*Sen.* 53). But productivity was often integrated with pleasure on rural property. For Varro, productivity was enhanced by careful and aesthetically pleasing plantings: "as to attention to appearance, what types are more attractive, I say that you should aim for the ones that are more productive" [*de formae cultura hoc dico, quae specie fiant venustiora, sequi ut maiore quoque fructu sint*] (*RR* 1.7.2).[5] Alternatively, "charm" might have been introduced as a type of *utilitas* connected strictly with urban properties where a water channel might serve no other practical purpose than domestic use. City property could, however, also be productive; many houses in and around Rome had kitchen gardens, some large enough to grow a surplus for the market.[6] Charm, then, did not necessarily exclude productivity, though it could suggest competition between ornamental and productive uses of water.

Competition for water shaped the development of the interdicts protecting water channels as well as the concept of *utilitas.* The concept of *utilitas,* or the "needs of the estate," was used to limit competition for water by defining a servitude to include some activities but not others, thereby enforcing excludability to ration a common resource by limiting access. Pomponius's mention of charm hints at such a broader debate, and Labeo's opinion in the earlier case also addresses these issues. In the earlier case, Labeo's

4. Biondi (*Categoria,* 367; cf. 635) sees in these cases a broader concept of utility implied by the multiplication of types of servitudes; that is, the new legal forms reflect the diversified aims of the landowner.

5. On the combination of pleasure and production in ideals for the villa, see at n. 23 in the introduction in the present study.

6. On gardens in the suburban areas near Rome, see chapter 1.

more abstract terms, *usus* (use) and *commodum* (convenience), acknowledge various possible uses of water without defining them. In other cases involving servitudes, these same terms are used to limit the rights created by servitudes—for example (as we saw in chapter 2), when repairs were distinguished from improvements. Labeo's choice of these terms may be intended to set a limit on the use of water channels, reaffirming their connection to the original purpose of servitudes—cultivation of the land.

The central place of the land persisted in legal definitions of servitudes even as the notion of utility evolved. Only in the postclassical period was the notion of a servitude separated from the land in the so-called personal servitudes, which could govern the same resources (e.g., water) but granted rights *in personam*, creating obligations between people (as opposed to rights *in rem*, or property rights).[7] The distinction between the two types of servitudes is formulated in terms of *utilitas* in a late classical legal opinion that sums up the rule. A servitude for grazing or watering animals is at issue, and the question is whether it should be treated as a personal or predial servitude.

> Servitudes for grazing a herd or for driving it to water seem to belong more to the estate than to a person, if the productivity of the estate is based mostly on the herd. If, however, the testator indicates a person to whom he wishes the servitude be assigned, this same servitude will not be assigned to a buyer or heir.
>
> [*Pecoris pascendi servitutes, item ad aquam appellendi, si praedii fructus maxime in pecore consistat, praedii magis quam personae videtur: si tamen testator personam demonstravit, cui servitutem praestari voluit, emptori vel heredi non eadem praestabitur servitus.*] (*D.* 8.3.4 Papin. 2 *Resp.*)

In this case, Papinian invokes utility to distinguish personal from predial servitudes; and utility, in turn, is defined as productivity (*fructus*). If the productivity of the land depended on the servitude, it should be treated as a predial servitude attached to the land; if not, it should be considered a personal servitude. Here, *utilitas* functions as an objective legal standard to limit

7. The concept of personal servitudes was developed on the basis of Marcianus's opinion (*D.* 8.1.1 Marcian. 3 *Reg.*): see Kaser, *RP* 1:440; Biondi, *Categoria*, 389, 434–39. For a Greek case about a personal servitude for water use, see *D.* 8.3.37 Paul. 3 *Resp.*, where the issue is similar; the personal servitude does not pass to an heir. For an exceptional type of temporary servitude, see Caiazzo, "In tema di servitù «*ad tempus*.»"

predial servitudes, restricting them to activities connected with making the land productive.[8]

The jurists took a similar approach in rules about the treatment of a farm's equipment when an estate was transferred by legacy: if the land was described as *uti optimus maximusque* in the legacy, equipment necessary to making the farm profitable went with it. The rule emerges from a case where hunting nets were transferred with an estate that derived its main revenue from hunting (*D.* 33.7.22 pr. Paul. 3 *Sent.*).[9] If a flock of sheep, for example, was kept on the land for its own profit, it was not included when the land was transferred. But if the sheep were an essential means to extract profit from woods on the property, they were treated as part of the property (*D.* 33.7.9 Paul. 4 *ad Sab.*). This standard is objective in that it applies equally to all estates and does not take into account the interests of an individual landowner. In this way, for the purpose of legal decisions, the interest of an estate can be expressed as a simplified concept of productivity. This approach is also economically rational, because raising a crop from the land—whether that meant raising a flock on woodland, producing milk and wool from a flock, or growing vegetables—was the most usual way for a Roman landowner to earn a return on his land. In practice, however, there could be a great deal of variety in landowners' ideas about how to make the land productive, what sorts of crops to produce, or even what constituted productivity: was it self-sufficiency, a surplus to sell on the market, or some combination of both?

In the previously cited case about the servitude for watering a herd, the term *fructus,* used to express utility, captures the ambiguity. In both legal and literary sources, the word can mean produce (crops or the offspring of animals) as well as cash profit. In Varro's *de Re Rustica,* for example, *fructus* and its cognates usually have an ambiguous meaning that straddles cash profit and the fertility or successful growth of plants and animals (in thirty-four of sixty-one passages in which *fructus* or *fructuosus* occur). Only ten passages unambiguously refer to cash and eleven to produce, while another twelve explain the relationship between cost and productivity. Varro also uses *utilitas*

8. Grosso, *Servitù prediale,* 71, 91–92; Biondi, *Categoria,* 370.

9. Similarly, for the equipment of a shop, see *D.* 33.7.23 Nerat. 2 *Resp.* For more examples illustrating the same principle, see *D.* 33.7.18 Paul. 2 *ad Vitell.,* with Steinwenter, *Fundus cum instrumento,* 73, 86–87. On the *uti optimus maximusque* clause and its role in the sale of land with servitudes, see chapter 4 in the present study.

and *utilis* to describe productivity (nine times, four times of which are in conjunction with *fructus* where *utilitas* denotes the means to productivity).[10] Similar usage occurs in the *Digest.* Labeo and Ulpian both use the term *fructus* when discussing what is at stake in a claim for ownership of property (*vindicatio*). Though there is no explicit mention of a monetary evaluation of *fructus,* it can be reconstructed from the situation: *fructus* is the plaintiff's interest in not being prohibited from exercising rights of ownership or in not letting the holder of the disputed servitude use his property (*D.* 8.5.4.2 Ulp. 17 *ad Ed.* citing Labeo).[11] In the practices of Roman landowners, there was a similar, unresolved ambiguity, as their estates frequently included both traditional, self-sufficient farming and rationalized, market-oriented activities.[12] Because landowners needed to raise a crop regardless of whether or not the market was good in a given year, they and the jurists could not always take into account market conditions.

The concept of utility, what it meant in practical terms, is explored in an unusually long case that focuses on the distinction between servitudes and usufruct. The case concerns two of the newer rustic servitudes connected with the manufacture of pottery: burning lime and digging chalk. A landowner could arrange with his neighbor to conduct these activities on his property either with a servitude or through usufruct, both of which created a right to use someone else's property. Usufruct was developed at the same time as servitudes were diversified in the second century BC, and both institutions reflect a growing interest in using legal tools to exploit natural resources and to improve productivity. While a servitude had a lasting attach-

---

10. In general for these definitions, see *OLD,* s.v. *fructus* 2 (useful products, including the children of slaves), 3 (the fruit of a plant), 4 (financial gain). *Utilitas, fructus,* and *fructuosus* occur in Varro's *de Re Rustica* as follows:

utilitas with *fructus* or *fructuosus:* 1.4.1, 1.4.3, 1.23.4, 2.4.22
utilitas alone: 1.2.12, 1.4.1, 1.23.1, 3.2.5
fructus or *fructuosus* implying a cash profit: 1.2.23, 1.4.1–2, 1.8.1, 1.11.1–2, 1.13.6, 1.16.6, 1.22.1–2, 1.65, 1.69, 2.1.24, 3.4.1, 3.5.1 (cf. 3.14.5), 3.16.9–11
fructus or *fructuosus* in the ambiguous sense of profit and fertility: 1.2.21, 1.3, 1.4.1, 1.23.1, 1.55.2–3, 2.praef.5, 2.1.11, 2.1.12, 2.1.13, 2.1.14, 2.1.24, 2.1.26, 2.2.3, 2.3.1, 2.4.17, 2.5.7, 2.6.1, 2.11, 3.1.9, 3.1.10, 3.2.10, 3.2.11–12, 3.2.13, 3.3.1, 3.4.2, 3.5.1, 3.6.1, 3.7.2, 3.10.5, 3.16.32–34, 3.17.2

11. Solazzi (*Specie ed estinzione,* 51) assumes that this case (discussed later in the present chapter) embraces both meanings of *fructus.*

12. Carandini, "Columella's Vineyard," 186, 191–92. De Neeve ("Price of Agricultural Land," 82–86) treats *fructus* and *reditus* (the monetary return from a property) as synonyms. See also Erdkamp, *Grain Market,* 112.

ment to the property, usufruct belonged to a person and could not be transferred to another user.[13] This case seeks to explain this distinction through the concept of a farm's productivity—or more precisely, the needs of the farm. The discussion unfolds through three extracts in the *Digest* that probably all refer back to the same treatment of the topic by the Flavian jurist Plautius. His opinion was reported by Neratius and then commented on by Paul and Ulpian, who also gives the opinion of his contemporary Maecianus. Plautius was a Flavian jurist. Neratius wrote a commentary on Plautius's work, and Ulpian's argument (*D.* 8.3.5.1 Ulp. 17 *ad Ed.*) comes from that commentary. The next excerpt, Paul's commentary (*D.* 8.3.6 pr.-1 Paul. 15 *ad Plaut.*), continues the argument, so it, too, may go back to Plautius. In any case, these two extracts represent part of a dialogue about the extent to which servitudes should be oriented toward the market, which may be traced back to the first century AD. Neratius seems to have had expertise in technicalities relating to farms.[14]

The case opens with the rule that restricts servitudes to adjacent property, which I have discussed in chapter 1 in the context of limitations inherent in servitudes. Here, I have omitted this sentence because it does not seem to be related to the comparison of servitude and usufruct and may have been added in the process of compilation, as it deals with some of the same types of servitude.[15] Most of the case explores the difference between servitude and usufruct, and it is in this context that utility is defined.

> (5) But [Plautius] himself says that for the most part a servitude for burning lime and digging chalk can be created, and only in so far as the needs of the estate itself require. (6 pr.) For example, if it had a ceramic works, in which pots were made in which the produce of the farm was shipped out (just as happens in certain places, where wine is transported in amphorae and *dolia* are made) or ceramic tiles were made for roofing the villa. But if the ceramic works are operated so that the pots can be sold, then it will be usufruct. (6.1) Likewise, far removed from usufruct is the right to burn lime or quarry stone or dig sand for the purpose of building what is on the farm, and likewise cutting wood, so that props for the vineyard will not be lacking. But what if

13. Grosso, *Servitù prediali,* 93–94; Kaser, *RP* 1:449–53.

14. On Neratius's knowledge of farming and on his letters on farm lease, see Frier, "Law, Technology, and Social Change," 204.

15. For the first sentence of *D.* 8.3.5.1 Ulp. 17 *ad Ed.,* see n. 2 of chapter 1 in the present study.

these [rights] make the condition of the property better? There is no doubt but that it should be a servitude. Maecianus also approved this, even to the point that he thought such a servitude could be established in order that I be allowed to have a shepherd's hut on your land, of course if I have a servitude for pasturing or watering my herd [on your land] so that if winter weather blows up I will have a place where I can shelter myself.

[(5) Sed ipse [Plautius] dicit, ut maxime calcis coquendae et cretae eximendae servitus constitui possit, non ultra posse, quam quatenus ad eum ipsum fundum opus sit. (6 pr.) Veluti si figlinas haberet, in quibus ea vasa fierent, quibus fructus eius fundi exportarentur (sicut in quibusdam fit, ut amphoris vinum evehatur autut dolia fiant), vel tegulae vel ad villam aedificandam. Sed si, ut vasa venirent, figlinae exercerentur, usus fructus erit. (6.1) Item longe recidit ab usu fructu ius calcis coquendae et lapidis eximendi et harenae fodiendae aedificandi eius gratia quod in fundo est, item silvae caeduae, ut pedamenta in vineas non desint. Quid ergo si praediorum meliorem causam haec faciant? Non est dubitandum, quin servitutis sit: et hoc et Maecianus probat in tantum, ut et talem servitutem constitui posse putet, ut tugurium mihi habere liceret in tuo, scilicet si habeam pascui servitutem aut pecoris appellendi, ut si hiemps ingruerit, habeam quo me recipiam.] (*D.* 8.3.5.1 Ulp. 17 *ad Ed.* and *D.* 8.3.6 pr.-1 Paul. 15 *ad Plaut.*)

The case examines a number of different activities to determine whether they fit better with usufruct or servitude. It turns out that the specific activity is inconsequential. What matters is the purpose of the activity. If it serves the needs of the farm, a servitude is appropriate; otherwise it should be considered usufruct. The resources supplied by a servitude may not exceed the needs of the farm itself (*non ultra posse, quam quatenus ad eum ipsum fundum opus sit*). The logic fits with the classification of servitudes among *res mancipi,* things closely connected with farmwork, and with the distinction between predial and personal servitudes in the case about watering herds and the *fructus* of the estate. This approach to utility also protected resources by limiting access and thereby providing excludability. In this rationale, servitudes appear to be connected with the goal of self-sufficiency, rather than with market-oriented production, which is connected with usufruct and the later personal servitudes.

Closer examination of the examples in this case, however, suggests that the distinction is not so clear. While usufruct might serve purely commercial interests, servitudes were not strictly limited to self-sufficiency.[16] Consider the main example in this case, digging chalk for pottery. If chalk was dug to make amphorae to transport wine produced on the farm, servitude was the appropriate legal mechanism. If the pots were made for sale, usufruct should be used. The contrast may be only apparent: why would the wine be transported? It is possible that some wine, pressed on rural land, was shipped to another property owned by the same person, where it served the needs of the estate. This interpretation would stretch the sense of *fundum,* broadening it to mean all property owned by the same person, not just the estate to which the servitude was attached. While legal terms are flexible, this extension seems too inconsistent with the treatment of servitudes, especially the rule that they were attached to a property.[17] In any case, shipping does raise the possibility of sale and market activity, undermining a clear distinction between the aims of servitude and usufruct.

Here again, it is helpful to compare the treatment of a farm's equipment in inheritance, as Steinwenter cites this case to illustrate types of operations that had dual purposes and could therefore be either included or excluded from property that was transferred with a farm in inheritance.[18] A pottery workshop, however, was not included in the inheritance, despite the fact that kilns could be used for either household or commercial production. The legal distinction between servitude and usufruct is based instead on the role of the servitude in providing materials for production on the land, but it leaves open the purpose of that production. Similarly, in the case about watering the herd, the term *fructus* brings out the ambiguity in utility, because *fructus* can have a purely agricultural meaning of growth or fruit or can connote the cash profit earned from that agricultural fruit. While the legal rationale is not entirely consistent, it is important because it highlights the dual purpose of servitudes and how they actually functioned in Roman society. In fact,

16. Grosso, *Servitù prediali,* 101–4, 42–43 (specifically on servitudes for water use).

17. For Biondi (*Categoria,* 419–20), manufacturing items for sale is not included in the needs of the estate, so activities connected with manufacturing must be treated as usufruct or as a personal servitude, not a predial one. Cf. *Categoria,* 376–78, where he emphasizes connection to a property (rather than to a person) as a basis for the distinction between servitude and usufruct. For revision of Biondi, see Franciosi, *Servitù prediali,* 1–86, distinguishing two kinds of ownership that are merged in Biondi. See also Kaser, *RP* 1:449–53.

18. Steinwenter, *Fundus cum instrumento,* 33 (this case), 26 (pottery workshop, citing *D.* 33.7.25.1. Iavol. 2 *ex Post. Labeo*). On the dual function of kilns and pottery works, see Marzano, *Villas in Central Italy,* 63–67.

the very inconsistency in the legal argument reflects the mixed motives of rural landowners, for whom productivity included both self-sufficiency and a surplus for the market.

Though the legal distinction between usufruct and servitude posits an opposition between self-sufficiency and market orientation, these purposes were integrated in Roman approaches to farming. Pliny's report of traditional wisdom about farming is typical, emphasizing cost control as a way of maximizing productivity: "their [i.e., our ancestors'] best advice was to spend as little as possible" [*summum providentiae illorum fuit ut quam minimum esset inpendi*] (*NH* 18.39). This advice refers to the cost of the land itself, but the cost of equipment was also a factor, so much so that "the man who buys what his farm could provide is a worthless farmer" [*nequam agricolam esse quisquis emeret quod praestare ei fundus posset*] (*NH* 18.40). Here, Pliny echoes Cato's famous maxim that the head of household should be a seller, not a buyer (*patrem familias vendacem, non emacem esse oportet, Agr.* 2.7). While Cato's rhetoric may be influenced by contemporary sumptuary laws that emphasized self-sufficiency, his advice also reflects a broader awareness and participation in commercial activities.[19] Cato's *de Agri Cultura* also includes catalogues of markets and good prices, reflecting his effort to obtain and communicate useful information about market conditions.[20] However limited Cato's information and his audience, his approach presumes that at least some landowners wanted to use this information as they evaluated costs and the choice between homegrown and purchased supplies. Cato's views continued to be popular, judging by the reference in Pliny just cited and also by the similar advice offered by Columella and Varro.

All the agricultural writers acknowledge that some participation in market exchange helps the landowner achieve self-sufficiency and possibly profit, though these aims tend to be combined in a more general goal of earning a steady return.[21] These mixed motives emerge, for example, in Varro's recommendations about supplies and the location of a rural estate. Varro preferred homemade equipment, even as he urged the landowner to calculate the monetary cost of purchasing supplies. Nearby villages and other estates could supplement the resources of the estate, providing venues for ex-

---

19. For the emphasis on self-sufficiency in second-century BC sumptuary laws, see Marzano, *Villas in Central Italy,* 83, with scholarship cited at n. 6.

20. Cato, *Agr.* 14.4 (price of building materials), 21.5 (price of mills at different towns—Suessa, Pompeii), 22.3–4 (price of fittings for mills), 135.1–5 (where to buy what, household supplies).

21. Kehoe, *Investment, Profit, and Tenancy,* 22; see, in general, 22–72.

change—the closer the better, in terms of controlling costs and increasing productivity.

> Likewise if these towns or villages are in the neighborhood or even large farms and villas of wealthy owners from which you can buy what you need for the farm at a moderate price and to whom you can sell your surplus, for example, props or poles or reeds, then the farm will be more profitable than if these things had to be brought in from a distance, sometimes even more profitable than if you were able to provide them by growing them on your own land.
>
> [*Item si ea oppida aut <vici in> vicinia aut etiam divitum copiosi agri ac villae, unde non care emere possis quae opus sunt in fundum, quibus quae supersint venire possint, ut quibusdam pedamenta aut perticae aut harundo, fructuosior fit fundus, quam si longe sint importanda, non numquam etiam, quam si colendo in tuo ea parare possis.*] (Varro, *RR* 1.16.3)

> As for the rest of the "mute" equipment, including baskets, jars, and other [such things], these are the recommendations. None of the things that grow on the property or can be made by the slaves should be bought, as, for example, things made from withes and rustic materials, such as hampers, baskets, threshing sledges, winnowing fans, rakes; in the same way things made from hemp, flax, rush, and palm, such as ropes, cords, and mats. (2) Things that cannot be gotten from the property, if they are purchased with an eye to usefulness rather than appearance, will not stretch expenses so much, especially if they are purchased most of all where good ones can be bought conveniently and for the lowest price.
>
> [*De reliquo instrumento muto, in quo sunt corbulae, dolia, sic alia, haec praecipienda. Quae nasci in fundo ac fieri a domesticis poterunt, eorum nequid ematur, ut fere sunt quae ex vimimibus et materia rustica fiunt, ut corbes, fiscinae, tribula, valli, rastelli; sic quae fiunt de cannabi, lino, iunco, palma, scirpo, ut funes, restes, tegetes.* (2) *Quae e fundo sumi non poterunt, ea si empta erunt potius ad utilitatem quam ob speciem, sumptu fructum non extenuabunt; eo magis, si inde empta erunt potissimum, ubi ea et bona et proxime et vilissimo emi poterunt.*] (Varro, *RR* 1.22.1–2)

Varro recognized that transport increased the cost of supplies but also that buying supplies could sometimes be more cost-effective than producing them at home. Columella offers a similar perspective on cost control: hiring animals for hauling is cheaper than raising them (1.3.3–4; cf. 1.2.3).[22] This advice acknowledges the traditional ideal of self-sufficiency and, at the same time, rejects it in favor of a calculation of costs that, combined with buying and selling on the market, could generate long-term security, even if the farm was not fully integrated into the market. But Columella is working with a false opposition. While procuring supplies and equipment from one's own property is a clear expression of self-sufficiency, buying and selling were also strategies for self-sufficiency as much as for market participation. This practice could draw a landowner into market exchange when there was a surplus on his estate, of equipment or materials, or when homegrown components were used to make products that were sold on the market. As Erdkamp has argued, the degree of market participation, especially for small-scale landholders, "depends on the balance between the farmer's vulnerability to risk and the extent of that risk."[23] Since a servitude could help reduce a farmer's risk by providing access to resources and a legal mechanism for compensation in the case of interruption, it is not surprising that the legal institution reflects the interests of landowners who raised crops for the market.

Careful accounting of costs represents a systematic approach to farm management that was limited by knowledge about markets—a kind of bounded rationality, to use Simon's term.[24] Cato's catalogue of markets and prices suggests both an awareness of this limitation and an attempt to overcome it. Servitudes represent another strategy for controlling costs by securing access to necessary resources without buying them. Like limited market participation, servitudes supplement self-sufficiency. The legal cases about servitudes reflect the varied strategies that landowners adopted for managing farmland and its resources, despite Neratius's attempt, in the case about digging chalk, to segregate servitudes and the needs of the farm from market practices. As with schedules, the concept of utility could advance several goals: protecting a common resource, increasing productivity, and supporting participation in local markets. Servitudes might originally have

22. On land transport in general, see Martin, "Land Transportation." Location close to markets was a key factor in assessing the nature or rationalism in the management of a given property. See De Neeve, "Price of Agricultural Land," 94–96.

23. Erdkamp, *Grain Market*, 103.

24. Simon, *Empirically Based Microeconomics*, 18; see at n. 97 in the introduction in the present study. Selling and buying on the market might be a rational approach to achieving long-term security, but it does not necessarily reflect a fully capitalistic approach to farming; see Erdkamp, *Grain Market*, 101–5.

been intended to serve the needs of the estate without regard for commercial factors; over time, as Rome's economy became more oriented toward the market, Roman landowners adapted the law of servitudes to respond to these new economic realities.

SPECIALIZATION AND PROFIT

Utilitas, or the "needs of the estate," was a key element in defining and limiting servitudes. Although *utilitas* was always connected with cultivation, it was a flexible concept that included both raising crops to support the household and commercial farming, as we have seen. In some legal cases, utility was evaluated in monetary terms, thus defining the needs of the estate in terms of commercial activity. Commercial interests are indicated indirectly in other cases, where servitudes were used in ways that suggest specialization—for example, to support a specific type of cultivation or to serve a particular part of a property (*D.* 8.1.6 Paul. 21 *ad Ed.*). These specialized uses seem to limit utility, narrowing the "needs of the estate" to one particular need. Cases involving specialized servitudes generated legal debate because they challenged the idea of a servitude as a broad and indivisible right. In their approaches to *utilitas,* the jurists strive to reconcile these sometimes contradictory ideas, accommodating the legal definitions to the changing needs of rural landowners.

The specialized use of a servitude is addressed in a short case about a vineyard. The case reports only the answers, but the questions can be reconstructed. Can a servitude be established for a specific type of cultivation? What happens to the servitude when the cultivation is changed?

> A servitude can be acquired for a specific type of land, for example, for a vineyard, because it applies to the land more than to buildings. For this same reason, if the vines are removed, the servitude remains; but if in setting up the servitude another agreement was made, a defense of fraud will be needed [to keep the servitude].
>
> [*Certo generi agrorum adquiri servitus potest, velut vineis, quod ea ad solum magis quam ad superficiem pertinet. Ideo sublatis vineis servitus manebit: sed si in contrahenda servitute aliud actum erit, doli mali exceptio erit necessaria.*] (*D.* 8.3.13 pr. Iavol. 10 *ex Cassio*)

While it was possible to establish a servitude for a particular type of crop (a vineyard in this case), the servitude was connected not to the use of the land but to the land itself. For this reason, the servitude continued to exist even after the vineyard was dug up. Only additional terms agreed to by the parties could change the situation, unless there was fraud involved in arranging the servitude (*doli mali exceptio erit necessaria*). The rules here reflect an unresolved tension between new uses of servitudes and old, enduring features of the institution, such as the concept of a servitude as attached to the land. In fact, Iavolenus cites this principle to support his argument (*quod ea ad solum magis quam ad superficiem pertinet*). The vines (i.e., the use of the land or the needs of the estate) are compared to buildings on property, something changeable and man-made, in contrast to the land itself and its attributes, which include the resources supplied by the servitude. The connection with the land recalls another old approach to servitudes, namely, their inclusion among *res mancipi,* the physical property necessary for farming. Both these old ideas and the new possibility of creating a servitude for a specific crop rely on a concept of utility that is directly connected to cultivation of the land. But the newer approach introduced a more flexible definition of *utilitas,* one that recognized the diversity in farming and responded to a landowner's plans for various types of cultivation. Indeed, the possibility of fraud suggests that access to resources could bring profit, legitimate or otherwise. The case considers fraud in the terms governing the servitude, where the terms dictated that the servitude should end if the vines were removed—this seems to be the implication of *aliud actum erit.* If the landowner wanted to keep the servitude, he would have to bring a defense of fraud (*doli mali exceptio*), alleging that the other party was trying to cheat him out of the servitude. While such a dispute over resources could reflect purely social antagonism, there were likely also economic motives, because servitudes were bound to cultivation of the land. In any case, controlling resources with a servitude could allow a landowner to change the way he cultivated his land, thereby increasing his productivity and possibly also making it possible for him to raise a market crop. A servitude could be especially helpful in managing a vineyard, because of a vineyard's special requirements.

Vineyards were generally considered the most costly and labor-intensive type of cultivation, as well as the most profitable: most of the later agricultural writers cite Cato (*Agr.* 1.7) as an authority for this view. Trenching, pruning, and staking are among the tasks that were familiar to readers of Vergil's *Georgics.* In the case cited earlier, there are no details about what type of servitude was set up for the vineyard or how it contributed to its cultivation. Water rights are a possibility, since some vines required irrigation, and if they were trained on trees, the trees could need watering, too (Pliny, *NH*

17.249–50; Col. 5.6.6, 8).[25] More likely, the servitude in this case involved a right to gather stakes for the vineyard, one of the new rustic servitudes (*D.* 8.3.3.1 Ulp. 17 *ad Ed.*). Such a servitude could save a great deal of expense, at least judging by Pliny's remarks about cultivating cypress trees for vine props. Their branches, trained upward and grown for twelve years, could be sold for a *denarius* each, making the cypress grove quite profitable, as suggested by its popular description as "a daughter's dowry" (*dotem filiae,* Pliny, *NH* 16.141).[26] The cypress bed itself could be improved with a servitude for channeling water, since it required watering. It should be built to hold water and be watered by hand or by a channel if dry, according to Cato's instructions. He also cautions landowners to use water sparingly if it is not available nearby (*Agr.* 151). Reeds were also used as vine props, so planting a reed bed could save on expense or contribute a cash profit (Pliny, *NH* 16.173; Cato, *Agr.* 6.3–4, 48). The value of vine props is also recognized in a late second-century AD bequest recorded in an inscription from Petelia in Bruttium.[27] On his death, one Manius Megonius established a fund to support a variety of public works, including the banquets of the Augustales, complete with a vineyard to supply the libations and wooden stakes for the vine trellises.

> I want this to be provided in addition by my heirs to government of the Petelini and to the body of the Augustales by the government of the Petelini, from the rest of my properties wooden support sufficient every year for staking the vineyard that I bequeathed to the Augustales.
>
> *[Hoc amplius ab heredibus meis volo praestar[i]*
> *rei P(ublicae) Petelinorum et a re p(ublica) Petelinorum corpori Au*
> *gustalium ex praedis ceteris meis palum ridica[m]*

---

25. Indirect evidence that a vineyard could require a water supply occurs in Cato's list of equipment for the vineyard, where he includes a watering can (*nassiterna, Agr.* 11.3); cf. Varro, *RR* 1.22.3. For more information about watering trees and vines, see appendix A in the present study.

26. Columella (4.30.1) seems to revise the adage when he describes the props, frames, and withes as a dowry for the vines: *haec enim quasi quaedam dotes vineis ante preparantur.* If, on the other hand, Pliny misinterprets the phrase in Columella, his mistake is even stronger evidence for the assumptions about the costs of vine-props.

27. Dennis Kehoe (email message to author) brought this inscription (*ILS* 6469, lines 33–37) to my attention, along with a comparison to Egypt, where vineyards "were commonly irrigated artificially" and "often have reed beds associated with them." On reed beds in Egypt, see Rathbone, *Economic Rationalism,* 191–92.

omnibus annis sufficiens pedaturae vineae
quam Augustalibus legavi.]

(*ILS* 6469.36–40)

The inclusion of vine props signals their value among the other gifts of money and land in this lengthy bequest.

Vine props could be viewed as a source of profit for the landowner who sold them. For the landowner who had to buy them, they represented a big expense, which Varro recognized in his advice to store them away and use them again next year (*RR* 1.8.6). A servitude to gather vine props was another cost-saving mechanism that could make the difference between earning a profit or not. The creation of a servitude for this specialized purpose suggests that landowners were using the law in systematic ways to manage resources and control costs. This use of law is not just reactive—it represents a forward-looking strategy and calculation about future costs and benefits. Specialized servitudes reflect the rationalized approaches that Roman landowners brought to farming, a rationality that both depended on social exchange and also was aimed at increasing profit; the cost saving could benefit the owner of a modest farm or a large estate alike.[28] The practical benefits of allowing specialized servitudes seem to outweigh the legal inconsistency, outlined earlier (namely, that the newer, more flexible concept of *utilitas* is not reconciled with older ideas about the connection of servitudes with the land). The servitude for gathering vine props may seem overly specialized and, for this reason, more easily reconciled with systematic planning, yet it is just one example illustrating a broader trend in the legal cases on rustic servitudes, especially those connected with water use. In the cases concerning schedules, for example, the rationing of water both conserved the supply and recognized its economic value for individual landowners.

When legal disputes arose over servitudes for water, economic issues came to the fore. In these cases, the servitude was measured both by productivity and by the monetary profits generated by that productivity. These two concepts are combined in the term *fructus,* which regularly bears both connotations in literary sources, as we saw earlier. A distinction begins to emerge in the legal evidence when *fructus* is defined as the landowner's interest in the servitude, as in the following case, which explains the relationship between interests and produce.

---

28. See Erdkamp, *Grain Market,* 55–105 ("The World of the Smallholder").

> Profits/produce [*fructus*] are relevant to a lawsuit that is brought to claim a servitude. But let us consider what profits/produce can belong to a servitude: the better view is that profit/produce should be calculated on the basis of the interest the holder has in not being prevented from [using] the servitude. But in a lawsuit to deny a servitude, as Labeo says, profit/produce [*fructus*] is also calculated, [namely,] how much interest the plaintiff has in the defendant's not using a right-of-way on his land. And Pomponius approves of this opinion.
>
> [*In confessoria actione, quae de servitute movetur, fructus etiam veniunt. Sed videamus, qui esse fructus servitutis possunt: et est verius id demum fructuum nomine computandum, si quid sit quod intersit agentis servitute non prohiberi. Sed et in negatoria actione, ut Labeo ait, fructus computantur, quanti interest petitoris non uti fundi sui itinere adversarium. Et hanc sententiam et Pomponius probat.*] (*D.* 8.5.4.2 Ulp. 17 *ad Ed.*, citing Labeo)

Labeo explains the owner's interest as a calculation of the *fructus* that comes from the servitude (*est verius id demum fructuum nomine computandum*). *Fructus* bridges the ambiguity between profits and produce, but the verb *computare* suggests that a financial interpretation is appropriate; while *computare* could be used in an abstract sense, it more often expresses real mathematical calculation.[29] Thus the purpose or *utilitas* of the servitude was connected not only with productivity but with the monetary evaluation of that produce.

The emphasis on the cash return of a servitude is articulated with extraordinary clarity in one case where a landowner brought suit because his neighbor cut off his water supply. The case reports Julian's opinion, and it comes from his commentary on a book of legal problems written by an otherwise unknown jurist named Minucius. The praetor's role in this case may have been of interest to Julian, who established a fixed form of the praetorian edict during Hadrian's reign. The remedy and the situation in this case may seem extreme; indeed, the case derives from a book of legal problems, many of which may have been pure hypotheticals invented by jurists to test legal rules. But this case, I argue, is typical in both its legal procedures and its assumptions about agriculture and the social relationships surrounding private water use.

According to the facts in the case, the defendant sent his slaves to block

29. On the usage of *computare*, see *OLD s.v. computo; TLL, s.v. computo* I.A.1.

a water channel and refused to appear in court. We are not told whether or not he had a legitimate grievance, only that he undertook a form of self-help or extralegal action to defend his interests. The plaintiff tried to take legal action, making a claim based on a servitude to channel water. Faced with his neighbor's intransigence, the plaintiff approached Julian to request a special hearing by the praetor, *cognitio*.[30] The plaintiff may have sought special protection out of ill will or because his neighbor was a nuisance, repeatedly interfering with the water supply. Though this kind of chronic conflict tends to be rare in shared water system, there are some chronic abusers—so described in Glick's study of the irrigation community in medieval Valencia—and the defendant in this case may have been just such a troublemaker.[31] In any event, Julian agreed that his claim should be protected and prescribed an order that the praetor should issue as a remedy.

> A man, whose slaves prevented a neighbor from channeling water, did not make himself available so that a suit could be brought against him. The plaintiff asked what he should do. I answered that, after the case had been heard, the praetor should order the defendant's property to be confiscated and he should not release it before he [the defendant] established for the plaintiff a right to channel water and made good any loss from the drought because he was prevented from channeling water, for example, if his meadow or trees had dried up.
>
> [*Is, cuius familia vicinum prohibebat aquam ducere, sui potestatem non faciebat, ne secum agi posset: quaerit actor, quid sibi faciendum esset. respondi oportere praetorem causa cognita iubere bona adversarii possideri et non ante inde discedere, quam is actori ius aquae ducendae constituisset et, si quid, quia aquam ducere prohibitus esset, siccitatibus detrimenti cepisset, veluti si prata arboresve exaruisset.*] (*D.* 8.5.18 Iul. 6 *ex Minucio*)

This case is interesting from the perspective of Roman legal procedure and the role of self-help in the legal system, and the importance of water rights emerges in the treatment of these procedural issues. Generally in Roman law, a plaintiff bore the responsibility for getting the defendant to court.

30. Kaser and Hackl (*Römische Zivilprozessrecht*, 391 at n. 34) interpret the procedure in *D.* 8.5.18 Iul. 6 *ex Minucio* as *cognitio*; see also Kelly, *Roman Litigation*, 29–30.

31. Glick, *Irrigation and Society*, 59–64.

The praetor had a limited role in compelling a defendant to appear.[32] The parties might make an agreement on the day to appear in court, and they might set a penalty for the defendant's failure to appear. The penalty was based on the amount claimed in the suit, and it was limited by a clause in the praetor's edict: the penalty could not exceed HS 100,000, nor could it be set very high just to cause trouble for the defendant—"vexatiously high," in Metzger's words.[33] When parties could not agree on the amount of the penalty (i.e., when the defendant objected to what the plaintiff proposed), they would bring the matter to the praetor. The case about the blocked channel appears to be a variation on this usual procedure. The role of the praetor may have been of special interest to the jurist in this case, Julian, who established a fixed form of the praetorian edict during Hadrian's reign. In any event, Julian instructed the praetor to intervene in an unusual but not unprecedented way. He recommended a special hearing, *cognitio*, and then a summary judgment, because the praetor was also instructed to restore the right to channel and to assess a penalty based on damage caused by interruption to the water supply.

The praetor's involvement in this case is part of a larger pattern of his involvement in private water rights, a pattern that can be traced to the second century BC, in the creation of the interdicts protecting springs and water channels examined in chapter 1. The praetor's role also recalls an earlier legal matter, the ownership of Q. Folvius's spring, documented by a second-century BC Campanian inscription, also discussed in chapter 1 (*CIL* X.8236). In Folvius's case, the urban praetor played a role in guaranteeing Q. Folvius's ownership of the spring, or at least Folvius expected that the praetor's guarantee, recorded on stone to remind potential trespassers, would protect his access to water. Similarly, in the case about the blocked channel, the praetor intervened to protect the plaintiff's access to water and, perhaps more important, his financial interest in it.

The plaintiff's financial interests were a key motive for the lawsuit and were addressed by the praetor's remedy. By the praetor's order, the plaintiff was authorized to hold his neighbor's property not just until he got his water back but until he was paid compensation for losses caused by the lack of

32. Metzger, *Litigation in Roman Law*, 3; see, more generally, 65–94, on the role of the parties and the praetor in setting the penalty. See also Kelly, *Roman Litigation*, 28–29; cf. 6–12.

33. Metzger, *Litigation in Roman Law*, 81. Metzger offers a helpful overview of the procedure.

water.[34] These terms chart a direct connection between the water supply, cash profit, and possibly also real estate value, if the loss of trees or meadow affected the selling price of the land. Compare the assumptions in lawsuits about mistakes in measuring land for sale: if the land was measured inaccurately, the seller could be held liable for the buyer's interest in proportion to the quality of the land (e.g., vineyard or olive grove), not just the simple quantity of it (*D.* 19.1.4.1 Paul. 5 *ad Sab.*; cf. *D.* 19.1.22 Jul. 7 *Dig.*). The presence of a servitude contributed to the quality of the land and, more directly, to its value, by improving productivity.

In the lawsuit about the blocked channel, the remedy proposed by Julian shows that water was critical to agricultural productivity. First, the order for summary judgment could protect the plaintiff from delays between the start of litigation and judgment, which could be long: even with an eighteen-month limit in which the trial must occur, the plaintiff could lose at least one and possibly two harvests.[35] Second, the order to restore the right to channel water also concerned productivity. While some grains could be grown without irrigation, most of the food crops grown in Roman Italy required some watering in the dry summer months. In the case under consideration, there are two examples of crops that could be damaged by interruption in the water supply: trees and meadows (*veluti si prata arboresve exaruisset*). These "crops" were recognized as profitable and were a regular part of the monetary economy, and both types of cultivation mentioned in the case, meadows and fruit trees, were most profitable when they had a water supply. According to Jashemski's analysis of trees and irrigation at Pompeii, rainfall was barely adequate for orchard trees, and extra water was needed for young trees.[36] The third part of Julian's remedy explicitly recognized the economic value of water. Since compensation probably meant a cash payment, the remedy assumes that the parties could calculate the value of the water, if not directly, then in terms of the crops that it supported.

A meadow could provide fodder for the estate's livestock, an indirect contribution to profit through cost saving. More directly, a meadow could be leased, as Cato knew (*Agr.* 149) and as Varro advised for landowners who had no animals to graze (*RR* 1.21).[37] For either purpose, an irrigated meadow

34. In Athenian law, the plaintiff had a similar right to seize the property of a recalcitrant defendant: see Christ, "Self-Help," 531–33.

35. Gaius, *Inst.* 4.104–5; Metzger, *Litigation in Roman Law,* 114–17; Kelly, *Roman Litigation,* 118–31.

36. Jashemski, *Gardens of Pompeii,* 253.

37. For more sources and details on meadows and the water supply, see appendix A.

would be more productive. Clover, for example, could be mowed as often as six times a year, if it was watered right after mowing to stimulate new growth (Col. 2.10.28). Kron's analysis of ley farming in the Roman agricultural writers affirms the pattern: in a regular rotation of tilled and fallow land, meadow might be mowed several times a year, or irrigated land could be set aside as a permanent meadow.[38] When Cicero and his brother considered buying an estate near Arpinum, they were favorably impressed by its water supply, particularly the possibility of irrigating a meadow (*Q.Fr.* 3.1.3, quoted in the next section of this chapter). If meadows were a reliable source of revenue, fruit trees were an especially rich crop.

Cultivating fruit trees required a steady water supply. Columella describes an apparatus to water seedling fruit trees in summer (5.10.8). This type of irrigation could also be used to water vines (known in the Roman sources as *ablaqueatio*).[39] The lay of the land could be used to advantage for passive irrigation and delivering fertilizer: gardens and orchards located downstream from the barnyard could catch enriching runoff (Col. 1.6.24).[40] Varro's etymology of *poma,* "fruit," encodes traditional wisdom about the need to water grafted fruit trees: "they can be called *poma* from the fact that they need to drink [*potu*]" [*a quo, quod indigent potu, poma dicta esse possunt*] (*RR* 1.31.5). He includes a colorful anecdote illustrating Scrofa's success as a farmer: the fruit grown on his estate is as marvelous as the fine art that adorns other villas.

> On account of its cultivation, his estate presents a more pleasing spectacle to many people than the royally refined buildings of other villa owners because they visit his villas to see the fruit galleries not the picture galleries, as at Lucullus's villa. The end of the Sacra Via, where fruit is sold for its weight in gold, is a picture of his orchard.
>
> [*Fundi enim eius propter culturam iucundiore spectaculo sunt multis, quam regie polita aedificia aliorum, cum huius spectatum veniant villas, non, ut apud Lucullum,*

38. Kron, "Roman Ley-Farming," 284–85 (mowed several times a year), 282 (irrigated meadow as a permanent pasture). See also White, *Roman Farming,* 152–53.

39. For more sources and details on watering fruit trees, see appendix A. On *ablaqueatio,* see Shaw, "Lamasba," 84–85, with Roman sources.

40. For a similar use of ditches to water olive trees planted on a slope, see Col. 5.9.13. In the garden of the house of Polybius at Pompeii, trees had soil around them built into a mound, surrounded by a channel for water; see Jashemski, "Use of Water in Pompeian Gardens," 51–52. This may be one circumstance in which runoff was valuable to farmers in nonarid areas. On runoff in arid Roman North Africa, see Shaw, "Water and Society," 137–38.

ut videant pinacothecas, sed oporothecas. Huiusce, inquam, pomarii summa sacra via, ubi poma veneunt contra aurum, imago.] (*RR* 1.2.10)

The fruit is beautiful because it is like art itself, but also because it provided the income that bought fancy art for the villa: it sold for its weight in gold.[41] This anecdote echoes the familiar connection between luxury and productivity on Roman villas, and it also connects that productivity with profits earned in the market.

Pliny the Elder observes another part of the same phenomenon when he remarks on the high price of apple trees, as an introduction to his discussion of how to make a good return from them.

> There was attention to trees in the ancient laws, and in the *Twelve Tables* it was prescribed that anyone who cut down someone else's trees wrongfully would pay a fine of twenty-five bronze pieces for each tree. What should we think? Should we think that those men who assessed the value of fruit-bearing trees at so great an amount believed that those trees would sell for the amount quoted above? (8) It is no less amazing in the case of the apple tree, when the annual produce of many apple trees in *suburbium* is sold for two thousand *sesterces,* and the revenue from a single tree is greater than that of farms in the old days.
>
> *[fuit et arborum cura legibus priscis, cautumque est XII tabulis ut qui iniuria cecidisset alienas lueret in singulas aeris xxv. quid existimamus, venturasne eas credidisse ad supra dictam aestimationem illos qui vel frugiferas tanti taxaverant?* (8) *Nec minus miraculum in pomo est multarum circa suburbana fructu annuo addicto binis milibus nummum, maiore singularum reditu quam erat apud antiquos praediorum.]* (*NH* 17.7–8)

Pliny emphasizes the value of fruit trees by comparing current prices with historical evidence. First, he cites the rule from the *Twelve Tables* (ca. 450 BC) prescribing a fine of twenty-five *asses* per tree for wrongfully cutting them down, a substantial fine that acknowledged the economic value of fruit trees in monetary terms. Then, the ancient fine is compared to a more recent (but still historical) price of trees in an anecdote related a couple of paragraphs earlier (*credidisse ad supra dictam aestimationem*), in which six shade trees were priced at a million *sesterces* (*NH* 17.5, cf. 3–6). By contrast, fruit trees should

41. On the posh fruit market on the Sacra Via, see Tilly, *Varro the Farmer,* 145.

be worth even more because their value was based on productivity, as Pliny explains with his evidence for contemporary prices. Apple trees, for example, could bring high profits if they grew in the *suburbium,* near the city markets, the same place where Varro saw the beautiful display of Scrofa's peaches.[42] In addition to a good water supply, an estate had to have the right location to make a profit from fruit. These literary sources, reminiscent of the landscape described in chapter 1, suggest both economic and geographic contexts for the lawsuit about the blocked water channel. The plaintiff sought monetary compensation for losses related to crops grown on an estate that was probably located in the *suburbium,* near Rome's markets, where fruit could be sold for a good price.

The lawsuit about the blocked channel affirms the economic value of a servitude for channeling water and corroborates the literary evidence for market-oriented agriculture. Whether the landowner was cultivating a meadow or an orchard or a garden, water was necessary for making it productive and profitable. Though the case about the blocked channel may date to the first century AD, the economic value of fruit crops, one of the examples in the case, was recognized long before, in the rules of the *Twelve Tables,* as cited by Pliny in the preceding passage. In the second century BC, Cato recognized the earning power of an orchard or irrigated garden on a suburban villa, second only to a vineyard, when located near a city (*Agr.* 1.7, 7.1, 8.1). The later agricultural writers make the same calculations; for example, Columella's advice about trenching a garden assumes irrigation (11.3.9–11).[43] The picture is most clear in Pliny's description of the villa garden.

> There is no question that gardens should be attached to a villa, and irrigated ones should most of all be cultivated, if it is available, from a stream flowing by, if not, from a well with a wheel or a windmill or irrigated by drawing water with a swing-beam. The soil should be broken up fourteen days after the west wind begins to blow in autumn by way of preparation, and again before the frost. It should be dug over by eight workers, and mulch should be dug in to a depth of three feet. It should be divided into plots with rounded sloping beds, each encircled

42. Even if Pliny's figure of HS 2,000 is an exaggeration or a conventional number rather than a report of an exact amount, it conveys the high price that apples brought in the Roman market. On conventional figures, see Scheidel, "Finances, Figures, and Fiction."

43. For sources and details of the water supply for gardens, see appendix A.

with a furrow for a path by which access is given for a person and a channel for the flow of water.

> *[Hortos villae iugendos non est dubium riguosque maxume habendos, si contingat, praefluo amne, si minus, e puteo rota organisve pneumaticis vel tollenonum haustu rigatos. Solum proscindendum a favonio in autumnum praeparantibus post XIIII dies iterandumque ante brumam. Octo iugerum operis palari iustum est, fimum tris pedes alte cum terra misceri, areis distingui easque resupinis pulvinorum toris, ambiri singulas tramitum sulcis qua detur accessus homini scatebrisque decursus.]* (*NH* 19.60)

Pliny took it for granted that a villa should have a garden and that the landowner should invest in its cultivation, working the soil and channeling water to irrigate it. His description of the garden caps the introduction to his catalogue of plants (*NH* 19.49–60). This moralizing introduction contrasts contemporary cultivation with old-fashioned garden plots: wild asparagus has been replaced by monstrous, cultivated varieties; salads are rejected in favor of vegetables cooked with imported spices and expensive oil; gourmet groceries divide rich and poor, threatening another secession of the plebs.[44] The rhetoric draws on economic realities. Produce, plain and fancy, was an important part of Rome's economy. Irrigated gardens provided much of the profit for villas near the city. The gardens at Pompeii—their layout, plantings, and water supply—show that practice did not much differ from Pliny's description.[45] Pliny would have recognized the importance of an efficient use of technology to cultivate the garden. Compare his enthusiasm for both the technology of the urban aqueducts and the cultivation of flowers in a controlled environment that depended on the positive cooperation between man and nature in a garden—topiary and ornamental plantings fall outside this category (*NH* 21.1).[46] Securing a water supply was thus a key el-

---

44. On Pliny's moral stance, see Healy, *Pliny the Elder,* 371–72, 350–52. The contrast also has political and philosophical implications, as argued by Wallace-Hadrill ("*Horti* and Hellenization," 5). Cf. Hor. *Serm.* 2.4.15–16 for the rejection of fancy food, including irrigated garden produce. The idea that the garden should be for self-sufficiency underlies Columella's quotation (11.3.3) of Vergil, *G.* 4.133 (*inemptas ruris dapes*).

45. For gardens laid out as in Pliny, *NH* 19.60, see Jashemski, *Gardens of Pompeii,* 19 (house of Pansa with large garden, probably for household), 191–92 (small shophouse garden near Porta di Nocera, possibly with surplus to sell), 235–42 (house of ship Europa with large market garden), 243–47 (garden of fugitives with a large plot and a smaller plot, possibly a nursery), 278–88 (Garden of Hercules).

46. Compare, too, Pliny's positive view of the technology of the urban aqueducts at *NH* 36.121–25 (with Beagon, *Roman Nature,* 79–91).

ement in a plan for cultivation on a suburban villa, the kind of plan that lay behind the lawsuit over the blocked channel.

When the broader contexts for garden crops and water use are taken into account, the lawsuit over the blocked channel illustrates the connection between market-oriented farming and rational planning. The plaintiff who sued his neighbor plainly anticipated a profit and had planned to use the water to this end. He recognized the economic value of this resource and used the legal system to advance his financial goals. Of course, his rational planning was probably imperfect because he did not have full or accurate information about the markets, whether for leasing his meadow or selling his fruit. Since he relied on a servitude for the water, he may have traded maximizing his supply for reliability, if the water was shared with his neighbors. All the same, the plaintiff's resort to the law is recognizable as a rational economic choice, because it could bring financial compensation. Moreover, Julian's ruling, specifically the award of compensation, implies a market where the plaintiff's losses could be evaluated in monetary terms. In this way, again, the priorities of the commons dovetail with the economic aims of an individual landowner but do not necessarily require a maximizing rationality. Social as well as environmental constraints limited the legal process and its rationality in this lawsuit, because implementing Julian's order had to rely on adequate social relationships that were already sorely strained, judging by the details of the case. Negotiation seems to have failed entirely with a defendant who refused either to respect the servitude or to participate in the legal process. Despite these limitations, the mechanisms of Roman law provided a framework for decisions that were economically rational—decisions based on calculations of the costs and benefits, measured in monetary terms. The aims of this plaintiff are consistent with participation in the market economy, at least on those properties close enough to transport crops to Rome, and thus represent one approach that Roman landowners brought to managing resources for their farms.

PLANNING AND INVESTMENT

A servitude provided a mechanism for protecting the water supply and a landowner's financial interest in it. Many of the legal cases examined so far concern problems in the past or present, correcting interruptions to water rights or preserving the status quo in local distribution schemes. But landowners also engaged in planning, looking ahead to how they might make better use of the resources available to them, for example, by making capital investment in hydraulic infrastructure. This type of investment was most likely to be made in properties with ready access to a market where surplus could be sold, such as those in the *suburbium* and near towns in Campania. As we saw in chapter 1, there is significant archaeological evidence for the development of water resources in this area. In the legal cases about servitudes, Roman landowners used law along with construction technology to improve their access to water, not just to serve ongoing operations, but to plan for the future by reserving a servitude. Indeed, the legal evidence opens a window on the calculations that landowners made about their needs for water and for building channels and about the costs of these projects as well as their likely return in increased productivity. The legal approaches cohere with attitudes toward investment expressed by the agricultural writers and by Pliny and Seneca. Cicero's letters offer specific information about how elite landowners evaluated and planned for an investment in a local aqueduct when a servitude was available.

Writing to his brother, Quintus, in September 54 BC, Cicero discussed the water supply on two of his brother's properties, one that Cicero had recently purchased and another that Quintus had decided not to sell (*Q.Fr.* 3.1.3). I mention Cicero's remarks again in chapter 4 in relation to the sale of property with servitudes, but here they are important for what they reveal about Cicero and his brother's approach to investment in the water supply. The new property, the Fufidian farm, gets a rave review from Cicero because of its ample water resources.

> From this place we set out right along the Via Vitularia to the Fufidian farm, which I had purchased from Fufidius for you at the most recent market at Arpinum for HS 110,000. I have never seen a spot with more shade in summer, water rising [i.e., from springs] in so many places and so plentiful itself. What more do you want? Caesius thought that you could easily irrigate fifty *iugera* of meadow. Indeed, on a topic that I understand better, I agree that you will have a villa of wondrous charm, with fountains added [and] a palaestra with manicured green woods.
>
> *[Ex eo loco recta Vitularia via profecti sumus in Fufidianum fundum, quem tibi proximis nundinis Arpini de Fufidio HS CCCIↃↃↃ CIↃ emeramus. Ego locum aestate umbrosiorem vidi numquam, permultis locis aquam profluentem et eam uberem. quid quaeris? Iugera L prati Caesius irrigaturum facile te arbitrabatur; equidem hoc*

> *quod melius intellego adfirmo, mirifica suavitate te villam habiturum piscina et salientibus additis, palaestra et silva viridi culta.]* (*Q.Fr.* 3.1.3)[47]

The water supply made the Fufidian farm an attractive investment as well as a pleasant place to stay. Since the water could be used to irrigate fifty *iugera* of meadow, the productivity of the land could be improved: an irrigated meadow could be mowed more often and so provided more fodder. Or the meadow could be leased, as Varro advised, if Quintus had no plans to keep livestock; since irrigation would make the lease more attractive, it would likely earn a higher rent, increasing Quintus's profits.[48]

Though Quintus's other property did not have a natural source of water, its water supply could be developed in useful ways. This other property is called, conjecturally, the Baebulian farm, based on Shackleton Bailey's discussion of the text. The real name of the estate is lost in a textual crux, but this conjecture is likely because similar names are known from inscriptions from the region.[49] In any case, there had been some trouble about the water supply on this property, according to Cicero's report: the water had been taken away, but access was now possible because a servitude for *aquae ductus* had been set up.[50]

> I hear that you would now like to keep the Baebulian farm, and you should do what seems right to you. Caesius said that we could still recover the cost if we wanted to sell since, though the water has been taken away, a right to this water has been established and a servitude has been imposed on the other property. I have Mescidius with me. He said that he had agreed with you on a price of three *denarii* a foot [to build an aqueduct] and that he had measured the distance at three thousand paces. It seems more to me; but I maintain that the money

47. On the crux in the last words, emending *silva viridicata* to *silva viridi culta,* see Harvey, "Cicero, *Epistulae ad Quintum Fratrem,*" 484.

48. On irrigated meadows, see discussion earlier in the present chapter; see also appendix A.

49. Shackleton Bailey, *Cicero: Epistulae ad Quintum Fratrem,* 204–5: Shackleton Bailey does not hazard a reconstruction of the texts but suggests that the property was named for its owner, who could have been a Babul(l)ianum or Baebuleianum, both names known in an inscription from the Liri Valley near Interamna (*CIL* 10.5370).

50. For the identification of this servitude as for *aquae ductus,* see Grosso, *Servitù prediali,* 59.

could not be better spent. I had summoned Cillo from Venafrum, but on that very day an underground channel killed four of his fellow slaves and workers.

[Fundum audio te nunc †Bobillianum† velle retinere; de eo quid videatur ipse constitues. Caesius aiebat aqua dempta et eius aquae iure constituto et servitute fundo illi imposita tamen nos pretium servare posse si vendere vellemus. Mescidium mecum habui. Is sese ternis nummis in pedem tecum transegisse dicebat, sese autem mensum pedibus aiebat passuum III CIↃ. Mihi plus visum est; sed praestabo sumptum nusquam melius posse poni. Cillonem arcessieram Venafro, sed eo ipso die quattuor eius conservos et discipulos Venafri cuniculus oppresserat.] (*Q.Fr.* 3.1.3)

To make use of the servitude, Cicero and his brother were prepared to construct an aqueduct to carry the water. Quintus had already negotiated with the contractor Mescidius and obtained an estimate of the costs. They had agreed on a price per foot, and Mescidius had measured the distance. Cicero's remark about the bid—that the distance seemed longer—suggests that he and Quintus were also calculating the overall cost. The project may have been expensive enough that Quintus needed a loan to cover it.[51] In any event, Cicero thought that the money would be well spent. His enthusiasm for Quintus's project matches the sentiment that he ascribed to Cato the Elder in *de Senectute* (quoted previously). The effort invested in managing the water and land was expected to reward the landowner in richer harvests.

Despite the advantages, building an aqueduct could be risky for both the landowner and the contractor, as is clear from Cicero's report of a collapsed tunnel that killed four men. There is also potentially a legal question about assigning liability for such a mishap or for less dramatic problems. In one legal case about a contract for the construction of a water channel, the channel subsided or the land around it sank so that it could not be used (*D.* 19.2.62 Labeo 1 *Pith.*). The landowner sued the contractor, presumably to compel him to fix the problem and to cover the costs. According to the legal rules, the contractor could be held liable only before the landowner approved the work and if his work had caused the problem. If there was a defect in the site, for example, that caused the water channel to sink, the contractor was not liable. Once the landowner approved the job, however, any problems were his alone, and he had to bear the continuing risk and had

51. Verboven, *Economy of Friends*, 166.

to cover the costs of damage if the earth sank from natural causes rather than because of the contractor's work.[52]

Cicero's letter shows that Quintus took an active role in developing the water supply on his land, using both law and technology to increase his access to water. Certainly he was not alone in calculating the costs and benefits of improving water management. Columella, for example, presented more than one method of trenching a vineyard, describing one method as less expensive (3.13.4).[53] Comparable, too, is the story, discussed in chapter 1, about G. Lucretius Gallus, who neglected his duty as praetor to supervise the construction of a water channel on his land (Livy 43.4.6–7). Gallus may indeed have been an irresponsible magistrate, but his excuse—building a water channel—indicates that he devoted attention to managing the resources on his land, an interest that he must have thought would appeal to the senators who were judging him.[54] As for Quintus's aqueduct, there is no evidence about how the water was to be used, but if it was supplied by the servitude, it had to be connected with the needs of the estate (*utilitas*), and the investment in an aqueduct could be expected to pay off in increased productivity and possibly also profits. The tone of Cicero's report is matter-of-fact, as if this was their usual approach to managing property—with attention to such details as price and ways to improve productivity and access to resources. Cicero brought a similar calculating approach to managing the water supply on his own property at Tusculum.

The water supply at Cicero's Tusculan villa also involved a servitude and investment in improvements. In late 47 BC, Cicero wrote to Tiro about improvements to the garden, its water supply, and its lease.

> Get Paredrus to rent the garden himself; that way you can get the real gardener going, too. That useless Helico used to pay one thousand *sestertii* [to lease it] when it had no sun, no drain, no wall, no shed. Should he now laugh at us when we've gone to such expense? Set a fire under the man, as I did with Motho. That way, I am lavish with flowers! (3)

---

52. On the broad liability of the contractor who built watercourses, see Martin, *Organization of Private Building*, 90–101. In general on the rules for liability in contracts for hire, see Kaser, *RP* 1:570–72.

53. See appendix A for sources on trenching and hydraulic infrastructure for the villa.

54. Compare Morley's conclusion (*Metropolis and Hinterland*, 160–61) that marketing the produce of one's estate was not grounds for censure among Roman elites in the second century BC.

I'd like to know what should be done about the Crabra, even if there is now rather too much water.

[Parhedrum excita ut hortum ipse conducat. Sic holitorem ipsum commovebis. Helico nequissimus HS ∞ dabat, nullo aprico horto, nullo emissario, nulla maceria, nulla casa. Iste nos tanta impensa derideat? Calface hominem, ut ego Mothonem. Itaque abutor coronis. (3) De Crabra quid agatur, etsi nunc quidem etiam nimium est aquae, tamen velim scire.] (*Fam.* 16.18.2–3)

Cicero had made several changes to the property: clearing the garden, installing a drain, building a wall and a shed. In addition, there was an ample water supply, so much water that Cicero may not have needed water from the Crabra system any longer.[55] In 45 BC, he was again engaged in some project related to the water channel at Tusculum. Atticus had taken some action, which Cicero approved: "You have done the right thing about the water channel" [*de aquae ductu probe fecisti*] (Cic. *Att.* 13.6.1). In fact, the success of these improvements to the water supply may be connected with Cicero's decision in the next year not to use a servitude that brought water to the property, as reported in a letter quoted and discussed in chapter 2 (*Att.* 15.26 from 44 BC). His ongoing attention to the water supply and other facilities can be understood in connection with his financial interest in the garden at Tusculum.

Cicero expected that the water supply would support crops and, in turn, profits from the lease.[56] The garden was leased to a tenant who would cultivate it and pay a cash rent, presumably after selling its produce. The profits from the garden at Tusculum are represented as a garland, suggesting also a likely crop, flowers (*Itaque abutor coronis*), which need irrigation and must be grown near to market because they cannot withstand long transport.[57] Shackleton Bailey explains:

55. Shackleton Bailey (*Letters to Atticus*, 3:212, on Cic. *Att.* 5.12.3) advances this interpretation of the passage quoted here (Cic. *Fam.* 16.18.2–3). Thomas and Wilson ("Water Supply for Roman Farms," 147) suggest that Cicero's garden was irrigated by water from the Crabra.

56. On the profits expected from this garden, see Scheidel, "*Coloni* und Pächter," 345–46. Purcell ("Roman Villa," 156) cites this passage as evidence that earning a profit from an elegant villa appeals to elites.

57. Rawson ("Ciceronean Aristocracy," 96) interprets this image as a possible indication that Cicero received some rent in kind. For similar imagery (a crown of flowers grown on various suburban properties, including Tusculum), see Mart. 9.60 and discussions in the introduction and chapter 1 of the present study.

> The gardener who looked after Cicero's garden at Tusculum apparently took part of the produce for himself, while keeping the owner supplied with flowers and, presumably, vegetables, as did one Motho elsewhere (on the Palatine?). But he was not delivering the goods (*iste nos . . . derideat?*). Cicero points out that he himself has made expensive improvements to the garden, and that even before he had done this a certain Helico . . . used to pay (or had been willing to pay) a rent of 1,000 sesterces.[58]

Cicero thought that the lease should earn a higher rent now because of improvements to the facilities and its abundant supply of water. Cicero's villa at Cumae had a similar garden that probably supplied the household and produced some crops to be sold in the market at Puteoli.[59]

Though there is no archaeological evidence for Cicero's garden at Tusculum, two comparable gardens at Pompeii (not supplied by the city aqueduct) preserve evidence of irrigated flower beds and probably also tree crops. The Garden of Hercules was a large, commercial enterprise, but similar design is found in the smaller, probably private Garden of the Fugitives. Jashemski concludes, "The ancient owner of this well-watered garden may well have found the advice of Varro [*RR* 1.16.3] very sound: flowers can be a very profitable crop."[60] In Cicero's letter to Tiro, the juxtaposition of flowers and water supply may be coincidental, but it signals an understanding about this fragile but profitable crop, grown for the city market. The water supply was a key factor in making the garden productive and attractive to potential tenants. Cicero expected his investment in hydraulic infrastructure to improve productivity and enhance his return on the garden lease. Cicero's expectations appear to have been realistic and typical when set against evidence from the Roman irrigation community in North Africa. Even in that more arid environment, improvements in the water supply could pay off, as Shaw has observed.[61]

---

58. Shackleton Bailey, *Ad Familiares,* 2:386.

59. On Cicero's villa at Cumae, see Cic. *Q.Fr.* 2.8.4 and *Att.* 14.16.1, with D'Arms, *Bay of Naples,* 199 (cf. 61); Shackleton Bailey, *Cicero: Epistulae ad Quintum Fratrum,* 188.

60. Jashemski, "Use of Water in Pompeian Gardens," 57; see 53–57 on gardens not served by the city aqueduct at Pompeii. See also Jashemski, "Commercial Flower Garden" (on the Garden of Hercules at Pompeii); Wallace-Hadrill, "*Horti* and Hellenization," 7–8 (the comparable situations of Pompeii and the Roman *suburbia*). For more on garden crops in the *suburbium* with comparison to gardens at Pompeii, see chapter 1 in the present study.

61. Shaw, "Water and Society," 141–42.

Cicero's approach to the garden at Tusculum is not very different from what is found in the legal cases previously discussed in regard to the use of law together with technology to improve the productivity of the land. For example, in the lawsuit about the blocked channel, the landowner depended on a channel to bring water for his meadow or fruit trees. When his neighbor interfered, he turned to the praetor to enforce the servitude and to obtain monetary compensation for the damage to his crops. Cicero also used a legal arrangement—leasing the garden—to secure a predictable return, and he made improvements to the garden with the express purpose of earning a higher rent. Cicero's approach to productivity, then, is forward-looking: he made an investment in infrastructure in the hopes of increasing his profit from the land. Like the landowner in the case about the blocked channel, Cicero treated the resources of his property as economic commodities that directly contributed to productivity or the *utilitas* of the property. Moreover, Cicero and his brother engaged in calculated planning about these resources and how best to use them.

The law of servitudes was also used to facilitate this kind of planning about the water supply. When land was sold, the buyer or the seller could add to the sale contract terms reserving a servitude on the sale property. When title to the property was transferred formally, the servitude was established in the same process because the same legal mechanisms were used for transferring title and for establishing servitudes (*mancipatio* or *in iure cessio*).[62] Terms to the sale contract are discussed in more detail in chapter 4, especially as they relate to litigation arising around the sale of land. The present discussion considers one kind of declaration that facilitated planning for investment.

While various terms could be attached to a sale contract, a specific declaration was required when a seller wanted to reserve a servitude for his own benefit. The practice is illustrated in a case about a seller who owned two adjacent properties, one with a water supply and another without. He planned

62. Kaser, *RP* 1:444. For cases where the seller reserves a servitude for himself, see *D.* 8.1.19 Iavol. 4 *Post. Labeo, D.* 8.3.30 Paul. 4 *Epit. Alf., D.* 8.4.3 Gaius 7 *ad Prov. Ed., D.* 8.4.5 Iavol. 2 *Epist., D.* 8.4.7 pr.-1 Paul. 5 *ad Sab., D.* 8.4.10 Ulp. 10 *ad Sab., D.* 8.4.13 pr. Ulp. 6 *Opin., D.* 8.6.19 pr. Pompon. 32 *ad Sab.* (cf. *D.* 8.3.33 pr.-1 Afric. 6 *Quaest.* for a similar use of declarations in division of common property, in a case probably relating to provincial law). The seller could not, however, reserve a servitude for his neighbor (*D.* 8.4.5 Iavol. 2 *Epist.*). For a general discussion of restrictions on informal sharing among neighbors, see chapter 2 in the present study.

to sell the one with the water supply and retain ownership of the other. To maintain access to water after the sale, he needed to reserve a servitude to channel water from the other property. The case provides instructions.

> Whatever the seller wants to receive for himself in a right of servitude, he should declare in detail. For the general declaration, "whoever has a servitude, let it be so," concerns external parties [i.e., parties other than the buyer and the seller], and does not serve the seller himself at all in protecting his right; for he has no rights, because no one owes a servitude to himself. But even if a servitude had been owed, and then ownership of the servient estate came to me, for this reason it would be said that the servitude was extinguished.
>
> [*Quidquid venditor servitutis nomine sibi recipere vult, nominatim recipi oportet: nam illa generalis receptio 'quibus est servitus, utique esto' ad extraneos pertinet, ipsi nihil prospicit venditori ad iura eius conservanda: nulla enim habuit, quia nemo ipse sibi servitutem debet: quin immo et si debita fuit servitus, deinde dominium rei servientis pervenit ad me, consequenter dicitur extingui servitutem.*] (*D.* 8.4.10 Ulp. 10 *ad Sab.*)

A general declaration could not cover the seller, Ulpian explains, because of the basic structure of a servitude: it was a right in someone else's property, and before the sale, both properties belonged to the same person. The seller must make a specific declaration in order to reserve a servitude. Either general or specific declarations could be aimed at preserving the status quo, an aim that we have seen before as neighbors sought to make the most of common resources. In fact, however, many specific declarations seem aimed at change or at least leave open the possibility of change. At the very least, these declarations indicate an interest in evaluating the resources on a property and their effect on productivity. In this case, the specific declaration created a servitude to take effect after the sale, making the property servient. As a result, the sale price was probably lower, but this loss was presumably offset by the benefit of the servitude in providing enhanced productivity. When water rights were involved, the landowner could have a plan to change production on the land that he did not sell, putting in a more profitable crop that required a good water supply—perhaps an irrigated meadow, as Cicero suggested for Quintus's newly purchased estate. Though we do not know exactly how Cicero and Quintus structured their servitudes, there is legal evidence indicating that some landowners used specific declarations to plan ahead.

Planning for the future is assumed in several legal cases with specific declarations about servitudes for water use. One of the cases is ascribed to the classical jurist Pomponius, and three others are ascribed to the Republican jurist Labeo, though two of these have been disrupted in compilation and are therefore more suggestive than diagnostic. In these cases, *utilitas* is understood in terms of not only current use but also future possibilities. The possibility of future use may represent an extreme view, but it accords well with the evidence from literary sources. In addition, because all these cases involve water servitudes, it appears that the water supply was a particular focus of planning.

In the first case, Labeo considers whether or not a servitude can be established even if it is not useful. Because a servitude could exist only to serve the needs of the estate, this should be impossible. But surprisingly, Labeo says that it is possible.

> I think that it is possible to impose a servitude on a property that someone is selling, even if it is not useful. Just as if there is no advantage in granting someone a right to channel water, nonetheless this servitude can be established: for we are able to owe [and] to have things even if they are not useful to us.
>
> *[Ei fundo, quem quis vendat, servitutem imponi, et si non utilis sit, posse existimo: veluti si aquam alicui [dedere] ducere non expediret, nihilo minus constitui ea servitus possit: quaedam enim debere habere possumus, quamvis ea nobis utilia non sunt.]* (*D.* 8.1.19 Iavol. 4 *Post. Labeo*)[63]

Though Labeo's opinion seems to reject the rule about the needs of the estate, this turns out to be only an apparent contradiction. The example in the case—the servitude to channel water—is key to understanding Labeo's approach. For Labeo, *utilitas* meant only the effective connection between the spring and the dominant estate, and "use" meant water flowing through the channel.[64] Without this connection, a servitude to channel water could not be used and thus could not fulfill any needs of the estate. But if the channel brought water from the spring to the dominant estate, the servitude had

---

63. In my translation, I follow Grosso (*Servitù prediali,* 99) in retaining *dedere* because it makes sense, and I follow Mommsen's edition of the *Digest* in deleting *debere.*

64. Grosso, *Servitù prediali,* 103–4; Capogrossi Colognesi, *Servitù d'acqua,* 172–75 (on *D.* 8.1.19).

achieved its purpose: it was useful, whether or not the landowner had any use for the water. This definition of *utilitas* simplified the complicated reality of how water was used in farming and, at the same time (somewhat paradoxically), made possible that complicated reality. A similar ambiguity characterizes the rule that a servitude continued to exist even after cultivation of the land was changed, as we saw earlier. The old legal idea of connection to the land provides a basis for new, unanticipated ideas about how to use servitudes and the resources they controlled.

Labeo's opinion may reflect older ideas about the servitude for channeling water, but it is not incompatible with the later juristic definitions of *utilitas.* In classical law, *utilitas* became a flexible but objective standard. A servitude could be established only if it served an objective, permanent use that was independent of the landowner's subjective and changeable needs and interests. Labeo's opinion prefigures this objective concept. Indeed, as we saw in chapter 1, the classical jurists adopted his notion of use as the physical connection between the properties, in a case where "use" was established simply on the basis of water flowing naturally through a channel (*D.* 8.6.12 Cels. 23 *Dig.*). In the case about the nonuseful servitude (*si non utilis sit*), the physical connection motivates an abstract concept of *utilitas.* Delivering water was useful in and of itself because it contributed to the resources of the property: "use" in this sense is equated with usefulness. The servitude could be established because it was useful in and of itself, if not to the particular landowner who reserved it.[65] While this legal analysis appears to reject the landowner's interests, it actually makes it possible to take them into account, because the specific declaration looks to the future: the landowner could choose to use the water any way he liked once the servitude was established.[66]

In the second case about a specific declaration, Pomponius addresses a legal question about the use-it-or-lose-it rule, and again the answer depends on the interpretation of use and *utilitas.* A landowner reserved a right to channel water when he sold a property, but he did not exercise the right for the statutory period, because there was no appropriate infrastructure. He had apparently been planning to build a channel, but he had not managed to do so before the two years ran out. According to Pomponius, despite the nonuse, the landowner did not lose his servitude, because it was not possible for him to channel water without suitable facilities.

---

65. Biondi, *Categoria,* 370; Grosso, *Servitù prediali,* 97–101.
66. For a similar conclusion, see Grosso, *Servitù prediali,* 140–41.

> If in selling part of my land I made a term in the conveyance that I could channel water across that part [of the property that is being sold] to the rest of my property, and the statutory period [for nonuse] passed before I built a channel, I do not lose my right because there was no passage for the water; but my right remains intact: but if I had built the channel and not used it, I would lose it [i.e., my right].
>
> *[Si partem fundi vendendo lege caverim, uti per eam partem in reliquum fundum meum aquam ducerem, et statutum tempus intercesserit, antequam rivum facerem, nihil iuris amitto, quia nullum iter aquae fuerit, sed manet mihi ius integrum: quod si fecissem iter neque usus essem, amittam.]* (*D.* 8.6.19 pr. Pompon. 32 *ad Sab.*)[67]

Pomponius's opinion is consistent with the approach we have seen in cases where natural phenomena interfered with the exercise of a servitude—for example, if a spring dried up and the holder of the servitude could not channel water, as happened in the Statilius Taurus lawsuit. There was some disagreement among the jurists about whether or not the right was lost in these cases, yet even if it was, the servitude could be restored if the water started flowing again. In the cases about natural phenomena, the legal rule relied on a concept of liability that was limited by human capability: where events were beyond human control, the landowner could not be held responsible for not using the servitude, because he could not control the spring and its water supply; therefore his right was protected.[68] The present case, however, is more complicated, because events may not be beyond the landowner's control. In fact, it appears that the landowner is in control, because he arranged the servitude ahead of time, before constructing the channel. Construction brought its own uncertainties, and it may be that Pomponius's opinion recognized such problems as beyond the landowner's control. In any case, his approach can be understood in terms of the relationship between use and *utilitas*.

Pomponius's rationale in the case about the not-yet-built channel shows how the objective concept of *utilitas* could be reconciled with the older, more physical notion of use. He explains his opinion by stating its converse: if the

---

67. There is some disagreement about whether the rule in this case belongs to classical or Justinianic law; see Solazzi, *Specie ed estinzione*, 167 n. 22. The economic contexts for the use of these servitudes supports the earlier date.

68. Cf. *D.* 8.6.14 pr. Javol. 10 *ex Cassio* and *D.* 8.3.35 Paul. 15 *ad Plaut.*, discussed in chapter 2 in the present study. Similar considerations were involved when a flood interfered with a servitude: see Grosso, *Servitù prediali*, 258–72.

landowner had built the channel and not used it, he would have lost his right. As in Labeo's opinion, a physical connection between the properties was sufficient for use and also could be used to ground an objective concept of *utilitas*. Delivering the water was itself objectively useful, regardless of how the landowner planned to use the water. Before the channel had been constructed, the servitude could not be used and therefore could not serve the needs of the estate (*utilitas*). Thus, when *utilitas* is defined by use, the right depends on construction of the channel, and the period of nonuse begins only after the channel has been constructed. But the implications of the case go beyond the physical connection between the properties, because Pomponius allows the right to exist even before the channel is constructed, which means that *utilitas* can include potential or future use. Pomponius's opinion is reminiscent of the incomplete distinction between servitude and usufruct discussed in the first part of this chapter. The jurists attempted to distinguish servitude from usufruct on the basis of their purpose, that is, agricultural production for the market or for the household. In fact, the legal category of servitudes proved to be flexible, allowing landowners to control resources needed for both kinds of productivity. A similar flexibility characterizes *utilitas*, which may serve present or future uses on the property.

The possibility of future *utilitas* also characterizes a pair of difficult cases that concern water rights. Because these cases present two contradictory opinions, both ascribed to Labeo, they were probably confused in compilation. Both cases discuss a seller who wanted to reserve a servitude but did not know whether or not there was a spring or stream that could be subject to a servitude. Was this possible? In one extract, Labeo says that it was (*D.* 8.3.10 Paul. 49 *ad Ed.*); in the other, he says that it was not (*D.* 8.5.21 Labeo 1 *Pith. Epit. Paul.*). It is most likely that it was not possible to create a servitude over an unknown source.[69] But even if compilation has obscured Labeo's opinion, the question posed by this case nevertheless suggests a kind of forward thinking that accords with the evidence for planning that we have seen in other cases and in the literary sources. In this view, *utilitas* embraces not only the present needs of the estate but also future eventualities, those that the current owner is planning or that he or another owner might undertake in the future. This latitude encouraged planning, as it enabled capital investment in infrastructure by guaranteeing the right to channel water that would

69. Capogrossi Colognesi, *Servitù d'acqua*, 177–79, especially n. 293. For the opposite interpretation of *D.* 8.3.10 Paul. 49 *ad Ed.* and *D.* 8.5.21 Labeo 1 *Pith. Epit. Paul.*, see Grosso, *Servitù prediali*, 140–41.

offset the cost of an aqueduct. Cicero's brother Quintus seems to have made just this sort of calculation about building a water channel on his property at Arpinum, as did Lucretius Gallus nearly a century earlier. A water channel or servitude for water could increase the price of land, as Cicero noted, and this indirect evidence for the financial benefit of such construction is discussed further in chapter 4. Thus, the legal approaches to *utilitas* are consistent with calculation in advance about investment that would improve productivity. Though these legal opinions may reflect extreme, limiting views, they appealed to some jurists and, presumably, some landowners as well, because they remained part of the legal discussion in the *Digest.* Such innovative ideas would have been attractive to landowners who were actively engaged in managing their rural properties.

The approaches to farming implied in the cases on servitudes may seem out of step with the caricatures of absentee landlords and elites averse to commerce and uninvolved with the management of their land. In fact, even the legal evidence may be misleading to some extent, because the legal cases discuss limiting (if suggestive) cases. Yet traditional farming methods involved regular planning in the rotation of fields, or more accurately, in the practice of ley farming, in which fields were left fallow for several years to rebuild nitrogen and other soil nutrients. This method was typical of Roman farming, according to Kron's analysis of evidence from the agricultural writers.[70] Varro recognized the trade-off of present effort and future return in this method: "some crops should not be sown so much for this year's harvest as for the following year, because when they are cut and left [in the field] they make the land better" [*quaedam etaim serenda non tam propter praesentem fructum quam in anuum prospicientem, quod ibi subsecta atque relicta terram faciunt meliorem*] (*RR* 1.23.3; cf. Pliny, *NH* 18.187; Col. 2.1.3). Cultivated meadows played an important role in this fallowing system, and it may be that servitudes for irrigating them helped landowners to grow the crops that enriched the soil, so that the investment in a servitude would pay off—not directly, but down the line—in improved productivity. Columella took a similar approach to several other areas of farming. In the selection of draft animals, large ones may cost more initially, but they do a better job of breaking up the soil, so the investment pays off in greater productivity. He endorsed this investment on the basis of a calculation of the benefits and costs, comparing his advice to that of Celsus, who emphasized reducing costs (*reformidans impensam,* Col. 2.2.24). When it came to the vineyard, Columella also accounted for start-

70. Kron, "Roman Ley-Farming," 278.

up costs, taking the long view that productivity repaid these expenditures over time. In support of his view that these plans often failed for lack of follow-through, however, he quoted an earlier authority, Graecinus: "in every kind of expenditure, so says Graecinus, most people start a new project more energetically than they oversee its completion" [*in omni genere impensarum, sicut ait Graecinus, plerique nova opera fortius auspicantur quam tuentur perfecta*] (Col. 4.3.1).[71] Columella expected landowners to be able to evaluate investment choices and their future returns, much as Labeo envisions them planning for future servitudes. Similarly, the careful record keeping in the Heroninos archive provided a basis for just this sort of calculation, according to Rathbone's interpretation.[72] We have already seen that at least two landowners, Quintus Cicero and Lucretius Gallus, invested in constructing water channels, and at least Quintus and his brother were attentive to the costs of such a project and to its potential for increasing the productivity and value of rural land.

While traditional farming practices offered scope for planning and investment, more innovative approaches were not unknown, and their potential for improving productivity was not unappreciated in Roman society. Columella, for example, when he set out the scope and purpose of his work, recommended both traditional and new approaches. Even old-fashioned diligence would reward the landowner with greater harvests if he worked hard (Col. 1.*praef.*19; cf. 1.*praef.*10–18, 1.1.18–20). But to really succeed, the landowner must have knowledge, resources to invest, and initiative (*prudentiam rei, facultatem impendendi, voluntatem agendi,* Col. 1.1.1–2). He should take a systematic approach to learning, evaluating, and applying both old and new techniques.

> Thus, the attentive head of household, whose aim is to follow a sure method of increasing his property by farming, will take special care to consult the wisest farmers of his own time about each topic and also the records of the old [writers], diligently to study and evaluate what

71. On following through, cf. Col. 3.4.3, 3.10.8. On what Columella includes in his calculations of cost, see Carandini, "Columella's Vineyard," 190–92. Julius Graecinus, Agricola's father, wrote a two-volume work on vineyards that took a similarly proactive approach to cultivation, based on Columella's quotations (e.g., Col. 3.3.4) as well as Pliny's opinion (*NH* 14.33). On Graecinus, see Tac. *Agr.* 4, with Gaheis, "Julius," 126, and Gossen, "Julius," 126.

72. Rathbone, *Economic Rationalism,* 394–403; cf. Tchernia, "Quelle rationalité?" 286–87, for a qualified acceptance of Rathbone's conclusions and, more important, for the recognition that modern accounting methods do not provide entirely robust information.

each of them thought [and] what he advised, [and] whether all the things which the [writers of] old recommended applied to the farming of this era or some of them were out of step.

[Itaque diligens pater familiae, cui cordi est ex agri cultu certam sequi rationem rei familiaris augendae, maxime curabit ut et aetatis suae prudentissimos agricolas de quaque re consulat et commentarios antiquorum sedulo scrutetur atque aestimet, quid eorum quisque senserit, quid praeceperit, an universa, quae maiores prodiderunt, huius temporis culturae respondeant an aliqua dissonent.] (Col. 1.1.3)

Columella sets the bar high for the "attentive head of household." The idealizing ambitions are rhetorical in part, an effort to motivate readers to study the eleven books of his *de Re Rustica.* But in order for such an appeal to work, it must have found some resonance in Columella's audience. Learning something new, thinking ahead, and investing money are all within reasonable expectations for Roman landowners. Of course, if everyone already did all these things, there would be no need for Columella's book.

Two well-known examples of innovative farming methods involve restoring old vines and olive trees that had stopped being productive, both from the middle of the first century AD. The first example, Acilius Sthenelus, was credited with developing new methods of trenching and planting the vineyard and using them most successfully to restore the vineyard on a property owned by the grammarian Remmius Palaemon, located on the Via Nomentana in the *suburbium* (Pliny, *NH* 14.48–51; Suet. *Gramm.* 23).[73] Palaemon's vineyard, once renovated, brought a rich return in fruit and cash within eight years.[74]

But, because of that same Sthenelus's work, the greatest fame belonged to Remmius Palaemon, otherwise renowned for his grammatical skill, due to his purchase in the last twenty years of a rural property, in the same area of Nomentana at the turnoff at the tenth milestone from the city, for HS 600,000. (50) The cheap price [of property] is known everywhere throughout the *suburbium,* and there especially so, since he bought a property after it had been neglected through carelessness but not even among the worst of the rather choice land. [Palaemon] began

73. In general on the difficulty of restoring a neglected vineyard, see Col. 3.11.2, 4–5, with Carandini, "Columella's Vineyard," especially 197–201.

74. On Palaemon's income, see Suet. *Rhet.* 23.4, with Kaster, *Suetonius de Grammaticis,* 229.

to cultivate this [land] not because of his virtuous character but at first out of pride—for which he was remarkably notorious. The vineyards were dug up [and planted] anew through the efforts of Sthenelus, and while he [Palaemon] played the farmer, he achieved a barely believable miracle: the sale of the vintage on the vine for HS 400,000 within eight years. (51) There was no one who did not run to see the piles of grapes in those vineyards, though the lazy neighborhood made his excessive studies an excuse [i.e., for its own failures].

[*sed maxima [fama], eiusdem Stheneli opera, Remmio Palaemoni, alias grammatica arte celebri, in hisce viginti annis mercato rus* $\overline{DC}$ *nummum in eodem Nomentano decimi lapidis ab urbe deverticulo.* (50) *est autem usquequaque nota vilitas mercis per omnia suburbana, ibi tamen maxime, quoniam et neglecta indiligentia praedia paraverat ac ne in pessimis quidem elegantioris soli. haec adgressus excolere non virtute animi, sed vanitate primo, quae nota mire in illo fuit, pastinatis de integro vineis cura Stheneli, dum agricolam imitatur, ad vix credibile miraculum perduxit, intra octavum annum* $\overline{cccc}$ *nummum emptori addicta pendente vindemia;* (51) *cucurritque non nemo ad spectandas uvarum in iis vineis strues, litteris eius altioribus contra id pigra vicinitate sibi patrocinante.*] (Pliny, *NH* 14.49–51)

The success of Sthenelus's methods are measured in the price that Palaemon earned for his grape harvest and in the speed with which his improvements paid off. The change is more notable by contrast with the poor condition of the farms in the neighborhood. In Pliny's report, Sthenelus's methods are recognized as new and improved, so to speak, by the arrangement of the discussion. Mention of Sthenelus directly follows a quotation from Cato's *de Agri Cultura* about varieties of grape grown in Italy, which was introduced to show how much life had progressed since Cato's time (*quantum postea ccxxx annis vita profecerit,* Pliny, *NH* 14.45). In addition, Palaemon's vineyard outperformed the rest of the neighborhood: his neighbors gawked at the piles of grapes and, making an excuse for their own failures, begrudgingly explained Sthenelus's success as the product of too much learning (*literis eius altioribus, NH* 14.51)—as if they had read, with disapproval, Columella's handbook. Though Pliny, on the whole, does not depict the neighbors sympathetically—they are described as lazy (*pigra vicinitate*)—his account also conveys some disapproval of Sthenelus, similar to the tone of another anecdote in which a freedman named Chresimus was charged with using magic to ruin his neighbors' crops (*NH* 18.41–43). That accusation seems to have been motivated by envy and status consciousness, since Chresimus was the most successful farmer in the area and also a freedman. Similar social stereotypes may explain the mixed messages about Sthenelus, who was a plebeian son of a freedman, as Pliny points out.

Despite undertones of class consciousness, Pliny's account takes a positive view of Sthenelus's success in the vineyards. His work is "the peak of achievement" (*summam gloriam*) and a perfect example of vine cultivation (*exempl[um] consummatae huius artis*). Pliny saves his real criticism for Sthenelus's boss, Remmius Palaemon, also a freedman, who was motivated by pride (*vanitate*) to renovate the vineyard. Instead of undertaking the project himself, Palaemon just "played the part" of a farmer (*dum agricolam imitatur, NH* 14.50), while Sthenelus worked wonders in his vineyard. In addition, Pliny not only rejects the neighbors' prejudice but also seems to reject the traditional wisdom that neighborhood practices determine productivity (cf. Cato, *Agr.* 1.2, 4).[75] Instead, the initiative and investment of one new farmer could turn the neighborhood around. Pliny's view of Sthenelus accords with his generally positive view of using technology and know-how to get things done, so long as it does no harm. Beagon notes that Pliny's discussion of agriculture includes "clear evidence of a personal interest in the latest developments" and that "its emphasis upon organization bears the unmistakable stamp of the military and administrative background of its author."[76] Taking an innovative approach to farming, then, might not be at odds with the old-fashioned ideals, once the class bias is filtered out of Pliny's account.

Pliny's contemporaries might also have appreciated Sthenelus's renovation of the vineyard and its financial success, as did, for example, the younger Seneca, who purchased the property from Palaemon for four times what he had paid for it just ten years earlier. According to Pliny, Seneca was so taken with the property that he bought it even though it meant giving a huge boon to an enemy: "Annaeus Seneca, . . . a man least prone to marvel at trivialities, was overcome by such a great desire for this estate that he was not ashamed to give this victory to a man otherwise hateful [to him] and ready to boast of it" [*Annaeo Seneca . . . minime utique miratore inanium, tanto praedii huius amore capto ut non puderet inviso alias et ostentaturo tradere palam eam*] (*NH* 14.51). Seneca's aversion to Palaemon may have stemmed from Palaemon's less-

75. For discussion of traditional ideas about neighbors, see chapter 2.

76. Beagon, *Roman Nature,* 21. For Pliny's positive attitude toward technology and nature, see, e.g., *NH* 36.104–8 (construction of the Cloaca Maxima), with Murphy, *Pliny the Elder's "Natural History,"* 188–93. In general on his view of nature and how humans should use it, see Wallace-Hadrill, "Man's Unnatural History"; Healy, *Pliny the Elder,* 371–79; Beagon, "Nature and Her Landscapes."

than-virtuous lifestyle, known to us from Suetonius's biographical sketch, which recalls, as Kaster put it in his commentary, "other stereotyped sketches of depraved and unworthy parvenus, including freedmen, who were thought to have risen above their station."[77] Pliny alludes to Palaemon's reputation in his comparison of Sthenelus and Palaemon, invoking class prejudice to motivate a distinction between two freedmen. As for Seneca, his delight in vistas of vines planted in neat arrays could have convinced him to pay a high price, though this may not be simply bald desire free from economic motives, as Saller assumes.[78] Aesthetic appeal was connected with productivity: according to Varro, if two estates were equally productive but not equally pleasing to look at, no one would pay a higher price for the unattractive one: *nemo enim eadem utilitati non formosius quod est emere mavult pluris, quam si est fructuosus turpis* (*RR* 1.4.2).[79] Moreover, in discussing the layout of the vineyard, Varro considers it traditional wisdom that attractive patterns of planting that required more careful attention from the farmer were more productive.

> I say this about the cultivation of beauty: it follows that those plantings that are more attractive in appearance also come with more produce, as, for example, those who have an *arbustum* [vines trained on trees], if [the trees] are sown in a pattern of five [*quincunx*], on account of the rows and the small spaces between them. Thus our ancestors produced much less and less good wine and grain from a field equally large but less well planted, because plants that are set each in their own places take up less space and each one blocks the other less from the sun and moon and wind.
>
> [*De formae cultura hoc dico, quae specie fiant venustiora, sequi ut maiore quoque fructu sint, ut qui habent arbusta, si sata sunt in quincuncem, propter ordines atque intervalla modica. Itaque maiores nostri ex arvo aeque magno{s} male consito et minus multum et minus bonum faciebant vinum et frumentum, quod quae {que} suo quicque loco sunt posita, ea minus loci occupant, et minus officit aliud alii ab sole ac luna et vento.*] (*RR* 1.7.2)

Varro refers specifically to planting trees for the vineyard in a *quincunx* pattern—five trees in a square array, with one at each corner of the square and

77. Kaster, *Suetonius de Grammaticis*, 232.

78. Saller, "Framing the Debate," 264.

79. For more on the combination of aesthetics and productivity on Roman estates, see also the introduction to the present study.

one at the center.[80] The functionality of this arrangement, which gives each plant enough space, air, and light, makes the vineyard both more productive and more pleasing to view. The sources do not describe the layout of Palaemon's vineyard, but it may have aroused Seneca's desire both for its aesthetically pleasing appearance and for its promise of revenue. As Pliny notes, Seneca was not generally swayed by trivialities (*minime utique miratore inanium*). In any case, Seneca had also seen and written about other new methods of cultivating a vineyard, employed by the second notable innovator in farming methods.

Vetulenus Aegilaus restored the vines and olive trees at the villa that was once owned by Scipio Africanus at Liternum on the coast south of Rome. He won a wide reputation for his work, according to Pliny, who mentions Aegilaus by way of introduction to Sthenelus, whose success exceeded even that of Aegilaus (*NH* 14.49). Aegilaus's methods are described by Seneca in his letter reporting a visit to Scipio's villa. In the first and second parts of the letter, ethical lessons are embedded in discussions of the villa and its landscapes, respectively (*Ep.* 86.1–13, 14–21). Renovation and innovation are prized features of the grounds outside the villa, where Aegilaus and his vineyard serve as a trope for Seneca's philosophical project. As Aegilaus improved trees and vines, so philosophy affects humans, even old men, according to Henderson's reading.

> This letter duly features agricultural images applied to human perfectability. . . . For Seneca, the suggestion might go, to "see with his own eyes," wherever it may be, people busy "sowing and reaping" their crops according to the season that suits their circumstances, amounts to a vindication of the anti-dogmatic ethical strategy articulated through the *Epistulae Morales,* where control is wrested away from cut-and-dried formulae, and handed back for embedding in the thick texture of ongoing life? . . . In the arboretum, we take "Tradition," in one form or another, as appropriate, to us and to the specific material. We prepare a fresh "setting," and put the old down in the ditch so it will grow anew.[81]

If Aegilaus's new methods were a model for Seneca's philosophical project, they could not be all bad, even though there is a hint of doubt at the end of

80. Cf. Vergil, *G.* 2.277–78; see Thomas, *Virgil: "Georgics,"* 1:206, for a handy diagram.
81. Henderson, *Morals and Villas,* 130, 138, 157.

the letter, where Seneca comments on the cistern that provided water for the trees: "if it works, we would have the rain in our power" *[quae si prodest, habemus pluvian in nostra potestate]* (*Ep.* 86.21). The apodosis of this condition undermines the protasis: since we cannot control the weather, the technological effort might seem to be misplaced, or in terms of philosophical renewal, it can only work within the parameters of mortality, a limit that the cycles of the natural world transcend. In effect, farming is the perfect environment for innovation, because it requires repetition and reinvention of tasks with careful attention to the outcome. This generally positive view of Aegilaus's innovative methods coheres with Seneca's expectations about farming as they are formulated in another letter: in answer to Posidonius's claim that philosophy invented all the arts, Seneca exclaims, "as if cultivators of the land are not now also finding many new [practices] through which productivity can be increased" *[tamquam non nunc quoque plurima cultores agrorum nova inveniant per quae fertilitas augeatur]* (*Ep.* 90.21). Seneca seems to have taken it for granted that farmers were always devising new ways of doing things, an attitude that suggests that Pliny's endorsement of innovation was not simply idiosyncratic.

Innovative methods of renovating a vineyard might have seemed worthwhile to Roman landowners, because vineyards were considered the most profitable type of cultivation. Similar efforts were made to improve the water supply when profitable market crops were at stake. As argued earlier, Cicero's improvements to the garden at Tusculum were aimed at increasing revenues, as was the aqueduct on Quintus's property at Arpinum. Also suggestive is the archaeological evidence for hydraulic facilities in the gardens at Pompeii, described by Jashemski: "The ingenuity exhibited in providing the necessary water for growing crops in this part of the city, where the aqueduct had not reached, is remarkable."[82] A similar, can-do attitude seems to have inspired the use of technology at Pompeii to process raw materials in commercial contexts, such as milling grain and processing hides, according to Oleson's analysis, which explains the development of water-lifting devices as part of a larger phenomenon of technological change.[83] The technology used in these urban businesses was different from what was typical on farms, and a dirt channel is admittedly not as sophisticated as a grain mill or even a waterwheel. Yet in both contexts, there is evidence of a drive to improve productivity by improving technology or making the most

82. Jashemski, "Use of Water in Pompeian Gardens," 53.
83. Oleson, "Water-Lifting Devices," 73–74.

of available resources or by doing both, as in the case of the water supply to Pompeian gardens. While some of the impetus for innovation may have come from the lower classes—Sthenelus and Aegilaus were both freedmen—elites like Pliny, Seneca, and Cicero were receptive to such new ideas. Labeo's forward-looking approach to servitudes is part of this picture, too. The legal evidence and Cicero's letters connect the interest in innovation and improvement to water resources in particular. Where water rights could be used to increase the productivity of market crops, reserving a servitude or building a water channel were two strategies for increasing productivity and revenue, and the success of such strategies depended on the calculation of costs and benefits.

CONCLUSION

Though there is no necessary opposition between economic rationalization and self-sufficiency, these principles could be seen as alternatives both in moralizing literature and in legal discussions of servitudes. The original concept of a servitude was based on a close connection to the land and its cultivation, and utility was narrowly defined in relation to current methods of production. The narrow definition functioned in legal analysis as an objective standard for distinguishing activities that supported productivity from those that did not. In this form, utility also promoted conservation of water, providing another mechanism for excludability to protect a common resource. As the definition of utility was broadened, it became a subjective standard that expressed the aims and interests of individual landowners. Financial compensation became the new objective standard, as we will see in the examination of lawsuits about servitudes in the following chapter. This change in terms shifted the focus of the discussion from the needs of cultivation to the evaluation of produce, or from input to outcomes, and it marks a significant change in ways of thinking about the use of resources for farming.

Alongside the goal of self-sufficiency, attention to market concerns gained greater influence in legal approaches to *utilitas* and changed the way a servitude might serve cultivation. In the preceding chapters, we saw that traditional ideas about neighborly behavior continued to influence the law of servitudes, even as Romans increasingly used private property rights to define their economic interest in water. The creation of schedules for use and of legal mechanisms to enforce these schedules shows that Roman landowners could calculate their need for water as well as its price. In this chapter, utility was defined in monetary terms—for example, in the lawsuit about the blocked channel. Similarly, landowners, such as Quintus Cicero, calculated the costs of constructing a water channel that would make it possible to benefit from a servitude. This approach to water rights shows that Romans understood the economic value of water and the landowner's interest in a reliable supply. As in the previous chapter, the argument here develops the idea that Roman landowners made calculated choices about farming their land, based on the limits inherent in their knowledge and resources. In arranging servitudes for water, Roman landowners had a flexible tool that could help them to make the most of the resources needed for productivity, as they pursued self-sufficiency and, in some cases, limited participation in the urban markets for produce. The legal institutions helped to provide the conditions in which the water supply could be managed well enough to support specialized agriculture.[84] In short, the rules of servitudes—their development to accommodate specialization and planning—reflect a partial rationalization in the Roman economy and, in turn, reveal that at least some landowners were actively engaged in managing their land, despite the moralizing rhetoric about absentee landlords and the decline of agriculture.

84. Horden and Purcell (*Corrupting Sea*, 242) observe, "So only in very favoured conditions has hydraulic control been effective enough to encourage specialization."

FOUR

SERVITUDES AND THE SALE OF LAND

When a property was sold, all servitudes were transferred with it, because servitudes were considered part of the land. This transfer of rights was not always smooth, however, as one legal case suggests.

> Once a servitude for channeling water has been established for the benefit of one of two farms that the seller kept [i.e., when he sold the other property], if this property is sold, the servitude that had been acquired goes with it, even when it is sold again [i.e., in a sale to a second, subsequent buyer]. It is not relevant that an agreement had been recorded in the name of the [first] buyer, by which it was agreed that a penalty would be paid if by chance he had not been allowed to have the benefit [of the servitude].
>
> *[Cum fundo, quem ex duobus retinuit venditor, aquae ducendae servitus imposita sit, empto praedio quaesita servitus distractum denuo praedium sequitur: nec ad rem pertinet, quod stipulatio, qua poenam promitti placuit, ad personam emptoris, si ei forte frui non licuisset, relata est.]* (*D.* 8.3.36 Paul. 5 *ad Plaut.*)

The case involves two subsequent purchases of the same property, and despite some disruption to the text in compilation, the situation can be reconstructed with some certainty. A servitude had been established to channel water to two properties owned by the same person. When one of these properties was sold, the servitude was transferred with the land even if it was not explicitly mentioned. At this time, the seller agreed to pay a penalty to compensate the buyer if, for some reason, he was unable to channel water. The property was purchased again, by a different buyer. But while the servitude was transferred automatically with the land in the second sale, the guarantee or the promise to pay a penalty could not be transferred, because it was a contract or a right *in personam,* that is, an agreement between two parties rather than a right attached to land. For this reason, if the second buyer wanted to have the same guarantee of water rights as the first buyer had had, he needed to make his own agreement with the first buyer, who was now seller of the property. This case highlights the importance of servitudes in the sale of land, as it illustrates some of the key legal mechanisms for protecting water rights when property changed hands.

The sale of rural land created a situation that drew attention to servitudes, or at least it should have. The arrival of outsiders could contribute to disputes about water, as may have happened in the Statilius Taurus case and in the irrigation community of North Africa studied by Shaw.[1] Cato's advice to buyers to scout out the neighborhood (*Agr.* 1.2–4, cited in chapter 1) suggests both that doing so was important and that not all buyers took this advice seriously, though the legal evidence suggests that they should have. But even a well-informed buyer—one who had inquired about servitudes and water resources on the land—might not know all his new neighbors or the local customs. Neighbors might not always be helpful, especially if it was in their interest to avoid making a servitude available, and a buyer who was unaware of servitudes owed to his land might lose out on a valuable resource. A seller, however, would favor disclosures that made the property more attractive to potential buyers, but he might want to conceal the fact that his property was servient, in order to get a higher price.

The law of sale offered mechanisms for managing water rights when property was sold. Already in the early law of sale, servitudes were protected by a general type of guarantee, related to *mancipatio,* the formal conveyance for transferring title of *res mancipi,* which included land and servitudes. When the ownership of land was transferred by other forms of conveyance (e.g., *in iure cessio* or *traditio*), guarantees about servitudes could be created by adding specific declarations or terms to the sale agreement, and these helped the parties to better manage the uncertainties surrounding the water supply on their property. The second part of this chapter explains the development of

1. Shaw, "Lamasba," 69.

these different types of guarantees and investigates how they were used to protect a landowner's interest in the water supply when he was buying or selling rural property. These declarations were discussed in chapter 3 as evidence for a systematic approach to managing resources on rural land. Here, the discussion focuses on problems with terms about servitudes, because legal disputes tended to arise when the buyer and the seller had not agreed on terms or if their terms were inadequate or had been based on misinformation. In the discussion that follows, I refer to such situations as "mistakes," but my use of the word *mistake* in this context does not necessarily imply a lack of fault: sometimes mistakes arose from deliberate and malicious intent (*dolus*). Whatever their cause, mistakes about servitudes could affect not only the sale price of the property but also the landowner's long-term plans for cultivating the land. In the last section of this chapter, I examine a famous lawsuit from the late republic involving servitudes and the purchase of an estate by G. Sergius Orata, who was known for building hypocaust baths and raising oysters. The analysis of this lawsuit sheds light on the economic interests that shaped the law regulating servitudes in sale and on Roman attitudes toward the use of law to pursue economic aims. The chapter opens with a consideration of the tacit transfer of servitudes and its basis in the connection between servitudes and the land. Some of the same issues arose when land was transferred by inheritance, and these cases are brought in for comparison.

THE TRANSFER OF WATER RIGHTS

In the usual course of events, a servitude went with the property in a sale, as explained in the *Digest of Justinian:* "when an estate is servient to an estate and it is sold, the servitudes also follow the estate" [*cum fundus fundo servit, vendito quoque fundo servitutes sequuntur*] (*D.* 8.4.12 Paul. 15 *ad Sab.*).[2] The same was true for dominant estates. The servitude was tacitly transferred because it was conceived as inhering in the land, an idea that is reflected in the inclusion of servitudes among *res mancipi*, the land and physical property necessary to cultivate the land.[3] Here again, the older physical concept of the servitude per-

2. The case cited has one more sentence (not quoted) that applies the same rule to servitudes attached to buildings rather than land. See also *D.* 8.3.25 Pompon. 34 *ad Sab.* (selling part of a property, discussed later in the present chapter); *D.* 8.3.27 Jul. 7 *Dig.* (applying the rule to the sale of jointly owned property); *D.* 41.1.20.1 Ulp. 29 *ad Sab.*

3. On tacit transfer and the servitude's inhering in the land, see Biondi, *Categoria*, 354–57; Grosso, *Servitù prediali*, 94–95 (where additional passages from the *Digest* are included). For the classification of servitudes as *res mancipi*, see the introduction in the present study.

sisted even after servitudes were defined as abstract rights based in use, as illustrated by the treatment of the rule on nonuse. As explained in the *Digest,* the period of nonuse was also transferred to the buyer: "the time [period], during which the preceding owner of the land, to which the servitude is owed, did not use [it], is charged to the person who enters into his place afterward" [*tempus, quo non est usus praecedens fundi dominus, cui servitus debetur, imputatur ei, qui in eius loco successit*] (*D.* 8.6.18.1 Paul. 15 *ad Sab.*).[4] The transfer of the period of nonuse made it all the more important for a buyer to know of servitudes, because he could lose his right rather quickly if the previous owner had not been using it.

When a servitude for channeling or drawing water was transferred in sale, along with it went the necessary infrastructure: pipes, cisterns, wellheads, well covers, troughs, basins, fountains, and taps—indoors or outdoors—as long as they were permanent installations.[5] All this equipment was necessary for exercising the right and making use of the water. In this respect also, the rules for tacit transfer connected utility with the older, more physical notion of a servitude inhering in the land. By contrast, equipment and natural resources were treated differently when a farm was transferred by legacy. Fixed equipment could be included with the land by describing the property as *fundus cum instrumento,* but as explained in the *Digest,* natural resources, such as reed beds or willow groves, could either be included in the *instrumentum* or not.[6]

> Cassius writes that those things that are contained in the earth are not part of the equipment of the farm, for example, reed beds and willow groves, before they are cut down, because the land cannot be equip-

4. For the transfer of the period of nonuse, see also *D.* 8.6.19 pr. Pompon. 32 *ad Sab.* (applying the rule to sale of part of a property, discussed in chapter 3 of the present study. Cf. Solazzi, *Specie ed estinzione,* 168–69.

5. On the transfer of equipment for using water, see *D.* 18.1.40.5–6 Paul. 4 *Epit. Alf.* (water jars and waterwheel); *D.* 18.1.47 Ulp. 29 *ad Sab.* (pipes); *D.* 18.1.48 Paul. 5 *ad Sab.* (outdoor fixtures); *D.* 18.1.49 Ulp. 29 *ad Sab.* (even if the servitude is lost, the pipes are transferred, citing Pomponius for this rule); *D.* 18.1.78 pr. Labeo 4 *Post. Epit. Iavol.* (pipes and cistern); *D.* 19.1.13.31 Ulp. 32 *ad Ed.* (well covers); *D.* 19.1.14 Pompon. 31 *ad Q. Muc.* (well covers); *D.* 19.1.15 Ulp. 32 *ad Ed.* (troughs, basins, fountains, channels—but not the fish in the ponds); *D.* 19.1.38.2 Cels. 8 *Dig.* (underground pipes only if specified).

6. Fixed equipment was included in *instrumentum;* movable items had to be specified individually. See *D.* 33.7.21 Pompon. 1 *Fidecom.,* with Steinwenter, *Fundus cum instrumento,* 82–84 (see 74–75 about reed beds and willows).

ment of the land; but if they are cut, I think they can be included, because they are used for acquiring produce. The same should be said in the case of stakes [i.e., vine props].

[Ea vero, quae solo continentur, instrumenti fundi non esse Cassius scribit, veluti harundineta et salicta, antequam caesa sint, quia fundus fundi instrumentum esse non potest: sed si caesa sint, puto contineri, quia quaerendo fructui deserviunt. idem et in palis erit dicendum.] (*D.* 33.7.12.11 Ulp. 20 *ad Sab.*)

When land was transferred by will or legacy, willows and reeds were considered part of the land itself while they were growing in the ground. Once cut, they became equipment and did not go with the land unless it was transferred *cum instrumento.* Both reed beds and water channels were treated as part of the property (rather than as tools) because of their natural connection to the land. Other equipment was included if it was used in activities that generated the main revenue for the property or contributed to making the property productive—for example, hunting nets went with an estate whose main profit came from hunting (*D.* 33.7.22 pr. Paul 3 *Sent.;* for similar treatment of the equipment of shops, see *D.* 33.7.23 Nerat. 2 *Resp.*).[7] The same principles operated in the law of sale where servitudes were concerned. Servitudes were transferred with the land because they, like the resources they governed, were considered part of the land itself. The second criterion also applies: servitudes were included because they were used to cultivate the land and produce revenue. Indeed, they could exist only if they were used to make the land productive, that is, to serve *utilitas.* Because servitudes were based in the concept of utility, there was no distinction between their connection to the land and their use, as the case makes for reeds. Instead, the connection to the land has two complementary components: the water supply is part of the physical landscape and also contributes to the cultivation of the land. This dualism was formalized and promoted in the legal concept of utility, and utility also underlies the treatment of servitudes in sale. Similarly, the concept of a servitude as a right based in use was critical to the effective transfer of the right when land was sold.

When a servitude was transferred in a land sale, the new owner had the same right to channel water as the previous owner had had, as long as he exercised that right (i.e., did not allow it to expire through nonuse). This rule

7. On the inclusion of equipment because it contributed to productivity or revenue, see Steinwenter, *Fundus cum instrumento,* 86–87. See also chapter 3 in the present study.

is formulated in a case about a right-of-way (*iter*), but it also applied to servitudes for water use.

> A person bought in good faith an estate belonging to someone other [than the seller] and has used a right-of-way that is owed to the estate. The right-of-way is maintained. This is so even if he takes possession of the estate through favor or by forcibly expelling the owner. For when a farm exists in a certain state and is taken in possession in that condition, the right is not lost. It does not make any difference whether the person who took possession did so wrongly. Therefore, it is even more strongly [argued] that the right of channeling water is maintained if water flows through a channel naturally; and this seemed right also to Sabinus, as is written in the fourth book of Neratius's *Parchments.*
>
> *[Qui fundum alienum bona fide emit, itinere quod ei fundo debetur usus est: retinetur id ius itineris: atque etiam si precario aut vi deiecto domino possidet: fundus enim qualiter se habens ita, cum in suo habitu possessus est, ius non deperit, neque refert, iuste nec ne possideat, qui talem eum possidet. Quare fortius et si aqua per rivum sua sponte perfluxit, ius aquae ducendae retinetur, quod et Sabino recte placet, ut apud Neratium libro quarto Membranarum scriptum est.]* (*D.* 8.6.12 Cels. 23 *Dig.*)

The point of the case is that the servitude was not lost, regardless of the circumstances of the sale, unless the right was not exercised.[8] Legal problems surrounding the transfer of title do not interfere with the transfer of the servitude, even if the buyer did not purchase the land in good faith. The connection of the servitude to the land is privileged over other considerations, including the circumstance of the sale of land, questions about title to the land, and the behavior of the parties to the sale. In the case of a servitude for channeling water, Celsus writes, this connection is even more obvious. Though Celsus does not set out his argument, we can reconstruct it. When water runs through the channel naturally (*sua sponte*) it appears to be an inherent part of the estate. It is more obviously connected to the land than is a path, because a stream or channel is a visible landmark that does not require human intervention. A right-of-way or path will fade from view if not used; flowing water will, if anything, create a deeper impression on the land over

8. *D.* 8.6.13 Marc. 17 *Dig.* (likely a hypothetical case testing the rule) maintains that even if the owner sells land with a servitude attached and repurchases it before the period of nonuse expires, he retains the servitude.

time. The legal notion of an inherent connection between the land and rights in servitudes is thus rationalized through ideas about nature or what is natural in land, as were also the concepts of daily and summer water (discussed in chapter 1). Treating the water supply as a natural resource, as this legal approach does, coheres with commons theory and provides a basis for strategies that conserve the water supply and aim at equitable distribution.

While the transfer of servitudes was usually automatic, questions about the allocation of water in a servitude could arise if a property was sold off in parcels. When a landowner divided his property into parcels and sold them individually, each parcel retained any servitudes that were attached to the original estate. A case about a right-of-way explains this rule and its implementation.

> Whatever servitude is owed to a property is owed to all parts of the property: and for this reason, even if it is sold in sections, the servitude goes with each section in such a way that each individual [sc., new owner] can claim a right-of-way for himself. In addition, if a property, to which a servitude is owed, is divided into specific parcels among a number of owners, even though the servitude is owed to each parcel, it still must be arranged so that those [owners] who will not own parcels adjacent to the servient estate nevertheless have passage by right through the other parcels of the divided property, or, if [their parcels] lie adjacent, they can cross [the servient estate].
>
> [*Quaecumque servitus fundo debetur, omnibus eius partibus debetur: et ideo quamvis particulatim venierit, omnes partes servitus sequitur et ita, ut singuli recte agant ius sibiesse eundi. Si tamen fundus, cui servitus debetur, certis regionibus inter plures dominos divisus est, quamvis omnibus partibus servitus debeatur, tamen opus est, ut hi, qui non proximas partes serventi fundo habebunt, transitum per reliquas partes fundi divisi iure habeant aut, si proximi patiantur, transeant.*] (*D.* 8.3.23.3 Paul. 15 *ad Sab.*)

The first part of this case is a fairly simple rule: the servitude must follow each parcel that is transferred in sale. The same rule applies in situations of joint ownership, including when land was inherited by several heirs: each of the co-owners or coheirs becomes a holder of the entire servitude.[9] Any of

9. For cases about shares in land and servitudes, see, e.g., *D.* 8.1.17 Pompon. 1 *Reg.* (each of several heirs can sue for the whole servitude); *D.* 8.3.19 Paul. 6 *ad Sab.* (each co-owner individually can bring an action to protect a servitude); *D.* 8.4.6.1 Ulp. 28 *ad Sab.* (servitudes cannot be owned in shares), with Kaser, *RP* 1:443.

the co-owners or coheirs or any of the new owners has a right to use the servitude. In all these situations, the rule coheres with the concept of a servitude as a unified right that applied to the entire property and could not be owned by shares. Jointly owned property might seem to contradict this rule, but where two people own a property that has a servitude, each owns the whole property and the whole servitude. Even when one of the co-owners sold his share in the property to another, the servitude might appear to be sold in shares, but it is only an apparent exception, because ownership of the servitude was seen as continuous (*D.* 8.3.32 Afric. 6 *Quaest.*; *D.* 8.1.8.1 Paul. 15 *ad Plaut.*).

Once the legal status of the servitude is determined, the case goes on to consider how the new owners would use the servitude in the new landholding configuration. The problem arises from the rule that a servitude can be established only on an adjacent property. In the case, the property has been divided in such a way that some of the new parcels are not contiguous but still possess the servitudes. The solution is not to limit the servitudes; rather, new servitudes are to be created and attached to the intervening properties so that the existing servitudes can be exercised. The legal solution rejects the rule about adjacent properties and focuses on preserving the connection between servitudes and the land, perhaps because this served the needs of the landowners.[10] Or it may be that the connection between servitudes and the land was simply more important. Yet the solution here seems limited by the particular circumstances of this case, namely, that the case deals with a right-of-way. Applying the rule to a servitude for channeling water would raise practical, if not also legal, problems. Though the servitude would remain undivided—owned fully by each new owner—the water itself would have to be divided, unless the supply were somehow increased. Other cases recognize this real environmental constraint on local water supplies and attempt to solve the problem in a different way that is more compatible with both utility and conservation.

When land was sold in two parcels the parties to the sale had to decide how the water would be shared between the two parts of the property, each now an independent estate. The answer to this question is deceptively simple. The water supply should be allotted in proportion to the size of the estate, regardless of the landowners' interests.

10. Biondi (*Categoria*, 218–19) assumes that this solution was the product of a lawsuit, the circumstances of which have been left out of the case as it is reported in the *Digest*.

> If I sell a specific part of my estate to you, the right of channeling water also passes to you, even if the water was channeled mostly for the sake of another part of the estate. There is no account taken of either quality of land or use of the water so that the right of channeling water would follow only that part of the estate that was most valuable [with the water] or needed the use of the water most. Instead there should be a sharing of the water in proportion to the amount of land that is retained or alienated.
>
> [*Si partem fundi mei certam tibi vendidero, aquae ductus ius, etiamsi alterius partis causa plerumque ducatur, te quoque sequetur: neque ibi aut bonitatis agri aut usus eius aquae ratio habenda est ita, ut eam solam partem fundi, quae pretiosissima sit aut maxime usum eius aquae desideret, ius eius ducendae sequatur, sed pro modo agri detenti aut alienati fiat eius aquae divisio.*] (*D.* 8.3.25 Pompon. 34 *ad Sab.*)

A strict proportional division of the water between the two parts of the estate creates a kind of "natural" equity, based in the inherent connection between land, water, and the right to water. The two owners have a right to as much water as land. A similar approach is found in a rescript by Marcus Aurelius (Antoninus) and Lucius Verus (AD 161–69) concerning the distribution of water from a public river for irrigation: allotments are in proportion to the size of the fields (*pro modo possessionum*).[11] Dividing water in proportion to the amount of land may have been the usual standard in public water systems, as, for example, in the irrigation communities described by the inscriptions from Roman Spain and North Africa.[12] This "natural" relationship provided an objective standard for a legal rule that could curtail wrangling and special pleading about subjective issues, such as how the owner planned to use the land and water. In the legal case, Pomponius explicitly rejects the landowners' rational calculations about land use, including how the land might be cultivated (*neque ibi aut bonitatis agri aut usus eius aquae ratio habenda est*) and how it might be made most profitable or productive (*quae [pars] pretiosissima sit aut maxime usum eius aquae desideret*). His argument is consistent with a ruling in another case by Iavolenus, who states as a general principle that the servitude remained after the land use changes, even if the

11. On *D.* 8.3.17 Papir. 1 *Const.*, see Biondi, *Categoria,* 361. For the same type of proportional division in North Africa, see Shaw, "Water and Society," 167–68; see also chapter 3 in the present study.

12. Shaw, "Lamasba," 82; Beltrán Lloris, "Irrigation Decree," 170. Cf. Glick, *Irrigation and Society,* 13.

servitude was established for a specific type of cultivation.[13] Thus, a servitude could be acquired to achieve a specific goal, but once established, its existence was independent of its function. These principles reflect a rigid notion of a servitude as a permanent feature of the land, like the resource it governs. Even as these rules attempt to create an equitable distribution of water, they seem to have the opposite effect by ignoring factors that make equity something other than equality or a strictly proportional allocation of water.

Reconstructing the circumstances surrounding the case, however, reveals that the rule does in fact serve the landowners' interests, by encouraging responsible planning about the water supply. In this case, the buyer might have had plans to change the way the land was cultivated or to build a new garden. Such plans would increase demand for water, which would put the seller at a disadvantage. If the two parties did not come to an agreement and include the terms in the sale, they would be stuck with this simple proportional allocation. The rule thus encouraged buyers and sellers to negotiate the terms of water sharing in advance, saving everyone the time and trouble of a lawsuit. This legal efficiency was recognized. In two cases, the jurists recommended appointing an arbiter to help the parties reach agreement about details, such as the width of a right-of-way (*D.* 8.3.13.2–3 Iavol. 10 *ex Cassio*) or the type of vehicle that could be driven along a right-of-way (*D.* 8.6.11 pr. Marcel. 4 *Dig.*). Where a servitude for water use was involved, negotiation among landowners could prevent conflicts arising from a proportional distribution: if the properties were of different sizes, the allocation of water would also be unequal, which could lead to dispute. The situation described in the previous case, where the new parcels of land were not all contiguous, might require careful negotiation to allocate the water within environmental as well as practical constraints, that is, not building too many expensive new channels. The cases about the transfer of servitudes suggest that land sale was not uncommon or at least that Roman landowners had moved away from Cato's idealistic, unchanging neighborhood, where a stable social structure supported traditional water-sharing arrangements. Instead, these legal cases emphasize individual aims, rather than common interests, and provide a mechanism through which landowners could negotiate changes in their rights to valuable natural resources.

---

13. *D.* 8.3.13 pr. Iavol. *ex Cassio.* The case involved a servitude attached to a vineyard and is discussed in chapter 3 in the present study.

GUARANTEES, MISTAKES, AND LIABILITY

Although the legal system provided incentives for buyers and sellers to make declarations about servitudes when land was sold, they did not always do so. Moreover, even when they had made such agreements, there could be problems—for example, if one or both parties had incorrect or incomplete information about servitudes on the sale property. Since these agreements and their terms functioned as warranties for free title and enjoyment of the property (including any attached servitudes), they could be the basis for a legal claim, especially if the buyer's financial interest in the property was harmed by problems with the terms. Most often, the buyer brought suit when the servitudes on the property turned out to be different than they had appeared when the sale was made: either a servitude was owed to the land but could not be exercised, or the land owed a servitude that had somehow been concealed. When a buyer or a seller had incomplete or inaccurate information about servitudes, he would not be able to plan effectively for the use of his property, nor could he add declarations to the sale contract in order to secure his interests. Mistakes or misinformation about servitudes, as well as sales based on misinformation, could create unfairness in negotiations over the sale price and could also have a negative impact on the estate's subsequent productivity.

As the following list shows, mistakes involved four kinds of misinformation about the servitudes on the property.

Land appears . . .	*Land is . . .*	*Advantage to . . .*
not dominant	dominant	buyer
to owe a servitude	free from servitude	buyer
free from servitudes	servient	seller
dominant	not dominant	seller

The first two mistakes represented the land as having fewer resources than it actually did. These mistakes put the seller at a disadvantage because the price might be lower, while the buyer reaped an unexpected boon when he discovered that his property did not owe any servitudes or was in fact the beneficiary of a servitude. Conversely, with the second two mistakes, the land appeared to have more resources than it actually did. They gave an advantage to the seller in negotiating a price and put the buyer at a disadvantage, because he was likely to pay more for the land than it was worth. These mistakes may have had long-term consequences as well, especially for the buyer who purchased a property with plans that relied on, for example, water governed by a servitude.

Roman landowners adapted the law of sale to mitigate the effects of these mistakes, creating remedies that provided economic compensation for the cost of the error. Typically in Roman law, the buyer bore a greater risk than the seller because of the structure of the Roman law of sale; our maxim "Let the buyer beware" [caveat emptor] comes from Roman law. While the seller's main risk in sale was payment of the price, the buyer risked title to the property, along with his enjoyment of the property and its amenities. Early Roman civil law (perhaps the *Twelve Tables*) protected the buyer's right to clear title of real estate and may have offered some protection for servitudes.[14] Broader protections for the buyer's interest in servitudes, on both servient and dominant estates, developed in the middle to late republican periods, as Romans recognized the economic value of servitudes both for the productivity of their estates and for their price on the real estate market. The development of broader protections for servitudes can be illustrated with a sketch of the historical development of guarantees in the sale of real estate.

The early civil law already provided some protection for the buyer when property was conveyed by *mancipatio* (the oldest form of conveyance for transfer of title). *Mancipatio* included a guarantee that the land was free from defect of title; that is, it guaranteed that the buyer would become owner of the property after the sale. If there was any question about title, the buyer could bring suit, using an *actio auctoritatis* (action for ownership). For example, if the seller did not own the property and the real owner came forward to take possession, the buyer could not obtain clear title and would be evicted from the property. In this case, the buyer could bring an *actio auctoritatis* against the seller to settle the issue, winning either clear title or double the sale price if he was evicted (*D.* 21.2.48 Nerat. 6 *Memb.*).[15] The *actio auctoritatis* did not, however, protect the buyer from the possibility that the estate owed unknown servitudes to its neighbors. The law's neglect of servitudes seems to fit landholding patterns of the early republic, when there was limited mobility: if land did change hands, buyers and sellers were likely to be familiar with the property because they were locals. Such a rural landscape

14. See Weber, *Agrarian Sociology*, 297, on this protection in the *Twelve Tables* (ca. 450 BC).

15. On the double penalty in the *actio auctoritatis*, see Kaser, *RP* 1:132, 545–46, 553–54; Zimmermann, *Law of Obligations*, 294–95. Cf. *D.* 21.2.10 Cels. 27 *Dig.* (applying the rule to sale by co-owners).

is idealized by Cato's advice to buyers of rural estates to buy land among farms that do not change owners often and where those who sell estates regret that they have sold (*Agr.* 1.4). Cato's audience would probably have reacted with nostalgia; what need would there have been for this advice if Romans were not already buying and selling property in ways that made it hard to find a property that fit this description? Assessments of the real estate market in Rome vary, and accurate measures may be impossible.[16] But in even a limited real estate market, protections for servitudes would have been helpful, if not strictly necessary. As with schedules, regulation of economic interests could also serve to protect a common resource, such as a local water supply.

Over the course of the second century BC, additional legal guarantees for servitudes were created in the form of declarations, formal and informal, that were added to the sale contract or conveyance.[17] Formal declarations could follow a fixed formula, the *uti optimus maximusque* clause, or they could be terms or statements that the parties made specifying the existence (or not) of servitudes on the sale property and promises not to interfere with the use of servitudes after the sale. Informal declarations included whatever the seller might say about the property during negotiations and, in some cases, what he did not say.

First in our discussion of guarantees and probably also first to develop was the *uti optimus maximusque* clause, which was used by the early first century BC, based on references to republican jurists in the legal cases about it.[18]

16. Love (*Antiquity and Capitalism,* 74–80) argues, on the basis of the previously quoted passage from Cato, that there was a Roman market for investment property. Kehoe (*Investment, Profit, and Tenancy,* 74–75) recognizes a more limited market for real estate; compare the more reserved judgment of Duncan-Jones (*Economy of the Roman Empire,* 324). There is some evidence for a lively real estate market at least in the first century (see Rawson, "Ciceronean Aristocracy"), and the proscriptions also stimulated buying and selling of land (see Shatzman, *Senatorial Wealth,* 37–44). G. Sergius Orata's activities, discussed later in this chapter, are evidence for investment in real estate around 100 BC; see Marzano, *Villas in Central Italy,* 76 (Orata), 75–81 (generally).

17. The development of the aediles' edict regulating sale, especially its treatment of the sale of slaves with defects, probably influenced this process. Some changes in the law of sale may have been earlier, perhaps from the third century BC, but the evidence does not allow certainty. See Watson, *Law of Obligations.* On the aediles' edict, see Monier, *La garantie contre les vices cachés,* 17–27.

18. For legal cases dating the *uti optimus maximusque* clause to the republican period, see *D.* 21.2.75 Venul. 16 *Stip.* (also with reference to Quintus Mucius); *D.* 19.1.39 Mod. 5 *Resp.* (*veteres,* "republican jurists"). Cf. *D.* 19.1.1.1 Ulp. 28 *ad Sab.; D.* 19.1.35 Ulp. 70 *ad Ed.; D.* 50.16.169 Paul. 5 *ad Sab.* See Kaser, *RP* 1:554; Zimmermann, *Law of Obligations,* 296–300.

Celsus quotes the rules from the writings of Quintus Mucius Scaevola (cos. 95 BC), though it is likely to have arisen earlier, along with other guarantees related to sale.

> When you sold a farm, you did not say, "As it is free from all encumbrances." It is true, as seemed right to Quintus Mucius, that you should deliver the property not free [i.e., unencumbered] but "as is." The same declaration is made about urban properties.
>
> [*cum venderes fundum, non dixisti "ita ut optimus maximusque," verum est, quod Quinto Mucio placebat, non liberum, sed qualis esset, fundum praestari oportere. Idem et in urbanis praediis dicendum est.*] (*D.* 18.1.59 Cels. 8 *Dig.*)

The quotation from Mucius appears to be a response to a seller (*cum venderes fundum*) after a buyer had brought suit on the sale because the land was encumbered (*non liberum*). Mucius's opinion, seconded by Celsus, would have been good news for the seller: because he had not included the *uti optimus maximusque* clause in the *mancipatio,* he could not be held liable for the land's being encumbered. Without this clause, the buyer takes the land "as is" (*qualis esset*), meaning that it might or might not owe servitudes. In this situation, the buyer was responsible for knowing about servitudes on the property, and the seller was freed from any liability arising from servitudes. When the *uti optimus maximusque* clause was added to the *mancipatio* in the sale of real estate, it provided a guarantee that the land owed no servitudes. If it was later discovered that the land was servient, the seller was liable to the buyer for a portion of the sale price (not the full double-price penalty for eviction from the whole property in the *actio auctoritatis*).[19]

The *uti optimus maximusque* clause made it easy to determine liability for servitudes owed by an estate. Not all sellers, however, used this clause, probably because of its sweeping warranty. A servitude might escape the notice of even a landowner more familiar with his estate than the stereotypical absentee landlord. Landholding patterns would have made it difficult to be certain of servitudes on one's land, as Roman elites tended to own several estates, usually not contiguous and often in different re-

19. For cases on compensation for a suit on the *uti optimus maximusque* clause, see *D.* 21.2.48 Nerat. 6 *Membr.* (compensation for excessive price; then, if eviction is from whole estate, total damages are limited to double the price); *D.* 21.1.61 Ulp. 80 *ad Ed.* (seller is liable for difference in price when the buyer pays more because of a mistake about a servitude); *D.* 21.2.69.5 Scaev. 2 *Quaest.* (seller not liable for eviction).

gions.[20] Even where landholdings were recorded in public archives, these records might not always be complete or up-to-date, and landowners might not consult them. Under Augustus, an administrative framework for landholding records began to be developed, though surveyors maps, for example, were typically meant to be not definitive records but working tools.[21] The very process of buying and selling land probably contributed to the confusion, as servitudes were forgotten or omitted from sale contracts. At least the number of cases reported in the *Digest* suggests that this was not uncommon. Moreover, simply including the *uti optimus maximusque* clause might not have been sufficient protection, since some buyers tried to expand it so that it meant not just "free" but dominant.[22] As a result, in many cases, a declaration tailored to the specific property might more effectively provide accurate information and thus prevent litigation and protect resources.

The second type of guarantee was a declaration about servitudes on the property. Such declarations could be informal statements or formal agreements or terms added to the sale contract. They created contracts between buyer and seller, rights *in personam* and not *in rem* like servitudes; for this reason, they applied only to the parties who made them and were invalid if the property was subsequently sold, as is illustrated by the case cited at the start of this chapter (*D.* 8.3.36 Paul. 5 *ad Plaut.*).[23] Declarations could follow any one of several legal forms (*stipulatio, cautio, exceptio, pactum*), but they are most commonly referred to as *dicta* in the legal sources.[24] Any of these declara-

---

20. The Younger Pliny's landholdings are probably typical; see De Neeve, "Roman Landowner"; De Neeve, *Colonus,* 167–69. For landholding patterns in general, see Vallat, "Structures agraires"; Gabba, "Strutture agrarie"; Duncan-Jones, "Configurations of Landholding." See also chapter 1 in the present study.

21. Campbell, "Shaping the Rural Environment," 95–98; Keppie, *Colonisation,* 8–14. On census records in the republican period, including the likelihood of local registration before Julius Caesar's veteran colonies and the *Tabula Heraclea,* see Brunt, *Italian Manpower,* 26–43.

22. *D.* 21.2.75 Venul. 16 *Stip.;* this case seems a bit confused, probably because of changes introduced by the compilers, but it is clear that the *uti optimus maximusque* clause did not guarantee a dominant estate and that Quintus Mucius is the authority for this opinion. Cf. *D.* 18.1.66.pr Pompon. 31 *ad. Q. Muc.* See Kaser *RP* 1.554.

23. Cf. *D.* 8.4.6.3a Ulp. 28 *ad Sab.; D.* 8.4.8 Pompon. 8 *ad Sab.* (sale of an *insula,* or apartment block, with, presumably, an urban servitude).

24. *Dictum* is the most common term, though *pactum* is also used. When the jurists use *promissum,* it is generally understood to mean *stipulatio.* All of these statements could be grounds for litigation. See Kaser, *RP* 1:443–44, 555–56; Zimmermann, *Law of Obligations,* 310; Watson, *Law of Obligations,* 83–89. These mechanisms could not be used to create servitudes, though two cases seem to indicate the opposite (*D.* 8.3.33.1 Afr. 9 *Quaest.; D.* 8.4.3 Gaius 7 *ad*

tions—general or specific, formal or informal—could be the grounds for a lawsuit after the sale.

For the most part, declarations about servitudes were made by the seller; the buyer usually made promises only about the price or schedule of payment. When the seller could not provide specific details about servitudes on the property, he might make a general disclaimer about servitudes, stating that servitudes owed by the property would remain in force: "whoever has a servitude, let it be so" [*quibus est servitus, utique esto*] (*D.* 8.4.10 Ulp. 10 *ad Sab.*, discussed in chapter 3). Such a declaration would have served as notice to the buyer that he was purchasing a servient estate and that he needed to work out the details with his new neighbors. In addition, when the sale property was dominant and when the seller owned land nearby, the seller might also promise not to interfere with the use of a servitude. In fact, the jurists encouraged buyers to get just such a promise when purchasing a dominant estate.[25] A general declaration could also protect the seller from an unexpected source of liability, such as a servitude that he did not know about. The rule and rationale are set out as the second part of a long case that opens with a discussion of mistakes about the boundary of the sale property, though only the part about servitudes is quoted here. The rule for general declarations is the same for boundaries as for servitudes.

> This rule is also reported in the writings of the old [i.e., republican] jurists in the case of a person who made a clause as follows: "if any servitudes are owed, they will be owed." For the legal experts responded, if the seller, though certain that particular servitudes were owed to specific individuals, had not advised the buyer, he can be held liable [in an action] on the sale, since this general clause ought not apply to things that the seller knew and that he could and should have declared specifically, but [the general clause applies] to those things that he did not know and about which he was unable to give the buyer sure

---

Prov. Ed.). These cases are generally interpreted as discussing law of the provinces, where, it seems, it was possible to create a servitude with a contract between the parties (*stipulatio* or *pactum*) rather than as a right in the land. For the mechanism to create servitudes, see the introduction in the present study, and for other cases with declarations and terms, see n. 62 to chapter 3 in the present study.

25. This guarantee not to interfere usually took the form of a *cautio:* see *D.* 8.1.20 Iavol. 5 *Post. Labeo* (*cavendum . . . per te non fieri, quo minus eo iure uti possit*); *D.* 8.3.29 Paul. 2 *Epit. Alf.* (*in lege ita dixerat*); *D.* 8.3.36 Paul. 2 *Resp.* (*stipulatio, qua poenam promittit placuit*); *D.* 18.1.40.1 Paul. 4 *Epit.* (*in lege ita dixerat*); *D.* 19.1.3.2 Pompon. 9 *ad Sab.* (*cavere debes per te non fieri quo minus utar*).

information. Herennius Modestinus replied, if the seller did anything of the sort that is in question for the purpose of entrapping the buyer, he can be sued in a suit on the sale.

> [*cum hoc et apud veteres sit relatum in eius persona, qui sic exceperat: "servitutes si quae debentur, debebuntur" etenim iuris auctores responderunt, si certus venditor quibusdam personis certas servitutes debere non admonuisset emptorem, ex empto eum teneri debere, quando haec generalis exceptio non ad ea pertinere debeat, quae venditor novit quaeque specialiter excipere et potuit et debuit, sed ad ea, quae ignoravit et de quibus emptorem certiorare nequivit. Herennius Modestinus respondit, si quid circumveniendi emptoris causa venditor in specie de qua quaeritur fecit, ex empto actione conveniri posse.*] (*D.* 19.1.39 Mod. 5 *Resp.*)

This case illustrates the form of a general declaration and allows us to observe how such a declaration could encourage the seller to be responsible in providing information about servitudes. The classical jurist Modestinus affirmed the opinions of republican jurists that a general declaration created broad liability for the seller. A general declaration protected the seller when he was unaware of servitudes on his land (i.e., from honest errors). But if the seller had specific information and used the general declaration, his action was interpreted as an attempt to entrap or defraud the buyer, and he could be held liable for fraud (*dolus;* cf. *D.* 21.2.69.5 Scaev. 2 *Quaest.; D.* 18.1.66.1 Pompon. 31 *ad. Q. Muc.*). It could be difficult to determine when fraud was involved, as is discussed in more detail shortly.

General declarations had drawbacks for both buyer and seller. They protected the buyer from only the third type of mistake about servitudes, when land appeared to be unencumbered but was in reality servient. A general declaration exposed the seller to greater liability, because it applied only to servitudes that were unknown to him before the sale. If a servitude appeared after the sale and if the buyer could demonstrate that the seller had known about it beforehand, the seller would be liable, even with a general declaration. Despite this advantage, buyers would probably have preferred specific declarations, because they provided more security about the resources available on the land (they could cover all four types of mistakes), as well as a more direct route to holding the seller liable and getting compensation for any mistake.

Specific declarations answered a number of questions: what servitudes existed on the land, owed to or by it? What servitudes would be created for the future? How should these rights be exercised? In the legal cases, specific declarations are described as *nominatim,* and a few are reported in enough detail to show their form. A declaration probably used the verb *servire* to indicate that the sale property owed a servitude, and presumably it named the property as well as the party or parties who would own the servitude, as in, for example, "if in transferring title anyone said that the estate owed a servitude to Titius" [*si quis in tradendo dixerit fundum Titio servire*] (*D.* 8.4.6.3a Ulp. 28 *ad Sab.*).[26] As we saw in chapter 3, the seller could use a specific declaration to reserve a servitude for himself after the sale, but these declarations could also be used to protect the buyer's access to resources and often led to dispute.

Even when the seller had made a specific declaration, questions or mistakes might arise that led to liability. Where a mistake in a specific declaration put the seller at a disadvantage, it was his own fault: he should have known about the servitudes on his land, and he was liable only to himself for the mistake. One case offers a chance at protection for a seller who made an informal declaration but failed to include it in the legal conveyance. This seller is allowed to file suit, but it is not clear that he would win his case (*D.* 8.2.35 Marc. 3 *Reg.*). When a mistake put the buyer at a disadvantage, however, he might try to hold the seller liable and win compensation. If the declaration was unclear or ambiguous, the buyer could sue for compensation in an action on the sale (*actio empti*),[27] as illustrated in the following example: "In the contract [for purchase] of land, he mentioned access to water; it was asked whether or not a right-of-way to the water was included. [Alfenus] responded that it seemed to him that it was agreed, and for this reason the seller should deliver the right-of-way" [*in lege fundi aquam accessuram dixit: quaerebatur, an etiam iter aquae accessisset. respondit sibi videri id actum esse, et ideo iter quoque venditorem tradere oportere*] (*D.* 18.1.40.1 Paul. 4 *Epit. Alf.*). Similarly, the seller could be liable for sloppy language, for example, by not specifying which part of the property was concerned. The rule is illustrated with an example of a servitude for drains or eavesdrip.

---

26. Some of the language in this case (*D.* 8.4.6.3a Ulp. 28 *ad Sab.*) might suggest a personal servitude (*si quidem Titio servitutem concesserit*), as argues Biondi (*Categoria*, 374–75). But it is better to interpret this clause as concerning servitudes attached to the land, because the case involves the transfer of ownership of a property (*aedes*) and recommends a suit on the sale of that property. Cf. *D.* 8.2.33 Paul. 5 *Epit. Alf.*, citing a clause from a sale contract that described an urban servitude for a supporting wall.

27. *D.* 19.1.1.1 Ulp. 28 *ad Sab.* (discussed shortly in the present chapter), with Kaser, *RP* 1:556. On liability for informal statements in particular, see Cic. *Off.* 3.55, with Watson, *Law of Obligations*, 89–90. In some cases, it might have been necessary to resolve a dispute about ownership of the land with *vindicatio* before proceeding with the claim about the servitude, because only the owner of land (i.e., the buyer with clear title) could sue for it (*D.* 19.1.6.5 Pompon. 9 *ad Sab.*). See Kaser, *RP* 1:446–47.

> When in the sale contract it was written thus, "The runoff and eavesdrip as they are now, so they should be," and it was not specified which runoff and eavesdrip, first you should consider what was meant. If this is not clear, then it should be interepreted to the disadvantage of the seller, for the expression was ambiguous.
>
> [*Cum in lege venditionis ita sit scriptum: 'flumina stillicidia uti nunc sunt, ut ita sint,' nec additur, quae flumina vel stillicidia, primum spectari oportet, quid acti sit: si non id appareat, tunc id accipitur quod venditori nocet: ambigua enim oratioest.*] (*D.* 18.1.33 Pompon. 33 *ad Sab.*)

Disputes tended to arise where the land was or might be encumbered, when the property appeared free but was servient, or if it appeared dominant when it was not. For this reason, most of the legal cases involve mistakes that put the buyer at a disadvantage, and in these cases, the seller could be held liable for real mistakes about servitudes and for mistakes involving fraud, depending on the circumstances of the case.

The decision about a seller's liability depended on what he knew about servitudes on the sale property and how he used that information. Four issues emerge:

> What did the seller know?
> To what extent did the seller share his knowledge with the buyer?
> What did the seller say about servitudes, both during negotiations and in formal declarations attached to the sale contract?
> What were the seller's intentions in his communication with the buyer about servitudes?

The buyer's knowledge could also be a factor: in some cases, the seller was not liable if the buyer already knew about the servitude. The legal interpretations of the buyer's and seller's knowledge changed over time, as Rodger has argued in a pair of articles.[28] I summarize his argument here.

---

28. Rodger, "Concealing a Servitude"; "Concealing a Servitude II." Rodger's argument is based on the analysis of a long legal case (*D.* 19.1.1.1 Ulp. 28 *ad Sab.*, discussed shortly in the present chapter) and on the lawsuit involving Gaius Sergius Orata that I discuss in the last section of this chapter. See also Apathy, "Sachgerechtighkeit," 102–13, for a similar interpretation of the legal rules in the late republic, based on *D* 18.1.45 Marc. 4 *Reg.*, a key case in the development of the seller's liability, involving a used garment sold as new. Cf. Kaser, *RP* 1:556.

In the republican period, the words of the seller's declaration were the basis of liability, and only the seller's knowledge was taken into account. If there was a servitude and the seller did not declare it, he could be held liable whether or not the buyer already knew about it. This rule is assumed in the opinion about the general declaration, cited earlier (*D.* 19.1.39 Mod. 5 *Resp.*), where it is ascribed to republican jurists (*veteres*). There, the seller was liable, despite his general declaration, because "this general clause ought not apply to things that the seller knew and that he could and should have declared specifically, but [the general clause applies] to those things that he did not know and about which he was unable to give the buyer sure information." In effect, the seller is liable just for concealing the servitude, not for intentionally misleading the buyer, which is central in the later rule. The earlier rule provided an adequate standard of good faith (*bona fides*) according to Rodger, because it put only a small burden on the seller, could be applied consistently, compensated for the lack of public records of servitudes, and protected against both sloppiness and fraud: "When a seller deliberately omits the simple step of mentioning the servitude, while there may be no question of actual fraud, there will nearly always be a suspicion that he hoped, even if only at the back of his mind, to obtain some advantage by not drawing attention to the defect."[29] With this rule, the decision about liability was based solely on rather straightforward evidence, often a written document of the sale contract and declarations, and there was no need to tackle the more difficult questions about fraud and what the buyer and seller knew.[30]

The later, classical rule takes the buyer's knowledge into account in evaluating what the seller knew and what he did with his knowledge. It also distinguishes fraud from unintentional mistakes; the seller was always liable for fraud but could in some circumstances avoid liability for a real mistake. The issues are laid out in a long case ascribed to Ulpian, which discusses four situations: (1) the seller failed to mention the servitude, (2) the seller denied the existence of the servitude when questioned by the buyer, (3) the seller made a general declaration omitting the servitude, and (4) the seller used unethical means to deceive the buyer about servitude. The case also considers the seller's motives and attempts to differentiate between concealing a servitude and misleading the buyer.

29. Rodger, "Concealing a Servitude," 145.

30. On the use of tablets to record contracts and *mancipatio*, see Meyer, *Legitimacy and Law*, 112–20.

If the seller, although he knew that a servitude was owed, concealed it, he will not escape an action on the sale <if the buyer did not know this fact:> for all acts done contrary to good faith come into the action on the sale. But we understand that the seller knew and concealed in this way, not only if he did not advise [the buyer] but if he denied that a servitude was owed, when he was asked by him [i.e., the buyer]. But if you imagine that he declared in this way, "no servitude is owed anyway, but lest an unanticipated one appears, I am not liable," I think that he is liable [in the action] on the sale, because a servitude was owed and he knew it. But if he did this so that the buyer could not know that a servitude was owed, I judge that he should be held liable. And in general I would say, if he relies on unethical practice in concealing the servitude, he should be held liable, but not if he wanted to protect his own security. These are the true [opinions], if the buyer did not know about the servitudes, because a person who knows does not seem to have been deceived and the one who is not unaware does not need to be informed.

[Venditor si, cum sciret deberi, servitutem celavit, non evadet ex empto actionem, <si modo eam rem emptor ignoravit:> omnia enim quae contra bonam fidem fiunt veniunt in empti actionem. sed scire venditorem et celare sic accipimus, non solum si non admonuit, sed et si negavit servitutem istam deberi, cum esset ab eo quaesitum. sed et si proponas eum ita dixisse: 'nulla quidem servitus debetur, verum ne emergat inopinata servitus, non teneor,' puto eum ex empto teneri, quia servitus debebatur et scisset. sed si id egit, ne cognosceret emptor aliquam servitutem deberi, opinor eum ex empto teneri. Et generaliter dixerim, si improbato more versatus sit in celanda servitute, debere eum teneri, non si securitati suae prospectum voluit. haec ita vera sunt, si emptor ignoravit servitutes, quia non videtur esse celatus qui scit neque certiorari debuit qui non ignoravit.] (*D.* 19.1.1.1 Ulp. 28 *ad Sab.*)

According to Rodger, the first sentence of this case should be ascribed to Massurius Sabinus, a jurist active in the early first century AD. Further, its last clause (*si modo eam rem emptor ignoravit*) is probably a postclassical gloss and therefore not part of the republican rule.[31] In this way, the first sentence reports the republican rule that the seller was liable, regardless of what the buyer knew or did not know.

In the rest of the case, Ulpian contemplates the classical rule and complications that could make it hard to determine liability. In general, the clas-

31. Rodger, "Concealing a Servitude II," 239.

sical rule freed the seller from liability when the buyer already knew about the servitude, unless there was evidence of fraud (*dolus*). As Rodger put it, "the obligation of the seller in their [i.e., the classical jurists'] eyes is not really to mention servitudes which he knows affect the property; rather his obligation is not to deceive the buyer by failing to mention a servitude which he knows affects the property."[32] In contrast to the republican rule, which focused on the declaration itself, the classical rule takes into account what both parties knew and the seller's motives. The buyer had to actually be deceived, as is brought out in the gloss at the end ("because a person who knows does not seem to have been deceived and the one who is not unaware does not need to be informed"). An ignorant buyer, however, could be deceived either intentionally or unintentionally, and Ulpian considers both scenarios. The seller was liable not just for failing to make a declaration informing the buyer about a servitude but also for denying the existence of a servitude when the buyer asked. In addition, a general declaration could be interpreted as implying fraud; in this respect, the classical rule was the same as the republican rule.

Ulpian's treatment of the general declaration is the most complicated, according to Rodger's analysis, starting from the hint of doubt (*puto*) that the seller should be held liable in this situation. Rodger understands Ulpian's opinion about the general declaration in connection with what looks like a summary at the end, taking together everything from *sed et si promonas* to *Et generaliter dixerim . . . prospectum voluit.* In this view, Ulpian considers two possible explanations for the seller's use of the general declaration: either to deceive the buyer or to protect his own interests. In the first case, he is liable for the declaration; in the second, he is not, though he might be held liable in a more general claim on title to the land. The classical rule thus involves a more nuanced view of mistakes about servitudes and the motives of the buyers and sellers in lawsuits about them.

Once it was determined that the seller was liable, he could be compelled to compensate for the mistake in two ways. First, the seller could be required to take action relating to the servitude itself. If the seller had promised that the estate was dominant, he could be compelled to provide the servitude (*D.* 18.1.40.1 Paul. 4 *Epit. Alf.* [cited earlier]; *D.* 19.1.6.6 Pompon. 9 *ad Sab.*). If the seller had declared that the property was servient when it was in fact free, the buyer could be released from the servitude (*D.* 19.1.8.1 Paul. 5 *ad Sab.*). Second, the seller could be compelled to pay monetary compensation to the buyer.

32. Rodger, "Concealing a Servitude," 147.

For example, when the buyer purchased property that was later found to be servient, he was compensated for the difference between the sale price and how much less he would have paid for the land if he had known about the servitude when the sale was negotiated: "As often as there is a claim about a servitude if [the seller] loses he should pay how much less the buyer would have paid, if he had known that this servitude was imposed [on the land]." [*quotiens de servitute agitur, victus tantum debet praestare, quanti minoris emisset emptor, si scisset hanc servitutem impositam*] (*D.* 21.1.61 Ulp. 80 *ad Ed.*). The buyer could also be compensated if he thought that he was purchasing an unencumbered property when it was in fact servient, because he could be forced to provide the servitude (*D.* 19.1.8 pr. Paul. 5 *ad Sab.*).[33]

Compensation might also extend to additional losses. For example, if the buyer discovered that his property lost water because of a servitude, his interest in having the water could be included in the settlement. Starting in the late republic, the concept of good faith, *bona fides,* was developed to protect the buyer's interests beyond clear title to the land (or whatever was purchased), and the idea is formulated in terms of interest by Ulpian: "if an object was sold but not delivered, there is a claim for the interest, that is, the interest of the buyer in having the object: this [interest], however, goes beyond the price, if his interest is worth more than what the object is worth or was sold for" [*si res vendita non tradatur, in id quod interest agitur, hoc est quod rem habere interest emptoris: hoc autem interdum pretium egreditur, si pluris interest, quam res valet vel empta est*] (*D.* 19.1.1 pr. Ulp. 28 *ad Sab.*).[34] The seller could be liable for more than the sale price, when the buyer's interest was taken into account, and thus it was in the interest of both buyer and seller for declarations to be as clear and specific as possible. Because terms to a sale made clear the limits on the local water supply, this part of the law of sale also helped to conserve water, preserving the existing system of excludability and reinforcing the social constraints on access to water. In this way, protecting economic interests also served environmental ends, as commons theory would prescribe. Thus the law of sale can be seen as another legal mechanism that re-

33. Should the buyer subsequently be evicted from the whole property, his total compensation was limited to twice the purchase price (*D.* 21.2.48 Nerat. 6 *Memb.*), that is, compensation plus penalty as provided in the *actio auctoritatis* (discussed earlier in the present chapter).

34. Kaser, *RP* 1:556; Honsell, *"Quod interest"*; Rodger, "Concealing a Servitude," 143–49 (building on Honsell's work, for the late republic). For cases illustrating the connection between the buyer's interest and the purpose of servitudes (*utilitas*), see chapter 3 in the present study.

inforced social constraints on the exploitation of natural resources, protecting access to a scarce resource.

Given the legal rules about liability and the general moral view, it appears to have been in the interest of the seller to make a full declaration about servitudes on sale property and not to conceal what he knew from the seller. Countering these factors, however, was the economic value of the resources governed by servitudes. Once a servitude's economic value was recognized, information about servitudes took on strategic importance in the sale negotiations, and there was sometimes reason to suspect manipulation or outright fraud. The tension between legal rules of liability and economic motives put the buyer and seller into a gamelike situation when the seller did in fact know about servitudes on the sale property. In this situation, the seller could decide how much information to share with the buyer, evaluating the odds that the buyer would (1) discover the servitude, (2) go to the trouble of bringing suit, and (3) prevail in the trial. The seller also had to assess the buyer's diligence in investigating the property. To what extent would he exercise common sense, following the advice in the agricultural writers—walk the land, get to know the neighbors, learn about all the amenities of the property (e.g., Cato, *Agr.* 1.2–4)? In so doing, would he discover a servitude before the sale, when he could use the information to bargain for a lower sale price? Or would the buyer adopt a laissez-faire attitude and not discover the servitude, even after he took possession of the property?

Where "buyer beware" was the operating principle, sellers may have gambled to get the best price for the land. The legal rules on liability are aimed at curbing such business practices, but the very existence of the rules implies that there was a need to discourage this type of shrewd dealing. Of course, it might have been the case that landowners were often simply ignorant of servitudes on their land, though, again, the rules punishing the informed but silent seller suggest not. Some ill-informed landlords—perhaps stereotypical absentee landlords—did resort to litigation and were to be discouraged. Columella, quoting Saserna, reports a generally negative view of this use of law: an absentee landlord was more likely to bring suit than profit (Col. 1.7.4 cited in chapter 2). More usual seems to be the well-informed landowner, since many legal cases show sellers using specific declarations in sophisticated ways to manage servitudes, demonstrating a familiarity and mastery of the resources on their property, much as we saw in Cicero's letters about the water supply on his own and his brother's land.

Shortly after Cicero had arranged the purchase of an estate at Arpinum for Quintus, he reported the price to his brother and described the amenities of the land, implying that Quintus had gotten his money's worth (*Q.Fr.* 3.1.3).[35] Abundant flowing water made the property desirable in terms of both charm and revenue. "Beauty, healthiness, or convenience provide rational reasons for enjoying a place," as Treggiari observes in her discussion of Cicero's ideas about a home.[36] Charm might initially attract a prospective buyer, as, for example, Seneca was enchanted by Palaemon's vineyard. But buyers will also have been interested in the land's productivity, and to these buyers, the water supply would be considered an asset. Compare Pliny's deliberations about the purchase of a neighboring estate. When he evaluated its productivity, first among his considerations were natural resources, the quality of the land and the water supply.

> Now this is the focus of my decision. The fields are productive, rich, and well watered, and they are comprised of meadows, vineyards, woods that provide the resource[s] and from these a moderate but reliable return.
>
> *[Iam, quod deliberationis nostrae caput est, agri sunt fertiles pingues aquosi; constant campis vineis silvis, quae materiam et ex ea reditum sicut modicum ita statum praestant.]* (Pliny, *Ep.* 3.19.5)

For Pliny, the resources of the land were explicitly linked to its productivity and thus were at the center of his decision about purchasing the property. In the case of Cicero's brother, Quintus's new property included a meadow and water sufficient to irrigate it. Of course, a meadow was worth more irrigated than dry, because an irrigated meadow produced more fodder, which could mean more food for the household's animals or a higher rent if the meadow was leased.[37] Cicero recognized that the abundant water on the estate at Arpinum was an asset, and he was also aware that the water supply on Quintus's other property needed attention and investment if it was to retain its value when it was sold. Happily, Quintus had already taken steps to remedy the situation, restoring a servitude and hiring a contractor to build an aqueduct. Cicero thought the price was good and the investment even better: "I maintain that the money could not be better spent" *[praestabo sumptum nusquam melius posse poni]* (*Q.Fr.* 3.1.3). Cicero and Quintus were not alone in

35. For quotation and more discussion of Cic. *Q.Fr.* 3.1.3, see chapter 3 in the present study.

36. Treggiari, "Upper-Class House," 36, with reference to this letter in n. 13.

37. On meadows, see chapter 3 and appendix A.

recognizing the economic value of a water supply on rural property. Nor were they unusual in taking steps to secure a water supply when they were planning to sell the land. Many of the legal cases involving the sale of land and declarations about servitudes reflect the same attitudes expressed in Cicero's remarks about the water supply on his brother's two estates.

The economic value of a private water supply was usually reflected in the purchase price of the land: the water supply contributed to productivity, and Romans regularly used the *reditus,* the net return from farming property, to set land values.[38] Where improvement to the water supply increased productivity, such investments would in turn be matched by an increased sale price when the land was sold. There is suggestive evidence that Romans understood these connections already in the early second century BC. When Cato the Elder was censor, he attempted to prevent the illegal use of public land and water, and connected with this effort is a fragment of his speech against L. Furius Purpureus (cos. 196): "Look how much he bought the land for, where he is channeling the water!" [*o quanti ille agros emit, qua aquam duceret!*] (*ORF* 42–43). This exclamation is generally understood to mean that Purpureus paid little for the land, but it also implies a comparison with the land's true value, which must have been increased by the water supply, even the water illegally appropriated.[39] Though any interpretation of a fragment can be at best suggestive, it does seem that Cato and his audience appreciated the value of water and its relation to the price that land could bring. This evidence is important because it comes from the same period when the protection of servitudes was beginning to develop in the law of sale. In the years that followed, other Romans paid close attention to servitudes and the water supply when rural land was bought and sold.

G. SERGIUS ORATA AND FISHPONDS

G. Sergius Orata was and perhaps still is best known for farming oysters and building hypocaust baths. The Roman sources say that he invented raised baths or hypocausts, but it is more likely that he developed their use in southern Italy, based on Fagan's analysis of the archaeological evidence.[40]

38. De Neeve, "Price of Agricultural Land," 97; cf. 78–85 on the various factors that affected the price of land.

39. For the interpretation of *ORF* 42–43, see Shatzman, *Senatorial Wealth,* 252. On Cato's attention to the water supply during his censorship, see Livy 39.44.4.

40. Cic. *Hort.* fr. 76; Val. Max. 9.1.1; Pliny, *NH* 9.168; Fagan, "Sergius Orata: Inventor of the Hypocaust?"

Orata was also sometimes associated with the fish fanciers who were treated as emblems of outrageous luxury. In Cicero's *de Finibus* (2.70), he figures as the prime example of a person who happily enjoys luxury despite his lack of integrity.[41] Orata is the subject of the first anecdote in Valerius Maximus's ninth book, *de Luxuria et Libidine.* Jokes about his cognomen involve false etymological plays on Orata and *aurata,* connecting him either with the gilthead, a fish that he raised, or with the gold rings that he wore, symbols of his wealth (Varro, *RR* 3.3.10; Festus p. 182). But unlike most of the fish fanciers, Orata appears to have been a successful fish farmer, energetic in pursuing his projects, even using private law to advance his interests.

Orata was associated with two lawsuits, both probably related to his business of raising oysters for the market. One of these lawsuits involved a mistake about a servitude in the purchase of rural land, so it nicely illustrates the importance that servitudes could have in decisions about property, both its initial purchase and further investment in developing its productivity. Though the sources do not indicate what kind of servitude was involved, the archaeological evidence for fishponds raises the possibility that a water servitude was at stake. In any event, Orata seems to have used law in a strategic way that fits with the previously discussed cases about the sale of land with servitudes, where landowners designed terms to articulate their interest in the water supply and relied on these terms to win compensation through litigation if a problem arose. In particular, Orata's lawsuit against M. Marius Gratidianus illustrates the potential for pursuing a profit through a calculated and aggressive use of the legal system.

Orata brought an action on the sale (*actio ex empto*) against M. Marius Gratidianus, based on a claim about a mistake concerning a servitude owed by a property on the Lucrine Lake near Baiae. The trial took place sometime around 100 BC, possibly as early as 107 BC or as late as 91 BC, the dramatic date of *de Oratore,* where it is mentioned as a recent event. This date is consistent with Gratidianus's age (he was probably born around 120 BC) and with Pliny's reference to Crassus and the Marsic War in his notice about Orata (*NH* 9.168).[42] Orata's involvement with Gratidianus began several

41. A good, recent review of the sources for Orata is Wikander, "*Senatores* and *Equites.*" For Orata's commercial orientation, see D'Arms, *Bay of Naples,* 18–20; Münzer, "Sergius," 1713–14. On the infamous fish fanciers, see D'Arms, *Bay of Naples,* 41ff. For an example of the notorious place of fish in Roman moralizing, see Juvenal's *Satire 4* on the enormous turbot given to Domitian.

42. Wikander ("*Senatores* and *Equites,*" 180) argued for the traditional date, with reference to Gratidianus's age. Dyck (*Commentary on Cicero, "De Officiis,"* 579) dates the lawsuit after 97 BC, when, he suggests, the censor Antonius first contracted fishing rights on the Lucrine Lake.

years before the trial. A rough chronology of the events leading up to the lawsuit can be reconstructed from the various sources that mention Orata.

Orata, who was connected with Baiae, owned a property on the Lucrine Lake, which he developed, probably building a villa with a hypocaust bath (Val. Max. 9.1.1; Pliny, *NH* 1.168). He then sold the property to Gratidianus (Cic. *Off.* 3.67). Subsequently, Orata invented artificial oyster ponds, and he purchased the property back from Gratidianus for the purpose of raising oysters on the Lucrine Lake. When Orata tried to set up an oyster farm, he wound up in a lawsuit with the tax farmer Considius, who had the contract to farm the fish on the lake. L. Licinius Crassus (cos. 95 BC) represented Orata in this legal action. This lawsuit and its connection with Orata's oyster farm is reported by Valerius Maximus (9.1.1) but with no details about the legal matter itself. Who brought the suit? Who won? What kind of a suit was it? Answers to these questions can be surmised on the basis of the legal sources for fishing rights in public waters, since Valerius Maximus describes the Lucrine Lake as *aqua publica.* These answers are important both for understanding the connection between Orata's two lawsuits and for appreciating the way he exploited his land and its resources.

Though Orata owned property on the shore of the Lucrine Lake, the waters of the lake itself were public, which meant that everyone had a free right of access to it, as to the ocean and most large rivers. The Lucrine Lake seems to have been treated as a commons, where public law was used to support fair and open access. If a landowner prevented fishermen from working on the shores, the fishermen could bring legal action to protect their right. Such complaints seem to have become common after Orata's day, as the *Digest* refers to numerous rescripts or legal rulings by the emperor in response to fishermen seeking protection for their fishing grounds: "It was also very often written in reply that no one could be prohibited from fishing." [*et est saepissime rescriptum non posse quem piscari prohiberi*] (*D.* 47.10.13.7 Ulp. 57 *ad Ed.*).[43] According to this case, if anyone interfered with a public contractor's fishing rights, he could use an interdict to stop them, and this is probably what Considius did in his lawsuit with Orata. Orata's construction of oyster ponds, if that is what he built on the shores of the Lucrine Lake, would not, in and of itself, have given Considius grounds to use the interdict, because the fishermen could work as long as they stayed clear of the structures (*D.* 1.8.4 pr. Marc. 3 *Inst.*). But if Orata had prevented or interfered with Considius's fishing operations, his actions could be grounds for a legal claim. A

43. On *D.* 1.8.4 pr. Marc. 3 *Inst.*, see Kaser, *RP* 1:380–81 and 396 (on the interdict). See also Fiorentini, "Ville marittime," 167–73; Costa, *Le acque*, 1–12.

motive for such interference can be found in the circumstances of oyster farming. In artificial oyster ponds, the shellfish were raised on strings attached to roof tiles in oyster enclosures. Since these structures were at risk of damage from Considius's boats or lines, it is likely that Orata chose extralegal self-help to prevent Considius from fishing nearby, filed a legal claim for compensation for the damage, or both. In any event, this first lawsuit hints at Orata's willingness to aggressively protect his interests in the oyster farm. His second lawsuit is more clearly a calculated financial strategy.

Orata's second lawsuit was related to his purchase of the property on the Lucrine Lake from Gratidianus. Although none of the ancient sources reports both lawsuits and their relationship, the case against Gratidianus is usually interpreted as evidence that Orata lost to the tax farmer. As a result, he was unable to farm oysters on the Lucrine Lake and, consequently, to earn a return from the property, and he filed suit against Gratidianus to recover the price of the property.[44] The first lawsuit, against the tax farmer, thus provides a motive for Orata's claim against Gratidianus. In the second lawsuit, Orata brought an action on the sale (*actio ex empto*), claiming, according to Cicero (*de Orat.* 1.178; *Off.* 3.67), that Gratidianus had not declared that the property was servient. Cicero does not specify the type of legal claim, but the language fits an action on the sale. If he won, Orata could recover the difference between the price that he actually paid for the property and what he would have paid if he had known about the servitude. At the trial, the parties were represented by two of the most notable orators of the day, Crassus and Antonius, who are the main characters in Cicero's *de Oratore,* an important source for this lawsuit.

Cicero reports Orata's lawsuit against Gratidianus twice, first in *de Oratore* and later in *de Officiis* (*de Orat.* 1.178; *Off.* 3.67). In both works, the lawsuit illustrates the tension between legal arguments based on the letter of the law and those based on the spirit of the law. In *de Oratore,* Crassus cited the case to support his contention that the orator needed to know the law.

---

44. For the connection between the lawsuits, see Rodger, "Concealing a Servitude," 138–39. Dyck (*Commentary on Cicero, "De Officiis,"* 579) mentions "opposition from the fish-farmers" but does not explicitly affirm a second lawsuit, nor does he refer to Rodger. D'Arms (*Bay of Naples,* 18–20) follows the reconstruction with one trial in Münzer, "Sergius," 1713–14, which assumes that there was only one lawsuit, the one with Gratidianus, presumably because of the lack of sources and because Crassus is depicted as defending Orata both times.

> Recently, when I pled the case of Gaius Sergius Orata against this Antonius of ours in a private lawsuit, didn't my whole defense turn on the law? For, since Marcus Marius Gratidianus had sold the house to Orata and he had not declared in the agreement for transfer of title that a certain part of the property was servient, I made the argument that he should make good whatever defect there was in the transfer of title, if he, as seller, had known about it and had not declared it.
>
> [*Nuper, cum ego C. Sergi Oratae contra hunc nostrum Antonium iudicio privato causam defenderem, nonne omnis nostra in iure versata defensio est? cum enim M. Marius Gratidianus aedis Oratae vendidisset neque servire quandam earum aedium partem in mancipi lege dixisset, defendebamus, quicquid fuisset incommodi in mancipio, id si venditor scisset neque declarasset, praestare debere.*] (Cic. *de Orat.* 1.178)

Crassus explained that his speech for Orata depended on a strict interpretation of the law of sale, namely, that Gratidianus should compensate Orata simply because he failed to declare the servitude. As we know from Cicero's account in *de Officiis,* Antonius made a case for equity, arguing that Gratidianus should not be held liable because his silence about the servitude did not hurt Orata: Orata could not have been deceived, because he already knew about the servitude, which had existed when he owned the property previously and before he sold it to Gratidianus. It was a "classic confrontation of the *summum ius* and *aequitas,*" as Dyck describes it in his commentary on *de Officiis,* where Cicero offers a different view of these rhetorical strategies and their implications for legal ethics.[45]

In *de Officiis,* Orata's lawsuit is the last of six legal cases illustrating Cicero's discussion of the problem of concealment in the sale of property—that is, when is a mistake fraud and when is it just a mistake, and what should the legal consequences be in either situation? (*Off.* 3.49–67). Cicero is interested in the relationship between integrity and expediency, what is *honestum* or *utile* in cases where one party's silence was turned to advantage. The silence in the Orata lawsuit was Gratidianus's failure to declare the servitude, and Orata tried to use it to his advantage, abetted by Crassus's argument from the letter of the law. In his closing quip, Cicero seems to disapprove of Orata's claim.

---

45. Dyck, *Commentary on Cicero, "De Officiis,"* 555.

> Marcus Marius Gratidianus, my relative, had sold to Gaius Sergius Orata the house that he himself had purchased from the same man a few years earlier. This [house] owed a servitude, but Marius had not declared it in the transfer of title. The case was brought to court, and Crassus represented Orata; Antony, Gratidianus. Crassus argued for the law: because the seller had not declared a defect when he knew [about it], he ought to provide compensation. Antonius argued for equity: since this defect was not unknown to Sergius, because he had sold, it had not been necessary for anything to be declared, nor was he deceived, because he possessed that house what he bought in the legal condition in which it was in [before]. Why say more? So that you know that these clever men did not please our ancestors.
>
> *[M. Marius Gratidianus, propinquus noster, C. Sergio Oratae vendiderat aedes eas quas ab eodem ipse paucis ante annis emerat. Eae [Sergio] serviebant, sed hoc in mancipio Marius non dixerat. Adducta res in iudicium est; Oratam Crassus, Gratidianum defendebat Antonius. Ius Crassus urgebat: quod vitii venditor non dixisset sciens, id oportere praestari, aequitatem Antonius: quoniam id vitium ignotum Sergio non fuisset, qui illas aedes vendidisset, nihil fuisse necesse dici, nec eum esse deceptum qui id quod emerat quo iure esset teneret. Quorsus haec? ut illud intellegas, non placuisse maioribus nostris astutos.]* (*Off.* 3.67)

This account provides some of the background information that is lacking in *de Oratore,* but the text as transmitted is inaccurate in one place and should be emended, as it is here following Winterbottom's edition.[46] The second mention of Orata's name, *Sergio,* must be deleted in order for the legal dispute to make sense: if the servitude had been owed to Orata, he probably would not have brought suit, because it would have been an asset rather than a cost. Instead, the servitude was owed not to Orata but to one of his neighbors, and the property was servient, not dominant. Thus, Orata was able to bring suit on the sale, claiming compensation for a mistake about the servitude, on the grounds that Gratidianus did not declare the servitude in advance.

The outcome of Orata's lawsuit depended on the law of liability for defect in sale, the rules governing mistakes about servitudes, analyzed in the second section of this chapter. Under what circumstances should a seller be liable when the property was in a condition that caused loss for the buyer?

---

46. Winterbottom, *De Officiis,* 136.

Was the seller liable for merely remaining silent about a servitude, even if the buyer already knew of it? Or was the seller liable only if his silence actually deceived the buyer because the buyer did not know about the defect? Depending on which rule was in force, Orata's lawsuit would have had a different outcome. The first rule would give Orata a victory; under the second, he would lose.

Interpretations of Cicero's accounts generally assume that Orata lost the suit, and they therefore conclude that the second rule on liability was in force (the seller was liable only when the buyer was unaware of the defect).[47] Since Orata knew about the servitude, Gratidianus's failure to mention it did not and could not have deceived him and, therefore, did not and could not have led him to lose out by paying more than he ought to pay. This interpretation of the legal issues seems consistent with Cicero's perspective in *de Officiis,* namely, that the claim was disingenuous, fraudulent in its own way, and therefore should not be protected by the law. But Cicero did not report either the outcome or the legal rules themselves, and he may have suppressed the verdict because he disagreed with it. As noted earlier, Rodger has argued that in the late republic at the time of Orata's lawsuit, the first rule was the law (the seller was liable merely for remaining silent, regardless of the buyer's knowledge). His reconstruction of the legal history reverses the logic of the standard view and depends on a reinterpretation of Cicero's accounts. In brief, he argues that Orata's lawsuit is cited in both *de Oratore* and *de Officiis* as an example supporting a larger question and that the example is effective only if Orata won the lawsuit; therefore, the law must have held the seller liable simply for failing to declare the defect, even if the buyer already knew about it. In *de Oratore,* citing Orata's case would not serve Crassus's argument unless he won, because he was trying to show that knowledge of the finer points of law was an advantage for the orator. Similarly, in *de Officiis,* the import of Orata's lawsuit depends on his winning: the story was meant "to illustrate the law taking a hard line on *reticentia,* failure to disclose."[48] Rodger's argument is persuasive both in its readings of Cicero and in its reconstruction of the legal developments. Moreover, if the legal rules were in Orata's favor, his decision to bring a claim can be better explained in economic terms.

---

47. For the assumption that Orata lost, see Dyck, *Commentary on Cicero, "De Officiis,"* 579; Rodger, "Concealing a Servitude," 136, 141. Both Dyck and Rodger cite other scholarship that takes this view.

48. Rodger, "Concealing a Servitude," 140; cf. 139–42 (on *de Officiis*), 142–43 (on *de Oratore*).

Since the law was on his side, Orata was likely to win his case. In addition, Orata probably knew about this legal advantage in advance, because he was represented in court by Crassus, who was associated with the jurist Q. Mucius Scaevola throughout his career.[49] Through his advocate, then, Orata had access to legal expertise that would have allowed him to calculate the risk of litigation in advance and to determine that by filing suit, he was likely to recover at least part of his investment in the property on the Lucrine Lake. Orata's strategy in filing suit against Gratidianus should also be understood in relation to the earlier lawsuit with the tax farmer, in which Orata lost both legally and financially. As a consequence of this loss, Orata's oyster farm was less productive, perhaps not productive at all. The decision to file suit against Gratidianus may well have been an attempt to recover this financial loss at least in part. The compensation that he won from Gratidianus could cover the costs of building the oyster farm, costs that Orata might have recovered by selling the property, since fishponds added to the value of real estate. For example, Pliny reported that Hirrus sold for HS 4,000,000 an estate on the Bay of Naples that is described as less than average (*infra quam modicam*) but equipped with fishponds (Pliny, *NH* 9.171; cf. Varro, *RR* 3.17.3).[50] Alternatively, Orata may have expected to recover his investment by selling oysters; even the conservative Cato (Cicero's contemporary, not the agricultural writer) turned a profit from the fishponds of his ward, the younger Lucullus.[51] According to Varro, Abbucius earned a sizable profit from these luxury products and claimed that he could increase his earnings if he added a coastal villa, presumably with more fishponds (*RR* 3.2.17). Thus, in bringing a legal claim against Gratidianus, Orata used the

49. Wikander, "*Senatores* and *Equites*," 181; Münzer, "Sergius," 1713–14.

50. For the likely location of Hirrus's estate on the Bay of Naples, see D'Arms, *Bay of Naples*, 188; Fiorentini, "Ville marittime," 150. Hirrus also owned property in Bruttium (Varro, *RR* 2.1.2). On the relationship between the price of land and its revenue, see De Neeve, "Price of Agricultural Land," 80–83, 85–91. The sale price reported by Pliny (HS 4,000,000) is probably not accurate but, rather, a conventional figure that represents a high price; for multiples of four hundred, see Scheidel, "Finances, Figures, and Fiction," in general. Scheidel (237) observes that "practically all numerical references may be no more than indicatory of a certain order of magnitude."

51. Varro, *RR* 3.2.17; Col. 8.16.5. Columella writes that Cato sold the fishponds for HS 400,000, and while this may be accurate, it is likely to be an error in reporting Varro's anecdote that Cato sold fish from the ponds for HS 40,000; numbers are especially susceptible to corruption in textual transmission. L. Cornelius Sulla (cos. 88) also had fisheries on his coastal property at Cumae, and he does not seem to have been mocked for it; see App. *BC* 1.104, with Shatzman, *Senatorial Wealth*, 272.

law of sale in a strategic way to pursue his long-term and short-term financial interests in the property on the Lucrine Lake. Such a calculating approach to fish farming also characterizes other portraits of Orata in the ancient sources, namely, Pliny and Valerius Maximus.

In Valerius Maximus's moralizing portrait, Orata appears as an ambitious inventor and entrepreneur. Because this is the only account of Orata's legal battle with the tax farmer, it forms the basis for the reconstruction of events previously presented, including Orata's aims in purchasing the property on the Lucrine Lake. Valerius Maximus's tone is openly critical, with hyperbolic descriptions of Orata's inventions and a moralizing adverb to convey his motivations. The account is frustratingly incomplete, focused as it is on a joke that was told at the trial. Nevertheless, some of the details point to a less critical perspective on Orata's commercial activities.

> Gaius Sergius Orata first set the example of building raised tanks. This project, though begun with small endeavors, ended up practically with an ocean of warm water suspended on high. The same man, surely so that he would not have to limit his taste according to Neptune's judgment, contrived individual oceans for himself, by catching the waves of the sea in estuaries and enclosing different species of fish separately with seawalls, so that no wild storm could break in and keep Orata's tables from overflowing with a variety of [seafood] plates. He surrounded the shores of the Lucrine Lake, empty at that time, with lofty and rambling buildings, so that he could profit from his recent experience with shellfish: there he was drawn into a lawsuit with Considius, a tax collector, while he plunged himself rather greedily into public water. In this [lawsuit] Lucius Crassus argued the case against him [Considius], saying that his friend Considius had made a mistake in thinking that if Orata could be removed from the lake, he would be without oysters: for if he had not been allowed to take them from there [i.e., from the Lucrine Lake], he could find them on the roof.
>
> [*C. Sergiuis Orata pensilia balnea primus facere instituit. Quae impensa <a> levibus initiis coepta ad suspensae caldae aquae tantum non aequora penetravit. Idem, videlicet ne gulam Neptuni arbitrio subiectam haberet, peculiaria sibi maria excogitavit, aestuariis intercipiendo fluctus pisciumque diversos greges separatim molibus includendo, ut nulla tam saeva tempestas inciderit, qua non Oratae mensae varietate ferculorum abundarent. Aedificiis etiam spatiosis et excelsis deserta ad id tempus ora Lucrini lacus pressit, quo recentiore usu conchyliorum frueretur: ubi dum se publicae aquae cupidius immergit, cum Considio publicano iudicium nanctus est. In quo L. Crassus,*

adversus illum causam agens, errare amicum suum Considium dixit, quod putaret Oratam remotum a lacu cariturum ostreis: namque ea, si inde petere non licuisset, in tegulis reperturum.] (Val. Max. 9.1.1)

In Valerius Maximus's portrait of Orata, the colorful details of excess seem to conceal a begrudging acknowledgment of his ability to plan and to realize his plans. The seawalls protected well-organized fishponds (*diversos greges separatim molibus includendo*), and the rambling buildings were designed with a purpose, namely, raising oysters (*quo . . . frueretur*). It even seems that the oyster ponds would have done well but for the tax farmer's lawsuit, which provides a setting for a joke that Crassus reportedly told in court (*namque ea, si inde petere non licuisset, in tegulis reperturum*). The humor resides in a pun where *tegula* refers both to the roof of a house (an unlikely place for oysters) and to the ceramic tiles that were used in oyster ponds as a platform for growing the shellfish (where Orata really did raise oysters). Though the joke may have appealed to senatorial bias against commerce, it also acknowledged Orata's ingenuity and energy.

Pliny is more straightforwardly positive in his assessment of Orata's commercial success. He introduces him as the inventor of oyster ponds and raised tanks, in the course of his chapters on discussion of sea creatures.

> Sergius Orata was the first to invent oyster farms in Baiae at the time of the orator Lucius Crassus, before the Marsic War, not for the sake of taste but for gain, earning large returns from such invention, just as he was the first to invent raised baths [or hypocausts], so [he also earned profit] by selling villas after he fixed them up [i.e., with hypocausts]. He was the first to decide that oysters from the Lucrine Lake had the best flavor, since the same kinds of seafood are better in different places, (169) for example, bass in the Tiber's channel. . . . Not yet did the British coast serve them up when Orata popularized Lucrine oysters; afterward it seemed worth a high price to seek oysters at the far reaches of Italy, at Brindisi, but so that there would be no contest between the two flavors, Orata decided to feed the hunger for [oysters delivered by] long transport with [oysters] on the Lucrine Lake.
>
> *[Ostrearum vivaria primus omnium Sergius Orata invenit in Baiano aetate L. Crassi oratoris, ante Marsicum bellum, nec gulae causa sed avaritiae, magna vectigalia tali ex ingenio suo percipiens, ut qui primus pensiles invenerit balneas, ita mangonicatas villas subinde vendendo. Is primus optimum saporem ostreis Lucrinis adiudicavit, quando*

> *eadem aquatilium genera aliubi atque aliubi meliora,* (169) *sicut lupi pisces in Tiberi amne. . . . nondum Britannica serviebant litoran, cum Orata Lucrina nobilitabat; postea visum tanti in extremam Italiam petere Brundisium ostreas, ac ne lis esset inter duos sapores, nuper excogitatum famem longae advectionis a Brundisio conpascere in Lucrino.]* (*NH* 9.168–69)

Orata turned both of his inventions—hypocaust baths and oyster ponds—into commercial enterprises, remodeling villas with his raised tanks and selling them, presumably at a profit (*magna vectigalia tali ex ingenio suo percipiens*). He probably also created a market for oysters from the Lucrine Lake (*excogitatum famem longae advectionis a Brundisio conpascere in Lucrino*). This passage is usually interpreted to mean that Orata brought oysters from Brundisium and fattened them in the Lucrine Lake for the market, based on Pliny's description of this practice (*NH* 32.61). But a second meaning is also possible, namely, that the hunger (*famem*) can be understood as belonging to consumers rather than to the oysters themselves. Orata's marketing of local oysters could have earned a good profit because transportation costs were lower, even if the price was not quite as high as what oysters from Brundisium cost. Though Pliny frames the issue as a matter of taste (*ac ne lis esset inter duos sapores*), he implies that Orata understood these economic relationships and profited from them.

Orata's approach to oyster farming, as depicted in both Pliny and Valerius Maximus, coheres with the economic strategies presented by Varro in his discussion of fish farming. Though Varro makes only a passing reference to Orata when he introduces specialized villa livestock (*pastio villatica, RR* 3.10), his approach to fish farming seems almost to be informed by Orata's strategies. Varro emphasized traditional cost control, but he also recognized that fish farms required extensive capital investment and careful management (*RR* 3.3.10; cf. 3.17). Fishponds were expensive to build, and if they were not properly maintained, the fish died. While Varro's presentation of elaborate fishponds is colored by moralizing rhetoric similar to that in Valerius Maximus, his judgment is based on economic, rather than ethical, factors, as much as is Columella's evaluation (8.16–17).[52] In essence, Varro draws a connection between ethical choices and their economic outcomes. Extravagant outlays on fishponds might be a sign of excessive luxury, if they were not productive. Fish farmers who made an investment in fishponds lost money when they

52. Marzano, *Villas in Central Italy*, 40; cf. 38–41.

did not supervise the operation effectively; that is, the landowners were incompetent or absent. For example, Hortensius did not make a profit from his fishponds because his costs exceeded his revenues: Varro compares the minimal costs of keeping his own mules with Hortensius's large staff and the expense of purchasing food for the fish (*RR* 3.17.6–7).[53] One of the Luculli so neglected his fishponds that they became scummy, while the other was so carried away by enthusiasm that he spent too much money building them (Varro, *RR* 3.17.8–9). Orata, by contrast, was persistent and attentive in managing his oyster farm and was successful until the tax farmer interfered.

Orata's decision to take legal action against Gratidianus is a signal example of his approach to making a profit from his land. He developed the technology to build oyster ponds to make his land more productive. He invested in land and in infrastructure to cultivate oysters. He may even have marketed his product to compete with oysters from Brundisium. When his oyster farm was challenged by the tax farmers, he participated in a legal battle to protect his interests. He also used the law of sale to recover his investment in the oyster farm, bringing a claim against Gratidianus based on a concealed servitude. He had the opportunity to know the legal rules in advance and thus to assess the risk of litigation. Both lawsuits, then, were part of Orata's use of the law as a strategy to pursue his economic interests. In one case, his claim for the right to use a public water supply was connected with the productivity of his land (i.e., farming oysters on the Lucrine Lake). In the other case, he may have used litigation in a strategic way to recover financial losses caused by an investment that would not pay off: if Orata had lost the suit with Considius and his right to farm the lake, he could not make a profit from the property he had purchased from Gratidianus. Moreover, the legal issue in the lawsuit against Gratidianus, the concealed servitude, may also have been directly related to Orata's economic interest in oyster farming.

Oysters thrive in brackish conditions that require a mix of freshwater and saltwater. In antiquity, the Lucrine Lake was probably naturally brackish, as it was separated from the sea by a narrow strip of land (Strabo 5.4.5–6). Yet Orata may have needed a supply of freshwater to maintain the proper balance of saltwater and freshwater. There is archaeological evidence to suggest that some of the fishponds on the Campanian coast were fed by streams and channels from inland springs. In some areas, freshwater could

53. Archaeological remains of hydraulic facilities (a canal at Puteoli and cisterns near Bacoli) have been associated with Hortensius's holdings or those of his son. See D'Arms, *Bay of Naples*, 181–82; Maiuri, *Phlegraean Fields*, 85–87.

be obtained from a public aqueduct, but many villas seem to have relied on private sources. Where the cistern or aqueduct was fed by a spring, stream, or local aqueduct, a servitude could be involved. At Torre Astura, for example, one of the fishponds was both open to the sea and connected to a freshwater aqueduct, allowing the owner to regulate the brackish water to improve cultivation of fish.[54] The installation at Puteoli that has been associated with Hortensius's fishponds could also have been supplied by an inland stream governed by a servitude. The site has cisterns that Maiuri believed held rainwater because they lacked the calcium deposit characteristic of water from the Serino aqueduct.[55] It is impossible to say how commonly servitudes were used to supply freshwater to fishponds, but the archaeological evidence is suggestive. The physical remains of Roman fishponds have been catalogued by Higginbotham in his book *Piscinae.* On more than half of the sites in his catalogue, the archaeological evidence indicates that the freshwater supply could have depended on a servitude. Most of these fishponds were built during the first century BC and the first century AD, when the law on servitudes was developing in response to new market conditions. During this period, landowners like Orata were actively using the available tools—technological and legal—to make the most of their investment in rural property, challenging nature with rock-hewn fishponds and setting up servitudes to secure a supply of freshwater that allowed them to engineer the perfect climate for cultivating gourmet species of seafood.[56]

In Orata's lawsuit against Gratidianus, the sources do not indicate what kind of servitude was at stake, though it is not impossible that it involved water. We know from Cicero that the property owed a servitude. If it was a water servitude, it would mean that one of the neighbors had a right to take water from a stream or spring on Orata's land. If the water flowed into the lake, the servitude would reduce the volume of water, changing the level of the lake or the quality of the water. Either change could affect oysters and

---

54. See Higginbotham, *Piscinae,* 135–40 (villa with aqueduct and fishpond at Astura), 115–18 (importance of brackish water). At least two private baths used a similar mix of saltwater and freshwater: one, on the property of M. Licinius Crassus Frugi (cos. AD 64), probably located on the coast near Pompeii, is known from an inscription (*CIL* 10.1063); the other, on property near Sorrento owned by Pollius Felix, is described by Statius (*Silv.* 2.2.18–19). See also D'Arms, *Bay of Naples,* 214–16 (Licinius), 220–22 (Pollius).

55. Maiuri, *Phlegraean Fields,* 85–87.

56. For the details behind my analysis of the evidence in Higginbotham and other sources, see appendix B; for hydraulic installations as a challenge to nature, see Higginbotham, *Piscinae,* 66. More generally on the manipulation of nature in villa design, see Newlands, *Statius' "Silvae."*

giltheads, both kinds of sea creatures raised by Orata, and requiring brackish conditions. While these details remain conjectural, the servitude could have had a real impact on Orata's fish farm. For this reason, his lawsuit against Gratidianus should be seen not as a dishonest use of the law but, rather, as a calculated way to recover an investment that was not going to pay off. Such an approach to making a profit from rural land seems to have been acceptable or at least uncontroversial, since only Cicero criticized Orata, and the other sources, while reflecting stereotypical views of fish farming, are generally positive. From Cicero's perspective in *de Officiis*, the example of Orata represented an extreme, an aggressive use of law to pursue financial profit. But this perspective itself may be an extreme, while Pliny and Varro conform to a more common perception of Orata's enterprising spirit. Thus, his legal claim based on a mistake about a servitude shows not only the importance of servitudes in the sale of rural property but also the strategic ways that Romans used the legal system to pursue their economic aims.

CONCLUSION

In the sale of rural land, the water supply was a factor that affected the sale price of the land as well as the types of cultivation that the new owner could pursue. When the water supply was governed by a servitude, this legal arrangement had to be taken into account in calculating the costs and benefits of the sale. A servitude was transferred tacitly with the property in a sale, as an integral part of the land. If the property was servient, it might bring a lower price, whereas a dominant estate could be sold for a higher price because it possessed more resources. Like Cato's advice, the law of sale encouraged buyers and sellers of rural land to find out about the resources of the property, including any servitudes attached to the property. Only full and accurate information could guarantee a fair deal and avoid the risk of litigation after the fact.

The law of sale protected buyers from sellers who tried to conceal the existence of servitudes that might lower the price. In early law, *mancipatio* provided a basic guarantee that the land was free of servitudes, because it protected title to the land. By the end of the second century BC, specific terms and declarations about servitudes were preferred because they could be tailored to individual circumstances, providing greater protection and predictability about the resources on a property. Sellers often used these terms to reserve a servitude for themselves and secure a water supply after the sale of land. Likewise, buyers relied on servitudes and information about them in planning how to cultivate their new property. The discussion between Cicero and his brother about Quintus's properties is a case in point: they investigated water resources and servitudes, paid close attention to the costs of developing the water supply, and evaluated these capital projects in terms of the potential profit to be earned from the land or from its subsequent sale.

G. Sergius Orata's activities illustrate how a Roman landowner could carefully manage the natural resources on his property by using both law and technology to his advantage. After he invented oyster ponds, he bought property on the Lucrine Lake and built oyster ponds in order to make the land productive, selling his crop in a market that he may have helped to create. When he lost the right to farm the Lucrine Lake, he turned to the law of sale to recoup his investment, claiming a return of part of the sale price because a servitude was not declared by the seller. Orata's lawsuit provides some historical grounding for the legal cases that involved such mistakes about servitudes, particularly by offering insight into the economic factors that could influence a landowner's decisions about servitudes, natural resources, and how to use the law to protect an investment in rural land. While the sources do not indicate that a water servitude was at stake in Orata's case, there is circumstantial evidence, in both the design of fishponds and the methods of fish cultivation, that his legal claim may have involved the water supply for his oyster farm. In any event, his approach to law is consistent with the assumptions behind the legal cases that focus on the treatment of servitudes in the sale of rural land. Natural resources and the rights to use them were treated as assets of rural land that merited special consideration when the land was bought or sold. Landowners who were able to use the law of servitudes and of sale to their advantage were in a better position to make their land productive and to earn a profit from crops, such as oysters and fish, that required capital investment and careful planning.

CONCLUSION

In Roman Italy, private water rights were governed by servitudes, a legal institution that afforded flexible solutions to managing a local water supply. This study has investigated the legal rules of servitudes in order to evaluate how and how well the regime of private water rights served the needs of rural landowners. We have observed the development of legal concepts relating to servitudes, such as daily/summer water and the use-it-or-lose-it rule, in which Roman ideas about nature were adapted to the needs of agricultural cultivation. Beyond a discussion of the legal rules in the abstract, we have examined the application of these rules and concepts to specific circumstances described in cases from the *Digest of Justinian.* Although some of the cases represent hypothetical situations created by the jurists to explore legal problems, they nevertheless shed light on issues and practices that both affected and were affected by the outcome of real legal disputes. Other sources—literary, epigraphical, archaeological—have been used to contextualize the legal sources. While the focus has been on water rights, cases about other types of servitudes have been considered where they help to reconstruct the jurists' approaches and the factors that influenced the law. Thus, this study of servitudes allows us to assess the relationship between the legal system and the practices and attitudes of Romans who relied on the law to answer the challenges and constraints inherent in their social, economic, and physical environments.

Because water sources were unevenly distributed in the physical landscape, managing a local water supply depended on cooperation between neighbors. To some extent, Roman landowners treated the water supply as a common good, in which the community shared rights and responsibilities. They had a common interest in sustaining the local water supply and protecting access to it, even though the legal system treated water as private property in the institution of servitudes. These common interests led them to practices that expressed the central principles of commons theory, subtractability and excludability. Social relations played an important role in allocating local water supplies and policing the system. In turn, the principles and priorities of this social system influenced the law of servitudes, not only in their asymmetrical structure, but also where they privileged negotiation over dispute, whether that meant encouraging landowners to specify the terms that would govern a servitude or punishing buyers and sellers who failed to come to an agreement about servitudes before the purchase of land. The jurists' flexible approach to local water-sharing customs follows a pattern observed by Dennis Kehoe in their treatment of farm tenancy.[1] Where landowners and farmers were engaged in long-term relationships, the institutions of Roman law were accommodated to local practices. Recall, for example, how the rules of servitudes reflect social norms of cooperation in Sabinus's and Celsus's instructions for exercising a servitude "in a civil manner" (*civiliter, D.* 8.1.9 Cels. 5 *Dig.*). Commons theory prescribes just such a role for law in communities with a developed legal system, that is, articulating and supporting social relationships. In this way, the regime of property rights helps to conserve water as well as resolve disputes about allocation.

The relationship between law and society in Roman private water rights is consistent with what we know about other water regimes, both ancient and modern. Inscriptions from Roman Spain and Africa document community water-sharing arrangements in which water was allocated in proportion to property holdings, a measure that reflected the social hierarchy. The local water system of medieval Valencia was organized in a similar way according to Glick's analysis. In Roman law, water could be allocated proportionally, or, more often, landowners crafted individualized solutions to meet specific needs. Such negotiations are also known from medieval Italy, where they may have been less successful: according to Squatriti's assessment, small-scale landholders were at a disadvantage because powerful elites monopolized local water supplies in the "patrimonialization of rural water rights," though his reconstruction may take this view at least in part because he underestimates the role of Roman law in local water systems and its likely

1. Kehoe, *Law and the Rural Economy*, 93–129.

legacy in later eras.[2] There is evidence that some Roman elites (Vegetus and Orata, perhaps) took advantage of the legal system, but overall, the regime of private water rights seems to have led to an efficient and equitable distribution of water. In both ancient and medieval water systems, maintenance and policing depended on social sanctions, which were buttressed by law when necessary. In the Roman communities, the law of servitudes supported neighborly cooperation around local water sources and provided an alternate venue for resolving disputes when social negotiation failed.

In their emphasis on social factors, servitudes cohere with a primitivist view of Roman society, where economic issues are embedded in social systems. Indeed, the allocation of a scarce resource, such as water, is typically considered an economic problem. In a pure commons, where the resource is communally owned, the system of allocation may depend entirely on social norms, and it is possible that local water systems in Roman Italy operated this way before and alongside the institution of servitudes. I draw this inference from the traces of social negotiation in the legal evidence and in Cicero's letters about his neighbor Aelius, though this remains only a suggestion because the evidence is purely circumstantial. More generally, I argue that the Romans recognized that managing the water supply involved both social and economic factors and that these two sometimes incompatible perspectives shaped the development of private water rights.

Servitudes offered an alternative to a purely social system of managing the local water supply. Neighbors could use the rules of servitudes to articulate their relationships and to resolve disputes. As we saw in the Statilius Taurus lawsuit, law could level the playing field, so to speak, protecting even modest landowners against the prerogatives of political and social status. Likewise, imperial policies on land tenure helped citizens of modest means by creating legal mechanisms through which they could protect their interests in farmland, as Kehoe has argued on the basis of legal cases from Egypt, North Africa, and Asia Minor.[3] Private water rights operated in a similar

---

2. Squatriti, *Water and Society*, 91; cf. 89–96. Squatriti mentions Roman evidence, including law, for drainage ditches; Pliny's remarks on irrigating grain around Salmo (*NH* 17.250); and the Venafro inscription (*CIL* 10.4842). But he does not discuss servitudes or private water rights in the Roman period, and he seems to assume that local water was treated as public property before the Lombard law code. In contrast, Glick's analysis of the water community of medieval Valencia uses the Roman evidence to chart continuity and change between the two eras; see especially *Irrigation and Society*, 149–206.

3. Kehoe, *Law and the Rural Economy*, 18, 53–91, 131–61.

way to allow landowners to defend their right to water when necessary and, at other times, to create a systematic method of allocating a scarce resource.

Water that arose or flowed on private property was considered part of that property, and servitudes were a kind of property right, as indicated by their classification as *res mancipi* in the *Twelve Tables.* Already in the early law, the cultivation of the land was central to the concept of servitudes. It is expressed in their classification as *res mancipi* and also in the principle of *utilitas,* which was fully developed only in later law. In the early law, a servitude was treated as physical property, like other *res mancipi.* But servitudes were different from other *res mancipi,* because they were intangible in a way, though the resources that they governed were not. By the second century BC, this inconsistency seems to have been recognized, or at least it was considered no longer useful as a basis for legal rules. At this time, a new understanding of servitudes emerged, in which a servitude was defined as an incorporeal or abstract right of use. The underlying connection between a servitude and the land persisted in the new configuration, in the rules for tacit transfer of servitudes in sale, for example, and in the fact that a servitude remained even when it was no longer used for the same kind of cultivation.

Once servitudes were treated as incorporeal rights of use, the institution became more flexible because of the concomitant development of the *modus servitutis.* The *modus* referred to the way a servitude was exercised, and it was defined by the parties when they set up the servitude. A *modus* did not create conditions for a servitude, because the servitude was still conceived as an integral and lasting attribute of the land. Instead, the *modus* was the legal concept that supported the terms that landowners designed to regulate use of a servitude, for example, schedules for use or limitations on repairs. The concept of *modus* reconciled the new abstract right with the original idea of a servitude as attached to property or as a kind of real property itself. While the servitude remained indivisible and permanent, the *modus* was variable. Because the *modus* was defined by the parties when the servitude was established, it could express individual landowners' interests and needs. In this way, the legal institution facilitated systematic approaches to farming, providing a mechanism through which landowners could articulate their plans and control resources to make their land productive. Schedules for water use are perhaps the clearest example, and they also imply that landowners measured and calculated their water use. These systematic approaches advanced both productivity and conservation, as commons theory anticipates, because they aim more to sustain the water supply than to maximize water use by individuals.

The concept of *utilitas* developed along a similar trajectory. A servitude could exist only if it served the needs of the dominant estate, an idea that is implicit in the classification of servitudes as *res mancipi* in the early law. In later cases where *utilitas* is problematized, however, we can trace the changing ideas about cultivation of the land and how servitudes contributed to the debate. Servitudes were at first connected with self-sufficiency of the dominant estate, rather than with production for the market, as becomes clear in a long case comparing servitudes and usufruct—two different kinds of right of use. While this legal discussion may oversimplify the contrast or take an anachronistic view, it reveals the terms of the debate that jurists and landowners applied to servitudes. Indeed, the contrast between self-sufficiency and market-oriented agriculture is familiar from ancient agricultural treatises, and it also shapes some modern scholarship on the Roman economy. Self-sufficiency and market orientation are useful categories, but they are not mutually exclusive, as the many other legal cases involving *utilitas* indicate. Rather, *utilitas* provided a conceptual space where landowners and jurists could plan and calculate how best to use the resources on agricultural land, as Roman landowners seem to have done, based on the evidence from Cicero's letters about the water supply on his brother's properties. Thus, through the concept of *utilitas,* we have a window on Roman ideas about how to make rural land productive and particularly about how to use legal institutions to develop the water supply in ways that improve productivity, whether to support the household (self-sufficiency) or to raise crops for a market.

While these developments in the legal concept of servitudes reflect systematic approaches to farming, another, more central feature of property rights involved explicitly financial calculations. Defining water as private property had the simple but important consequence of creating a right that could be defended in court. When a landowner brought suit over a servitude, he could win a judgment restoring his right to water and also compensation for damages, which were measured in monetary terms. Through this process, Romans put a price on water that corresponded to its role in agricultural production. Essentially, the legal right to water was treated as an economic commodity whose value could be determined by the costs of damage from a lack of water and/or the profits that could be earned from water-dependent crops, as we saw in the lawsuit over the blocked channel. In this way, the institution of servitudes provided a mechanism that mediated the relationship between natural resources and the market. Landowners could plan to meet their needs for water and could also evaluate the costs and benefits of a reliable water supply in monetary terms that allowed them to compare different options and choose what seemed most advantageous. As the careful calculations of Cicero and Quintus suggest, many Roman landowners will have sought to make the most of the water supply both in ongoing production on their land and when it came time to sell the property itself.

The legal cases about servitudes reflect landowners' strategies for cultivation and, in turn, offer insight into the nature of their economic rationality. Effective management of the water supply could improve the productivity of rural land, especially near market towns where water-dependent garden crops could be sold for a profit. A servitude for water rights could provide some insurance against drought, some limited control over the unpredictable natural forces that affect farming. With a servitude, the landowner could raise different, more profitable crops or a larger surplus for the market. If the servitude did not work out as planned, he could file suit to recover his losses. In all these ways, a servitude increased the wealth of the household. Private water rights contributed to economic growth within individual households and possibly, through a cumulative effect, in the Roman economy as a whole. The effect of servitudes on economic growth cannot be measured, and I do not argue that private water rights caused dramatic growth, but it is clear from the legal cases that private water rights had an economic value for the Romans and an impact on their decisions about the purchase and cultivation of land. This use of law not only sustained productivity but also contributed to economic growth, because servitudes allowed landowners to change or increase cultivation and to invest in technology that improved their access to resources.

The effect of servitudes on economic growth can be appreciated using insights from economic development theory, as outlined by Richard Saller.[4] To evaluate the potential for growth, Saller considers five factors that support economic growth, according to economic development theory: trade, capital investment, improved technology, human capital, and institutional framework. Private water rights involved four of these factors. Only human capital seems unrelated to water rights, though labor was needed to tend the crops and to construct and maintain water channels. First among the four factors that were directly affected by water rights is trade, which could be increased by servitudes that facilitated the cultivation of market crops. Second, because a servitude could provide access to otherwise unavailable re-

4. Saller, "Framing the Debate," 261–62.

sources, this legal arrangement functioned as an alternative to capital investment. Private water rights could be especially helpful to small-scale landholders with little access to capital, because a servitude could take the place of capital investment by providing additional resources to the land.[5] Third, a servitude could facilitate the development of technology or at least its more effective deployment. Secure access to water would make it worthwhile for a landowner to invest in improvements to his land (as Quintus Cicero planned to do), whether that meant digging a dirt channel or building a stone aqueduct or improving a dirt channel by lining it with waterproof cement. In addition, a servitude was like an insurance policy that reduced the risk of such an investment by providing a legal mechanism through which a landowner could obtain financial compensation if problems arose down the line. A savvy investor like G. Sergius Orata might even know the law well enough to plan ahead for such eventualities.

The institutional framework for economic activity, the fourth applicable factor for growth, is an essential part of my approach to private water rights. Servitudes, as an institution of private law, were part of the institutional framework that supported economic activity in ancient Rome. There were some limitations in the structure of Roman legal institutions; for example, long-distance buying and selling was impossible under the law of sale, as Tchernia has observed.[6] But Kehoe has demonstrated that law was effective in protecting property rights, and his conclusions are apposite to my argument about servitudes.[7] The cases about servitudes show clearly that when it came to determining the compensation for interfering with a water channel, Roman landowners were assessing the water supply in economic, even monetary, terms. Servitudes, like other kinds of property rights, provided a means of economic development that was particularly important since the Roman economy was largely agricultural: the economic well-being of individual landowners depended on successful farming. It must be noted, however, that these economic decisions were integrated into broader social and moral contexts. This combination may well have been essential to the successful management of local water supplies, based on a study by the International Irrigation Management Institute. This analysis of modern water

5. On the limited access to capital and the resulting restrictions on small-scale landholders, see Erdkamp, *Grain Market*, 14–15.

6. Tchernia, "Quelle rationalité?" 289.

7. Kehoe draws on new institutional economics to analyze the way law affected economic decisions; see especially *Law and the Rural Economy*, 29–51.

systems shows that treating water as an economic commodity works best in societies where

> there are in place: laws assigning rights, laws describing how rights may be traded; legal systems that enforce the rights and punish infringements on those rights; farmers who are accustomed to working with laws and rules that are enforced; and a physical irrigation infrastructure and irrigation management system capable of allocating water in accordance with market-friendly principles and the changing needs and priorities that flow from these principles.[8]

The law of servitudes addressed most of these issues directly, while indirectly revealing, in the rules on repairs and improvements, some of the efforts that Roman landowners made to sustain the physical infrastructure, though the archaeological evidence may never give us a full picture of this critical component.

Romans recognized the importance of water rights and the power of the legal system to protect them. The inscription recording Q. Folvius's claim to water rights exemplifies both the early and the widespread use of law to control private water sources (*CIL* 10.8236). In Folvius's case, the urban praetor played a role in guaranteeing Q. Folvius's ownership of the spring and, therefore, access to water. His inscription is dated to the second century BC and was found in Campania. Both the date and the provenance of this inscription are important for our understanding of the later legal developments: if the praetor was involved in water rights already in the late second century BC and even in a rural area distant from local administrative centers (Capua and Cumae)—never mind Rome itself—then the application of Roman law to local water supplies was early recognized by rural landowners as a powerful tool, and praetorian intervention may have been more common than the sources indicate. Later legal cases, especially the case where Julian directed the plaintiff to seek a remedy from the praetor, show striking continuity in practice through the early imperial period. While economic and political conditions changed, the water supply remained a constant concern, because climate and settlement patterns made water a scarce resource and because agriculture remained central to the economy throughout the Roman period.

8. Perry, Rock, and Seckler, *Water as an Economic Good,* 12.

Servitudes for water use provided a means of managing a key natural resource for agricultural production. In fact, the natural landscape itself was a starting point for many of the approaches to private water rights and sharing arrangements. A change in the environment could lead to a lawsuit, as happened when the spring began to flow again on Statilius Taurus's property near Sutrium. More generally, the physical environment and Roman ideas about nature set the first constraints on legal definitions as well as social patterns and economic possibilities relating to servitudes. For example, the distribution of springs and streams in the landscape shaped not only settlement patterns but also local water-sharing arrangements. Similarly, definitions of summer and daily water started from observable natural phenomena (i.e., the alternation of day and night and of the seasons) and adapted them to serve landowners' plans for cultivation. Indeed, servitudes were included in the legal category of *res mancipi,* the most valuable possessions for the cultivation of the land.[9] This categorization recognized an organic relationship between farming and the natural resources of the land and reflects the unavoidable fact that prosperity in the Roman world, like agriculture itself, depended on natural conditions. The vulnerability of the farmer to wind and weather is practically a cliché, and Roman law did insure tenant farmers against losses caused by unexpected storms.[10] Water rights engaged Roman landowners in a less catastrophic, but no less critical, negotiation with their environment.

Roman ideas about nature and man's relationship to it tend to fall into two contrasting tropes: an opposition of nature and culture (or civilization) and a primitivizing ideal of the harmonious coexistence of man and nature.[11] Scholarly discussions of nature are similarly polarized, even if self-consciously, sharing the Romans' nostalgia for a golden age when the earth bore fruit without human toil, as well as their fear or disdain for engineering projects that appeared to defy nature in financially and morally irresponsible ways. In the preceding chapters, this opposition emerges most clearly in the discussion of attitudes toward fish cultivation. The Romans seem to take delight in mocking the fish fanciers, yet fish farming appears to have been one type of cultivation where an investment in infrastructure could pay off. While the jurists participate in such cultural discourses, they

9. On servitudes as *res mancipi,* see the introduction in the present study.

10. Kaser, *RP* 1:566–67; Kehoe, *Investment, Profit, and Tenancy,* 203–4, 215–16, 221–34.

11. Compare the epic battle of the farmer to cultivate his land in, for example, Vergil, *G.* 1.160–75 (with Thomas, *Virgil: "Georgics,"* 1:95–98).

do not engage with them in literary terms. The jurists define the relationship between farming and the environment in their own terms, and in the process, they revise the familiar tropes, generating a new vision of human interaction with nature.

The trope of man, nature, and their relationship is reflected in legal ideas about servitudes in several ways. First, in some cases, the jurists construct an ideal of their own, an unchanging and idealized landscape in which water rights can be defined and regulated. Second, where human activity is risky or where the natural world itself is dangerous, the opposition between man and nature informs legal rules that limit human intervention and imposition on the environment. Finally, legal approaches to engineering, improvements, and investments are often positive, and here the jurists are most revisionist, crafting a third alternative to the prevailing tropes. In this third mode, the human exploitation of natural resources fits comfortably within the constraints of the environment, and human endeavor is coordinated with the natural world to increase productivity and allow landowners to realize their plans, as in the concept of summer water. I mean to suggest not that these legal ideals were in any way poetic or idealistic but simply that they continue, in a different context, a larger cultural conversation about man's place in the natural world.[12] More important, the legal evidence has heuristic value because it opens new perspectives on literary and material evidence for Roman farming, economics, and management of natural resources.

The underlying importance of the environment in the law of servitudes coheres well with commons theory and helps to explain why the commons is an especially useful model for servitudes despite their different type of ownership. Conservation of resources and respect for the environment are central aims of commons theory. These goals are achieved by preserving the status quo, and Roman law takes a similar approach in cases where the natural landscape is constructed as an unchanging ideal. In a true commons, shared ownership gives individuals a stake in conserving a resource like water. The same aim is supported by a regime of private ownership in the law of servitudes, in part, perhaps, as a carryover of social practices from the early period when water may have been communally owned. More important in Roman law, however, landowners were motivated to carefully manage competition for scarce resources because it was economically efficient for them. In this way, the rationality of commons theory coheres with the cal-

12. These issues are addressed in Mantovani and Schiavone, *Testi e problemi del giusnaturalismo romano,* which I was unable to include in my discussion because of its recent publication.

culations that landowners made in using private law to regulate the water supply necessary to their commercial success. Finally, both commons theory and Roman private law emphasize the coordination of human activity and natural constraints.

The complementarity of commons theory and Roman water rights might give rise to some optimism about modern environmental issues and how we might better adapt our legal institutions to manage the water supply and other scarce resources in our world. In a recent book, *When the Rivers Run Dry: Water—the Defining Crisis of the Twenty-first Century,* Fred Pearce has argued that local, traditional strategies are often more effective than high-tech, high-cost solutions to managing the water supply, from both economic and environmental perspectives. These traditional methods are often embedded in social practice, much like servitudes, and they can be combined with appropriate technological interventions, such as improving springs or building ponds to collect water. In some places, private law or government institutions have played a role in supporting and structuring traditional practices of water sharing, in much the same way as Romans developed private water rights to protect and allocate local water supplies. Circumstances surrounding water use in the modern world may be more complicated, because there are more interested parties (international corporations, governments and nongovernmental agencies, as well as local elites and nonelites) and because there is more cultural conflict arising from colonization and current politics. But if Pearce's marshaling of the evidence is credible, the need to act is urgent. There is much experience in history to draw on, including the examples presented in this study. The Roman evidence may offer a model not for managing local water supplies but for investigating them. As the study of the International Irrigation Management Institute noted, the systems of law and hydraulic infrastructure in many societies operate so smoothly that even specialists may be unaware of them.[13] Though the Roman institution of servitudes was not perfect, it provided a robust mechanism for negotiating, allocating, and conserving water in the countryside through many changes in government and economic activity, beginning in the second century BC and continuing beyond Justinian's codification of Roman law in the sixth century AD.

---

13. Perry, Rock, and Seckler, *Water as an Economic Good,* 13.

APPENDICES

APPENDIX A

SOURCES FOR USES OF WATER AND HYDRAULIC FACILITIES ON THE FARM

This appendix gathers passages about the use of water in farming from the following Roman literary works:

Cato, *de Agri Cultura*
Varro, *de Re Rustica*
Columella, *de Re Rustica*
Pliny, *Natural History*

The passages are grouped into topics that are arranged alphabetically, as follows:

Bees
Fish and Shellfish
Fowl, Domestic and Exotic
Fruit Trees
Gardens—Choosing a Site
Gardens, Irrigated
Gardens, Not Irrigated
Grapes and Olives
Land—Choosing Suitable Crops
Land—Choosing a Site for the Villa

Land—Physical Features and the Lay of the Land
Land—Trenching and Drainage
Livestock—Cattle, Sheep, Pigs
Livestock—Diseases
Meadows
Vine Props
Wild Game

BEES

Varro, *RR* 3.16.14 (sprinkle the fodder planted for bees with a mixture of thyme and water), 3.16.27 (near the hive, a clear stream should flow into a pond with rocks near the water for bees to perch on while drinking), 3.16.28 (in bad weather, provide food for bees near the hive, figs cooked in water or honey water or mash of figs and raisins soaked in water).

Columella 9.5.4–5 (flowing water for bees, citing Vergil, *G.* 4.20–24, 27–29), 9.8.6–9 (bees may be captured near springs where flowers grow; a lure may be used; cf. 9.8.12), 9.14.7 (pour freshly drawn water into hives after fumigating).

FISH AND SHELLFISH

Varro, *RR* 3.3.5 (fish cultivation began with raising freshwater fish culled from rivers; cf. 3.3.9–10 on the switch to ocean fish), 3.14 (snails should be kept on a man-made island surrounded by water and with a continuous spray of water piped in), 3.17.2–4 (construction of freshwater and saltwater fishponds, more than one at a villa; separate ponds for different species), 3.17.8 (Hortensius made greater effort to provide freshwater for his fish than to care for sick slaves properly by preventing them from drinking cold water; M. Lucullus did not provide proper circulation of saltwater in his fishponds), 3.17.9 (L. Lucullus dug a channel through a hill to bring saltwater to his fishponds at Baiae, at great expense: his fishponds had tides twice daily).

Columella 8.1.3 (the villa should have fishponds where water is available), 8.16.2 (even people from long ago [the descendants of Romulus and Numa!] stocked artificial fishponds and inland lakes, including Velinus [Lago di Piedi di Luco, Umbria], Sabatinus [Lago di Bracciano], Volsiniensis [Lago di Bolseno], and Ciminius [Lago di Vico]), 8.16.7–10 (types of fish for different coastal environments; cf. 8.17.7–10), 8.17.1–11 (designs of fishponds), 8.17.11–16 (feeding different kinds of fish).

Pliny, *NH* 9.79 (Sergius Orata invented oyster ponds on the gulf of Baiae in the early first century BC), 9.80 (Licinius Murena invented fishponds; Lucullus built a channel through a mountain near Naples to let the sea into his fishponds), 9.81 (C. Hirrius invented a pool for raising moray eels; Hortensius fell in love with one of his eels, and Drusus's wife, Antonia, put earrings on her eel), 9.82 (in the first half of the first century BC, Fulvius Lippinus invented snail ponds and devised a method of fattening them to prodigious sizes).

FOWL, DOMESTIC AND EXOTIC

Cato, *Agr.* 89 (when force-feeding chickens, give them water for just one hour per day; geese may have water twice a day), 90 (food for wood pigeons should be dipped in water).

Varro, *RR* 1.13.3 (a villa should have an outer enclosure with a reservoir for geese; cf. Varro under "Livestock—Cattle, Sheep, Pigs"), 3.3.5 (chickens were the first livestock to be raised in the villa, then boars, bees, and freshwater fish), 3.5.2 (the "for-profit" aviary should have water brought in by pipe and drained by pipe; cf. 5.5.4 on drinking water on the ground), 3.5.9, 12, 14–16 (Varro's pleasure aviary is built around two natural streams that feed fish pools and a pond for ducks), 3.7.5 (a dovecote should have running water so that the birds can drink and bathe), 3.7.10–11 (expensive equipment for pigeons), 3.8.1 (clear water for turtledoves), 3.9.13 (to fatten chickens, prepare a mix of barley meal and cress seed mashed with water; otherwise keep them away from water; cf. 3.9.20–21 on similar feed for hens from Media), 3.10.3 (geese are driven to a stream or pond to mate), 3.10.4 (goslings are driven daily to a pond or swamp), 3.10.5 (geese feed in swamps; fodder plants can be grown for additional profit, *quod aliquem ferat fructum,* presumably either from selling the surplus or from saving the expense of buying fodder), 3.10.6 (when they are sitting on their eggs, fatten geese and goslings on barley meal soaked in water), 3.11.1 (choose a place with a pond or swamp to raise ducks, or build an artificial pond), 3.11.2 (an enclosure for ducks should have a continuous trough for food and flowing water), 3.11.3 (ponds in the duck enclosure should have a large supply of water flowing in so that it is fresh).

Columella 8.3.8 (chickens need very clean water to drink; otherwise the poultry yard should be dry), 8.5.20–21 (prevent disease by giving chickens the cleanest possible water), 8.5.23 (disease afflicts chickens if, *inter alia,* they drink water from puddles in the barnyard), 8.7.3–4 (to fatten birds, feed them barley meal mashed with water or honey water), 8.8.5 (an apparatus for watering pigeons should be designed the same as that for chickens, allowing the birds to drink but not to wash), 8.9.4 (same watering apparatus for turtle doves), 8.10.6 (same watering apparatus for thrushes), 8.11.1 (peafowl can be raised on wooded islands off the coast to deter thieves), 8.11.4 (a peacock house needs to be very dry; cf. the warning at 8.11.16 that they are subject to the same diseases as other fowl), 8.11.6 (supply peafowl with water suitable for drinking), 8.13.2–3 (citing Celsus, geese cannot be raised without a good supply of grass and water), 8.14.1–2 (to raise swimming birds, build goose pens near a pool or river; if there is none on the land, build a reservoir or pond; they cannot live without water; a swamp nearby provides food for geese), 8.14.4 (geese mate in a river or pond), 8.14.10 (feed sitting geese and goslings on barley soaked in water), 8.15.1–6 (similar accommodations for ducks, but more expensive [*maior impensa est*], including a water channel to carry food and water), 8.15.3–4 (finish the sloping edges of the duck pond with *opus signinum* so they are not broken by the wash of waves; part of the floor should be plaster, while the center should be dirt where plants can be grown for the ducks to eat), 8.15.6 (build a channel into the ground to carry food mixed with water; food may be grains or shrimp).

FRUIT TREES

Cato, *Agr.* 3–4 (fertilizing with amurca and water to make olive and fruit trees bear; cf. Col. 2.14.3), 7.1, 3–4 (a suburban property is particularly well suited to an orchard; fruits to grow there include but are not limited to quinces, apples, pomegranates, pears), 8.1 (grow vegetables and flowers for wreaths on a farm near the city), 40.1 (plant fig and apple trees in heavy, wet soil).

Varro, *RR* 1.31.5 (during dry periods, water grafted fruit trees every evening; etymological explanation for their need for water: *a quo, quod indigent potu, poma dicta esse possunt;* cf. the advice at 1.39.2 that since grafting is usually done in spring, some watering would be necessary over the summer months when it does not rain), 1.37.4 (making trenches for an *arbustum* or an orchard; also listed under "Land—Trenching and Drainage"), 1.41.1–2 (apparatus for constant, slow watering of grafts on hard plants; softer stems should be grafted in the dry days of summer so that they will not rot from too much water).

Columella 1.6.24 (orchards and gardens where they catch runoff from the barnyard and baths; also listed under "Gardens—Choosing a Site" and "Land—Physical Features and the Lay of the Land"), 2.14.3 (add amurca, oil lees, to water for fruit-bearing trees, especially olive trees), 5.6.6 (water trees after planting nursery), 5.6.8 (in summer, water trees twice a day, before sunrise and after sunset; frequent sprinkling works better than soaking), 5.9.11 (olive trees must be watered if they are transplanted during a drought), 5.10.4 (in planting fruit trees, shape the hole so as to minimize erosion), 5.10.7 (transplant fruit trees into a damp field), 5.10.8 (to facilitate watering seedling fruit trees in summer, place a bunch of branches as a conduit into the planting hole), 5.13 (water fruit trees after transplanting if no rain), *Arb.* 19.2 (planting holes should be shaped like an oven to minimize erosion), *Arb.* 20.3 (apparatus for watering roots of seedling trees).

Pliny, *NH* 17.249 (irrigation is good for trees in summer, bad in winter, variable in autumn; saplings and trees growing in dry places need the most), 17.259 (some say that pomegranate trees should be watered four times a year with a mixture of urine and water, an amphora per tree; boil lupines in water used for watering fruit trees).

GARDENS—CHOOSING A SITE

Cato, *Agr.* 9 (plant osier beds in damp land or near a stream).

Varro, *RR* 1.37.4 (trenching an *arbustum* or an orchard).

Columella 1.2.4 (streams running down to meadows, gardens, and willow groves), 1.6.24 (plant orchards and gardens where they catch runoff from the barnyard and baths), 10.11 (garden soil should be neither too wet nor too dry), 10.23–26 (nearby streams or a spring or a well for watering a garden), 10.329–36 (too much rain can ruin vegetables), 11.3.8 (choose a site close to the villa, with rich soil that can be irrigated with flowing water or from a well), 11.3.9–11 (spring is best for trenching well-watered gardens, but where water cannot be brought in, rely on winter rain and deep trenching).

GARDENS, IRRIGATED

Cato, *Agr.* 36 (fertilizing with amurca and watering trees, with shallow trench to hold liquid).

Varro, *RR* 1.35.1 (planting violets is not recommended [*non utile*] because they must be grown in raised beds that are easily eroded by rain and irrigation).

Columella 2.10.26 (prepare a bed for growing clover like a garden, with footpaths that provide access for bringing in water and for weeding; cf. 5.12.3 on making beds for clover like those for basil; cf. *Arb.* 28.3 on making beds for clover like those for vegetables and sowing clover in autumn like basil), 10.23–28 (nearby streams or a fountain should be used to water the garden), 10.47–49 (in autumn, irrigate if no rain), 10.143–48 (in spring, after planting, water abundantly), 10.263–310 (invites nymphs to rest by cool fountains after picking flowers in the garden), 10.318–19 (plant basil in well-trenched and well-watered, fallow ground), 11.3.25, 27 (lettuce needs a lot of water to have tender leaves and can be grown all year in a sunny climate where there is plenty of water), 11.3.32 (water leeks after transplanting and after you cut them), 11.3.33, 37 (parsley and mint like damp soil and grow well near springs), 11.3.44 (transplant asparagus into a sunny, well-watered and well-manured plot; cf. the advice at 11.3.46 to allow an asparagus bed to absorb winter rains), *Arb.* 30 (violets need occasional watering).

Pliny, *NH* 19.130 (lettuce and endive are grown year-round in irrigated and manured soil or planted in spring), 19.182–83 (instructions for watering the garden; the best source is a stream, then a pool or channels).

GARDENS, NOT IRRIGATED

Columella 10.41–49, 150–54 (advice about when to irrigate includes directions for unirrigated gardens: wait for winter rains and use raised beds), 11.3.33 (transplant parsley in autumn if no irrigation, in May if can water), 11.3.42 (transplant beets in summer if soil is well watered), 11.3.43–44 (plant asparagus in a furrow when soil is dry, on top of a ridge where it is swampy), 11.3.48, 51 (cucumbers and gourds require less care where water is abundant; in a dry place, plant them in a ditch, and to have early fruit, water them only until they sprout; they will have a better taste if not irrigated over the summer; follow the same regimen for growing them in carts over the winter), 2.10.19 (chickpeas cannot endure the heat and thus seldom thrive; presumably they were not irrigated).

Pliny, *NH* 19.133 (beets like a damp place), 19.145 (grow asparagus in reed beds; cf. Cato, *Agr.* 141), 21.20 (roses have more perfume when grown in dry soil and do not grow well in irrigated soil).

GRAPES AND OLIVES

Cato, *Agr.* 1.7, 144–48 (a vineyard was for Cato the most profitable part of a farm, based on sale of the grapes or the wine), 7.1 (vines to plant on a suburban property), 7.4 (olives to grow on a suburban farm), 10.2, 11.3 (equipment for a vineyard and olive grove includes water buckets, but they could be used for tasks other than irrigating; the one watering can [*nassiterna*] recommended for the vineyard does not suggest large-scale irrigation), 33.3 (instructions for improving the soil in an old vineyard), 37.3 (how to improve a poor vine), 40.4 (plant olives and elms [presumably to train vines] in heavy, wet soil), 61.2 (mulch olive trees so that water will not harm them; plant olive trees in fall in a dry field, in spring in rich land [*agro laeto*]), 93 (to improve fruit on an olive tree, treat with a mixture of amurca and water in equal parts).

Varro, *RR* 1.8.7 (choice of vine prop depends on climate: on damp soil, the vine must be trained higher, because the vine needs sun, not water, while the grape grows).

Columella 2.14.3 (add amurca to water for olive trees), 3.1.8 (soils that are too dense or too crumbly cannot adequately absorb rainwater; cf. 3.11.6, 3.12.2), 3.2.4 (the best vines neither rot in rain nor die in drought; this description implies that the vines were not irrigated), 5.6.6, 8, 9 (trees to which vines were trained did need watering, at least when they were saplings), 5.9.13 (dig trenches around olive trees planted on slopes to bring water from higher ground to lower), 6.9.11 (water olive saplings after transplanting), *Arb.* 17.1 (in damp places, an olive tree grows lush foliage without fruit).

Pliny, *NH* 17.76 (elms grown to support vines should be watered when grown from seed if no rain), 17.247 (manuring and irrigation kill a cypress but nourish vines and pomegranate trees), 17.250 ("harsher" vines [*asperiora vina*] need irrigation, at least in the territory of Sulmo where even the grain fields are irrigated, in part as a way of weeding), 17.258 (swine dung may burn vines unless mixed with water or if used in too large quantities).

LAND—CHOOSING SUITABLE CROPS

Cato, *Agr.* 5.6 (don't plough thin soil), 6 (soil for wheat, olives, trees, and vines; plant poplars and reeds on riverbeds, also asparagus and willows), 9.1 (in well-watered, damp, shady places near streams, plant willows); 27 (in a dry spot, plant olives when legumes are sown); 35, 40, 151.2, 151.4 (sow cypress in tender soil with water nearby, and water the beds lightly where there is no rain and the soil dries out; if there is no water nearby, carry it in, and use it sparingly).

Varro, *RR* 1.6–7, 1.9.1, 1.9.4–7, 1.23, 1.23.5 (plant willows and reeds in wet places; cf. 1.24.4, citing Cato to the same effect), 1.24, 1.25 (land for the vineyard), 1.42 (land that is neither very wet nor very dry is best).

Columella 1.4.4–5, 2.10.4 (sow peas where it rains a lot), 2.10.5 (beans grow well in a valley that receives water from above), 2.10.18 (sesame likes to be well watered), 2.10.21 (hemp grows best in rich, watered soil), 2.10.22 (turnips grow in well-watered soil), 3.1.1–10 (general advice on choosing trees and vines to suit the soil and climate), 3.2.6–32 (varieties of grapes grown in regions of Italy; suitability based on soil and climate), 3.5 (plant vine cuttings in suitable soil), 3.11 (soil in the vineyard), 5.8.6 (good soils for olive trees).

Pliny, *NH* 18.34 (citing Cato on crops for different soil types), 18.163–66 (citing Varro's advice about soil and suitable crops), 18.170 (methods must fit the soil, too), 18.188–89 (exceptionally fertile land in Africa has well-watered soil), 18.190 (among well-watered places, quality of soil and crops varies), 18.230 (drain vineyard with ditches in autumn), 18.235 (clean ditches in winter), 18.242 (make new ditches in early spring; cf. 18.243 for Cato's instructions about ditches for planting).

LAND—CHOOSING A SITE FOR THE VILLA

Cato, *Agr.* 1.3 (farmland should have a good supply of water and of laborers, both necessary to cultivation; the preference for a site at the foot of the hills may reflect the possibility of a mountain stream to supply water; cf. Varro, *RR* 1.7.1).

Varro, *RR* 1.6.6 (it is best if the lay of the land creates natural drainage), 1.11.2 (property with a villa should have a water supply inside the structure or as close as possible; first choice is a spring on site, second choice is water that flows all the time [*perennis*], and if that fails, build reservoirs, one for livestock and one for people), 1.13.7 (villa should be on a hill; cf. the advice at 1.12.3–4 to build on high land to get the healthiest air and avoid flash floods).

Columella 1.2.3 (property should have meadows, arable land, and willow groves and reed thickets near the farmhouse/barns), 1.2.4 (recommending a hillside site, some land for grain, some for vines and olive trees, with streams running down into meadows, gardens, and willow plantations, with water also for the villa [*colles . . . tum rivos decurrentes in prata et hortos et salicta villaeque aquas salientes demittant*]), 1.3.4 (good water is essential), 1.4.10 (the best site for a farm is halfway up a slope where a rain-fed torrent will not damage the foundations), 1.5.1 (property should have water from a spring that flows year-round [*fons perennis*], either on the property or channeled in, or if not, then a well), 1.5.1–4 (a perennial source within or outside the villa [*sit autem vel intra villam vel extrinsecus inductus fons perennis*]), 1.5.2 (if no well, then have cisterns to collect rainwater or water from a hillside stream), 1.5.3 (swamp water is unhealthful but may be purified by winter rains), 1.5.4 (bubbling brooks [*salientes rivi*] make the property more charming and bring useful supply of freshwater for the villa), 1.5.6 (locate a villa on the shore but not near a marsh), 2.16.4–5 (locate a villa on a gentle slope where water neither pools nor runs off before it can soak in; cf. 2.2.20 on finding springs and wells by the plants that grow above them; cf. Vitr. 8.1.5–6 and Palladius 4.8–12), 8.17.3 (using the natural slope for channels to a fishpond, on which see also entry on fish and shellfish in this appendix).

LAND—PHYSICAL FEATURES AND THE LAY OF THE LAND

Cato, *Agr.* 6.3 (on the banks of streams or in marshy places, plant poplars and reeds and wild asparagus and willows that will provide withes to tie up vines).

Varro, *RR* 1.6.6 (a location on the plain is preferable if it all slopes in one direction, rather than being completely flat, so that water runs off and the land does not become marshy), 1.13.4 (runoff from the barnyard should be collected for soaking the manure pit, cf. 13.2 recommending that there be two farmyards, an outer yard with a reservoir for animals, and a pond to soak lupines and other supplies that are more suitable for use after soaking).

Columella 1.6.24 (plant orchards and gardens where they catch runoff from the barnyard and baths, cf. 1.6.21–22 for the design of manure pits, stepping down in a gentle slope to retain moisture), 2.10.5 (beans, too, should be grown in a valley which receives water from above), 1.6.21–22 (manure pits should be constructed like fishponds, with 2.14.6–7 on the manure pit), 2.17.7 (let water carry manure down hill for fertilizer), cf. 2.17.5 (irrigating to restore a meadow, cf. Cato, *Agr.* 29 for manuring the meadow).

LAND—TRENCHING AND DRAINAGE

Cato, *Agr.* 2.4 (cleaning ditches is work for holidays), 27 (trenching around transplanted olive trees), 29 (trench and manure olive trees at the time when you sow fodder crops in the same field), 40 (trenching in the spring), 43 (ditches to drain land for olive grove), 155 (drain the land in the winter; dangers of rain: the whole household should turn out with shovels when it rains).

Varro, *RR* 1.12.4 (sudden rains and torrents are harmful to farm buildings in low-lying areas; surprise attacks of robbers are similarly dangerous), 1.14.2–3 (trenches and bulwarks to keep water from the fields), 1.29.2 (at the third plowing, ditches are cut alongside the rows so that rain can drain away), 1.35.2 (in the winter, dig new ditches and clear old ones), 1.36 (in winter, be sure that the grain lands are drained), 1.37.4 (making trenches for an *arbustum* or an orchard; cf. Cato, *Agr.* 1.7), 1.45.2 (drain winter rains from grain crops so that they are not killed by frost or ice), 1.51.1 (build a threshing floor with an elevated center so that it drains well), 2.2.7 (damp ground damages fleece and sheep's hooves).

Columella 2.2.9–11 (design of open and closed ditches), 2.4.1, 6, 11 (plowing schedule based on wetness of soil), 2.8.3 (furrows to drain grain fields), 2.9.9 (trenches or furrows to drain wet soil), 3.13.4 (alternate, less expensive way to trench a vineyard), 4.1.1–2, 5.5.4–6, 5.6.18–19, 5.9.13 (trenching an olive grove; cf. 3.16 on plant cutting when the trenches are dry), 5.10.4 (when planting fruit trees, dig holes shaped like an oven to minimize erosion), 10.329–36 (too much rain can ruin vegetables), 11.1.13 (among its skilled workmen, the farm should have an excellent digger [*optimus fossor*]), 11.2.82–83 (clean out ditches and make drain furrows in late October), 11.3.2 (choose a garden enclosure that allows least damage from drainage), 11.3.5 (drain furrows around the garden in mid-February), 11.3.9 (spring is the best time for trenching well-watered areas), 11.3.10 (where water cannot be carried in and the garden must rely on winter rain, dig deep trenches in winter), 11.3.11 (where garden is irrigated, trenches may be shallow).

Pliny, *NH* 17.139–40 (trenching around trees, including fruit trees), 18.47 (ditches to drain land), 18.152 (rain is beneficial when seeds are sprouting but damages grains as they mature).

LIVESTOCK—CATTLE, SHEEP, PIGS

Cato, *Agr.* 54 (soak acorns in water to feed oxen in the evening, and let them forage during the day; cf. 27 on plants to sow as forage), 73 (see that cattle always have good running water in summer to keep them strong and healthy), 96 (to avoid scabs on sheep and other quadrupeds, apply a mixture of amurca and water in equal parts, let sweat for two or three days, then wash with saltwater, from the sea if possible), 103 (to keep oxen healthy, give them a drink of amurca and water in equal parts, every fourth or fifth day).

Varro, *RR* 1.13.3 (a villa should have an outer enclosure with a reservoir where cattle and hogs can drink and bathe in the summer and a second reservoir for soaking lupines and other fodder more suitable when softened in water; cf. 1.11.2), 2.1.22–23 (the cure for cattle sick with fever includes a cold bath), 2.2.10–12 (water sheep at dawn and just after sunset in summer, once at mid-day in winter), 2.2.14 (sheep should drink the same water during pregnancy so as not to harm the womb or change the color of the fleece), 2.4.6 (in summer, pigs should be driven to a shady spot with water before the day heats up), 2.4.8 (sows are driven to swampy places for mud baths when breeding; cf. Pliny, *NH* 8.207 on wallowing in mud), 2.4.15 (feed sows barley soaked in water, morning and evening; cf. 2.4.21 on similarly feeding the suckling pigs if the sow lacks milk), 2.4.18 (the sow should drink twice a day to produce enough milk for the piglets; cf. the advice at 2.4.19 that the sow be driven out of her pen only to drink in the first ten days after the piglets are born), 2.5.12 (cows should have their fill of food and drink in the month before breeding), 2.5.14 (cattle should be pastured in a well-watered area [*locis viridibus et aquosis*] and driven to water twice a day in summer, once a day in winter), 2.5.17 (calves should be watered twice a day), 2.7.7 (water horses twice a day), 2.9.14 (a cure for ulcers on dogs' feet is a rub made from hazelnuts crushed in water).

Columella 1.6.21 (a villa should have two ponds, one for geese and cattle, the other for soaking withes, twigs, etc.), 2.10.35 (soaking grain for oxen to eat), 2.21.2 (among tasks for holidays is washing sheep in a river or stream to prevent disease), 6.3.2 (so much fodder for cattle can be found in well-watered places that fewer herdsmen are needed; cf. the observation at 6.24.4 that with rich fodder, a cow can produce a calf every year), 6.22 (man-made pools filled by rainwater are better for watering cattle than rivers and streams, because cold water from natural streams can cause miscarriages), 6.27.2 (a horse pasture should be well watered), 6.30.2 (horses' vigor can be maintained by a proper regimen of water, feeding, and exercise), 7.3.23–24 (water sheep at dawn and dusk in summer, but n.b. cite of Vergil, *G.* 3.324–29, 332–34), 7.3.25 (water only at dusk in cold, damp seasons), 7.3.8 (avoid standing water in the sheepfold), 7.4.5 (wash fleece three times to clean wool; cf. 11.2.35), 7.8.2–7 (water used in making cheese), 7.9.7 (pigs prefer marshy, muddy ground; it benefits them to use water freely, especially during the summer), 7.9.8 (store mast in water in cisterns for pigs), 7.10.6–7 (in summer, thirst is especially harmful to pigs, and they should be kept near a stream or pond so that they can drink and wallow; if there are no natural ponds, canals should be kept full with water from wells).

Pliny *NH* 8.169 (the ass's aversion to water; they must drink at a spring where they can approach by a dry track), 18.254 (wash sheep at the spring equinox).

LIVESTOCK—DISEASES

Varro, *RR* 2.1.23 (bathing as a remedy for fever), 2.7.8 (use of water in a poultice).

Columella 7.3.8 (too much water could be a problem: standing water in a sheepfold can cause disease), 7.5.14 (sheep contract lung disease if they lack water during summer, so they should be given plenty to drink), 8.5.23 (chickens; cf. the observation at 8.11.16–17 that peafowl are vulnerable to the same diseases).

MEADOWS

Cato, *Agr.* 8 (for a supply of hay, let grass grow long, irrigated if possible), 9 (have an irrigated meadow if you have water; if not, a dry one), 50 (manure pastures at the start of spring or, if not irrigated, in late February; see Dalby, *Cato,* 115 for the date), 149 (in a contract for lease of winter pasture, lease of an irrigated meadow ends when neighbors above and below begin to irrigate and the owner reserves water and other amenities for himself).

Varro, *RR* 1.7.10 (popular etymology of meadow as multipurpose land, *prata* from *parata;* cf. Col. 2.16; Pliny, *NH* 18.29; Isid., *Orig.* 15.3), 1.21 (if you own a meadow but no cows or sheep, sell the fodder and let your neighbor keep his sheep on your meadow), 1.31.5 (irrigate a meadow right after haying; cf. 1.33 on a second mowing of an irrigated meadow in the fall), 1.37.5 (irrigate the meadow at the right time, and close it from grazing when the pear tree blossoms), 1.47 (the risks of a path across a meadow).

Columella 2.10.28 (water clover right after mowing to stimulate growth, for six mowings per year), 2.16.3 (hay grown in moist soil is superior to what grows in an irrigated meadow; irrigation makes it possible to grow a meadow in even poor soil), 2.16.4 (in an irrigated meadow, the soil may erode if the slope is steep, or the water may pool if the land slopes inward), 2.16.5 (a meadow must be drained with ditches if it has boggy patches), 2.17.7 (in a sloping meadow, rain carries manure from high to low areas), 5.12.4, 8 (water shrubs for fodder if no rain; cf. *Arb.* 28.3), 6.27.2 (the horse meadow should be well watered and never dry), 11.2.7–8, 16, 18, 40 (instructions for the *vilicus* about meadow maintenance), 12.3 (water *cytisus* [a fodder plant] after transplanting seedlings if no rain).

Pliny, *NH* 18.137 (vetch, a fodder plant, grows well in dry soil), 18.145 (lucerne, another fodder plant, grows in either dry or watered soil), 18.254 (irrigate meadows at the spring equinox; when grass has grown stalks, shut off the water), 18.258 (cultivate a meadow in rich or damp soil or land that is watered by rain or a public aqueduct), 18.260 (some farmers irrigate a meadow on the day before mowing), 18.263 (a meadow should be irrigated after mowing; with irrigation, a meadow can usually be mowed three times a year, though at Terni in Umbria, meadows are mowed four times a year without irrigation).

VINE PROPS

Cato, *Agr.* 6.3–4 (plant a reed bed on riverbanks or in waterlogged soil; plant willows around the reeds, to have something to use in tying the vines to the reeds), 33.5 (cut, soak, and store willow withes for tying up vines), 47 (instructions for sowing reeds directly precede a description of the vine nursery, where, presumably, the reeds will be used as props), 151 (cultivation of cypress).

Varro, *RR* 1.8.1–5 (types of trellises and vine props, including bundles of reeds in clay pipes with open bottoms to allow proper drainage; least costly vineyard does not use vine props), 1.8.7 (choice of vine prop depends on climate: on damp soil, the vine must be trained higher, because the vine needs sun, not water, while the grape grows), 1.15 (plant trees along the land lines to avoid lawsuits over boundaries; elms are best and very profitable [*maxime fructuosa*], because they can provide support for vines, fodder for cattle, and firewood for the hearth and furnace; cypresses are also good to plant along boundaries, though Varro does not connect them with vine props here), 1.16.2 (if props, poles, or reeds can be bought nearby, the cost of buying may be less than that of growing them on one's own property).

Columella 1.6.21 (a villa should have two ponds, one for geese and cattle, the other for soaking withes, twigs, etc.; not strictly vine props but withes were used to tie the vine to a trellis), 3.3.8 (vine props and withes as dowry of the vineyard, perhaps recasting the traditional maxim?), 4.12 (reeds and briar canes may be used as vine props), 4.13 (bind a vine to a prop with withes of willow, elm, broom, rush, or sedge or with rush leaves), 4.26.1 (vine props may be made from olive wood, oak, juniper, laurel, cypress, pine, and elder; vine props must be replaced when they rot or when the vine outgrows them, and new bindings are needed with them; cf. 11.2.38), 4.30.1 (props, frames, and withes must be prepared in advance, like dowries for the vineyard [*quasi quaedam dotes vineis*]), 11.2.11–13, 90, 92 (instructions for the *vilicus* about making vine props), *Arb.* 29.1 (plant willow and broom in damp areas near the vineyard, because they grow ties for the vines), *Arb.* 29.2 (water reeds after cutting).

Pliny, *NH* 16.141 (vine props are "a daughter's dowry"), 16.173 (reeds used as vine props), 17.73 (after planting cypress seeds, water them lightly every three days after sunset), 17.141–43 (willows are the first choice for vine props [cf. 17.147 on chestnut tree]; plant them in damp places), 17.144–46 (reeds grown as vine props like even wetter soil than willows), 17.147–50 (chestnut tree grown as vine prop, preferred to all others; one *iugera* of trees provides enough props for twenty *iugera* of vines), 17.151 (oak trees grown for vine props), 17.209 (osier or willow for tying vines to props or trees), 17.247 (manuring and irrigation kill a cypress but nourish vines and pomegranate trees), 18.341 (plant reeds just before a rainstorm).

WILD GAME

Columella 9.1.1 (wild animals are raised for pleasure in an enclosed park and for profit in a nearby woodland), 9.1.2 (if there is no natural source of water, build channels or a reservoir lined with *opus signinum* to hold rainwater for wild game), 9.1.4 (abundant springs are good for wild animals).

APPENDIX B

FISHPONDS AND FRESHWATER SUPPLY

To determine how commonly fishponds might have relied on servitudes for supplies of freshwater, I analyzed the evidence collected in the "Gazetteer of Fishponds in Roman Italy" in James Higginbotham's *Piscinae* (69–226). I rely on that publication because it presents a comprehensive collection of the physical evidence for fishponds in Roman Italy and examines this archaeological evidence in the context of the relevant literary and epigraphical sources. A few fishponds are omitted from Higginbotham's study, mostly those published after his work, and I include those in my analysis. The lists in this appendix, like Higginbotham's gazetteer, are arranged geographically and cover the Tyrrhenian coast from near Cosa in Etruria in the north to Paestum in Lucania in the south.

A few of the sites have more than one fishpond, and in some of these cases, the freshwater supply seems to be connected with all the ponds. For example, at Formia, the "Villa of Cicero" has three fishponds, two near the villa on the shore and one in the sea on a small promontory, and all seem to have been supplied with freshwater from a source on the shore that also served the villa (*Piscinae,* 163–67). On other sites, each pond has its own freshwater supply. For example, at Torre Astura, the rectangular fishpond was supplied by an aqueduct from the shore (as mentioned in chapter 4 of the present study), while a freshwater spring rose inside the round fishpond (the so-called Piscina di Lucullo) to supplement the water from the sea (*Piscinae,* 151, 156).

Among the fifty-four sites with fishponds examined in *Piscinae* by Higginbotham, there is ample evidence for freshwater supplies that could have relied on servitudes.

Sixteen have remains of a channel that can be connected with a nearby, natural water source.
Eight have remains of a channel but no indication of a water source.
Six have channels from cisterns on the property that either collected rainfall or were fed by a local source.
Thirteen are located where access to municipal water was possible and likely.
Eleven have too little evidence to draw conclusions about the freshwater supply.

The sites in the first two categories in the preceding list—sites with a channel and a local source and sites with remains of a channel—could have relied on servitudes to bring freshwater to their fishponds. Together, the twenty-four sites in these first two categories make up nearly half of the fifty-four sites in Higginbotham's gazetteer. The third category, sites with cisterns, could also have been connected to local distribution systems that involved servitudes, bringing the total to thirty of fifty-four sites. In the fourth category, sites with access to municipal water, some sites may still have relied on servitudes at least in the republican era. In the city of Rome, no servitudes would be needed for the imperial properties on the Palatine. But in Campania—at Pompeii, Herculaneum, Puteoli, and Baiae—servitudes could have been used before the construction of the Serino aqueduct by Augustus, which brought municipal water.[1] Similarly, a public water supply was brought to Capua by Augustus.[2] Of the sites with access to municipal water, ten could have relied on servitudes in the republican period, and

1. For dating the Serino aqueduct to the Augustan period, see *CIL* 10.1805, with Sgobbo, "serino," 78–79. See also Frederiksen, *Campania,* 42, 331, 334; D'Arms, *Bay of Naples,* 79–80; Potenza, "Gli acquedotti romani di Serino," 93–97. On the later history (second through fourth centuries AD) of the branch of the Serino serving Herculaneum, see Pagano, "Alcuni acquedotti romani," 101–3. On water from the Sarno and springs on the slopes of Vesuvius for Pompeii in the late republic, on dating the Augustan aqueduct serving Pompeii to around 35 BC, and for a survey of Pompeii's water supply, see Eschebach, "Wasserwirthschaft in Pompeji."

2. For the Augustan aqueduct for Capua, see Frederiksen, *Campania,* 331; D'Arms, *Bay of Naples,* 80. For the smaller, probably older aqueduct at Puteoli, see Frederiksen, *Campania,* 345 n. 133.

if these are added to the preceding categories, the total comes to forty. It is not unlikely that owners of fishponds would have developed the water supply, at least if, as in the gardens at Pompeii, there is evidence for irrigation before the construction of the aqueduct and in areas beyond its reach.[3] The last category, sites poorly preserved, allows few, if any, inferences, except the mere possibility of servitudes. Thus, by any measure, on well over half of the sites in Higginbotham's gazetteer, the infrastructure is consistent with a servitude to channel water from another property.

The page numbers in the following lists of fishpond sites refer to Higginbotham's *Piscinae,* which also provides a handy map locating the fishponds (70–71).

Fishponds with Freshwater by Channels from Nearby Natural Sources (servitudes likely because channels draw on streams, springs, or local aqueducts)

Cosa, Ansedonia, 82–84 (channel from hillside)
Isola di Giglio, Bagno di Saraceno, 86 (*cuniculi*), 255 n. 33 (lead pipes)
Pian di Spille, near Gravisca, 87 (clay tubing)
Torre Valdaliga, 92 (channels bringing water from rain-fed streams)
Fosso Guardiole, 104 (canal along mole from shore)
Rome, Grottarosa, 111 (supplied from Tiber or cisterns), 115 (channels not from Tiber)
Tivoli, Villa of Quintilius Varus, 122 (cisterns fed by two aqueducts from the river Anio)
Tivoli, Villa of Manlius Vopiscus, 128 (aqueduct cut into hillside)
Licenza, Villa of Horace, 131 (nearby spring)
Torre Astura, 156 (a freshwater spring "bubbled through the floor of the . . . pond")
Circei, Torre del Fico (Villa Prato), 157–58 (channels emerge from the beach)
Sperlonga, Grotto of Tiberius, 163 (springs in the grotto)
Formia, "Villa of Cicero," 164 (channels brought freshwater from "supplies on shore" to both a pond and an offshore *piscina*)
Sorrento, Villa del Convento dei Cappucini, 215 (the villa was served by a branch of an aqueduct originating near Formiello that could also have supplied the fishpond)

3. Jashemski, "Use of Water in Pompeian Gardens."

Sorrento, Villa of Agrippa Postumus, 218 (freshwater from hill above)
Paestum, Santa Venera (sanctuary of Venus), 221 (water from the Capodifiume in an open canal lined with brick and mortar)

Fishponds with Channels for Freshwater, Sources Not Apparent (servitudes possible, if water is from streams or aqueducts and not cisterns)

Martanum, near Gravisca, 88 (channel at northwest end probably carried freshwater)
La Mattonara, near Civitavecchia, 94 (channels on north side, along shore, to distribute freshwater)
Punta della Vipera, between Civitavecchia and San Marinella, 101 (damaged channel, could have brought freshwater)
Torre Flavia, 107 (possibly a channel)
Nettuno, opposite the Villino del Adolfo Nesi, 132–33 (freshwater canal into the triangular pool, source unknown)
Astura, La Saracca, 138 (freshwater aqueduct on east side)
Astura, La Banca, 142–43 (probable freshwater supply: western wall could have supported a canal from the hills)
Paestum, sanctuary of Hera, 222 (*piscina,* possibly for fish)

Fishponds with Channels from Cisterns (no servitudes necessary if rain-fed cisterns, no evidence for natural sources)

Pianosa, I Bagni di Agrippa, 74 (seaside)
Santa Liberata, Villa Domiziana, near Porto Santo Stefani, 79 (seaside)
Grottacce, 106 (seaside)
Isola di Ponza, 168 (island fishponds, rain-fed cisterns, conduits to fishponds)
Ventotene, 181 (island fishponds, channel possibly for water from cisterns)
Pausilypon, 192–93 (island fishponds; a rock-cut channel brought water from the mainland or from cisterns on the island)

Fishponds with Possible Access to Municipal Water (servitudes not necessary)

Rome, Monteverde, 118 (probably supplied from the Aqua Alsietina)
Rome, Palatine, Domus Tiberiana, 118–19
Rome, Palatine, Domus Augustana (Aqua Claudia), 120–22

Santa Maria Capua Vetere, 185 ("Its location inland indicates that freshwater . . . filled this pond"; municipal aqueduct of the Augustan era)
Baiae, Terme di Baia, 187 (cistern adjacent to fishpond, fed by aqueduct)
Puteoli, glass flasks, 189–91 (no information about freshwater supply, but Higginbotham conjectures oyster beds, and these require a mix of saltwater and freshwater; probably supplied by the Serino aqueduct from the Augustan era)
Herculaneum, Villa dei Papiri, 194 ("fed by freshwater"; probably supplied by the Serino aqueduct from the Augustan era)
Herculaneum, Palaestra, 196 (with fountain; fed by the Serino aqueduct from the Augustan era)
Pompeii,[4] house near the forum, Regio VII.2.14, 198–200 (water probably circulated in lead pipes, though no traces remain)
Pompeii, Casa di Gavisius Rufus, Regio VI.2.16, 201 (no indication of water source)
Pompeii, Casa di Melagro, Regio VI.9.2, 202–4 (fishpond with fountain, no source indicated)
Pompeii, Villa di Diomede, 206 ("Water jets, which supplied freshwater to the pond, were arranged around the perimeter")
Pompeii, Praedia di Julia Felix, II 4, 207 (water from lead pipe at top of north wall and clay conduit near center of western side)
Pompeii, Casa di D. Octavius Quartio, 212 (two long narrow ponds, *nymphaeum*)

Fishponds with No Channels and No Indications of Freshwater Supply (too little evidence to speculate about servitudes)

Orbetello Lagoon, 84–85 (remains of concrete walls in the water)
Punta San Paolo, near Civitavecchia, 96 (badly damaged remains)
Pyrgi, 107 (remains of underwater concrete walls, possibly a fishpond, possibly the foundation of a tower)
Fosso Sanguisuga, 109 (scattered concrete walls)
Palo, Alsium, 110 (poorly preserved)

4. On Pompeii in general, cf. Higginbotham, *Piscinae,* 198: "Many of the houses and villas at Pompeii were designed with pools and ponds which could have been used to hold fish." But there are no remains of fish in the houses. The city was supplied by the municipal aqueduct from Serino from the Augustan era.

Sperlonga, Villa Prato (poorly preserved)[5]
Nettuno, below the Castello del Sangallo, 133–34 (landward sides of pond obscured by later buildings and beach sand)
Nettuno, fishpond east of the city, 135 (no evidence for freshwater supply)
Scauri, villa and two tanks, 167 (construction of modern port destroyed most of remains)
Paestum, gymnasium, 222–24 (uncertain whether for ritual bathing in a shrine or the centerpiece of a public garden)
Paestum, residential zone west of temple of Hera, 224–26 (*piscina* takes up almost an entire block; design is consistent with fishponds)

5. For a description of the fishpond and its likely commercial orientation, see Broise and Lafon, *La Villa Prato,* 192–96.

BIBLIOGRAPHY

ABBREVIATIONS

AE	*L'année épigraphique*
CIL	*Corpus Inscriptionum Latinarum*
FIRA	S. Riccobono. *Fontes Iuris Romani Antejustiniani.* 2nd ed. 3 vols. Florence: S. A. G. Barbèra, 1940–43.
ILS	H. Dessau. *Inscriptiones Latinae Selectae.* 3 vols. Berlin: Weidmann, 1892–1916.
Kaser, *RP*	M. Kaser. *Das Römische Privatrecht.* 2nd ed. 2 vols. Munich: Beck, 1972.
ORF	H. Malcovati, ed. *Oratorum Romanorum Fragmenta.* 2d ed. Turin: Paravia, 1955
RE	A. F. von Pauly, G. Wissowa, W. Krall. *Paulys Real-Encyclopadie der classischen Altertums wissenschaft.* 34 vols. Stuttgart: Metzler, 1894–1972.

WORKS CITED

AA.VV. *Il trionfo dell'acqua: Acque e acquedotti a Roma IX sec. a.C.–XX sec.* Commune di Roma, Assessorato alla Cultura. Rome: Paleani Editrice, 1986.

AA.VV. *Misurare la terra: Centuriazione e coloni nel mondo romano. Città, agricoltura, commercio: Materiali da Roma e dal suburbio.* Ministero dei Beni Culturali, Soprintendenza Archeologica di Roma. Modena: Edizioni Panini, 1985.

Akerlof, G. A. "The Market for 'Lemons': Quality Uncertainty and the Market Mechanism." In *An Economic Theorist's Book of Tales,* 7–22. Cambridge: Cambridge University Press, 1984.

Alcock, S. *Archaeologies of the Greek Past: Landscape, Monuments, and Memories.* Cambridge: Cambridge University Press, 2002.

Andreussi, M. "Stanziamenti agricoli e ville residenziali in alcune zone campione del Lazio (sulle base degli studi pubblicati nella Forma Italiae)." In *Società romana e produzione schiavistica,* ed. A. Giardina and A. Schiavone, 1:349–90. Rome and Bari: Editori Laterza, 1981.

Apathy, P. "Sachgerechtigkeit und Systemdenken am Beispiel der Entwicklung von Sachmängelhaftung und Irrtum beim Kauf im klassischen römischen Recht." *ZRG* 111 (1994): 95–154.

Argoud, G., L. Marangou, V. Panagiotopoulos, and C. Villain-Gandossi, eds. *L'eau et les hommes en Méditerranée et en Mer Noir dans l'antiquité de l'époque mycénienne au règne de Justinien: Actes du Congrès International, Athènes, 20–24 mai 1988.* Athens: Centre national de recherches sociales, 1992.

Arrow, K. J. "Gifts and Exchange." *Philosophy and Public Affairs* 1, no. 4 (1972): 343–62.

Arthur, P. *Romans in Northern Campania: Settlement and Land-Use around the Massico and the Garigliano Basin.* Archaeological Monographs of the British School at Rome 1. London: British School at Rome, 1991.

Ashby, T. *The Roman Campagna in Classical Times.* London: E. Benn, 1927.

Ashby, T. *The Aqueducts of Ancient Rome.* Oxford: Clarendon Press, 1935.

Astin, A. E. *Cato the Censor.* Oxford: Oxford University Press, 1978.

Baden, J. A., and D. S. Noonan, eds. *Managing the Commons.* 2nd ed. Bloomington: Indiana University Press, 1998.

Barker, G., and R. Hodges, eds. *Archaeology and Italian Society.* Papers in Italian Archaeology 2. BAR 102. Oxford: British Archaeological Reports, 1981.

Barker, G., and J. Lloyd, eds. *Roman Landscapes: Archaeological Survey in the Mediterranean Region.* Archaeological Monographs of the British School at Rome 2. London: British School at Rome, 1991.

Baronowski, D. W. "Roman Treaties with Communities of Citizens." *CQ* 38 (1988): 172–78.

Beagon, M. "Nature and Views of Her Landscapes in Pliny the Elder." In *Human Landscapes in Classical Antiquity: Environment and Culture.* Ed. G. Shipley and J. Salmon, 284–309. London: Routledge, 1996.

Beagon, M. *Roman Nature: The Thought of Pliny the Elder.* Oxford: Clarendon, 1992.

Beltrán Lloris, F. "An Irrigation Decree from Roman Spain: The *Lex Rivi Hiberiensis.*" *JRS* 96 (2006): 147–97.

Bergamini, M., ed. *Gli Etruschi maestri di idraulica.* Perugia: Electa, Editori Umbri, 1991.

Biondi, B. *La categoria romana delle "servitutes."* Milan: Società Editrice "Vita e Pensiero," 1938.

Bizzarri, C. "Bonifica idraulica ed opere di canalizzazione nel territorio orvietano." In *Gli Etruschi maestri di idraulica,* ed. M. Bergamini, 61–65. Perugia: Electa, Editori Umbri, 1991.

Borda, M. *Tuscolo.* Rome: Libreria dello stato, 1958.

Borsari, L. "Terracina." *NSc* (1891) 232–35.

Bouckaert, B., and G. de Geest, eds. *Encyclopedia of Law and Economics.* 5 vols. Cheltenham, UK: Edward Elgar, 2000. On-line edition (1999): http://users.ugent.be/~gdegeest/.

Brandizzi Vitucci, P. *Antium: Anzio e Nettuno in epoca romana.* Roma: Bardi, 2000.

Brehaut, E. *Cato the Censor on Farming.* New York: Columbia University Press, 1933.

Brennan, T. Corey. *The Praetorship in the Roman Republic.* 2 vols. Oxford and New York: Oxford University Press, 2000.

Broise, H., and V. Jolivet. "Il giardino e l'acqua: L'esempio degli *horti Luculliani.*" In *Horti Romani: Atti del convengo internazionale, Roma, 4–6 maggio 1995,* ed. M. Cima and E. La Rocca, 189–202. Bullettino della commissione archeologica comunale di Roma, Supplement 6. Rome: "L'Erma" di Bretschneider, 1998.

Broise, H., and X. Lafon. *La Villa Prato de Sperlonga.* Collection de l'École française de Rome 285. Rome: École française de Rome, 2001.

Brunt, P. A. "*Amicitia* in the Late Roman Republic." In *The Fall of the Roman Republic,* 351–81. Oxford: Clarendon, 1988.

Brunt, P. A. *Italian Manpower, 225 B.C.–A.D. 14.* Oxford: Clarendon, 1971.

Brunt, P. A. "Two Great Roman Landowners." *Latomus* 34 (1975): 620–35.

Bruun, C. "The Roman World." In *Handbook of Ancient Water Technology,* ed. O. Wikander, 575–604. Leiden: Brill, 2000.

Bruun, C. "Water Shortage and Surplus in the Ancient World." In *Cura Aquarum in Sicilia: Proceedings of the Tenth International Congress on the History of Water Management and Hydraulic Engineering in the Mediterraean Region, Syracuse, May 16–22, 1998,* ed. G. C. M. Jansen, 215–24. Leiden: Stichtung Babesch, 2000.

Bruun, C. *The Water Supply of Ancient Rome: A Study in Roman Imperial Administration.* Commentatione Humanarum Litterarum 93. Helsinki: Societas Scientiarum Fennica, 1991.

Buck, R. J. *Agriculture and Agricultural Practice in Roman Law.* Historia Einzelschriften 45. Wiesbaden: Franz Steiner, 1983.

Buonocore, M. "Fra topografia ed epigrafia: L'acquedotto di *Amiternum* (L'Aquila)." *JAT* 4 (1994): 185–94.

Buonocore, M. "Insediamente e forme economiche nell'Abruzzo romano dei primi due secoli dell'impero." *SCO* 36 (1986): 279–92.

Caiazzo, E. "In tema di servitú «*ad tempus*»" *Index* 25 (1997): 333–43.

Camilli, A., and G. Vitali Rosati. "Nuove ricerche nell'Agro Capenate." In *Settlement and Economy in Italy, 1500 BC–AD 1500: Papers of the Fifth Conference of Italian Archaeology,* ed. N. Christie, 403–12. Oxford: Oxbow, 1995.

Campbell, B. *The Writings of the Roman Land Surveyors.* Journal of Roman Studies Monograph, no. 9. London: Society for the Promotion of Roman Studies, 2000.

Campbell, B. "Shaping the Rural Environment. Surveyors in Ancient Rome." *JRS* 86 (1996): 74–99.

Capogrossi Colognesi, L., ed. *L'agricoltura romana: Guida storica e critica.* Rome and Bari: Editori Laterza, 1982.

Capogrossi Colognesi, L., ed. *La struttura della proprietà e la formazione dei "iura praediorum" nell'età repubblicana.* Milan: Giuffrè, 1976.

Capogrossi Colognesi, L., ed. *Richerche sulla struttura delle servitù d'acqua in diritto romano.* Quaderni di "Studi senesi" 14. Milan: Giuffrè, 1966.

Carandini, A. "Columella's Vineyard and the Rationality of the Roman Economy." *Opus* 2 (1983): 177–203.

Carandini, A. "I paesaggi agrari dell'Italia romana." In *L'Italie d'Auguste à Dioclétien: Actes du colloque international (Rome, 25–28 mars 1992),* ed. C. Nicolet, 167–74. Collection de l'École française de Rome 198. Rome: École française de Rome, 1994.

Carandini, A., ed. *La Romanizzazione dell'Etruria: Il Territorio di Vulci.* Milan: Electa, 1985.

Carandini, A. "*Hortensia.* Orti e frutteti intorno a Roma." In AA.VV., *Misurare la terra: Centuriazione e coloni nel mondo romano: Città, agricoltura, commercio: Materiali da Roma e dal suburbio,* 66–74. Ministero dei Beni Culturali, Soprintendenza Archeologica di Roma. Modena: Edizioni Panini, 1985.

Carlsen, J., P. Ørsted, and J. E. Skydsgaard, eds. *Landuse in the Roman Empire.* Rome: "L'Erma" di Bretschneider, 1994.

Castagnoli, F., et al. "Resti di divisioni agrarie nel territorio del'odierno Lazio." In AA.VV., *Misurare la terra: Centuriazione e coloni nel mondo romano: Città, agricoltura, commercio: Materiali da Roma e dal suburbio,* 38–61. Ministero dei Beni Culturali, Soprintendenza Archeologica di Roma. Modena: Edizioni Panini, 1985.

Champlin, E. "Owners and Neighbors at Ligures Baebiani." *Chiron* 11 (1981): 239–64.

Champlin, E. "The *Suburbium* of Rome." *AJAH* 7 (1982): 97–117.

Chastagnol, A., S. Demougin, and C. Lepelley, eds. *Splendidissima civitas: Études d'histoire romaine en hommage à François Jacques.* Paris: Publications de la Sorbonne, 1996.

Christ, M. R. "Legal Self-Help on Private Property in Classical Athens." *AJP* 119 (1998): 521–45.

Christie, N. *Settlement and Economy in Italy, 1500 BC–AD 1500: Papers of the Fifth Conference of Italian Archaeology.* Oxford: Oxbow, 1995.

Cifani, G. "Notes on the Rural Landscape of Central Tyrrhenian Italy in the 6th–5th c. B.C. and Its Social Significance." *JRA* 15 (2002): 247–60.

Cima, M., and E. La Rocca, eds. *Horti Romani: Atti del convengo internazionale, Roma, 4–6 maggio 1995.* Bullettino della commissione archeologica comunale di Roma, Supplement 6. Rome: "L'Erma" di Bretschneider, 1998.

Cornell, T. J. *The Beginnings of Rome: Italy and Rome from the Bronze Age to the Punic Wars (c.1000–264 B.C.).* London: Routledge, 1995.

Corrente, M. "Alcuni esempi di forme economiche nel settore Est del suburbio romano." In AA.VV., *Misurare la terra: Centuriazione e coloni nel mondo romano: Città, agricoltura, commercio: Materiali da Roma e dal suburbio,* 112–18. Ministero dei Beni Culturali, Soprintendenza Archeologica di Roma. Modena: Edizioni Panini, 1985.

Costa, E. *Le acque nel diritto romano.* Bologna: Zanichelli, 1919.

Coste, J., and P. Schutzmann-Bolzon. "Il cippo arcaico della tenuta Sbardella." *NSc* (1970): 364–71.

Crawford, M. H., et al. *Roman Statutes.* 2 vols. *BICS* Supplement 64. London: Institute for Classical Studies, 1996.

Crook, J. A. "*Lex 'Rivalicia.'* (*FIRA* I, no. 5)." *Ath* 64 (1986): 45–53.

Dalby, A., ed. and trans. *Cato on Farming: De Agricultura.* Blackawton, Devon: Prospect Books, 1998.

Dall'Aglio, P. L., and G. Marchetti. "Settlement Patterns and Agrarian Structures of the Roman Period in the Territory of Piacenza." In *Roman Landscapes: Archaeological Survey in the Mediterranean Region,* ed. G. Barker and J. Lloyd, 160–68. Archaeological Monographs of the British School at Rome 2. London: British School at Rome, 1991.

D'Arms, J. H. *Romans on the Bay of Naples: A Social and Cultural Study of the Villas and Their Owners from 150 B.C. to A.D. 400.* Cambridge, MA: Harvard University Press, 1970.

De Francesco, D. "Insediamenti a Monte Savello presso Albano." *StudRom* 39 (1991): 217–35.

De Haan, N., and G. C. M. Jansen, eds. *Cura Aquarum in Campania: Proceedings of the Ninth International Congress on the History of Water Management and Hydraulic Engineering in the Mediterranean Region, Pompeii, 1–8 October 1994.* Leiden: Stichting Babesch, 1996.

De Kleijn, G. "Die Fundorte der Fistulae Aquariae in Rom." In *Cura Aquarum in Campania: Proceedings of the Ninth International Congress on the History of Water Management and Hydraulic Engineering in the Mediterranean Region, Pompeii, 1–8 October 1994,* ed. N. De Haan and G. C. M. Jansen, 153–57. Leiden: Stichting Babesch, 1996.

Del Chicca, F. *De aquae ductu urbis Romanae.* Rome: Herder, 2004.

Del Nero, R. *The Towns of the Tusculum and Algidus Areas.* Frascati: Azienda Autonoma di Soggiorno e Tursimo "Del Tuscolo," 1996.

De Neeve, P. W. *Colonus: Private Farm-Tenancy in Roman Italy during the Republic and the Early Principate.* Amsterdam: J. C. Gieben, 1984.

De Neeve, P. W. "*Fundus* as Economic Unit." *RHD* 52 (1984): 3–19.

De Neeve, P. W. *Peasants in Peril: Location and Economy in Italy in the Second Century B.C.* Amsterdam: J. C. Gieben, 1984.

De Neeve, P. W. "The Price of Agricultural Land in Roman Italy and the Problem of Rationalism." *Opus* 4 (1985): 77–109.

De Neeve, P. W. "A Roman Landowner and His Estates: Pliny the Younger." *Ath* 78 (1990): 363–402.

de Zulueta, F. *The Institutes of Gaius.* 2 vols. Oxford: Clarendon, 1946.

di Mazano, P., G. Messineo, and A. R. Staffa. "Le ville nel settore Nord-est del suburbio." In AA.VV., *Misurare la terra: Centuriazione e coloni nel mondo romano: Città, agricoltura, commercio: Materiali da Roma e dal suburbio,* 83–90. Ministero dei Beni Culturali, Soprintendenza Archeologica di Roma. Modena: Edizioni Panini, 1985.

Duncan, G. "Sutri (*Sutrium*). (Notes on Southern Etruria, 3)." *PBSR* 26 (1958): 63–134.

Duncan-Jones, R. P. *The Economy of the Roman Empire: Quantitative Studies.* 2nd ed. Cambridge: Cambridge University Press, 1982.

Duncan-Jones, R. P. "Some Configurations of Landholding in the Roman Empire." In *Studies in Roman Property,* ed. M. I. Finley, 7–33. Cambridge: Cambridge University Press, 1976.

Dyck, A. *A Commentary on Cicero, "De Officiis."* Ann Arbor: University of Michigan Press, 1996.

Dyson, S. L. "Settlement Patterns in the *Ager Cosanus:* The Wesleyan University Survey, 1974–1976." *J. Field Arch.* 5 (1978): 251–68.

Dyson, S. L. "Settlement Reconstruction in the *Ager Cosanus* and the Albegna Valley: Wesleyan University Research, 1974–1979." In *Archaeology and Italian Society,* ed. G. Barker and R. Hodges, 269–74. Papers in Italian Archaeology 2. BAR 102. Oxford: British Archaeological Reports, 1981.

Eck, W. "Die Wasserversorgung im römischen Reich: Sozio-politische Bedingungen, Recht und Administration." In *Die Wasserversorgung antiker Städte: Pergamon, Recht/Verwaltung, Brunnen/Nymphäen, Bauelemente,* ed. W. Eck, F. Glaser, and H. Fahlbusch, 51–101. Geschichte der Wasserversorgung 2. Mainz am Rhein: Verlag Philipp von Zabern, 1987.

Eck, W., F. Glaser, and H. Fahlbusch. *Die Wasserversorgung antiker Städte: Pergamon, Recht/Verwaltung, Brunnen/Nymphäen, Bauelemente.* Geschichte der Wasserversorgung 2. Mainz am Rhein: Verlag Philipp von Zabern, 1987.

Eder, W. "The Political Significance of the Codification of Law in Archaic Societies: An Unconventional Hypothesis." In *Social Struggles in Archaic Rome: New Perspectives on the Struggle of the Orders,* ed. K. Raaflaub, 262–300. Berkeley and Los Angeles: University of California Press, 1986.

Ellickson, R. C. *Order without Law: How Neighbors Settle Disputes.* Cambridge, MA: Harvard University Press, 1991.

Ellis, S. "Pooling Resources: The Use of Water for Social Control in the Roman Empire." In *TRAC 96: Proceedings of the Sixth Annual Theoretical Roman Archaeology Conference,* ed. K. Meadows, C. Lemke, and J. Heron, 144–50. Oxford: Oxbow, 1997.

Erdkamp, P. *The Grain Market in the Roman Empire: A Social, Political, and Economic Study.* Cambridge: Cambridge University Press, 2005.

Eschebach, L. "Wasserwirtschaft in Pompeji." In *Cura Aquarum in Campania: Proceedings of the Ninth International Congress on the History of Water Management and Hydraulic Engineering in the Mediterranean Region, Pompeii, 1–8 October 1994,* ed. N. De Haan and G. C. M. Jansen, 1–12. Leiden: Stichting Babesch, 1996.

Evans, H. B. "In Tiburtium Usum: Special Arrangements in the Roman Water System (Frontinus, *Aq.* 6.5)." *AJA* 97 (1993): 447–55.

Evans, H. B. *Water Distribution in Ancient Rome: The Evidence of Frontinus.* Ann Arbor: University of Michigan Press, 1994.

Fagan, G. "Sergius Orata: Inventor of the Hypocaust?" *Phoenix* 50 (1996): 56–66.

Farrar, L. *Gardens of Italy and the Western Provinces of the Roman Empire From the 4th Century BC to the 4th Century AD.* BAR International Series 650. Oxford: Tempus Reparatum, 1996.

Feeny, D., F. Berkes, B. J. McCay, and J. M. Acheson. "The Tragedy of the Commons: Twenty-Two Years Later." In *Managing the Commons,* ed. J. A. Baden and D. S. Noonan, 76–94. 2nd ed. Bloomington: Indiana University Press, 1998.

Fentriss, E. "Saturnia: Figures in a Centuriate Landscape." In *Splendidissima civitas: Études d'histoire romaine en hommage à François Jacques,* ed. A. Chastagnol, S. Demougin, and C. Lepelley, 79. Paris: Publications de la Sorbonne, 1996.

Fernea, R. A. "Conflict in Irrigation." *Comparative Studies in Society and History* 6 (1963–64): 76–83.

Finley, M. I. *The Ancient Economy.* 2nd ed. Berkeley and Los Angeles: University of California Press, 1999.

Finley, M. I. *Studies in Roman Property.* Cambridge: Cambridge University Press, 1976.

Fiorentini, M. "Sulla rilevanza economica e giuridica delle ville marittime durante la Repubblica e l'Impero." *Index* 24 (1996): 143–98.

Forsythe, G. *The Historian L. Calpurnius Piso Frugi and the Roman Annalistic Tradition.* Lanham, Maryland: University Press of America, 1994.

Franciosi, G. *Studi sulle servitù prediali.* Naples: Jovene, 1967.

Frayn, J. M. *Subsistence Farming in Roman Italy.* Fontwell: Centaur, 1979.

Frederiksen, M. *Campania.* Rome: British School at Rome, 1984.

Frederiksen, M. "I cambiamenti delle strutture agrarie nella tarda repubblica: La Campania." In *Società romana e produzione schiavistica,* ed. A. Giardina and A. Schiavone, 1:265–88. Rome and Bari: Editori Laterza, 1981.

Frier, B. W. *Landlords and Tenants in Imperial Rome.* Princeton, NJ: Princeton University Press, 1980.

Frier, B. W. "Law, Technology, and Social Change." *ZRG* 96 (1979): 204–28.

Frier, B. W. "Urban Praetors and Rural Violence: The Legal Background of Cicero's *Pro Caecina.*" *TAPA* 113 (1983): 221–41.

Frier, B. W. "Why Law Changes." Review of *The Evolution of Law,* by A. Watson. *Columbia Law Review* 86 (1986): 888–900.

Friggeri, R. "Epigrafi sull'agricoltura a Roma." In AA.VV., *Misurare la terra: Centuriazione e coloni nel mondo romano: Città, agricoltura, commercio: Materiali da Roma e dal suburbio,* 75–79. Ministero dei Beni Culturali, Soprintendenza Archeologica di Roma. Modena: Edizioni Panini, 1985.

Gabba, E. "Strutture agrarie dell'Italia Romana (III–I a.C.)." In *L'agricoltura romana: Guida storica e critica,* ed. L. Capogrossi Colognesi, 104–33. Rome and Bari: Editore Laterza, 1982.

Gabba, E., and M. Pasquinucci. *Strutture agrarie e allevamento transumante nell'Italia romana (III–I sec. A.C.).* Pisa: Giardini Editori e Stampatori, 1979.

Gaheis, A. Iulius (Agricola). *RE* 10.1: 125–43.

Gallant, T. W. *Risk and Survival in Ancient Greece: Reconstructing the Rural Domestic Economy.* Stanford, CA: Stanford University Press, 1991.

Getzler, J. *A History of Water Rights at Common Law.* Oxford: Oxford University Press, 2004.

Giardina, A., and A. Schiavone, eds. *Società romana e produzione schiavistica.* 3 vols. Rome and Bari: Editori Laterza, 1981.

Gilkes, O., S. Martin, and M. Matheus. "Excavation and Survey at Prati San Martino, Sutri." *PBSR* 68 (2000): 371–80.

Glick, T. *Irrigation and Society in Medieval Valencia.* Cambridge, MA: Harvard University Press, 1970.

Gossen, H. Iulius (Graecinus). *RE* 10.1: 613.

Grosso, G. *Le servitù prediali nel diritto romano.* Turin: G. Giappichelli Editore, 1969.

Gvozdeva, I. A. "The Land Cadastre of Augustus." *Acta Universitatis Carolinae, Philologica 2 Graecolatina Pragensia* 13 (1991): 9–21.

Hanson, V. *The Other Greeks: The Family Farm and the Agrarian Roots of Western Civilization.* New York: Free Press, 1995.

Hardin, G. "The Tragedy of the Commons." In *Managing the Commons,* ed. J. A. Baden and D. S. Noonan, 95–118. 2nd ed. Bloomington: Indiana University Press, 1998.

Harris, W. V. *Rome in Etruria and Umbria.* Oxford: Clarendon Press, 1971.

Harvey, P. "Cicero, *Epistulae ad Quintum Fratrem:* Three Notes." *Ath* 64 (1986): 482–86.

Healy, J. F. *Pliny the Elder on Science and Technology.* Oxford: Oxford University Press, 1999.

Heitland, W. E. *Agricola: A Study of Agriculture and Rustic Life in the Greco-Roman World from the Point of View of Labour.* Cambridge: Cambridge University Press, 1921.

Henderson, J. "Columella's Living Hedge: The Roman Gardening Book." *JRS* 92 (2002): 110–33.

Henderson, J. *Morals and Villas in Seneca's Letters.* Cambridge: Cambridge University Press, 2004.

Higginbotham, J. *Piscinae: Artificial Fishponds in Roman Italy.* Chapel Hill: University of North Carolina Press, 1997.

Hinker, H. "Grundzüge des öffentlichen Römischen Wasserrechts." In *Vestigia Iuris Romani: Festschrift für Gunter Wesener zum 60. Geburtstag am 3. Juni 1992,* ed. G. Klingenberg, J. M. Rainer, and H. Stiegler, 177–85. Graz: Leykam Verlag, 1992.

Hodge, A. T., ed. *Future Currents in Aqueduct Studies* Leeds: Francis Cairns, 1991.

Hodge, A. T. *Roman Aqueducts and Water Supply.* London: Duckworth, 1992.

Honsell, H. *Quod interest im Bonae-Fidei Iudicium: Studien zum römischen Schadensersatzrecht.* Münchener Beiträge zur Papyrus forschung und antiken Rechtsgeschichte 55. Munich: Beck, 1969.

Hopkins, K. "Rome, Taxes, Rents, and Trade." In *The Ancient Economy,* ed. W. Scheidel and S. von Reden, 190–230. New York: Routledge, 2002. Originally published in *Kodai: Journal of Ancient History* 6–7 (1995–96): 41–75.

Horden, P., and N. Purcell. *The Corrupting Sea: A Study of Mediterranean History.* Oxford: Blackwell, 2000.

Hunt, R. C., and E. Hunt. "Canal Irrigation and Local Social Organization." *Current Anthropology* 17 (1976): 389–411.

Jansen, G. C. M., ed. *Cura Aquarum in Sicilia: Proceedings of the Tenth International Congress on the History of Water Management and Hydraulic Engineering in the Mediterraean Region, Syracuse, May 16–22, 1998.* Leiden: Stichtung Babesch, 2000.

Jashemski, W. *The Gardens of Pompeii: Herculaneum and the Villas Destroyed by Vesuvius.* New Rochelle, NY: Caratzas Brothers, 1979.

Jashemski, W. "'The Garden of Hercules at Pompeii' (II. viii.6): The Discovery of a Commercial Flower Garden." *AJA* 83 (1979): 403–11.

Jashemski, W. "The Use of Water in Pompeian Gardens." In *Cura Aquarum in Campania: Proceedings of the Ninth International Congress on the History of Water Management and Hydraulic Engineering in the Mediterranean Region, Pompeii, 1–8 October 1994*, ed. N. De Haan and G. C. M. Jansen, 51–57. Leiden: Stichting Babesch, 1996.

Johannowsky, W. "La situazione in Campania." In *Hellenismus in Mittelitalien: Kolloquium in Göttingen vom 5. bis 9. Juni 1974*, ed. P. Zanker, 1:267–99. Göttingen: Vandenhoeck und Ruprecht, 1976.

Jones, G. D. B. "Capena and the *Ager Capenus.*" *PBSR* 30 (1962): 116–210; 31 (1963): 100–158.

Jongman, W. *The Economy and Society of Pompeii.* Amsterdam: J. C. Gieben, 1988.

Jonkers, E. J. *Social and Economic Commentary on Cicero's "De Lege Agraria Orationes Tres."* Leiden: Brill, 1963.

Kahane, A., L. Murray Threipland, and J. Ward-Perkins. "The *Ager Veientanus,* North and East of Rome." *PBSR* 36 (1968): 1–218.

Kaser, M. *Das Römische Privatrecht.* 2nd ed. 2 vols. Munich: Beck, 1972.

Kaser, M., and K. Hackl. *Das Römische Zivilprozessrecht.* 2nd ed. Munich: Beck, 1996.

Kaster, R. A., ed. *Suetonius, De Grammaticis et Rhetoribus.* Oxford: Clarendon Press, 1995.

Kehoe, D. P. "Approaches to Profit and Management in Roman Agriculture: The Evidence of the Digest." In *Landuse in the Roman Empire,* ed. J. Carlsen, P. Ørsted, and J. E. Skydsgaard, 45–58. Rome: "L'Erma" di Bretschneider, 1994.

Kehoe, D. P. *Investment, Profit, and Tenancy: The Jurists and the Roman Agrarian Economy.* Ann Arbor: University of Michigan Press, 1997.

Kehoe, D. P. *Law and the Rural Economy in the Roman Empire.* Ann Arbor: University of Michigan Press, 2007.

Kehoe, D. P. *Management and Investment on Estates in Roman Egypt during the Early Empire.* PTA 40. Bonn: R. Habelt, 1992.

Kelly, J. M. *Roman Litigation.* Oxford: Clarendon Press, 1966.

Keppie, L. *Colonisation and Veteran Settlement in Italy, 47–14 B.C.* London: British School at Rome, 1983.

Klingenberg, G., J. M. Rainer, and H. Stiegler, eds. *Vestigia Iuris Romani: Festschrift für Gunter Wesener zum 60. Geburtstag am 3. Juni 1992.* Graz: Leykam Verlag, 1992.

Knapp, C. "Irrigation among the Greeks and Romans." *CW* 12 (1919): 73–74, 81–82.

Kolendo, J. "Praedia suburbana e loro redditività." In *Landuse in the Roman Empire,* ed. J. Carlsen, P. Ørsted, and J. E. Skydsgaard, 59–71. Rome: "L'Erma" di Bretschneider, 1994.

Koot, C. W. "Marching through Marshes: An Historical Survey of the Agro Pontino." In *The Agro Pontino Survey,* ed. A. S. Voorrips, S. H. Loving, and H. Kamermans, 9–10. Studies in Prae- en Protohistorie 6. Amsterdam: Universiteit van Amsterdam, 1991.

Kron, G. "Roman Ley-Farming." *JRA* 13 (2000): 277–87.

Kunkel, W. *An Introduction to Roman Legal and Constitutional History.* Trans. J. M. Kelly. Oxford: Clarendon, 1966.

Lafon, X. "À propos des villas de la zone de Sperlonga." *MEFRA* 93 (1981): 297–353.

Lanciani, R. *Le acque e gli acquedotti di Roma antica.* Rome: Edizioni Quasar, 1975. Reprint of "Topografia di Roma antica: I commentarii di Frontino intorno le acque e gli acquedotti; Silloge epigrafica aquaria," *MAL,* 3rd ser., 4 (1880–81): 215–616.

Leveau, P. "Dal paesaggio naturale al paesaggio coltivato: Dati archeologi relativi ai grandi lavori agricoli in età romana; Il drenaggio delle paludi nella Bassa Provenza." In *Landuse in the Roman Empire,* ed. J. Carlsen, P. Ørsted, and J. E. Skydsgaard, 73–78. Rome: "L'Erma" di Bretschneider, 1994.

Leveau, P. "La recherche sur les aqueducts romains depuis les dix dernieres années." In *L'eau et les hommes en Méditerranée et en Mer Noir dans l'antiquité de l'époque mycénienne au règne de Justinien: Actes du Congrès International, Athènes, 20–24 mai 1988,* ed. G. Argoud et al., 95–109. Athens: Centre national de recherches sociales, 1992.

Leveau, P. "Research on Roman Aqueducts in the Past Ten Years." In *Future Currents in Aqueduct Studies,* ed. A. Trevor-Hodge, 149–62. Leeds: Francis Cairns, 1991.

Levy, E., and E. Rabel. *Index Interpolationum.* 3 vols. Weimar: Hermann Böhlaus Nachfolger, 1929–35.

Lilli, M. "La villa alla Civitana, presso Velletri." *ARID* 26 (1999): 24–45.

Lirb, H. J. "Partners in Agriculture: The Pooling of Resources in Rural *Societates* in Roman Italy." In *De Agricultura: In Memoriam Pieter Willem De Neeve (1945–1990),* ed. H. Sancisi-Weerdenburg et al., 263–95. Dutch Monographs on Ancient History and Archaeology 10. Amsterdam: J. C. Gieben, 1993.

Liverani, P. "L'Ager Veientanus in Età Repubblicana." *PBSR* 52 (1984): 36–48.

Lo Cascio, E., ed. "Forme dell'economia imperiale." In *Storia di Roma,* ed. A. Momigliano, A. Schiavone, and C. Ampolo, 2:313–65. Turin: Guilio Einaudi Editore, 1988.

Lo Cascio, E., ed. *Mercati permanenti e mercati periodici nel mondo romano: Atti degli Incontri capresi di storia dell'economia antica, Capri 13–15 ottobre 1997.* Bari: Edipublia, 2000.

Love, J. *Antiquity and Capitalism: Max Weber and the Sociological Foundation of Roman Civilization.* London: Routledge, 1991.

Lugli, J. *Ager Pomptinus. Pars 1. Anxur-Terracina. Pars 2. Circeii* vol. 1 of *Forma Italiae. Regio 1. Latium et Campania.* Roma: Danesi, 1926.

Luisi, A. "Campania: Dalla felicità alla fertilità." *InvLuc* 10 (1988): 201–13.

Maiuri, A. *Passeggiate campane.* Florence: G. C. Sansoni Editore, 1957.

Maiuri, A. *The Phlegraean Fields.* Trans. V. Priestly. Rome: Libreria dello stato, 1947. Originally published as *I campi flegrèi: Dal sepolcro di Virgilio all'antro di Cuma.* Itineri dei musei e monumenti d'Italia 32. Rome: Libreria dello stato, 1934.

Manacorda, D. "Produzione agricola, produzione ceramica e proprietari nel'*ager Cosanus* nel I a.C." In *Società romana e produzione schiavistica,* ed. A. Giardina and A. Schiavone, 2:3–54. Rome and Bari: Editori Laterza, 1981.

Mantovani, D., and A. Schiavone, ed. *Testi e problemi del giusnaturalismo romano.* Pavia: IUSS Press, 2007.

Martin, S. D. *The Roman Jurists and the Organization of Private Building in the Late Republic and Early Empire.* Collection Latomus 204. Brussels: Latomus, 1989.

Martin, S. D. "Roman Law and the Study of Land Transportation." In *Speculum Iuris: Roman Law as a Reflection of Social and Economic Life in Antiquity,* ed. J.-J. Aubert and B. Sirks, 151–68. Ann Arbor: University of Michigan Press, 2002.

Marzano, A. *Roman Villas in Central Italy: A Social and Economic History.* Leiden: Brill, 2007.

Mayer, J. W. *Imus ad villam: Studien zur Villeggiatur im stadtrömischen Suburbium in der späten Republik und frühen Kaiserzeit.* Stuttgart: Franz Steiner, 2005.

McGinn, T. J. A. *Prostitution, Sexuality and the Law in Ancient Rome.* New York: Oxford University Press, 1998.

Meadows, K., C. Lemke, and J. Heron. *TRAC 96: Proceedings of the Sixth Annual Theoretical Roman Archaeology Conference.* Oxford: Oxbow, 1997.

Metzger, E. *Litigation in Roman Law.* Oxford: Oxford University Press, 2005.

Meyer, E. A. *Legitimacy and Law in the Roman World:* Tabulae *in Roman Belief and Practice.* Cambridge: Cambridge University Press, 2004.

Mills, N. T. W. "Luni: Settlement and Landscape in the Ager Lunensis." In *Archaeology and Italian Society,* ed. G. Barker and R. Hodges, 261–68. Papers in Italian Archaeology 2. BAR 102. Oxford: British Archaeological Reports, 1981.

Momigliano, A., A. Schiavone, and C. Ampolo, eds. *Storia di Roma.* 4 vols. Turin: Guilio Einaudi Editore, 1988.

Mommsen, T. "Inschrift aus Caiatia." *Hermes* 16 (1881): 495–98.

Mommsen, T. "Romische Urkunden: Edict Augustus über die Wasserleitung von Venafro." *ZGR* 15 (1895): 287–370. Reprinted in *Gesammelte Schriften* (Berlin: Weidmann, 1905–13), 3:75–124.

Mommsen, T., and P. Krueger. *Digesta Iustiniani Augusti.* 2 vols. Berlin: Weidemann, 1868–70.

Monier, R. *La garantie contre les vices cachés dans la vente romaine.* Bibliothèque d'histoire du droit 3. Paris: Recueil Sirey, 1930.

Morley, N. "Markets, Marketing, and the Roman Élite." In *Mercati permanenti e mercati periodici nel mondo romano: Atti degli Incontri capresi di storia dell'economia antica, Capri 13–15 ottobre 1997,* ed. E. Lo Cascio, 211–21. Bari: Edipublia, 2000.

Morley, N. *Metropolis and Hinterland: The City of Rome and the Italian Economy, 200 B.C.–A.D. 200.* Cambridge: Cambridge University Press, 1996.

Morley, N. "The Transformation of Italy, 225–28 B.C." *JRS* 91 (2001): 50–61.

Münzer, F. Sergius (Orata). *RE* 2.A.2: 1713–14.

Murphy, T. *Pliny the Elder's "Natural History": The Empire in the Encyclopedia.* Oxford: Oxford University Press, 2004.

Musco, S., and P. Zaccagni. "Carrateri e forme di insediamenti rustici e residenziali nel suburbio orientale tra il IV e il I secolo a.C." In AA.VV., *Misurare la terra: Centuriazione e coloni nel mondo romano; Città, agricoltura, commercio: Materiali da Roma e dal suburbio,* 90–106. Ministero dei Beni Culturali, Soprintendenza Archeologica di Roma. Modena: Edizioni Panini, 1985.

Nagl, M.A. Statilius (Taurus). *RE* 3.A.2: 2195–2203.

Newlands, C. E. *Statius' "Silvae" and the Poetics of Empire.* Cambridge: Cambridge University Press, 2002.

Nicholas, B. *An Introduction to Roman Law.* Oxford: Clarendon, 1962.

Nicolet, C., ed. *L'Italie d'Auguste à Dioclétien: Actes du colloque international (Rome, 25–28 mars 1992).* Collection de l'École française de Rome 198. Rome: École française de Rome, 1994.

Oakley, S. P. *A Commentary on Livy, Books VI–X.* Oxford: Clarendon Press, 1997–2005.

Oleson, J. P. "Irrigation." In *Handbook of Ancient Water Technology,* ed. O. Wikander, 183–216. Leiden: Brill, 2000.

Oleson, J. P. "Water-Lifting Devices at Herculaneum and Pompeii in the Context of Roman Technology." In *Cura Aquarum in Campania: Proceedings of the Ninth International Congress on the History of Water Management and Hydraulic Engineering in the Mediterranean Region, Pompeii, 1–8 October 1994,* ed. N. De Haan and G. C. M. Jansen, 67–78. Leiden: Stichting Babesch, 1996.

Olson, M. "Group Size and Group Behavior." In *Managing the Commons,* ed. J. A. Baden and D. S. Noonan, 39–50. Bloomington: Indiana University Press, 1998.

Östenberg, C. E., and M. Pallottino. *Case Etrusche di Acquarossa.* Rome: Multigrafica Editrice, 1975.

Ostrom, E. "Private and Common Property Rights." In *Encyclopedia of Law and Economics,* ed. B. Bouckaert and G. deGeest, 2.332–79. Cheltenham, UK: Edward Elgar, 2000.

Ostrom, E. "Reflections on the Commons." In *Managing the Commons,* ed. J. A. Baden and D. S. Noonan, 95–118. 2nd ed. Bloomington: Indiana University Press, 1998.

Pagán, V. E. *Rome and the Literature of Gardens.* London: Duckworth, 2006.

Pagano, M. "Note su alcuni acquedotti romani in Campania." In *Cura Aquarum in Campania: Proceedings of the Ninth International Congress on the History of Water Management and Hydraulic Engineering in the Mediterranean Region, Pompeii, 1–8 October 1994,* ed. N. De Haan and G. C. M. Jansen, 101–8. Leiden: Stichting Babesch, 1996.

Palma, A. "Derivazioni di acqua 'ex castello.'" *Index* 15 (1987): 439–57.

Palma, A. *Iura vicinitatis: Solidarietà e limitazioni nel rapporto di vicinato in diritto romano dell'età classica.* Turin: G. Giappichelli Editore, 1988.

Parisi, F. "Spontaneous Emergence of Law: Customary Law." In *Encyclopedia of Law and Economics,* ed. B. Bouckaert and G. de Geest, 9:603–30. Cheltenham, UK: Edward Elgar, 2000.

Parkins, H. M. "The 'Consumer City' Domesticated." In *Roman Urbanism: Beyond the Consumer City,* ed. H. M Parkins, 83–111. London: Routledge, 1997.

Pasqualini, A., ed. *Alba Longa: Mito storia archeologia; Atti dell'Incontro di studio Roma-Albano Laziale 27–29 gennaio 1994.* Studi pubblicati dall'istituto italiano per la storia antica 60. Rome: Istituto italiano per la storia antica, 1996.

Peachin, M. *Frontinus and the* Curae *of the* Curator Aquarum. HABES 39. Stuttgart: Franz Steiner, 2004.

Pearce, F. *When the Rivers Run Dry: Water—the Defining Crisis of the Twenty-first Century.* Boston: Beacon, 2006.

Perry, C. J., M. Rock, and D. Seckler. *Water as an Economic Good: A Solution, or a Problem?* Colombo: International Irrigation Management Institute, 2002.

Potenza, U. "Gli acquedotti romani di Serino." In *Cura Aquarum in Campania: Proceedings of the Ninth International Congress on the History of Water Management and Hydraulic Engineering in the Mediterranean Region, Pompeii, 1–8 October 1994,* ed. N. De Haan and G. C. M. Jansen, 93–100. Leiden: Stichting Babesch, 1996.

Potter, T. W. *The Changing Landscape of South Etruria.* New York: St. Martins Press, 1979.

Potter, T. W. *A Faliscan Town in South Etruria.* London: British School at Rome, 1976.

Purcell, N. "The Roman Villa and the Landscape of Production." In *Urban Society in Roman Italy,* ed. T. J. Cornell and K. Lomas, 151–79. New York: Routledge, 1995.

Putnam, M. C. J. *Tibullus: A Commentary.* Norman: University of Oklahoma Press, 1973.

Quilici, L. "Centuriazione e paesaggio agrario nell'Italia centrale." In *Landuse in the Roman Empire,* ed. J. Carlsen, P. Ørsted, and J. E. Skydsgaard, 127–33. Rome: "L'Erma" di Bretschneider, 1994.

Quilici, L. "La campagna romana come suburbio di Roma antica." *PP* 29 (1974): 410–38.

Quilici Gigli, S., ed. *Archeologia laziale V: Quinto incontro di studio del Comitato per l'archeolgoia laziale.* Rome: Consiglio Nazionale delle Ricerche, 1983.

Quilici Gigli, S. "Sistemi di cunicoli nel territorio tra Veletri e Cisterna." In *Archeologia laziale V: Quinto incontro di studio del Comitato per l'archeologia laziale,* ed. S. Quilici Gigli, 112–23. Rome: Consiglio Nazionale delle Ricerche, 1983.

Rainer, J. M. *Bau- und Nachbarrechtliche Bestimmungen im Klassischen Römischen Recht.* Grazer Rechts- und Staatswissenschaftliche Studien 44. Graz: Leykam Verlag, 1987.

Rathbone, D. W. "The Development of Agriculture in the 'Ager Cosanus' during the Roman Republic: Problems of Evidence and Interpretation." *JRS* 71 (1981): 10–23.

Rathbone, D. W. *Economic Rationalism and Rural Society in Third-Century A.D. Egypt. The Heroninos Archive and the Appianus Estate.* Cambridge: Cambridge University Press, 1991.

Rawson, E. "The Ciceronean Aristocracy and Its Properties." In *Studies in Roman Property*, ed. M. I. Finley, 85–102. Cambridge: Cambridge University Press, 1976.

Reggiani, A. M. "La villa rustica nell'agro Sabino." In AA.VV., *Misurare la terra: Centuriazione e coloni nel mondo romano: Città, agricoltura, commercio: Materiali da Roma e dal suburbio*, 61–65. Ministero dei Beni Culturali, Soprintendenza Archeologica di Roma. Modena: Edizioni Panini, 1985.

Reid, J. S., ed. *M. T. Ciceronis L. Cornelio Balbo Oratio ad Iudices.* Cambridge: Cambridge University Press, 1908.

Rendeli, M. *Città aperte: Ambiente e paesaggio rurale organizzato nell'Etruria meridionale costiera durante l'età orientalizzante e arcaica.* Rome: Gruppo editoriale internazionale, 1993.

Richardson, J. S. "The *Tabula Contrebiensis:* Roman Law in Spain in the Early First Century B.C." *JRS* 73 (1983): 33–41.

Robinson, O. "The Water Supply of Rome." *SDHI* 46 (1980): 44–86.

Rodger, A. "Concealing a Servitude." In *Studies in Justinian's "Institutes" in Memory of J. A. C. Thomas*, ed.. P. G. Stein and A. D. E. Lewis, 134–50. London: Sweet and Maxwell, 1983.

Rodger, A. "Concealing a Servitude II." *Index* 22 (1994): 237–48.

Rodgers, R. H., ed. *Frontinus, De Aquaeductu Urbis Romae.* Cambridge: Cambridge University Press, 2004.

Saliou, C. *Les lois des bâtiments: Voisinage et habitat urbain dans l'empire romain; recherches sur les rapports entre le droit et la construction privée du siècle d'Auguste au siècle de Justinien.* Beirut: Institut français d'archéologie du Proche-Orient, 1994.

Saller, R. P. "Framing the Debate over Growth in the Ancient Economy." In *The Ancient Economy*, ed. W. Scheidel and S. von Reden, 251–69. New York: Routledge, 2002.

Salmon, E. T. *Roman Colonization Under the Repuiblic.* Ithaca: Cornell University Press, 1970.

Sancisi-Weerdenburg, H., R. J. Van Der Spek, H. C. Teitler, and H. T. Wallinga, eds. *De Agricultura: In Memoriam Pieter Willem De Neeve (1945–1990).* Dutch Monographs on Ancient History and Archaeology 10. Amsterdam: J. C. Gieben, 1993.

Scheidel, W. "*Coloni* und Pächter in den römischen literarischen Quellen vom 2.Jh.v.Chr. bis zur Severerzeit: Eine kritische Betrachtung (*Colonus*-Studien I)." *Ath* 70 (1992): 331–70.

Scheidel, W. "Finances, Figures, and Fiction." *CQ* 46 (1996): 222–38.

Scheidel, W., and S. von Reden, eds. *The Ancient Economy.* New York: Routledge, 2002.

Schmidt, S. W., L. Guasti, C. H. Landé, and James C. Scott, eds. *Friends, Followers, and Factions: A Reader in Political Clientism.* Berkeley and Los Angeles: University of California Press, 1977.

Schulz, F. *History of Roman Legal Science.* Oxford: Clarendon, 1946.

Scott, E. *TRAC: Theoretical Roman Archaeology, First Conference Proceedings.* Aldershot, UK, and Brookfield, VT: Avebury, 1993.

Segenni, S. "Regio IV. Sabina et Samnium. Amiternum-Ager Aniterninus." *Supp. Ital.* n.s. 9 (1992): 11–209.

Semple, E. C. *The Geography of the Mediterranean Region: Its Relation to Ancient History.* New York: Henry Holt, 1931.

Sgobbo, I. "Serino." *NSc* (1938): 75–97.

Shackleton Bailey, D. R., ed. *Cicero: Epistulae ad Familiares.* 2 vols. Cambridge: Cambridge University Press, 1977.

Shackleton Bailey, D. R., ed. *Cicero: Epistulae ad Quintum Fratrem et M. Brutum.* Cambridge: Cambridge University Press, 1980.

Shackleton Bailey, D. R., ed. *Cicero's Letters to Atticus.* 6 vols. Cambridge: Cambridge University Press, 1965–70.

Shatzman, I. *Senatorial Wealth and Roman Politics.* Collection Latomus 142. Brussells: Latomus, 1975.

Shaw, B. "Lamasba: An Ancient Irrigation Community." *Ant. Afr.* 18 (1982): 61–103.

Shaw, B. "Water and Society in the Ancient Maghrib: Technology, Property, and Development." *Ant. Afr.* 20 (1984): 121–73.

Sherwin-White, A. N. *The Letters of Pliny: A Historical and Social Commentary.* Oxford: Clarendon, 1966.

Shipley, G. and J. Solomon, eds. *Human Landscapes in Classical Antiquity: Environment and Culture.* London: Routledge, 1996.

Silverio, A. L. "Iconografia delle acque antiche." In AA.VV., *Il trionfo dell'acqua: Acque e acquedotti a Roma IX sec. a.C.–XX sec.,* 173–75. Commune di Roma, Assessorato alla Cultura. Rome: Paleani Editrice, 1986.

Silverman, S. "Patronage and Community-Nation Relationships in Central Italy." In *Friends, Followers, and Factions: A Reader in Political Clientism,* ed. S. W. Schmidt et al., 293–304. Berkeley and Los Angeles: University of California Press, 1977.

Simon, H. A. *An Empirically Based Microeconomics.* Cambridge: Cambridge University Press, 1997.

Solazzi, S. *La tutela e il possesso delle servitù prediali.* Naples: Jovene, 1949.

Solazzi, S. *Specie ed estinzione delle servitù prediali.* Naples: Jovene, 1948.

Spera, L. *Il paesaggio suburbano di Roma dall'antichità al Medioevo: Il comprensorio tra le vie Latina e Ardeatina dalle Mura Aureliane al III miglio.* Rome: "L'Erma" di Bretschneider, 1999.

Squatriti, P. *Water and Society in Early Medieval Italy, AD 400–1000.* Cambridge: Cambridge University Press, 1998.

Stefani, E. "Veio." *NSc* (1953): 29–112.

Stein, P. G., and A. D. E. Lewis, eds. *Studies in Justinian's "Institutes" in Memory of J. A. C. Thomas.* London: Sweet and Maxwell, 1983.

Steinwenter, A. *Fundus cum instrumento: Eine agrar- und rechtsgeschichtliche Studien.* Akademie der Wissenschaften in Wien, Philosophisch-historische Klasse, Sitzungsberichte 221, no. 1. Vienna: Hölder-Pichler-Tempsky, 1942.

Stiglitz, J. E. "Alternative Approaches to Macroeconomics: Methodological Issues and the New Keynesian Economics." Working Paper 380, National Bureau of Economic Research, Cambridge, MA, 1991.

Syme, R. *The Augustan Aristocracy.* Oxford: Clarendon, 1986.

Syme, R. *The Roman Revolution.* Oxford: Oxford University Press, 1939.

Taylor, R. A. *Public Needs and Private Pleasures: Water Distribution, the Tiber River, and the Urban Development of Ancient Rome.* Studia Archaeologica 109. Rome: "L'Erma" di Bretschneider, 2000.

Taylor, R. A. "Torrent or Trickle? The Aqua Alsietina, the Naumachia Augusti, and the Transtiberim." *AJA* 101 (1997): 465–92.

Tchernia, A. "Quelle rationalité?" *Topoi orient-occident* 12–13 (2005): 283–91.

Temin, P. "A Market Economy in the Early Roman Empire." *JRS* 91 (2001): 169–79.

Thaler, R. H. *Quasi Rational Economics.* New York: Russell Sage Foundation, 1991.

Thomas, R. F., ed. *Virgil: "Georgics."* 2 vols. Cambridge: Cambridge University Press, 1988.

Thomas, R., and A. Wilson. "Water Supply for Roman Farms in Latium and South Etruria. " *PBSR* 62 (1994): 139–96.

Tilly, B. *Varro the Farmer: A Selection from the "Res Rusticae."* London: University Tutorial Press, 1973.

Tomei, M. A. "Il suburbio di Roma: *Tibur* et il territorio Tiburtino." In AA.VV., *Misurare la terra: Centuriazione e coloni nel mondo romano: Città, agricoltura, commercio: Materiali da Roma e dal suburbio,* 107–9. Ministero dei Beni Culturali, Soprintendenza Archeologica di Roma. Modena: Edizioni Panini, 1985.

Torelli, M. *Etruria.* Rome: Laterza, 1980.

Tortorici, E. *Castra Albana.* Vol. 11 of *Forma Italiae, Regio I.* Rome: De Luca, 1975.

Traina, G. *Paludi e bonifiche del mondo antico: Saggio di archeologia geografica.* Rome: "L'Erma" di Bretschneider, 1988.

Treacy, J. M., and W. M. Denevan. "The Creation of Cultivable Land through Terracing." In *The Archaeology of Garden and Field,* ed. N. F. Miller and K. L. Gleason, 91–110. Philadelphia: University of Pennsylvania Press, 1994.

Treggiari, S. "The Upper-Class House as Symbol and Focus of Emotion in Cicero." *JRA* 12 (1999): 33–56.

Valenti, G. P. "I *loca Albana* nei manoscritti di Rodolfo Lanciani alla Biblioteca Vaticana." In *Alba Longa: Mito storia archeologia: Atti dell'Incontro di studio Roma-Albano Laziale 27–29 gennaio 1994,* ed. A. Pasqualini, 67–99. Studi pubblicati dall'istituto italiano per la storia antica 60. Rome: Istituto italiano per la storia antica, 1996.

Valieri, D. "Terracina" *NSc* (1907): 144–45.

Vallat, J.-P. "Les structures agraires de l'Italie républicaine." *Annales (ESC)* 42 (1987): 181–218.

Van Dommelen, P. A. R. "Roman Peasants and Rural Organisation in Central Italy: An Archaeological Perspective." In *TRAC: Theoretical Roman Archaeology, First Conference Proceedings,* ed. E. Scott, 167–86. Aldershot, UK, and Brookfield, VT: Avebury, 1993.

Vera, D. "Dalla 'villa perfecta' alla villa di Palladio." Parts 1 and 2. *Ath* 83, no. 1 (1995): 189–211; 83, no. 2 (1995): 331–56.

Verboven, K. *The Economy of Friends: Economic Aspects of* Amicitia *and Patronage in the Late Republic.* Brussels: Latomus, 2002.

Voorrips, A. S., S. H. Loving, and H. Kamermans, eds. *The Agro Pontino Survey.* Studies in Prae- en Protohistorie 6. Amsterdam: Universiteit van Amsterdam, 1991.

Wallace-Hadrill, A. "Elites and Trade in the Roman Town." In *City and Country in the Ancient World,* ed. J. Rich and A. Wallace-Hadrill, 241–72. London: Routledge, 1991.

Wallace-Hadrill, A. "*Horti* and Hellenization." In *Horti Romani: Atti del convengo internazionale, Roma, 4–6 maggio 1995,* ed. M. Cima and E. La Rocca, 1–12. Rome: "L'Erma" di Bretschneider, 1998.

Wallace-Hadrill, A. "Pliny the Elder and Man's Unnatural History." *G&R* 37, no. 1 (1990): 80–96.

Ward-Perkins, J. B. "Central Authority and Patterns of Rural Settlement." In *Man, Settlement, and Urbanism,* ed. P. J. Ucko et al., 867–82. London: Duckworth, 1972.

Ward-Perkins, J. B. "Luni: The Prosperity of the Town and Its Territory." In *Archaeology and Italian Society,* ed. G. Barker, and R. Hodges, 179–90. Papers in Italian Archaeology 2. BAR 102. Oxford: British Archaeological Reports, 1981.

Ward-Perkins, J. B. "Notes on Southern Etruria and the Ager Veientanus." *PBSR* 23 (1955): 44–72.

Ward-Perkins, J. B. "Veii: The Historical Topography of the City." *PBSR* 29 (1961): 1–123.

Watson, A. *Law Making in the Later Roman Republic.* Oxford: Clarendon, 1974.

Watson, A. *The Law of Obligations in the Later Roman Republic.* Oxford: Clarendon, 1964.

Watson, A. *The Law of Property in the Later Roman Republic.* Oxford: Clarendon, 1968.

Weber, M. *The Agrarian Sociology of Ancient Civilizations.* Trans. R. I. Frank. London: Verso, 1988.

White, K. D. *Roman Farming.* Ithaca, NY: Cornell University Press, 1970.

Whittaker, C. R. "The Consumer City Revisited: The *Vicus* and the City." *JRA* 3 (1990): 110–17.

Wikander, O. *Handbook of Ancient Water Technology.* Leiden: Brill, 2000.

Wikander, O. "The Iron Age and the Archaic and Classical Periods." In *Handbook of Ancient Water Technology,* ed. O. Wikander, 617–30. Leiden: Brill, 2000.

Wikander, O. "*Senatores* and *Equites.*" *ORom* 20 (1996): 177–82.

Wilson, A. "Deliveries *extra Urbem:* Aqueducts and the Countryside." *JRA* 12 (1999): 314–31.

Winterbottom, M. *M. Tulli Ciceronis De Officiis.* Oxford: Clarendon, 1994.

Yntema, D. "Greeks, Natives, and Farmsteads in South-Eastern Italy." In *De Agricultura: In Memoriam Pieter Willem De Neeve (1945–1990)*, ed. H. Sancisi-Weerdenburg et al., 78–97. Dutch Monographs on Ancient History and Archaeology 10. Amsterdam: J. C. Gieben, 1993.

Zaccagni, P. "Lo sfruttamento agricolo del suburbio." In AA.VV., *Misurare la terra: Centuriazione e coloni nel mondo romano: Città, agricoltura, commercio: Materiali da Roma e dal suburbio*, 79–82. Ministero dei Beni Culturali, Soprintendenza Archeologica di Roma. Modena: Edizioni Panini, 1985.

Zanker, P., ed. *Hellenismus in Mittelitalien: Kolloquium in Göttingen vom 5. bis 9. Juni 1974*. 2 vols. Göttingen: Vandenhoeck und Ruprecht, 1976.

Zimmermann, R. *The Law of Obligations: Roman Foundations of the Civilian Tradition.* Cape Town: Juta, 1990.

Zuccotti, F. "Il *Locus Servitutis* e la sua tutela interdittale." *SDHI* 60 (1994): 159–260.

INDEX OF SOURCES CITED IN THE TEXT

(N. B. This index includes sources cited in the main text but not all those in Appendix A: Sources for Water Use on Farms and Villas)

LEGAL SOURCES

LITERATURE

GENERAL INDEX

Note: Roman names that appear in the text primarily as authors of sources cited are not listed here, but may be found in the Index of Sources.